DISPUTATION
and
DIALOGUE

*Readings in the
Jewish-Christian Encounter*

DISPUTATION
and
DIALOGUE

Readings in the
Jewish-Christian Encounter

Edited by

FRANK EPHRAIM TALMAGE

Foreword by
REVEREND EDWARD A. SYNAN

KTAV PUBLISHING HOUSE INC.
NEW YORK

ANTI-DEFAMATION LEAGUE OF B'NAI B'RITH
NEW YORK

Library of Congress Cataloging in Publication Data
Main entry under title:

Disputation and dialogue.

   Bibliography: p.
   1. Judaism—Relations—Christianity. 2. Christianity
and other religions—Judaism. I. Talmage, Frank.
BM535.D53   296.3'87'2   75-25590
ISBN 0-87068-284-9

For

DAVID AND RAANAN ABUSCH

"They shall never be ravaged by the nations again nor shall wild beasts devour them; they shall live in peace of mind, with no one to alarm them."

Ezekiel 34:28

The Anti-Defamation League of B'nai B'rith
dedicates this volume to the memory of
Dr. Esther Feldblum.

"And Esther charmed all who saw her."

TABLE OF CONTENTS

FOREWORD

One way to understand the present volume is to locate it in its historical setting. A useful point of reference has been provided by the appearance on January, 1975, of "Guidelines" from the Vatican for Catholics who wish to engage in dialogue with Jews. Those Guidelines constitute a significant step in the not very rapid implementation of *Nostra aetate,* the Declaration by Vatican II on the Jews which the Council issued on October 28, 1965.

It is no secret that the Council Declaration disappointed many who had hoped for a more radical document. Disappointment was only exacerbated by publicity given to preliminary formulations of the Declaration which included specific provisions missing from the version that finally emerged after long debate and with the inevitable compromises. Nor can it be hoped that Guidelines issued more than nine years after the Council document will assuage that disappointment. We live in a world given to quick solutions, a world in love with instant transformations, whereas Rome breathes another air. If not literally "eternal," Rome has been remarkably durable, so durable in fact that, should we wish to identify a religious entity more long-lived than *Roma aeterna* we must look to the Jewish People.

After so many centuries and so much tragedy, improbably not to say impossibly, the Jews survive. Can Christians who ponder the fact of Jewish survival avoid weighing the advice that a Christian Scripture ascribes to Rabbi Gamaliel in their own regard? Speaking to a Council of his peers who were puzzled almost two thousand years ago by "The Way" to which Christian Rome traces her own beginnings, Gamaliel produced this memorable bit of theological common sense:

> If this project, or its working out, is from men, it will be destroyed, but if it is from God, you will never be able to destroy them, and you may find yourselves at war with God (Acts 5:38).

Christians now read this admonition with comfort, even with a degree of complacency for Gamaliel's disjunction would entail a reassuring conclusion: The two Christian millennia must be accepted as evidence that the Christian Way is "from God," *ex Theou.* But the thing cuts two ways; already venerable in Gamaliel's day, the Synagogue is with us still. If the Synagogue were no more than a human construct, would it not have gone the way of all merely human projects? There can be no explanation for the stubborn fact of Jewish survival unless it be that the Holy One refuses to revoke His covenanting with His People. Paul of Tarsus assured the Christian community at Rome, and through them all who count him a man inspired by the Holy Spirit, that this is the case:

> I ask, therefore, Has God in fact rejected His People?
> That cannot come to pass . . . (Romans 11:1).

Rightly or wrongly, Rome has chosen the present juncture as "the opportune moment," what Scripture would term the *kairos,* for her most recent intervention in the dialogue beween Catholics and the Jews who remain the People chosen for God's everlasting Covenant.

A telling criticism of the Council Declaration, *Nostra aetate,* is that, although it speaks with sympathy, of the Israel of old and looks forward with hope to the mysterious Messianic moment when Jew and Gentile will speak to the Lord with one voice (Zephaniah 3:9), its only word on the Jews and Judaism of our day is a categoric condemnation of anti-Semitism in all forms. This is an exception, most welcome to be sure but an exception for all that, to what is otherwise a disconcerting silence on the Jews with whom we live.

Indeed, official Christianity has traditionally found it easy to concede a glorious past of the Jews, for Christians count themselves among the sons of Abraham. So too, with regard to the future; the Last Days, it was proclaimed consistently by Christian exegetes, will surely see the "ingathering" of a Jewish remnant. Put more bluntly, this means that, as Christians have read the Scriptures in times gone by, the Hebrew Bible as well as their own, a mass conversion of Jews to the Church must be expected. Church leaders often pointed to a dismaying possibility: how embarrassing it would be to have exterminated every remnant of the predestined converts, even under the guise of zeal for the Church.

In sorry contrast to this esteem for the Judaism of the Patriarchs and for the glowing Messianic future, Judaism incarnate in the Jews of any given period seems to have been a baffling enigma to the official Church of every Christian generation. One witness will suffice to make the point. Pope Gregory IX (1227-1241) defended his Jewish contemporaries against persecution much as Vatican II was to speak out against anti-Semitic outrage, but Pope Gregory thought it right to explain that the Jewish past which had been and the Jewish future which was to be counted as the ground for the protection of Jews in his present:

> They [the Jews] must not be destroyed by those who believe in Christ: It is the Lord who forbids it! Now, to whatever point their median group [*medietas*] may be perverse, their Fathers were rendered friends of God, and their remnants will be saved (*Les registres de Grégoire IX, éd. L. Auvray;* Paris: Thorin et fils, 1896-1910; t. I, pp. 691-692; no. 1216)

The "median group," that is, Jews between the Advent of Jesus at Bethlehem and his Second Coming in the Eschaton, ought to be secure from persecution because a remnant must be present in the End Time to witness a final divine mercy. If 13th century Jews and Judaism had any religious value proper to themselves, the Pope did not think it worth mentioning. Given that *Nostra aetate* is silent on, for instance, the State of Israel, we may ask how Vatican II has gone beyond this 13th century document and how the Council initiative fares in our world.

If the Guidelines of January, 1975 are right, Roman Catholics will do well "to learn by what essential traits the Jews define themselves in the light of their own religious experience," for indeed (and the Guidelines have not failed to mention this almost universal misconception of Jewish experience on the part of gentile observers) "The history of Judaism did not end with the destruction of Jerusalem. . . ." Thus has Rome, with all the caution born of her long tradition, entered into the meeting of Jews with Christians. This meeting, as the very title of this volume invites us to put it, can be an instance either of destructive disputation or of creative dialogue. With regard to the Vatican Guidelines, it would be an error to see this volume as a "response" for Professor Talmage had his work on the way long before January, 1975. Still, it would be an error too should we fail to note both productions as evidence of a new mind-set in the gentile world. If it can be said without a patronizing air, Rome seems to have been right that this is indeed "the opportune moment."

Above all, it is the opportune moment for the introduction into Christian-Jewish dialogue of this rich collection of materials from every period of our historical encounter. At the very least, these materials, collected and presented in accord with Professor Talmage's rigorous scholarship, provide both sides with unimpeachable evidence of the unexpected ways in which questions have been canvassed and texts interpreted. To give one instance from among many, the text of Acts 5:38 to which reference is made above, will be found cited in a controversy between a Lutheran Christian and the sixteenth century Karaite, Isaac ben Abraham of Troki. For the Lutheran, Gamaliel's criterion had evidently been met by the Christian faith; for the Karaite Jew, a text from the "gospel" was "not accredited among us," and Lutheran disclaimers against "image-worship" by Catholics sufficed to show that Christianity cannot have been the work of God, no matter how long it might have perisited. Did the thousand years of Islam count with Christians as evidence that this too was the work of God? Did "popery's" sesquimillennium convince Lutherans? Thus the *tu quoque*, the "you too" dialectic of sterile efforts to score debating-points, has dominated and enervated our counsels in the past.

The bane of many a grass-roots meeting between Jews and Christians is that their goodwill has been dissipated in a vacuum of mutual ignorance. Not only our words, but our conceptual schemes, can seem alien and unintelligible; this book provides a precious fund of facts, points of view, perspectives, and suggestions. To say that the components are of uneven quality is but to accord the collection an accolade in the dimension of historical accuracy; neither Jews nor Christians have always been at their best when confronting "the others." No matter; a shrewdly chosen assembly of spokesmen from across all the ages since the Destruction of Jerusalem cannot fail teach us all something of "the others" and—who knows?—perhaps something of ourselves as well.

Edward A. Synan

The Pontifical Institute of Mediaeval Studies

Toronto, 1975

PREFACE

This reader is one of several projects inspired by a conference of academicians convened by the Anti-Defamation League of B'nai B'rith in New York several years ago. Since that time, the A.D.L. has sponsored bibliographies, textbooks and other teaching materials designed to make Judaism and Judaica more accessible to the general community of scholars—teachers and students—in institutions of higher learning. A volume presenting a cross-section of the two thousand year debate between Judaism and Christianity has its place in such a setting.

Judith Herschlag Muffs of the Anti-Defamation League has been with this project from the beginning. She has functioned as editor and has allowed me to benefit often from her great experience and creativity. Emil Fackenheim has been my mentor in this undertaking. He has done everything from advising on the choice of materials to revising the translation of Buber's letter to Kittel—and much, much more. I have gained greatly from Rose Fackenheim's comprehensive knowledge of contemporary theological literature and from her keen sense of taste and judgment. Barry Walfish has read and proofread the manuscript and made helpful suggestions in matters of style and bibliography. Beyond these more tangible forms of assistance, all these people, in ways perhaps not fully realized by them, removed the burden from what might otherwise have been a burdensome task.

Frank Ephraim Talmage

Toronto, Canada
Purim 5735 (1975)

ACKNOWLEDGEMENTS

Selections 1, 13, 21—from Joseph Kimhi, *The Book of the Covenant,* The Pontifical Institute of Mediaeval Studies, Toronto, Canada, 1972, pp. 32-35; 46-49; 43-53. By permission of the publisher.

Selection 2—from Abraham Troki, *Faith Strengthened,* trans. M. Mocatta, KTAV, New York, 1970, pp. 18-20. By permission of the publisher.

Selection 3—from Jacob Neusner, *Aphrahat and Judaism,* E. J. Brill, Leiden, pp. 60-67. Copyright 1971 E. J. Brill. By permission of the publisher.

Selection 5—from J. R. Marcus, *The Jew in the Medieval World,* Jewish Publication Society of America, Philadelphia, pp. 166-169. Copyright 1938 Union of American Hebrew Congregations. By permission of U.A.H.C.

Selection 6—from Karl Barth, *Church Dogmatics,* T. & T. Clark, Edinburgh, pp. 205-213. Copyright 1957 T. & T. Clark. By permission of Charles Scribner's Sons.

Selection 7—from Martin Buber, *Die Stunde und die Erkenntnis*: *Reden und Aufsatre,* Schocken, Berlin, 1936, pp. 171-177. By permission of the Estate of Martin Buber.

Selection 8—from Joseph Klauser, *The Messianic Idea in Israel,* Macmillan, New York, pp. 519-531. Copyright 1955 Macmillan. By permission of the publisher.

Selection 9—from Frank Talmage, *David Kimhi: The Man and the Commentaries,* Harvard University Press, Cambridge. (Forthcoming) Copyright 1975 by the President and Fellows of Harvard College. By permission of the publisher.

Selection 10—from O. S. Rankin, *Jewish Religious Polemic of Earlier and Later Centuries,* KTAV, New York, pp. 187-194. Copyright 1956 Edinburgh University Press. By permission of Edinburgh University Press.

Selection 11—from Thomas B. Falls, ed., *The Complete Writings of St. Justinius Martyr,* Catholic University of America Press, Washington, D.C., 1948. pp. 202-210, 212-214. By permission of Catholic University of America Press.

Selection 12—from E. N. Stone, trans., *Adam: A Religious Play of the 12th Century,* University of Washington Press, Seattle, 1926, pp. 184-193. By permission of the publisher.

Selection 14—from F. Kobler, *Letters of Jews Through the Ages from Biblical Times to the Middle of the Eighteenth Century,* Ararat and East & West Library, London, 1953, pp. 276-282. By permission of the publisher.

Selection 15—from Solomon Schechter, *Aspects of Rabbinic Theology,* Schocken Books, New York, 1969, pp. 116-126.

Selection 16—from Frederick H. Chase, Jr., trans., *Orthodox Faith,* Fathers of the Church, New York, 1959, pp. 389-393. By permission of Catholic University of America Press.

Selection 18—from Harvey Cox, *The Secular City,* rev. ed., Macmillan, New York, pp. 46-49. Copyright 1965, 1966 Harvey Cox. By permission of the publisher.

Selections 19, 20—from Daniel Callahan, *The Secular City Debate,* Macmillan, New York, pp. 145-155, 183-185. Copyright 1966 Macmillan. By permission of the publisher.

Selection 22—from I. Heinemann, ed., *Kuzari,* East & West Library, London, 1947. pp. 64-70. By permission of the publisher.

Selection 24—from Abraham Joshua Heschel, *Israel: An Echo of Eternity,* Farrar, Straus & Giroux, New York, pp. 139-147, 161-167. Copyright A. J. Heschel 1967, 1968, 1969. By permission of publisher.

Selection 25—from D. B. Robertson, ed., *Love and Justice,* Westminster Press, 1951, pp. 132-142. Copyright *The Nation,* 1942. By permission of *The Nation.*

Selection 26—from Maurice Samuel, *The Professor and the Fossil,* Alfred A. Knopf, New York, pp. 183-216, *passim.* Copyright 1956 Alfred A. Knopf, Inc. By permission of the Estate of Maurice Samuel.

Selection 27—from Willard Oxtoby, "Christians and the Mideast Crisis," *Christian Century,* Chicago, July 26, 1967, pp. 961-965. Copyright 1967 Christian Century Foundation. By permission of the publisher.

Selection 28—from A. Roy Eckardt, "The Devil and Yom Kippur," *Midstream,* New York, Vol. XX, 1974, pp. 67-75. By permission of author and publisher.

Selection 29—from Frank Talmage, "Christianity and the Jewish People," *Commentary*, New York, Feb., 1975, pp. 57-62. By permission of the publisher.

Selection 30—from Moses Mendelssohn, *Jerusalem and Other Jewish Writings*, trans. and ed. by A. Jospe, Schocken Books, New York, pp. 113-122. Copyright 1969 Schocken Books. By permission of the publisher.

Selection 31—from Martin Buber, *Israel and the World*, Schocken Books, New York, pp. 28-40. Copyright 1948, 1963, Schocken Books. By permission of the publisher.

Selection 32—from Eliezer Berkovits, "Judaism in the Post-Christian Era," *Judaism*, New York, Vol. XV, 1966, pp. 74-84. By permission of the author and publisher.

Selection 33—from Emil Fackenheim, "The People Israel Lives," *Christian Century*, Chicago, May 6, 1970, pp. 563-568. Copyright 1970 Christian Century Foundation. By permission of the publisher.

Selection 34—from Gregory Baum, "Salvation Is from the Jews: A Story of Prejudice," *Christian Century*, Chicago, July 19, 1972, pp. 775-777. Copyright 1972 Christian Century Foundation. By permission of the publisher.

Selection 35—from Rosemary Radford Ruether, *Faith and Fratricide*, Seabury Press, New York, pp. 251-261. Copyright 1974 Seabury Press. By permission of the publisher.

Selection 36—from Krister Stendahl, "Judaism and Christianity II: After a Colloquium and a War," *Harvard Divinity Bulletin*, Cambridge, N.S.I., 1967. Copyright 1967 by the President and Fellows of Harvard College. By permission of the publisher.

Selection 37—from Abraham Joshua Heschel, "No Religion Is an Island," *Union Seminary Quarterly Review*, New York, Vol. XXI, 1966, pp. 117-133. Copyright 1966 Sylvia Heschel. By permission of Farrar, Straus, Giroux.

INTRODUCTION

The emergence of Christianity from Judaism and its subsequent development involved an ongoing literary polemic with the mother religion.[1] The function of this extensive literature *adversus Judaeos* (against the Jews) was not necessarily the winning over of the Jews themselves. Often, Christian polemicists do not address the Jews explicitly. At other times, the "Jews" they seem to debate are merely literary devices. In a like fashion, the Church father Origen's pagan adversary Celsus (3rd century) invented a Jew to present his refutations of Christianity. The primary purpose of this literature then, at least in the patristic period, was the bolstering of Christianity—the confirmation of Christians in their own faith and the stemming of judaizing within the Church.

In the Jewish anti-Christian polemic, one may discern a similar process. In the Middle Ages (anti-Christian polemic in the talmudic period is sparse), Jews often wrote disputational works—in Hebrew—not to convince Christians but to dissuade wavering Jews from leaving the fold. For the medieval Jewish skeptic, it was often more profitable to be a Christian non-believer than a Jewish non-believer and there were those who were tempted to follow the path of least resistance.

Nonetheless, real encounters between Jews and Christians did take place. In private dwellings, in bishops' palaces, and in royal courts, Church and Synagogue recalled the old arguments and elaborated the new. In the protocols of these debates, such as those of Joseph Kimhi or Moses Nahmanides, one can at times feel the tension and strain of the antagonists as they grapple with each other. Such medieval disputations never really went out of style. In the twentieth century, Arthur Lukyn Williams of Cambridge was at work refuting a sixteenth century Lithuanian Jew. The same arguments, in differing guises, were presented by the missionaries known to Mendelssohn in the eighteenth century and to Buber in the 1930's. They are still echoed by evangelistic groups on college campuses across the continent.

It is partly because of this that polemical literature is so often associated with a relentless sameness, with monotony, with repetition, with endless *déjà vu*. By and large, this is so. The formulation may

---

1. See Bibliographic Survey, nos. 4, 11, 32, 41a, 41b, 44a, 45, 59, 62, 69, and most recently R. Ruether, *Faith and Fratricide*, New York: Seabury Press, 1974.

1

change in accord with the language of the age but the fundamental argument remains the same. Now it is the thought-world of Avicenna and Averroes, now of Kant and Hegel, now of the existentialists—but *plus ça change, plus c'est la même chose.* Is there any novelty in the justification for the execration of Israel from early Christianity to post-Christianity? Are Halevi or Mendelssohn or Buber dissimilar when they insist that the Christian cannot challenge the faith of Israel because he is ignorant of the experience of Israel? Is there any difference between Pablo Cristiá and Professor Oxtoby's attempting to refute Judaism by using Jewish sources (except that Pablo used more authoritative material)? Do not Isaac Troki and Abraham Joshua Heschel both seek to teach the gospel to Christians?

Yet if content does not change, personal styles and moods do vary. Some are the essence of restraint. We marvel at a Buber who could face those who would abolish Judaism and invite them to "wait for the advent of the One together;" at a Buber who could stand before one who would abolish Jews and coolly return his Teutonic *werter Herr Kollege.* Not all can achieve such studied composure; some of the writers here represented might even be accused of emotionalism. As Cynthia Ozick lived through the Yom Kippur War, she too was accused of being emotional or, more precisely, overwrought. In a sea of indifference, she cried:

> Who . . . was thinking about the death of Jews? Only Jews; the mass of Jews. . . . The Jews of dust, of ordinariness, alone with each other. Day by day it became more and more plain *how* alone —the aloneness of those who feel themselves condemned. . . . Oh the huddling of those days. We went to synagogues, to rallies, in a manyness that was as the dust of the earth.[2]

Emotion, overwroughtness, too, has its place.

"Polemics" appear in many places other than the obvious. Not only the disputational tract but the biblical commentary, the philosophical treatise, the sculpture, the oratorio, the drama, the poem, and many another medium all become vehicles for religious propaganda. More significantly, religious polemics need not be found only in a religious context. Even after heirs to a particular tradition have ceased to

2. C. Ozick, "All the World Wants the Jews Dead," *Esquire* LXXXII:5 (Nov., 1974), p. 208.

adhere to its formal doctrines, they may often retain its preconceptions and prejudices. Thus no study of the Jewish-Christian controversy would be complete until one takes note as well of its continuous and tenacious survival in secular or post-religious thought.

The selections in this reader are drawn from a wide variety of sources, Jewish and Christian, ancient, medieval, and modern. Highly technical material—such as medieval discussions of Christology—has been avoided. A principal criterion for selection of the readings was that they be stated clearly and frankly. For two millennia, Jewish-Christian relations have been characterized by polarization. Bland or timid formulations would only serve to obfuscate this fact.

The readings have been arranged according to topic in order to provide thematic units for discussion. *"Verus Israel"* (Part I), the dispute over the identity of the "true Israel"—heir to God's election—is at the foundation of the debate between Church and Synagogue. It was this which would have the greatest implications for the social and political status of Jews throughout history. From the Jewish point of view, it has been the central issue. For Israel, the debate over "Messiah and Christ" (Part II) was tangential; for the Church, of course, it was pivotal. In perusing these selections, one will note then that there has been disagreement not only on specific issues; there has been disagreement on the very question of which issues should be debated at all. "Law and Gospel, Letter and Spirit" (Part III) presents the conflicting views on the proper mode of interpretation of a common sacred text. Here too, Judaism will not recognize the manner in which Christianity formulates the question, viz. letter *or* spirit; it insists rather on both letter *and* spirit. "The Scepter of Judah" (Part IV) draws upon all of the preceding. The debate on theological grounds over the Jewish right to a homeland in Zion has been carried forth on many levels. A representative sampling is presented here. Finally, "Impasse, Coexistence, Dialogue" (Part V) deals with the question of whether the history of Jewish-Christian relations is to proceed unchanged indefinitely or whether there are in fact possible alternatives.

While this reader provides a broad overview, one may wish to use it in conjunction with a more intensive examination of one or several individual texts. A list of such works, currently in print, may be found at the end of the volume. Biblical references are according to the Masoretic Text unless otherwise indicated. The footnotes which originally appeared with these readings have generally been omitted.

The texts in this collection must be read with the awareness that they tell only part of the story. Despite the controversy between Judaism and Christianity in the Middle Ages—indeed, perhaps as an indirect result of it—there was much positive contact and mutual influence between the two religious communities. In the areas of biblical exegesis, philosophy, liturgy, art, literature, and social structure, the mark of the one is clearly stamped upon the other. In this sense, there is a certain irony in Vatican II's recently reiterated encouragement of "brotherly dialogues" stemming from common biblical and theological studies. From a historian's point of view, in the area of biblical studies alone, there was far greater cultural interpenetration in an age of "non-dialogue" eight hundred years ago. A companion to the present volume, which will provide this additional perspective, is now being planned.

Many of the readings in this anthology were written in a spirit of despair; they have been gathered here in a spirit of hope. The rabbis relate that Abraham set his tent at a crossroads. It was to be open on four sides that every wayfarer might find refreshment therein. Since the time of Abraham, men continue to travel their separate highways; yet they seldom pause to meet at the crossroads. To say that they ought not is to underestimate God; to say that they cannot is to underestimate man.

PART I

VERUS ISRAEL

THE FIRST CHRISTIANS were Jews. They saw Jesus as the Jewish Messiah and his coming as the redemption of Israel. When the majority of the Jewish people failed to share this belief, the early Church denounced them as obtuse and unable to perceive what had happened to them. Against them Matthew invoked the words of Isaiah: "You shall indeed hear but never understand, and you shall indeed see but never perceive" (Isa. 6:9f., Mt. 13:14f.). Yet the mystery that Israel refused to recognize their own salvation had to be explained. It became clear to the Christians that God had chosen to elect a new people from among the Gentiles. Conversely, the faithless Jews had lost the promises of the covenant and were rejected. This is expressed in a number of ways—among them, the vilification of the Jews in the gospels and the parable of Paul in Romans 11. There he compares Israel to an olive tree. The trunk represents those Jews who had acknowledged Christ. Those Jews who did not believe were likened to branches which were broken off. The Gentiles, the new Church, were grafted on in their place. This rejection of the old Israel is not irrevocable for when "the full number of the Gentiles come in, . . . all Israel will be saved" (vss. 25ff.) through their conversion. Until then, however, they have no positive role in the divine economy.

The transfer of the covenant from the old Israel to the new Israel meant that all the promises made to the former were now reassigned to

5

the latter. It was the Gentile Church who were the children of Abraham, the first Christian, who was himself saved by faith and not by the Mosaic law. Jacob was the Church; Esau the rejected Synagogue. As medieval Jewish polemicists complain, all prophecies of redemption and consolation were applied to Christians; all prophecies of chastisement to the Jews. The Jews were entitled only to divine wrath but not to divine love.

The theology of rejection was elaborated in many ways. There was, it was maintained, clear evidence for it. The Temple of the Jews lay in ashes; they themselves were excluded from Jerusalem and were scattered to the four corners of the earth. The Jews were typified by Cain, who murdered the Just One, and were therefore condemned to wander the earth forever. Their sole value lay in the fact that their very destitution was proof of the truth of Christianity.

In contrast, the Jewish claim to divine election did not entail a rejection of the nations: "Blessed be Egypt My people and Assyria the work of My hands and Israel My inheritance" (Isa. 19:25). All nations were equally righteous before the Lord so long as they kept the Noachide commandments which represent the basic principles of morality and social responsibility. Israel is called to spread a knowledge of God throughout the world but is not required—indeed, they are even discouraged—to call the Gentiles to abandon their own ethnicity and become Jews or to adopt the Torah of Moses. It is here that we encounter a remarkable paradox. When addressing each other, Jews throughout the Middle Ages spoke of Christianity with considerable esteem. The Church was viewed as a vehicle for the proclamation of the one God throughout the world. (Cf. sel. 37.) Yet in a disputational context, this was not the case. It was not enough for the Jews to defend themselves by claiming that the prophetic utterances referred to them. They had to go on the offensive and demonstrate that Christians had little claim to being called God's elect.

This debate was carried out on many levels. There was the philological and exegetical level which attempted to refer biblical names and passages to the Synagogue or the Church. Alongside this, there was the social critique: Only those who behave as Israel ought to behave are entitled to the name of Israel. It is here that Jews would claim not only that Christians failed to observe the commandments (an argument which would not especially impress a Christian) but that they ignored the very fundamentals of the morality which they asserted could be ascribed to them alone. It is here that Christian doctrine and ritual are pronounced idolatrous and the Christian clergy denounced as corrupt. Jews, on the other hand, prided themselves on their family life, their concern for education, and their solicitude for each other in the face of Christian oppression.

It was the doctrine of the divine rejection of Israel which, of all anti-Jewish teachings, was the most pernicious in terms of its practical applications. Cast off by God, they were to be despised by man. Jews were to dwell apart, have their opportunities for earning a livelihood restricted, wear special clothing, have no Christian servants, limit their social contacts with Christians. . . . The list is lengthy. With the passage of time, the condemnations grew more severe. Martin Luther, after his great disillusionment with the Jews, burst forth in a fit of invective which few of his predecessors could rival. Luther's denunciations were widely circulated as Luther's Germany became Hitler's Germany. It is here that one senses the sheer power of the anti-Jewish myth. For, as Karl Barth and Buber's letter to Kittel will show, nazi anti-Christians, nazi Christians, and anti-nazi Christians all drank from the same wells of hatred. Of the classic sources, Aphrahat stresses the election of the Gentiles, while Augustine emphasizes the rejection of the Jews. Joseph Kimhi and Isaac Troki present typical Jewish responses to this Christian challenge.

THE ELECTION OF THE JEWS

Joseph Kimhi (1110?-1170?) was a Provençal Jewish scholar who specialized in Bible and philology and translated several philosophical works from Arabic into Hebrew. His diverse intellectual activities led him into contacts and ultimately disputations with Christians. His *Book of the Covenant* (*Sefer ha-Berit*) is probably the first Jewish anti-Christian polemic to have been written in Europe. The work is written in the popular dialogue form with the bulk of the space given to the Jewish disputant. The account appears to be a composite of various discussions Kimhi held with Christian theologians.

Kimhi's main argument in the selection cited here is that the true Israel is to be known by her behavior—a behavior worthy of God's own people. Thus, in addition to the scripturally based arguments which are the substance of medieval polemical treatises, there emerges here a strong social critique, both implicit and explicit, of Christianity. The Jews are portrayed as the only ones who are faithful to the Ten Commandments, live ordered and moral lives, train their children to fear God, and act charitably. Christian asceticism is discounted as having no intrinsic value and as not being representative of Christian behavior in general.

The author's Christian antagonist counters that the Jews do not observe God's law because they take interest or, in the parlance of the day, usury. While money-lending was far from being the exclusive activity or the exclusive prerogative of the medieval Jew, it occupied a major place in the polemical literature. Kimhi's argument is straightforward: The taking of interest from a Gentile is permitted to the Jew by the Torah. Christians, on the other hand, circumvent the law by using legal fictions.

The passage cited is from J. Kimhi, *The Book of the Covenant,* Toronto: Pontifical Institute of Mediaeval Studies, 1972, pp. 32-35.

In selection 2, the rejection of Christianity's "Israelite" status is developed in a rather piquant fashion by Isaac ben Abraham of Troki. Troki (1533-1594) was a Lithuanian Karaite, a member of that sect of

9

Judaism which abandoned the Talmud and rabbinic Judaism in the early Middle Ages. However, in polemics with the Christians, Karaites and Rabbanites (followers of the Talmud) were one. It is no wonder that Troki's book, *Faith Strengthened* (*Ḥizzuq 'Emunah*), could become one of the most popular Hebrew disputational works ever written. Indeed, Christian theologians continued to write refutations of it through the twentieth century. (See, for example, A. Lukyn Williams, *A Manual of Christian Evidence for Jews,* 2 vols., Cambridge: Cambridge University Press, 1911-19).

The value of Troki's work lies in its order or, more precisely, its studied disorder. It is divided into one hundred chapters, a standard medieval representation of wholeness. Theoretically, fifty chapters are allotted for passages from the Hebrew Bible and fifty for a New Testament critique. Yet this division is purely artificial. The second half, far shorter than the first, actually begins with chapter forty-five. Furthermore, critiques of New Testament passages are liberally interspersed throughout the first section, while abundant interpretations of texts from the Hebrew Bible are to be found in the latter. There results a remarkable integration of a centuries old polemical tradition with the key passages being reinforced repeatedly in the reader's mind.

In terms of strategy, it must be recalled that the Hebrew Bible was accepted as binding in some sense by both sides in the Jewish-Christian debate. Not so the New Testament. From the twelfth century on, Jews took particular pains to point out what they felt were the weak points and contradictions in the Christian Scriptures. On the other hand, a Jew would not mind adducing them as evidence if it suited his argument. In this passage from *Faith Strengthened,* Troki uses the gospel in this way, even though it is "not accredited among us."

The Christianity which Isaac Troki knew was considerably different from that with which Joseph Kimhi was familiar. Sixteenth century Lithuania knew not *one* Christian Church but several—Lutheran, Roman, Greek, and Arian—and Troki disputed with them all. On the subject of *Verus Israel,* the very divisions within Christianity bolstered his case. If the Church is the New Israel, which church is it to be? Against this background, Troki argues with a Lutheran that as long as Roman Catholic "idolatry" (use of icons) exists, Christians cannot claim to be the people of the Lord.

The selection is adapted from *Faith Strengthened,* trans. M. Mocatta, New York: Ktav, 1970, I:4, pp. 18-20.

1.

THE BOOK OF THE COVENANT

Joseph Kimhi

The Christian said: You have neither faith nor deeds, dominion nor sovereignty, for you have lost all. I have many verses in your Torah which support me in this belief. Now finish your words.

The Jew said: Know that all the good which a man achieves in this world is of two kinds: good works and faith. If I can attribute good works and faith to the Jews, then they have everything. I shall begin to tell of these good works which you cannot deny and I shall start with the Ten Commandments: *I [am the Lord,* etc.] (Exod. 20:2). The Jews declare God's unity; *You shall have no [other gods besides Me]* (vs. 3). The Jews do not make idols; *You shall not take [the name of the Lord in vain]* (vs. 7). There is no nation in the world which avoids vain oaths as does Israel: *Remember [the Sabbath day]* (vs. 8). Only Israel keeps the Sabbath; *Honor [your father . . .]* (vs. 12); likewise, *You shall not murder, You shall not commit adultery* (vs. 13). Similarly, there are no murderers or adulterers among them. Oppression and theft are not as widespread among Jews as among Christians who rob people on the highways and hang them and sometimes gouge out their eyes. You cannot establish any of these things with respect to the Jews. These Jews and Jewesses who are modest in all their deeds, raise their children, from the youngest to the oldest, in the study of the Torah. If they hear a vile word from the mouth [of a child], they beat him and chastise him so that he would no longer swear with his lips. They train him too to

11

pray every day. If they hear that he has become accustomed to swearing, they keep him from [doing] so. Their daughters, with modesty, are not to be seen about nor found wanton like the daughters of the Gentiles who go out everywhere to streetcorners. The Holy One, blessed be He, has prevented all this [among the Jews]. Are you not then ashamed and embarrassed to say that you are a good people since you regularly and publicly encourage these sins. [You are] not from a people that will prevent this sort of thing. On the contrary, [your children] become accustomed to sin. [The sins] may be light as cobwebs in the windows of a house. Yet [such cobwebs] keep out the light [as] these sins keep the light from you.

I tell you further that whenever a Jew stops at the home of his fellow for a day or two or [even] a year, he will take no payment for food from him. This is so with all the Jews in the world who act toward their brethren with compassion. If they see their brother a captive, they ransom him; [if] naked, they clothe him and do not allow him to go about begging. They send him provisions in secret. You see with your own eyes that the Christian goes out on the highways to meet travelers—not to honor them—but to swindle them and take all their provisions from them. No one can deny that all these good traits which I mentioned are found among the Jews and [that] their opposites [are found] among Christians. Further, the Jews keep their Sabbaths and festivals conscientiously, while the Christians do all manner of work and travel about even on Sunday which is their holy [day]. What more can you ask for in the way of good deeds found among Jews and bad deeds found among Christians?

He answered: You are right in part. Yet what good are their deeds if they have no faith? I shall show you other deeds which you do that are contrary to religion. You lend with usury, although David said *Who will dwell in Your tabernacle? He who has not lent his money with usury* (Ps. 15:1, 5). I shall show you other good deeds which Christians do. There are people among them who separate themselves in their way of life from the world and from its pleasures and dwell in forests and deserts in affliction all their days.

The Jew said: Usury, to which you refer is mentioned in the Torah of Moses: *You may take usury on loans to foreigners but not on loans to your countrymen* (Deut. 23:21). Thus when David said *he who has not lent his money with usury* (Ps. 15:5), he reiterated what had been forbidden them. Do you not see that although Scripture said *You shall not kill* (Exod. 20:13), David killed thousands from among the nations? This is because *you shall not kill* means that you shall not kill one who is innocent. Similarly, *he who has not lent his money with usury* is to be interpreted with reference to what the Torah forbade. There was no need for David to refer to this since Moses had already stated it. The Jews are indeed scrupulous about usury and the taking of interest from their brethren as the Torah forbade. They are also very scrupulous about *'avaq ribbit* [that which is tantamount to usury, e.g., postponing payment while increasing the price at the same time]. A Jew will not lend his brother wheat, wine, or any commodity on a term basis in order to increase his profit, while you, who have disdained usury, sell all commodities to your brethren on a term basis at twice the price. You should be ashamed to say that you do not lend with usury for this is enormous usury. Furthermore, many Gentiles clearly lend on interest to [both] Jews and Gentiles, although Jews do not lend to their fellow Jews.

Now with respect to your statement that there are many holy people among them [the Gentiles] who separate themselves from this world in their lifetime, [it must be said] that they are one in a thousand or ten thousand, while the rest are contaminated by the ways of the world. It is well known that your priests and bishops who do not marry are fornicators. Now when Israel were in their land, there were few righteous men among them. Because there were many wicked men, Nebuchadnezzar came and exiled and slaughtered them. Thus David said *O God, Gentiles have invaded Your domain, etc. They have given the corpses of Your servants to the fowl of heaven for food, the flesh of Your righteous ones to the beasts of the earth* (Ps. 79:1f.). What good will it do you then if you have one man in a million who is conscientious about serving his God? Even more so, I do not believe that one who has isolated himself in the forest is perfect in his actions and his belief. Yet if he *is* perfect in his actions, they will do him no good if his faith is not perfect.

2.

FAITH STRENGTHENED

Isaac ben Abraham of Troki

An eminent disciple of Martin Luther one day, thus argued with me:—
"You know that in our gospel, Acts 5:34, it is mentioned that Rabbi
Gamaliel, a learned and distinguished man, addressed some Jews present
in the following terms: (vs. 38) 'Refrain from these men, and let them
alone, for if this counsel, or this work be of men, it will come to naught;
(vs. 39) but if it be of God, you cannot overthrow it, but it will continue firm, or else you may even be found fighting against God.' To
this he adduces an example in Theudas and Judas of Galilee, who came
forward as Messiahs of their own accord, without approbation and
decree of the Almighty, and were in a short time utterly destroyed, with
all their followers.

"You see then with your own eyes (said the Lutheran) that this
faith, that is to say, the faith of Jesus and his apostles, has not been
destroyed these 1500 years and more; consequently this trial (of the
veracity of the Christian faith proposed by the Jewish doctor) is a
convincing and perfect proof, that the words and acts of the founders of
Christianity met with the full approbation of God."

Upon this, I gave him the following reply:—The words reported
in the gospel as having been used by Rabbi Gamaliel are not accredited
among us; but were it even acknowledged that Rabbi Gamaliel did thus
express himself, we know that he did not speak in a prophetic spirit,
for he was no prophet, but that he merely expressed his views from

14

what he had experienced in his own time of Theudas and Judas of Galilee. Hence it is possible he might have uttered his views, as Scripture says (Psalm 19:12), "Who can be aware of errors," etc. On the other hand, you may perceive incontrovertible testimony of the contrary from the idolatry which preceded Jesus, and which was renewed after his time, and did not cease for so many centuries. You well know that the worship of idols was introduced prior to the existence of our ancestor Abraham; for Terah the father of Abraham was an idolater, as is recorded in Scripture, Joshua 24:2, concerning the father of Abraham and Nahor, "and they served other gods."

Since that period to the present time, 3000 years and more have elapsed; and the worship of images still continues. For we see your Evangelists, who follow in the steps of Martin Luther, accuse those who walk in the faith of the Pope of Rome of rendering homage to images in their houses of worship; yet it is manifest, that image-worship proceeds not from the will of God.

Thus has also the infidel Mohammed instituted the spurious religion of Islam—a religion the falsity of which you yourself acknowledge. Nevertheless, this delusion lasted for more than 1000 years and is to this day not put down.

Would you say then that these two creeds, viz., Popery and Mohammedanism because they are not yet abolished, were established by the approbation or command of God? I have not the slightest idea that a reasonable being can entertain such a supposition: but the fact is, that the Almighty says, "leave the foolish-minded to themselves, for in the future they will have to render account of their actions." Moreover, it is known, from the words of the prophets, that idolatry will continue till the time of the Messiah, whose advent we expect; for concerning that period see Isaiah 2:18, "And the idols he shall utterly abolish." Again, Zephaniah 2:11, "The Lord will be terrible unto them, for He will bring low all the gods of the earth," "and men shall worship Him every one from his place, even all the isles of the heathen." Again, Zechariah 13:2, "And it shall come to pass in that day, says the Lord of hosts, that I will cut off the name of the idols out of the land, and they shall no more be remembered," etc. Then will be fulfilled the passage contained in the same prophet, 14:9, "And the Lord shall be King over all the earth; in that day the *Lord shall be One, and His name One.*"

THE ELECTION OF THE GENTILES

The Iranian or Syriac church in the fourth century had a closer connection to Judaism than did its Byzantine or Latin counterparts. Its language, Syriac, was virtually that of the Babylonian rabbis; its Bible, the Peshitta, would have been perfectly intelligible to one conversant with the Targum, the Jewish Aramaic translation. Syriac Christianity grew alongside the flourishing eastern Jewish communities. Its adherents were themselves Semites and often the descendants of converts from Judaism. Yet this very proximity made it necessary for the Syriac church, no less than for the non-Semitic churches, to define itself over against Judaism.

Aphrahat, bishop at Mar Mattai near Nineveh, wrote a number of theological treatises or "demonstrations" several of which were dedicated to a refutation of Judaism. The sixteenth of these, written in 344, is entitled "On the Peoples Which Are in Place of the People" and deals with the question of the relation between the Old and the New Israels.

It is the judgment of some of those scholars who have studied Aphrahat that he "showed not the slightest traces of personal ill-feeling toward the Jews; and his calm, dispassionate tone proves that it was only his firm conviction of Christianity that caused him to assail Judaism" (L. Ginzberg, *Jewish Encyclopedia,* I, 665). Certainly, in comparison to other patristic writers such as John Chrysostom, he is not to be labeled antisemitic. The Jews are not generally vilified or abominated. Yet they are by necessity portrayed as rejected by God.

Aphrahat's chief witness in his argument is Scripture. His writings are part of a literary genre which is an outgrowth of the early "testimonies," "chains" of scriptural passages which in themselves were thought to expound a theological doctrine. Aphrahat adduces his texts with a minimum of commentary; yet there can be no doubt concerning his exegesis: The "rulers of Sodom and people of Gomorrah" (Isa. 1:10) are the Jews; yet the "House of Jacob" (Isa. 2:5) is the Church, the new people in place of the people. If the Jews pridefully claim that "we are the people of God and the children of Abraham," Aphrahat

17

ironically replies with Deut. 32:21: "I shall provoke you with a people which is *no people*. . . ." The peoples ("no people") provoke the Jews ("the people") by their resolute monotheism which shames the Jews themselves and restrains them from backsliding into idolatry. Here then is a response to Jewish allegations of Christian "idolatry" such as those stated in Joseph Kimhi and Troki. (See above, sels. 1 and 2.)

The passage from Aphrahat (sel. 3) was translated by Jacob Neusner in his study, *Aphrahat and Judaism,* Leiden: E. J. Brill, 1971, pp. 60-67.

The views on Judaism of St. Augustine (354-430), bishop of Hippo in North Africa, are better known than those of Aphrahat and served as guidance to the Church on the Jewish question throughout the Middle Ages. Like Aphrahat, Augustine, the author of the *City of God,* avoided the harsh invective used by Chrysostom. Yet unlike the Syriac father, he could not rest content with establishing the election of the Gentiles. Rather, he elaborated on the place of the Jews, the Old Israel, in the divine plan. Because of their sin against Christ, the Jews rightly deserved death. Yet, as with Cain who murdered the just Abel, they are not to die. Indeed, anyone who slays them shall himself be punished! For they are doomed to wander the earth—the *testes iniquitatis suae et veritatis nostrae*—the "witnesses of their iniquity and of our truth," the living proof of Christianity. Thus was the legend of the wandering Jew born. The Jews were to be tolerated because of their theological usefulness—witnesses for the Church and "slave-librarians," preservers of the Hebrew Scriptures which themselves witness to the Church.

Augustine's remarks on the Jews are scattered throughout various writings, a special tract devoted to the subject and his expositions on Psalms among them. Himself a convert from Manichaeism, a gnostic dualist religion with a large following at the time, Augustine wrote several treatises against his former faith as well. Selection 4, the classical passage which bestows the curse of Cain on the Jews is taken from the "Reply to Faustus the Manichaean" (12:9-13), reprinted with minor changes from *A Select Library of Nicene and Post-Nicene Fathers,* Buffalo, 1887, IV, 186-88. Biblical references are according to the Vulgate.

The translation of theological contempt into social contempt is a complex problem. Official spiritual rejection of the Jews did not universally preclude a productive coexistence between Jew and Christian. Nor must one presume that hostility to the Jews was always motivated primarily by the writings of the fathers and the theologians; economic rivalry might be at the root of the matter. Thus, while Christian writings taught of the perdition of the Jews, each and every Christian could make as much or as little of these writings as he saw fit.

One of the most remarkable of these reactions was that of Martin Luther (1483-1546) who both radically rejected and then radically reaccepted the antisemitic tradition. In 1523, six years after Luther's open break with Rome, he wrote a treatise called *That Jesus Christ Was Born a Jew*. With great sympathy, he rejected social antisemitism and maintained that if the Jews were properly treated, they would learn to respect Christianity, i.e. Protestantism, and convert. Indeed, tolerance is expressed even toward those who might remain obstinate. However, the Jews were to be no more responsive to Lutheran Christianity than to Roman Catholicism. Twenty years after the first treatise, Luther completely reversed himself in such writings as *Concerning the Jews and their Lies*. Giving full vent to his disillusionment, he advocates in explicit terms how the pariah people are indeed to be treated as pariahs. Drawing on older sources, he yet manages to outstrip them and goes far beyond such anti-Jewish legislation as the decrees of the Fourth Lateran Council in 1215. Selection 5 is taken from J. R. Marcus, *The Jew in the Medieval World,* Philadelphia: The Jewish Publication Society of America, 1938, pp. 166-69.

3.

ON THE PEOPLES WHICH ARE IN THE PLACE OF THE PEOPLE

Aphrahat

I. VOCATION OF THE GENTILES

The peoples which were of all languages were called first, before Israel, to the inheritance of the Most High, as God said to Abraham, "I have made you the father of a multitude of peoples" (Gen. 17:5). Moses proclaimed, saying, "The peoples will call to the mountain, and there will they offer sacrifices of righteousness" (Deut. 33:19). And in the hymn of testimony he said to the people, "I shall provoke you with a people which is no people, and with a foolish nation I shall anger you" (Deut. 32:21). Jacob our father testified concerning the peoples when he blessed Judah, saying to him, "The staff shall not depart from Judah, the lawgiver from between his feet, until there shall come he who possesses dominion, and for him the peoples will hope" (Gen. 49:10).

Isaiah said, "The mountain of the house of the Lord will be established at the head of the mountains and high above the heights. All the peoples will look to it, and many peoples from a distance will come and say, Come, let us go up to the mountain of the Lord, to the house of the God of Jacob. He will teach us his ways, and we shall walk in his paths. For from Zion law will go forth, and the word of the Lord from Jerusalem. He will judge among peoples and will correct all the distant peoples" (Is. 2:2-4). When he judges and corrects them, then will they

20

accept instruction, be changed, and be humbled from their hard-heartedness. "And they shall beat their swords into ploughshares, and their spears into pruning hooks. No longer will a nation take the sword against a nation; no longer will they learn how to make war" (Is. 2:4). From of old, those peoples who did not know God would do battle against robbers and against wrong-doers with swords, spears, and lances. When the redeemer, the Messiah, came, "he broke the bow of war and spoke peace with the peoples" (Zech. 9:10). He had them turn "their swords into ploughshares, and their spears they made into pruning hooks," so that they would eat from the works of their hands, and not from spoil.

Furthermore, it is written, "I shall turn chosen lips for the peoples, so that they will all of them call upon the name of the Lord" (Zeph. 3:9). From of old the nations did not have chosen lips, nor did they call on the name of the Lord, for with their lips they would praise the idols which they had made with their hands, and on the name of their gods they would call, but not on the name of the Lord. Furthermore, also the prophet Zechariah said, "Many and strong peoples will adhere to the Lord" (Zech. 2:11). Jeremiah the prophet publicly and clearly proclaimed concerning the peoples, when he said, "The peoples will abandon their idols, and they will cry and proclaim, saying, The lying idols, which our fathers left us as an inheritance, are nothing" (Jer. 16:19).

II. REJECTION OF ISRAEL

To his people Jeremiah preached, saying to them, "Stand by the ways and ask the wayfarers, and see which is the good way. Walk in it." But they in their stubbornness answered, saying to him, "We shall not go." Again he said to them, "I established over you watchmen, that you might listen for the sound of the trumpet." But they said to him again, "We shall not hearken." And this openly, publicly did they do in the days of Jeremiah when he preached to them the word of the Lord, and they answered him, saying, "To the word which you have spoken to us in the name of the Lord we shall not hearken. But we shall do our own will and every word which goes out of our mouths, to offer up incense-offerings to other gods" (Jer. 44:16-17). When he saw that they would not listen to him, he turned to the peoples, saying to them,

"Hear O peoples, and know, O church which is among them, and hearken, O land, in its fullness" (Jer. 6:18-19). And when he saw that they rashly rose against him and impudently responded to him, then he abandoned them as he had prophesied, saying, "I have abandoned my house. I have abandoned my inheritance. I have given the beloved of my soul into the hands of his enemies. And in his place a painted bird has become my inheritance" (Jer. 12:7-9). And this is the church which is of the peoples, which has been gathered together from among all languages.

So that you will know he has truly abandoned them [listen to this]: Isaiah further said concerning them, "You have abandoned your people, the house of Jacob" (Is. 2:6). He called their name Sodomites and the people of Gomorrah, and in their place he brought in the peoples and he called *them* 'House of Jacob.' For Isaiah called the peoples by the name of the House of Jacob, saying to them, "O House of Jacob, come and let us go in the light of the Lord" (Is. 2:5-6), for the people of the house of Jacob has been abandoned and they have become "the rulers of Sodom and people of Gomorrah" (Is. 1:10). "Their father is an Amorite and their mother is a Hittite" (Ez. 16:3, 45); "they have been changed into a strange vine" (Jer. 2:21). "Their grapes are bitter and their clusters are bitter for them" (Deut. 32:32). [They are] rebellious sons (Is. 30:1), and rejected silver (Jer. 6:30). [They are] "the vine of Sodom and the planting of Gomorrah" (Deut. 32:32); "a vineyard which brings forth thorns instead of grapes" (Is. 5:2). [They are] "a vine whose branches the fire has consumed, they are good for nothing, they are not serviceable, and they are not wanted for any use" (Ez. 15:4).

Two did he call Jacob, one to go in the light of the Lord, one to be abandoned. In place of Jacob they are called "rulers of Sodom." By the name of Jacob [now] are called the people which is of the peoples. Again the prophet said concerning the peoples that they shall bring offerings in place of the people, for he said, "Great is my name among the peoples, and in every place they are offering pure sacrifices in my name" (Mal. 1:11). Concerning Israel the prophet said, "I am not pleased by your sacrifices" (Jer. 6:20). Again he said, "Your sacrifices do not smell good to me" (Jer. 6:20).

Furthermore Hosea also said concerning Israel, "In lying they seek the Lord" (Hos. 5:7). Isaiah said that his heart is distant from his God, for he said, "This people honors me with its lips, but its heart is distant from me" (Is. 29:13). Hosea said, "Ephraim has encircled me in lying, and the house of Israel and Judah in deceit until the people of God go down" (Hos. 11:12). And which people [of God go down], if not the righteous and faithful people? If then he said concerning Israel, "He has surrounded me with lying and deceit," and concerning Ephraim, "Lo, the sinning kingdom of Ephraim has arisen in Israel,"—since the name of Judah is not mentioned in this saying, [then] they respond, *Judah* is the holy and faithful one that has gone down and [still] adheres to the Lord. But the prophet openly and articulately declared, "Ephraim *and* Israel have surrounded me with lying, for Jeroboam the son of Nabat has publicly turned them aside after the calf." "And Judah in deceit" (Hos. 11:12)—for in deceit and in concealment they were worshipping idols, as he furthermore showed Ezekiel their uncleanness (Ez. 8:10ff). Concerning them Hosea preached when he called them a licentious and adulterous woman. He said concerning the congregation of Israel, "Remove her licentiousness from her face," and concerning the congregation of the house of Judah he said, "Remove her adultery from between her breasts" (Hos. 2:2). Now, so that you should know that the prophet spoke concerning both of their congregations and called them [both] licentious and adulterous, he said at the end of the verse, "If she does not remove her licentiousness from before her face and her adultery from between her breasts, then I shall throw her out naked, and I shall abandon her as on the day on which she was born, and as on the day on which she went forth from the land of Egypt" (Hos. 2:2, 3, 15). [These are] *both* their congregations, one of Israel and one of Judah. The one of Israel has played the whore, and the one of Judah has committed adultery. And the people which is of the peoples is the holy and faithful people which has gone down and adhered to the Lord. Now why does he say that it has gone down? Because they have gone down from their pride. Ezekiel moreover called them by the name of Ohola and Oholibah, and *both* of their congregations he called two shoots of the vine which the fire has eaten (Ez. 23:4). David further proclaimed and said concerning the peoples, "The Lord will count the peoples in a book" (Ps. 87:6), and concerning the children of Israel he prophesied, saying, "They shall be blotted out of your book of the living. With your righteous they will not be inscribed" (Ps. 69:28).

You should know, my beloved, that the children of Israel were written in the book of the Holy One, as Moses said before his God,

"Either forgive the sin of this people, or blot me out from the book which you have written." He [God] said, "Him who sins against me shall I blot out of my book" (Ex. 32:31-33). When they sinned, David said concerning them, "They are wiped out of your book of the living. With your righteous will they not be inscribed" (Ps. 69:28). But concerning the peoples he said, "The Lord will number the peoples in the book" (Ps. 87:6). For the peoples were not recorded in the book and in the Scripture.

See, my beloved, that the vocation of the peoples was recorded before the vocation of the people. When they sinned in the wilderness, he said to Moses, "Let me blot out this people, and I shall make you into a people which is greater and more worthy than they" (Ex. 32:10). But because the time of the peoples had not come, and another was [to be] their redeemer, Moses was not persuaded that a redeemer and a teacher would come for the people which was of the peoples, which was greater and more worthy than the people of Israel. On this account it is appropriate that we should name the son of God [with] great and abundant praise, as Isaiah said, "This thing is too small, that you should be for me a servant and restore the scion of Jacob and raise up the staff of Israel. But I have made you a light for the peoples, that you may show my redemption until the ends of the earth" (Is. 49:6). Isaiah further preached concerning the peoples, "Hear me, O peoples, and pay attention to me, O nations, for the law has gone forth from before me, and my justice is the light of the peoples" (Is. 51:4). David said, "Alien children will hear me with their ears," and these alien children, "will be kept back and will be lamed from their ways" (Ps. 18:45, 46), for the peoples have heard and have been lamed from the ways of the fear of images and of idols.

If they should say, "Us has he called alien children," they have *not* been called *alien* children, but sons and heirs, as Isaiah said, "I have raised up and nurtured children, and they have rebelled against me" (Is. 1:2). The prophet said, "From Egypt I have called him my son" (Hos. 11:1). And the Holy One said to Moses, "Say to Pharaoh, let my son go that he may serve me" (Ex. 4:23). Further he said, "My son, my first born [is] Israel" (Ex. 4:22). But the peoples are those who hearken to God and were lamed and kept back from the ways of their sins. Again Isaiah said, "You will call the peoples who have not known you, and peoples who do not know you will come to you and turn" (Is. 55:5). Again Isaiah said, "Hear, O peoples, the thing which

I have done, and know, O distant ones, my power" (Is. 33:13). Concerning the church and the congregation of the peoples, David said, "Remember your church which you acquired from of old" (Ps. 74:2). Again David said, "Praise the Lord all peoples, and praise his name, O nations" (Ps. 117:1). Again he said, "Dominion belongs to the Lord, and he rules over the peoples" (Ps. 22:28). Again the prophet said, "At the end of days I shall pour my spirit over all flesh, and they will prophesy. No longer will a man teach his fellow-citizen nor his brother, and say, 'Know our Lord,' for all will know me from the least of them even to the oldest" (Jer. 31:34).

Concerning the children of Israel he said, "I shall send a famine in the land, not that they shall hunger for bread, nor that they shall thirst for water, but for hearing the word of the Lord. They shall go from the west to the east and from the south to the north to seek the word of the Lord, but they shall not find it, for he has withdrawn it from them" (Amos 8:11, 12). Moses earlier wrote about them, "When in the end of days many evil things will happen to you, you will say, Because the Lord is not in my midst, these evil things have happened to me" (Deut. 31:17). So it was that they said in the days of Ezekiel, "The Lord has abandoned the land, and the Lord no longer sees us" (Ez. 8:12). Isaiah said about them, "Your sins have separated between you and your God, and your iniquities have held back good things from you" (Is. 59:2). Again he said, "You will call in my ears with a loud voice, but I shall not hear you" (Ex. 8:18). Concerning the people which is from the peoples David said, "All you peoples clap hands, and praise God with the sound of praise" (Ps. 47:1). Again he said, "Hear this, all of you peoples, and pay attention, all who dwell on earth" (Ps. 49:1).

III. ISRAEL AND THE NATIONS

Even from of old, whoever from among the peoples was pleasing to God was more greatly justified than Israel. Jethro the priest who was of the peoples and his seed were blessed: "Enduring is his dwelling place, and his nest is set on a rock" (Num. 24:21).

And [to] the Gibeonites from among the unclean peoples Joshua gave his right hand, and they entered, took refuge in the inheritance of the Lord, and were hewers of wood and drawers of water for the congregation and the altar of the Lord. When Saul wanted to kill them, the heavens were closed up from [giving] rain until the sons of Saul were slaughtered. Then the Lord turned toward the land and blessed its inheritors.

Rahab, the prostitute who received the spies, and the house of her fathers received an inheritance in Israel.

Obededom of Gath of the Philistines, into whose house the ark of the Lord entered and by whom it was honored more than by all Israel, and his house were blessed by the Lord. Ethai, the Gathite, fed David when he was persecuted, and his name and seed were honored.

Ebedmelech the Ethiopian, the man of faith, raised up Jeremiah from the pit when the children of Israel his people imprisoned him. This is the matter concerning which Moses said concerning them, "The stranger that is among you will be higher, and you will be lower" (Deut. 28:33). They imprisoned and lowered Jeremiah the prophet into the lowest pit, but Ebedmelech the sojourner from Ethiopia raised up Jeremiah from the pit.

Ruth the Moabite, from the people smitten with wrath, came and was assimilated with the people of Israel, and from her seed arose the leader of kings, from whom was born the redeemer of the peoples.

Uriah the Hittite, from an unclean people, was chief among the men of David. Because David killed him with deceit in the war with the children of Ammon, desired his wife, and married her, David received the judgment that the sword would never depart from his house (II Sam. 12:10).

Furthermore Isaiah said concerning our redeemer, "I have set you as a covenant for the people and as a light for the peoples" (Is. 42:6). Now how was this covenant for the people? From the time that the light and the redeemer of the peoples came, from that time Israel was restrained from the worship of idols, and they had a true covenant. Concerning this matter Moses said, "I shall provoke you with a people which is no people, and with a foolish people I shall anger you" (Deut. 32:21). By us they are provoked. On our account they do not worship idols, so that they will not be shamed by us, for we have abandoned idols and call lies the thing which our fathers left us. They are angry, their hearts are broken, for we have entered and have become heirs in their place. For theirs was this covenant which they had, not to worship other gods, but they did not accept it. By means of us he provoked them, and ours was the light and the life, as he preached, saying when he taught, "I am the light of the world" (John 8:12). Again he said, "Believe while the light is with you, before the darkness overtakes you" (John 12:35). And again he said, "Walk in the light, so that you may be called the children of light" (John 12:36). And further he said, "The light gave light in the darkness" (John 1:5). This is the covenant which the people had, and the light which gave light for all the peoples, and lamed and hindered them from crooked ways, as it is written, "In his coming the rough place will be smooth, and the high place will be plain, and the glory of the Lord will be revealed, and all flesh will see the life of God" (Is. 40:4, 5; Luke 3:5, 6).

This brief memorial I have written to you concerning the peoples, because the Jews take pride and say, "We are the people of God and the children of Abraham." But we shall listen to John [the Baptist] who, when they took pride [saying], 'We are the children of Abraham', then said to them, "You should not boast and say, Abraham is father unto us, for from these very rocks can God raise up children for Abraham" (Matthew 3:9). Our redeemer said to them, "You are the children of Cain, and not the children of Abraham" (John 8:39, 44). The apostle said, "The branches which sinned were broken off. We were grafted on in their place and are partners in the fat of the olive tree. Now let us not take pride and sin so that we too may not be broken off. Lo, we have been grafted onto the olive tree" (Rom. 11:17, 18). This is the apology against the Jews, because they take pride saying, "We are the children of Abraham, and we are the people of God."

The demonstration on the people and the peoples is completed.

4.

REPLY TO FAUSTUS, THE MANICHEAN

Augustine

As Cain's sacrifice of the fruit of the ground is rejected, while Abel's sacrifice of his sheep and the fat thereof is accepted, so the faith of the New Testament praising God in the harmless service of grace is preferred to the earthly observances of the Old Testament. For though the Jews were right in practicing these things, they were guilty of unbelief in not distinguishing the time of the New Testament when Christ came, from the time of the Old Testament. God said to Cain, "If you offer well, yet if you divide not well, you have sinned." If Cain had obeyed God when He said, "Be content, for to you shall be its reference, and you shall rule over it," he would have referred his sin to himself, by taking the blame of it, and confessing it to God; and so assisted by supplies of grace, he would have ruled over his sin, instead of acting as the servant of sin in killing his innocent brother. So also the Jews, of whom all these things are a figure [a prefiguration], if they had been content, instead of being turbulent, and had acknowledged the time of salvation through the pardon of sins by grace, and heard Christ saying, "They that are whole need not a physician, but they that are sick; I came not to call the righteous, but sinners to repentance" (Matt. 9:12f.); and, "Every one that commits sin is the servant of sin;" and, "If the Son make you free, you shall be free indeed" (John 8:34, 36),—they would in confession have referred their sin to themselves, saying to the Physician, as it is written in the Psalm, "I said, Lord, be merciful to me; heal my soul, for I have sinned against You" (Ps. 41:4). And being

28

made free by the hope of grace, they would have ruled over sin as long as it continued in their mortal body. But now, being ignorant of God's righteousness, and wishing to establish a righteousness of their own, proud of the works of the law, instead of being humbled on account of their sins, they have not been content; and in subjection to sin reigning in their mortal body, so as to make them obey it in the lusts thereof, they have stumbled on the stone of stumbling, and have been inflamed with hatred against him whose works they grieved to see accepted by God. The man who was born blind, and had been made to see, said to them, "We know that God hears not sinners; but if any man serve Him, and do His will, him He hears" (John 9:31); as if he had said, God regards not the sacrifice of Cain, but he regards the sacrifice of Abel. Abel, the younger brother, is killed by the elder brother; Christ, the head of the younger people, is killed by the elder people of the Jews. Abel dies in the field; Christ dies on Calvary.

God asks Cain where his brother is, not as if He did not know, but as a judge asks a guilty criminal. Cain replies that he knows not, and that he is not his brother's keeper. And what answer can the Jews give at this day, when we ask them with the voice of God, that is, of the sacred Scriptures, about Christ, except that they do not know the Christ that we speak of? Cain's ignorance was pretended, and the Jews are deceived in their refusal of Christ. Moreover, they would have been in a sense keepers of Christ, if they had been willing to receive and keep the Christian faith. For the man who keeps Christ in his heart does not ask, like Cain, Am I my brother's keeper? Then God says to Cain, "What have you done? The voice of your brother's blood cries unto me from the ground." So the voice of God in the Holy Scriptures accuses the Jews. For the blood of Christ has a loud voice on the earth, when the responsive Amen of those who believe in Him comes from all nations. This is the voice of Christ's blood, because the clear voice of the faithful redeemed by His blood is the voice of the blood itself.

Then God says to Cain: "You are cursed from the earth, which has opened its mouth to receive your brother's blood at your hand. For you shall till the earth, and it shall no longer yield unto you its strength. A mourner and an abject shall you be on the earth." It is not, Cursed is the earth, but, Cursed are you from the earth, which has opened its mouth to receive your brother's blood at your hand. So the unbelieving people of the Jews is cursed from the earth, that is, from the Church, which in the confession of sins has opened its mouth to receive the blood shed for the remission of sins by the hand of the people that would not be under grace, but under the law. And this murderer is cursed by the Church; that is, the Church admits and avows the curse pronounced by the apostle: "Whoever are of the works of the law are under the curse of the law" (Gal. 3:10). Then, after saying, Cursed are you from the earth, which has opened its mouth to receive your brother's blood at your hand, what follows is not, For you shall till it, but, you shall till the earth, and it shall not yield to you its strength. The earth he is to till is not necessarily the same as that which opened its mouth to receive his brother's blood at his hand. From this earth he is cursed, and so he tills an earth which shall no longer yield to him its strength. That is, the Church admits and avows the Jewish people to be cursed, because after killing Christ they continue to till the ground of an earthly circumcision, an earthly Sabbath, an earthly Passover, while the hidden strength or virtue of making known Christ, which this tilling contains, is not yielded to the Jews while they continue in impiety and unbelief, for it is revealed in the New Testament. While they will not turn to God, the veil which is on their minds in reading the Old Testament is not taken away. This veil is taken away only by Christ, who does not do away with the reading of the Old Testament, but with the covering which hides its virtue. So, at the crucifixion of Christ, the veil was rent in twain, that by the passion of Christ hidden mysteries might be revealed to believers who turn to Him with a mouth opened in confession to drink His blood. In this way the Jewish people, like Cain, continue tilling the ground, in the carnal observance of the law, which does not yield to them its strength, because they do not perceive in it the grace of Christ. So, too, the flesh of Christ was the ground from which by crucifying Him the Jews produced our salvation, for He died for our offenses. But this ground did not yield to them its strength, for they were not justified by the virtue of His resurrection, for He arose again for our justification. As the apostle says: "He was crucified in weakness, but He lives by the power of God" (II Cor. 13:4). This is the power of that ground which is unknown to the ungodly and unbelieving. When Christ rose, He did not appear to those who had crucified Him. So Cain was not allowed to see the strength of the ground which he tilled to sow his seed in it; as God said, "You shall till the ground, and it shall no longer yield unto you its strength."

"Groaning and trembling shall you be on the earth." Here no one can fail to see that in every land where the Jews are scattered they mourn for the loss of their kingdom, and are in terrified subjection to the immensely superior number of Christians. So Cain answered, and said: "My case is worse, if You drive me out this day from the face of the earth, and from Your face shall I be hid, and I shall be a mourner and an outcast on the earth; and it shall be that every one that finds me shall slay me." Here he groans indeed in terror, lest after losing his earthly possession he should suffer the death of the body. This he calls a worse case than that of the ground not yielding to him its strength, or than that of spiritual death. For his mind is carnal; for he thinks little of being hid from the face of God, that is, of being under the anger of God, were it not that he may be found and slain. This is the carnal mind that tills the ground, but does not obtain its strength. To be carnally minded is death; but he, in ignorance of this, mourns for the loss of his earthly possession, and is in terror of bodily death. But what does God reply? "Not so," He says; "but whosoever shall kill Cain, vengeance shall be taken on him sevenfold." That is, It is not as you say; not by bodily death shall the ungodly race of carnal Jews perish. For whoever destroys them in this way shall suffer sevenfold vengeance, that is, shall bring upon himself the sevenfold penalty under which the Jews lie for the crucifixion of Christ. So to the end of the seven days of time, the continued preservation of the Jews will be a proof to believing Christians of the subjection merited by those who, in the pride of their kingdom, put the Lord to death.

"And the Lord God set a mark upon Cain, lest any one finding him should slay him." It is a most notable fact, that all the nations subjugated by Rome adopted the heathenish ceremonies of the Roman worship; while the Jewish nation, whether under Pagan or Christian monarchs, has never lost the sign of their law, by which they are distinguished from all other nations and peoples. No emperor or monarch who finds under his government the people with this mark kills them, that is, makes them cease to be Jews, and as Jews to be separate in their observances, and unlike the rest of the world. Only when a Jew comes over to Christ, he is no longer Cain, nor goes out from the presence of God, nor dwells in the land of Nod, which is said to mean commotion. Against this evil of commotion the Psalmist prays, "Suffer not my feet to be moved" (Ps. 66:9); and again, "Let not the hands of the wicked remove me" (Ps. 36:11); and, "Those that trouble me will rejoice when I am moved" (Ps. 13:4); and, "The Lord is at my right hand, that I should not be moved" (Ps. 16:8); and so in in-

numerable places. This evil comes upon those who leave the presence
of God, that is, His loving-kindness. Thus the Psalmist says, "I said in
my prosperity, I shall never be moved." But observe what follows,
"Lord, by Your favor You have given strength to my honor; You did
hide Your face, and I was troubled" (Ps. 30:6f.) which teaches us that
not in itself, but by participation in the light of God, can any soul
possess beauty, or honor, or strength.

5.

WRITINGS ON THE JEWS

Martin Luther

A. That Jesus Christ Was Born a Jew—1523

I will therefore show by means of the Bible the causes which induce me to believe that Christ was a Jew born of a virgin. Perhaps I will attract some of the Jews to the Christian faith. For our fools—the popes, bishops, sophists, and monks—the coarse blockheads! have until this time so treated the Jews that to be a good Christian one would have to become a Jew. And if I had been a Jew and had seen such idiots and blockheads ruling and teaching the Christian religion, I would rather have been a sow than a Christian.

For they have dealt with the Jews as if they were dogs and not human beings. They have done nothing for them but curse them and seize their wealth. Whenever they converted them, they did not teach them either Christian law or life but only subjected them to papistry and monkery. When these Jews saw that Judaism had such strong scriptural basis and that Christianity [Catholicism] was pure nonsense without Biblical support, how could they quiet their hearts and become real, good Christians? I have myself heard from pious converted Jews that if they had not heard the gospel in our time [from us Lutherans] they would always have remained Jews at heart in spite of their conversion. For they admit that they have never heard anything about Christ from the rulers who have converted them.

33

I hope that, if the Jews are treated friendly and are instructed kindly through the Bible, many of them will become real Christians and come back to the ancestral faith of the prophets and patriarchs. . . . [Luther considered the heroes of the Old Testament good Christians.]

I would advise and beg everybody to deal kindly with the Jews and to instruct them in the Scriptures; in such a case we could expect them to come over to us. If, however, we use brute force and slander them, saying that they need the blood of Christians to get rid of their stench and I know not what other nonsense of that kind, and treat them like dogs, what good can we expect of them? [Mediaeval Christians believed in a *Foetor Judaicus,* a "Jewish stench."] Finally, how can we expect them to improve if we forbid them to work among us and to have social intercouse with us, and so force them into usury?

If we wish to make them better, we must deal with them not according to the law of the pope, but according to the law of Christian charity. We must receive them kindly and allow them to compete with us in earning a livelihood, so that they may have a good reason to be with us and among us and an opportunity to witness Christian life and doctrine; and if some remain obstinate, what of it? Not every one of us is a good Christian.

I shall stop here now until I see what the results will be. May God be gracious to us all. Amen.

B. CONCERNING THE JEWS AND THEIR LIES—1543

What then shall we Christians do with this damned, rejected race of Jews? [The Jews were rejected by God since they refused to accept Jesus as the Messiah.] Since they live among us and we know about their lying and blasphemy and cursing, we can not tolerate them if we do not wish to share in their lies, curses, and blasphemy. In this way we cannot quench the inextinguishable fire of divine rage (as the prophets say) nor convert the Jews. We must prayerfully and reverentially practice a merciful severity. Perhaps we may save a few from the fire and the flames [of hell]. We must not seek vengeance. They are surely being punished a thousand times more than we might wish them. Let me give you my honest advice.

First, their synagogues or churches should be set on fire, and whatever does not burn up should be covered or spread over with dirt so that no one may ever be able to see a cinder or stone of it. And this ought to be done for the honor of God and of Christianity in order that God may see that we are Christians, and that we have not wittingly tolerated or approved of such public lying, cursing, and blaspheming of His Son and His Christians. . . . [Luther and others believed that the Jews cursed the Christians in their daily prayers.]

Secondly, their homes should likewise be broken down and destroyed. For they perpetrate the same things there that they do in their synagogues. For this reason they ought to be put under one roof or in a stable, like gypsies, in order that they may realize that they are not masters in our land, as they boast, but miserable captives, as they complain of us incessantly before God with bitter wailing.

Thirdly, they should be deprived of their prayer-books and Talmuds in which such idolatry, lies, cursing, and blasphemy are taught.

Fourthly, their rabbis must be forbidden under threat of death to teach any more. . . .

Fifthly, passport and traveling privileges should be absolutely forbidden to the Jews. For they have no business in the rural districts since they are not nobles, nor officials, nor merchants, nor the like. Let them stay at home. I have heard that there is a rich Jew riding around the country with a team of twelve horses—he wants to be a Messiah—and he is exploiting princes, nobles, land, and people to such an extent that important people look askance at this. [This was "the wealthy Michael," court-Jew of Joachim II of Brandenburg, a famous commercial magnate of the time.] If you princes and nobles do not close the road legally to such exploiters, then some troop ought to ride against them, for they will learn from this pamphlet what the Jews are and how to handle them and that they ought not to be protected. You ought not, you cannot protect them, unless in the eyes of God you want to share all their abomination. . . . [Luther seems to be inciting the robber barons to attack the Jews on the roads. Michael, the wealthy Jew, was actually seized in 1549 by highwaymen acting as agents for some of the most prominent citizens of Magdeburg.]

Sixthly, they ought to be stopped from usury. [Usury means any degree of interest, not only an exorbitant rate.] All their cash and valuables of silver and gold ought to be taken from them and put aside for safe keeping. For this reason, as said before, everything that they possess they stole and robbed from us through their usury, for they have no other means of support. This money should be used in the case (and in no other) where a Jew has honestly become a Christian, so that he may get for the time being one or two or three hundred florins, as the person may require. This, in order that he may start a business to support his poor wife and children and the old and feeble. Such evilly acquired money is cursed, unless, with God's blessing, it is put to some good and necessary use. . . .

Seventhly, let the young and strong Jews and Jewesses be given the flail, the ax, the hoe, the spade, the distaff, and spindle, and let them earn their bread by the sweat of their noses as is enjoined upon Adam's children. For it is not proper that they should want us cursed *Goyyim* [Gentiles] to work in the sweat of our brow and that they, pious crew, idle away their days at the fireside in laziness, feasting, and display. And in addition to this, they boast impiously that they have become masters of the Christians at our expense. We ought to drive the rascally lazy bones out of our system.

If, however, we are afraid that they might harm us personally, or our wives, children, servants, cattle, etc. when they serve us or work for us—since it is surely to be presumed that such noble lords of the world and poisonous bitter worms are not accustomed to any work and would very unwillingly humble themselves to such a degree among the cursed *Goyyim*—then let us apply the same cleverness [expulsion] as the other nations, such as France, Spain, Bohemia, etc., and settle with them for that which they have extorted usuriously from us, and after having divided it up fairly let us drive them out of the country for all time. For, as has been said, God's rage is so great against them that they only become worse and worse through mild mercy, and not much better through severe mercy. Therefore away with them. . . .

To sum up, dear princes and nobles who have Jews in your domains, if this advice of mine does not suit you, then find a better one so that you and we may all be free of this insufferable devilish burden—the Jews.

THE SPECTER OF THE SYNAGOGUE

Karl Barth (1886-1968) has been the most influential Christian theologian of the twentieth century. Raised in Swiss Calvinism, he moved into a Christologically centered scripturally oriented theology which has affected not only Christian thinkers but Jewish thinkers as well. Jews (and not a few orthodox Jews) have found his conception of God's movement towards man and his biblical orientation appealing. In his writings, especially the *Church Dogmatics,* Barth acknowledged the continuity of the Israel of old with the Israel of the present, the Jewish people. During the rise of nazism, Barth lost his position at the University of Bonn because of his theologically based opposition to the regime. Later, in 1942, he was to write: "A church that becomes anti-semitic or even only a-semitic sooner or later suffers the loss of its faith by losing the object of it" (*Church Dogmatics,* II, pt. 2, 236). In an even later essay, Barth wrote:

> Without any doubt the Jews are to this very day the chosen people of God in the same sense that they have been so from the beginning, according to the Old and New Testaments. They have the promise of God; and if we Christians from among the Gentiles have it too, then it is only as those chosen with them; as guests in their house, as new wood grafted onto their old tree. ("The Jewish Problem and the Christian Answer," in *Against the Stream,* London: SCM Press, 1954, p. 200).

Yet Barth's acceptance and recognition of the old Israel is dialectical. (See below, Bibliographic Survey.) In many passages in his writings, the Jews remain recalcitrant, perfidious, and rebellious in conformity with Christian theological molds.

The truth is that Barth's position towards Jews is ambivalent. Because of the authenticity of his Christianity, because he reads Scripture obediently, he becomes aware of the centrality of Israel in God's relation with man and in the very message that Christianity proclaims to the world. There is little doubt that Barth's experience with Nazism taught him just how equivalent the anti-Christian is to anti-semitism, how necessary the destruction of the Jewish people is to those who make war on the God of Israel and his commandments. But there is also in Barth an anti-semitism made up of two parts: the traditional anti-semitism of European Christendom . . . and the anti-semitism of Christian theology. As far as the first sort of anti-semitism is concerned, it may surprise some that a man of Barth's stature is not completely immune to it. But we must never forget that Barth is a human being subject to human frailties. [The other aspect of Barth's antisemitism stems from the Christian] tradition that Israel, the elect people, is also from the very first a rebellious people who kills its prophets. . . . (M. Wyschogrod, "Why Was and Is the Theology of Karl Barth of Interest to a Jewish Theologian?," in H. M. Rumscheidt, ed., *Footnotes to a Theology: The Karl Barth Colloquium of 1972,* Corporation for the Publication of Academic Studies in Religion in Canada, 1974, pp. 107f.).

Selection 6 is taken from Barth's *Church Dogmatics* (Edinburgh: T. & T. Clark, 1957, II, 205-213). Written during the Holocaust, it seems that—as in the past (see above, sel. 4.)—the very misery and suffering of European Jewry is called upon as a witness to Christianity. Whether this can be ascribed to human frailty is left to the reader to decide. The fact remains that on this topic the thinking of a Christian anti-nazi and that of a Christian nazi (see below, sel. 7.) are not very far apart.

6.

THE JUDGMENT AND THE MERCY OF GOD

Karl Barth

In the eternal election of the one man Jesus of Nazareth, God makes Himself the covenant-partner of the sinful man who has fallen away from Him and therefore fallen a victim to death according to His just judgment. The purpose of the election of this one man is God's will to save this lost man and to make him a participant of the glory of eternal life in His kingdom by taking his place in the person of this one man, by taking to Himself man's misery in Him, by making it His own concern, by clothing him in return with His own righteousness, blessedness, and power. Thus the election of this one man is His election for the execution of the judgment and mercy of God.

As the environment of the elected man, Jesus of Nazareth, the elected community of God is the place where God's honor dwells, i.e., where this Jesus as the Christ (Messiah) and Lord, and therefore in Him God's covenant purpose, His intervention for lost man, the execution of His judgment and mercy, is effective and visible among men. It is elected to serve the presentation (the self-presentation) of Jesus Christ and the act of God which took place in Him—as a testimony and summons to the whole world. The whole community of God— Israel and the Church—is elected for this as surely as it is elected in Jesus Christ. The whole community exists in this service as surely as Jesus Christ founds and constitutes it in both its forms, as surely as He is its unity and in its midst. Wherever the community is living, there

39

—in the power and commission of Him who is in its midst—it will at all events exist in the service of this presentation, the presentation of the judgment and mercy of God.

The specific service for which Israel is determined within the whole of the elected community is to reflect the judgment from which God has rescued man and which He wills to endure Himself in the person of Jesus of Nazareth. If in faith in Jesus Christ Israel is obedient to its election, if it is given to it to come to the Church and rise to life again in it, to attain in it the goal of its determination, the special contribution which it will make within the whole of the community to the work of the community will be this. It will express the awareness of the human basis of the divine suffering and therefore the recognition of man's incapacity, unwillingness and unworthiness with regard to the divine mercy purposed in Jesus Christ; the recognition of the justice of the judgment passed on man in the suffering of Jesus Christ. The Church needs this contribution. It cannot voice its witness to Jesus Christ and its summons to faith in Him without at the same time expressing this testimony which is peculiarly Israel's. Indeed there can be no witness borne to Jesus Christ without a confession of His saving passion, and therefore without a confession of the human misery that in His passion He has taken upon Himself and taken away. But the Church knows of man's misery only in so far as Israel too lives in it—as a reflection of the divine judgment. If this is lacking, if for any reason or in any form the Church has become estranged from its Israelite origin, sooner or later this will inevitably be seen and avenged in a loss of power in its witness to man's misery, and therefore in a similar loss in its witness to the cross and saving passion of Jesus Christ, so that in equal measure it will be a debtor to the world for both of these. But what power at all will there then be within it? What will it *not* then owe to the world? It will face the threatened loss of its character and commission as the Church; its name "Church" may well be on the point of becoming sound and fury. The Church has every reason to see that Israel's particular service is rendered in the community of God.

The Israelite form of God's community reveals what God elects for Himself when in His eternal election of grace He elects fellowship with man. It is not an obedient but an obdurate people that He chooses. He does not choose a people which has something to give Him but one which has everything to receive from Him. He chooses for Himself suffering under the obduracy of this people, and suffering under the curse and shame and death which this inevitably brings in its train. He burdens Himself with rebels and enemies and at the same time with their merited fall. This is the twofold burden that God chooses for Himself when He elects to make His fellowship with man radically true by becoming man Himself in the person of the Son of David, Jesus; when He elects the people of Israel for the purpose of assuming its flesh and blood. What is really meant by the humanity of the whole elected community of God, what it costs God to make Himself one with it, to be its God, emerges in its Israelite form. Over and above this, there emerges what is really meant by the humanity of the man in general and as such to whom God's electing love is addressed—that the price which God pays for this great love of His is no less than to make Himself a curse. Judgment has overtaken man, and if it is borne and suffered by God Himself, this only emphasizes its supreme reality and validity. What can we say, then, for man's good-will, his capacity and dignity, in view of the fact that he has been snatched from destruction only because God was pleased to take upon Himself this twofold burden, making Himself a curse? One thing is sure: since this is God's good-will with him he will not pit himself a second time against God; he will not suppose that he can abide in God's sight otherwise than by His mercy. One thing is sure: he will no longer be able to cast doubt upon the justice of the judgment that has overtaken him (just because it has been carried out in this way), nor on the truth of the verdict passed on him. The witness to all this is Israel's crucified Messiah (delivered up *by* and crucified *for* Israel). To testify to all this in His service is now also the duty of the whole community of God. It can and does do this in virtue of the fact that it is the community of Israel's Messiah and that accordingly it has also an Israelite form, so that Israel may and should come to life and live on even in its form as the Church. It acknowledges the misery of man for which God's mercy is the only help. By showing forth the mercy of God that passes understanding, it also shows to the world that on its own it can only plunge into ruin, that it cannot save itself from ruin. When Israel becomes obedient to its election—coming to life and living on in the Church—it then becomes the guarantee that this (the negative) side of the Church's message remains actual until the end of the world.

It is also God's aim that Israel should become obedient to its election, that it should enter the Church and perform this special office in the Church, in order that in this way the differentiation within the community should confirm its unity. But God does not wait till Israel is obedient before employing it in His service. This is settled and completed in and with its election as such, so that Israel cannot in any way evade it, whether it is obedient or disobedient. God does not make the purpose He has with Israel dependent on Israel's attitude to it. The situation is rather that Israel's attitude is itself dependent on God's purpose with it. Whatever its attitude, it necessarily takes place in the course of the fulfilment of the service assigned to and required of Israel in and with its election. It necessarily benefits the work of God's community as it is carried on in the Church. It necessarily witnesses to Jesus Christ. It necessarily confirms His election, and with His election the election of Israel, and with this the election of the Church as well.

If Israel were to be obedient to its election, this attitude would at once mean that its special witness about God's judgment would become the undertone to the Church's witness about God's mercy, and that sustained, covered and (in the best sense of the word) softened by the voice of the Church it would be taken up into the praise of the elected community. As a reminder of the settled dispute, the cancelled indictment, the forgiven sin, its witness would lend critical salt to the message of the accomplished reconciliation of the world with God without calling it in question. The special honor of Israel would then consist in continually consoling and exhorting the Church by magnifying to it the judgment which has overtaken man in and with the mercy of God, and therefore holding before it the cross of its Lord as its one and only hope, not to assail but to confirm the faith that the Church as such has to confess.

As things stand, however, Israel as such and as a whole is not obedient but disobedient to its election. What happens is that Israel's promised Messiah comes and in accordance with His election is delivered up by Israel and crucified for Israel. What happens further is that in His resurrection from the dead He is established as the promised One and believed on by many even of the Gentiles. What does not happen, however, is that Israel as such and as a whole puts its faith in Him. What happens, on the contrary, is that it resists its election at the very moment when the promise given with it passes into fulfilment. Israel refuses to join in the confession of the Church, refuses to enter upon its service in the one elected community of God. Israel forms and upholds the Synagogue (even though the conclusion of its history is confirmed by the fall of Jerusalem). It acts as if it had still another special determination and future beside and outwith the Church. It acts as if it could realize its true determination beside and outwith the Church. And in so doing it creates schism, a gulf, in the midst of the community of God.

But Israel's unbelief cannot in any way alter the fact that objectively, and effectively, even in this senseless attitude beside and outwith the Church, it is the people of its arrived and crucified Messiah, and therefore the people of the secret (concealed from it as yet) Lord of the Church. It cannot evade its electing God nor His elected community, and it cannot therefore escape its appointed service in it. It must now discharge it in a manner corresponding to its adopted attitude. Over against the witness of the Church it can set forth only the sheer, stark judgment of God, only the obduracy and consequent misery of man, only the sentence and punishment that God in His mercy has chosen to undergo Himself to prevent them from falling on us . . . only the realm of darkness as covered and removed and destroyed by the saving passion of Jesus Christ, only the existence and nature of fallen man in his futile revolt against God as completely outmoded and superseded in virtue of the mercy of God in Jesus Christ. This is how Israel punishes itself for its sectarian self-assertion. But it cannot alter the fact that even in this way it discharges exactly the service for which it is elected. Even in this way it really gives to the world the very witness that is required of it. How it is with man, the nature of the burden which God in His great love assumes, the nature of the curse which God has made Himself for the good of man, man himself by whom and for whom Jesus Christ was crucified—these things and all that they mean it reveals even in this way, even in and with its unbelief even in the spectral form of the Synagogue. The existence of the Jews, as is generally recognized, is an adequate proof of the existence of God. It is an adequate demonstration of the depths of human guilt and need and therefore of the inconceivable greatness of God's love in the event in which God was in Christ reconciling the world to Himself. The Jews of the ghetto give this demonstration involuntarily, joylessly and ingloriously, but they do give it. They have nothing to attest to the world but the shadow of the cross of Jesus Christ that falls upon them. But they, too, do actually and necessarily attest Jesus Christ Himself.

But they cannot again reverse what for the sake of man and therefore for their sakes God has put right in this Jesus Christ. They cannot restore to the sentence and punishment borne and taken away by Jesus

Christ, to the rule of Satan abolished by Him, to the existence and condition of fallen man superseded by His saving passion, the power which in God's eternal counsel these were allowed to hold only at once to lose it again, which in God's eternal counsel is denied and taken from them. They cannot give to the judgment willed and completed by God a meaning that runs counter to God's purpose. They cannot give the lie to the mercy of God in this judgment. By their resistance to their election they cannot create any fact that finally turns the scale against their own election, separating them from the love of God in Jesus Christ, cancelling the eternal decree of God. They can put themselves in the wrong, but not God's offering of His Son and the ordering of human affairs accomplished by it. They can be unthankful, but they cannot efface the reason and occasion they have for thanksgiving. They can disturb but not destroy the community of God of which they are the elected basis. They can assault but not overthrow the Church elected in and with their own election. They cannot prevent it from being called and gathered from among themselves and the Gentiles. They cannot weaken the effectiveness and truth of its message (the subject of which is their own Messiah and therefore their own salvation). They can do nothing to hinder the application and objective validity even for themselves of the testimony of God's mercy in Jesus Christ. They can do nothing to alter the fact that Jesus Christ, delivered up by them, is crucified for their sakes too. They can continually ratify the sin of this betrayal by failing to recognize the hand of God which in this very sin was undeservedly over them and at work for them. But they cannot reduce to impotence this work of God's hand which by their very sin has procured and accomplished forgiveness for the whole world and therefore for them also. They cannot prevent the fact that even in and with their obduracy they stand in the realm of this work of God's power. They can, indeed, deny their only hope, but no denial that they can make can render it ineffective. They cannot deny that Jesus of Nazareth is—primarily and supremely—theirs. As the promise irrevocably given them with this fact is maintained their membership of the one elected community of God is confirmed and ratified. It is confirmed and ratified not only with respect to the service which they cannot evade, but also with respect to the grace of God addressed to them, which they can indeed resist but cannot nullify.

The service for which the Church as the perfect form of the one elected community is determined, whether Israel obeys its election or not, consists always in the fact that it is the reflection of the mercy in which God turns His glory to man. The community in the form of the Church is the community of the risen Lord Jesus Christ. As the Church is elected, called and gathered from among Jews and Gentiles, the task laid upon it consists in the proclamation of its knowledge of the divine meaning of the judgment that has overtaken man in the death of Jesus, in witness to the good-will, readiness and honor of God with respect to man accepted and received by Him in Jesus Christ. This knowledge and insight it owes to its Lord, the crucified Messiah of Israel. In distinction from that of Israel the service of the Church is not a specific service beside which there might yet be another in the community of God. On the contrary, it includes in itself the particular service of Israel as a necessary auxiliary service. It takes it up, using and applying it as a contribution. As the one service of God's community is really discharged by the Church in so far as Israel too lives in the Church, so it is also by Israel in so far as in and with the crucified Messiah the Church lives in Israel also; in so far as in and with His resurrection the Church arises from Israel; in so far as Israel's determined purpose is fulfilled in the form of the Church. Israel in itself and as such can have only the involuntary share in the service of God's community described above. Israel in itself and as such lives actually—to its hurt—by the fact that it cannot renounce this share in the life of the community, that it *must* serve as a witness to the divine judgment. It can live to its salvation only as its special witness to God's judgment becomes the undertone of the Church's witness, the witness to God's mercy.

The Church form of the community reveals what God chooses for man when He elects him for communion with Himself in His eternal election of grace. He chooses for man His whole selflessly self-giving love. He chooses out of the treasures of His own nature righteousness and holiness, peace and joy, life and blessedness. He chooses for man His own self as Brother but also as Leader, as Servant but also as Master, as Physician but also as King. He therefore chooses for man the reflection of His own glory. He does this by electing flesh and blood from Judah-Israel to be His tabernacle and the Church of Jews and Gentiles to be His sanctuary, to declare to the world His gracious turning. All this happens wholly for *our* benefit, for our *benefit*. All that is implied in the nature and will of the electing God, all that God has given and gives and will give, all that is in any circumstance to be expected from Him, is what the community of God reveals in its final

form as the Church. It reveals that the primal, basic decision of God
with regard to man is His mercy, the engagement of His heart, and
therefore His most intimate and intensive involvement in the latter's
existence and condition. It reveals that even God's judgment is sustained
and surrounded by God's mercy, even His severity by His kindness,
even His wrath by His love. If the judgment that has overtaken man
(according to Israel's commission) forbids us to seek any refuge except
in the mercy of God, even more strictly does the mercy of God laying
hold of man (according to the Church's commission) forbid us to fear
His judgment without loving Him as Judge, without looking for our
justification from Him. All this is attested by the Lord of the Church;
the Lord who has created the Church by revealing Himself as such;
the Lord in whom the Church puts its faith as it has received it from
Him. All this the community of God must attest in His service. It can
and does so in virtue of the fact that it is the Church called and gathered
by this Lord; Israel gathered from Jews and Gentiles. In face of the
great misery of man it acknowledges the still greater grace of God. It
attests to the world its own misery by attesting to it first and foremost
the divine mercy. The Church is the bearer of God's positive message
to the world in which the negative is—necessarily, but still only sub-
ordinately—included.

The Church is the perfect form of the elected community of God.
In this form the unity of the community is revealed in its differentiation.
In this form it enters on its mediating function as the provisional environment of the man Jesus, on its mission in relation to the world.
The Church form of the community stands in the same relation to its
Israelite form as the resurrection of Jesus to His crucifixion, as God's
mercy to God's judgment. But this means that the Church is older than
its calling and gathering from among Jews and Gentiles which begins
with the ascension or the miracle of Pentecost. It is manifested at this
point, but it has already lived a hidden life in Israel. It is the goal and
therefore the foundation of the election of the people of Israel too. Nor
can Israel's obduracy do anything to alter the fact that His Church
exists in its midst from the beginning—since it is from the first the
natural root of the existence of Jesus of Nazareth—and that it is revealed over against Israel's own obduracy in the shape of a special
revelation of the promise, special blessing, special calling, guidance,
sanctification and claim, special faith and special service and obedience.
If this pre-existence of the Church in Israel does not abrogate its

peculiar determination for the setting forth of the divine judgment, the peculiar determination of Israel cannot and will not exclude the fact that in virtue of these special events occurring in its midst Israel too is already a witness to the divine mercy and therefore participates in advance in the definitive form of God's community, in its function and mission in relation to the world.

The election of Israel, then, is not only negatively confirmed by the fact that Israel as such and as a whole has in any case to fulfil its determination and to serve as a reflection of the divine judgment, but also positively by the fact that from the very first the Church pre-exists and is prefigured in its midst. With *Israel's* election in view God has, according to Scripture, acted among men from the beginning of the world in the form of election. And on the basis of Israel's *election,* in order continually to reveal and attest it, God proceeds to elect men in and from its midst for special appointment, mission and representative function, as exponents and instruments of the mercy in which He has made this people His own. Their existence does not alter in the very least the determination of Israel as such and on the whole. But it sets in relief what Israel has to reveal in reflection of the divine judgment: the misery of man, not as it is left to take its course, but as it is taken to heart by God and considered and limited from all eternity; not the wrath of God raging for its own sake, but the fire of His love which consumes and yet does not destroy, but rather purifies and saves. It is, indeed, in this sense that the crucifixion of Christ is the fulfilment of the divine judgment. It is in this sense, too, that the negative side of the Church's message (as the Word of the cross of Jesus Christ) should and will retain its actuality until the end of the world. That it has been present with this meaning from the very first is shown by the existence of the elect from the foundation of the world, and within the elected people Israel by the pre-existence of the Church in Israel.

The existence of the elect in and from Israel does not alter at all the determination of Israel as such as a whole because these elect are exceptions which as such do not suspend the rule that Israel has to serve the revelation of the divine judgment. Again, it is only partially that in their function and mission they point beyond this rule. Again, in Israel they are only too consistently opposed by "reprobates" in whom the rule appears to be expressly confirmed. And finally, the circle of the elect grows continually smaller, or at least continually less visible, in the course of Israel's history, until it is ultimately reduced to the person of one man, Jesus of Nazareth. Strictly speaking, the pre-existent life of the Church in Israel consists only in the light which, without changing its character, is provisionally cast on the history of Israel by this one man, who is Israel's future and goal, making visible within this history certain individual, fragmentary, contradictory and transitory prefigurations of the form of the community which will be revealed in and with the appearance, death and resurrection of Jesus Christ. The pre-existent life of the Church in Israel consists in the fact that again and again in its history there is revealed a contradiction against the sin of man, an illumination and clarification of the divine judgment, an obedience and faith which are disclosed and validated in their reality, not indeed by the course and character of this history in itself and as such, but by its future and goal in the person of Jesus of Nazareth and the existence of His Church. The pre-existent life of the Church in Israel consists, then, in what the fulfilment shows to be the real prevision and prophecy of the Church itself occurring in and with the existence of these elect in and from Israel and constituting the purpose of their special election.

But if, for its part, the Church as the perfect form of the elected community has as such and as a whole the universal, uncontradicted and constant determination to praise God's mercy, it will not refuse to recognize itself in the prototype, prevision and prophecy of the elect in and from Israel, and therefore to see its interrelationship with them. More than that, it will understand and acknowledge that in and with these elect the election of all Israel is established. It will thus regard itself as united and bound to all Israel—in spite of the very different form of its membership in the community of God. Even more, it will reckon it as a special honor to have in its midst living witnesses to the election of all Israel in the persons of Christian Israelites. And, finally, it will interpret its own existence, its calling and gathering from Jews and Gentiles, only in analogy to that of these elect in Israel. It can never by any chance fail to recognize that—in its Jewish and, above all, its Gentile members—it is snatched with them from the judgment to which (according to Israel's mission) the whole world as well as Israel is liable, and that it no less than they is called by special mercy to proclaim to the same world (and also to all Israel itself) the victorious mercy of God. To be sure, the Church waits for the conversion of Israel. But it cannot wait for the conversion of Israel to confess the unity of the mercy that embraces Israel as well as itself, the unity of the community of God.

A REPLY TO A CHRISTIAN NAZI

The historian of antisemitism, Jules Isaac, has written: "Christian anti-Semitism is the powerful, millenary, and strongly rooted trunk upon which (in the Christian world) all other varieties of anti-Semitism are grafted, even those of a most anti-Christian nature." (Cited from E. L. Flannery, *The Anguish of the Jews,* New York: Macmillan, 1964, p. 273.) In accord with this, the principles established by the theology of rejection were brought to a new metamorphosis in nazism. Here, the problem of the accursed, homeless, alien race was to be treated in a manner now well known to all. Many, of course, deny such a connection, since, as they rightly maintain, nazism was anti-Christian. Obviously then, many Christians vehemently opposed nazism. Yet for a peculiar segment of German Christianity, national socialism was the fulfilment of the Christian religion. One such Christian nazi was Gerhard Kittel (1888-1948). Kittel's father, Rudolph, had been a distinguished biblical scholar and had edited the *Biblia Hebraica.* Gerhard specialized in New Testament research and was the first editor of the *Theological Dictionary of the New Testament.* "Kittel affirmed the national renewal through national socialism, with which he dubiously associated a 'Christian' antisemitism." (*Religion in Geschichte und Gegenwart*[3], Tübingen: J. C. B. Mohr, 1959, III, 162b.) In his belief that the "national socialist labor party clings to a positive Christianity," he contributed to nazi racist propaganda from the early 1930's. In the first phases of nazism, Kittel considered the possibility of solving the Jewish problem through extermination. (See the footnote to Buber's letter below.) He rejected it, however, on the grounds that it was inexpedient. Later, he came to agree with established policy. In a classic instance of projection, Kittel wrote *The Treatment of the Stranger According to the Talmud* (1943), in which he alleged Jewish exclusivity and Jewish practice of genocide in the second century. (See M. Weinreich, *Hitler's Professors,* New York: YIVO, 1946.)

In 1933, Kittel sent his *The Jewish Question* with an accompanying letter to Martin Buber (1878-1965). In this work, Kittel advocated the imposition of "alien status" upon the Jews as part of his "lending

49

a Christian meaning to the struggle against Judaism." On their part, *authentic* Jews should accept this willingly as "God's just dispensation." (The echo of patristic and medieval antisemitic writings is unmistakable.) Kittel's letter was sent as a challenge which Buber could not ignore. The situation strikingly resembled the encounter between Mendelssohn and Lavater in Germany two hundred years earlier. (See below, sel. 30.) Both challenges came at critical junctures in German Jewish history—the first, at a time when the Jews were obtaining their civil rights; the second, when they were losing those rights and about to lose their very lives. Both men, Mendelssohn and Buber, were reluctant to speak out; but both responded to the challenge when there was no choice left to them. Buber's action was in a real sense heroic since his temerity could have led to his end in a concentration camp.

Buber's response has been translated from *Die Stunde und die Erkenntnis: Reden und Aufsätze,* Berlin: Schocken, 1936, pp. 171-77. The national socialist overtones of such terms as *Volk* (people), *Volksgenossen* (fellow members of a people), and *Volkstum* (character of a people) cannot be adequately conveyed in English. These words have therefore been left in the original as has Buber's icily correct *werter Herr Kollege* ("worthy colleague").

7.

AN OPEN LETTER TO GERHARD KITTEL

Martin Buber

You have sent me your essay on the Jewish question, *werter Herr Kollege*. From the accompanying letter and from the text itself I conclude that you believe yourself to be in agreement with me; not, to be sure, on your specific judgments about Judaism and your suggestions on how to treat it but on the essential issue: our basic religious commitment.

Since your statements were made publicly, I must contradict them publicly.

I need say nothing of your judgments and demands; they are the prevailing ones. I learned from your essay that which I neither knew nor suspected: that they are yours as well; that you maintain that "a member of a foreign people" has "no business in German literature;" that "if he wants to be a writer," he should "work in a literature which is clearly marked as Jewish and which is intended for his coreligionists and *Volksgenossen*;" that "if his book is of general literary value and transcends that particular *Volkstum*," there would be "nothing to prevent its being read by Germans in the same way that Swedish and French literature is translated and read by us." You and the public will, I hope, understand that I have nothing to say to this or to anything of this sort in your essay; especially since you make your intention of "lending a Christian meaning to the struggle against Judaism" clear in your introduction.

Yet it is incumbent upon me to object, especially since you welcome in this lending the participation of Jews, namely those Jews who, as I, look forward to a religious renewal of Judaism. According to you, the problem is "whether it will be possible to arouse a living religion in that part of Jewry which says yes to alien status." The "authentic Jewry of the future" would be that which practices "obedience under alien status." But what you understand by "alien status" is clarified by the answer to the question of what should happen to Jewry. There you have stated that one should "resolutely and consciously preserve the historical fact" of "alien status" among nations. You explained your understanding of this in this fashion: the "right of the guest" must be sharply set off from that of the citizen; the Jew must give up "all claims to civil equality." If he proves a "decent guest," "there may then come a time" when he appears only "relatively unequal" and no longer "absolutely inferior." You take "obedience under alien status," which according to you belongs to a pious Jewish attitude, to mean that discrimination against and defamation of Judaism must be accepted in faith; that it must therefore be viewed as God's just dispensation and as the just action of men. Hence, you presuppose the identity of that which you mean by alien status with that which God, to whom we owe obedience, means by alien status. But this is not so.

That which the God of the Bible means by alien status, more correctly guest status (a *ger* is one who is a guest in a land), can be learned from the Pentateuch. In an extraordinary appeal, the community is admonished (Num. 15:16; cf. Lev. 24:22): "Congregation! There shall be one law for you and for the resident guest; it shall be a law for all times throughout the generations. You and the guest shall be alike before YHVH (the LORD); the same instruction and the same rule shall apply to you and to the guest who resides among you." Thus no discrimination! But it is not only a question of law; it is a question of love. "When a guest resides with you in your land, you shall not wrong him. The guest who resides with you shall be to you as one of your citizens. You shall love him as yourself for you were guests in the land of Egypt" (Lev. 19:33f.). In Deuteronomy, with even greater emphasis, love is not only found with the dative [showing love to him] but with the accusative [loving him] in a way at once holy and paradoxical. "For YHVH your God is the God of gods and the Lord of lords, the great, the mighty, the awesome God, who shows no favor and takes no bribe but upholds the cause of the fatherless and the widow, who loves the guest and gives him food and clothing. You too must love the guest for you were guests in the land of Egypt" (Deut. 10:17ff.). Love of the guest is an aspect of biblical *imitatio Dei*: As God loves the unprotected, so must you love him! The acceptance of this stance has consequences which extend to a redemption and a mystery that unites all. It is said of the peace-offering which is offered by the community because of an error (Num. 15:26): "The whole Israelite community and the guest residing among them shall be forgiven for it happened to the entire people through error."

Yet, *Herr Kollege*, although you quote a passage from Deuteronomy in which we read that one may not subvert the rights of the alien [Deut. 24:17], you quote none of those passages in which we read that this right of the alien is not separate from that of the natives of the land but that both rights are the "same right." Only if you start from this Magna Carta of biblical faith, which should be binding not only upon Israel but upon all nations among whom guests reside (or is it your belief that God no longer asks this justice and love from nations), and only if you believe that this was not abrogated by the New Testament (for how could the gospel intend a diminishing of justice and love between nation and nation?), only then is it possible to talk in an attitude of faith of an "alien status" and of an "obedience under alien status." However, if one does this in the seriousness of faith as a believer among the nations, then surely one must first of all inquire into the obedience *of the nations.*

However, an obedience under alien status as you understand it (but as God does not understand it) God does not order us to give. It does not become us to rebel against it but it does not become us either to yield to the will of a *Volk* as if it were the will of God. Psalm after psalm of our Book, adopted by the Church, utters an appeal to the liberator from oppression. Psalm after psalm would be blasphemy if God not only demanded of us that we should endure, but also that we resign ourselves without appeal to whatever He has ordained. We pray today as well. The "enemy" against which the psalmist inveighs means, as we utter the psalm in prayer, not men or human powers but the original tempter, who hinders redemption in history.

"Authentic Jewry," as you say, "remains faithful to the symbol of the restless and homeless alien who wanders the earth." Judaism does not know of any such symbol. The "wandering Jew" is a figure of Christian legend, not a Jewish figure. Authentic Jewry is ever aware that *in the very next moment* the promise may be fulfilled and its wandering may end. It does not believe that it is ordered to affirm the dispersion but believes that it must prepare itself in the dispersion for the ingathering. It knows of no "tragedy willed by God" which it must needs recognize but knows only the mercy which calls man to His work.

History is no throne speech of God but His dialogue with humanity. He who does not wish to miss everything must be mindful to discern the voice of the Partner. The "historical fact" of "alien status," the reinstatement of which you, *Herr Kollege,* hold to be the "solution of the Jewish question,"* is partly the question itself—God's question to the nations and to Israel which He poses in history; partly it is the lack of an answer. To be sure, emancipation as it took place was not the true answer either.[1] But it does not follow from this that one must go back to that lack.

July, 1933

---

* Of the other three "attempts at solution" which you mention, extermination, assimilation, and Zionism, we wish to touch upon the last only. The arguments which you put forward against Zionism are partly exaggerated. (As one who has constantly fought for a more serious consideration of Arab claims, I have the right to say that there is no ground for speaking of a "frightful violation of the *fellaḥin.*") Partly they are false. I am hardly able to understand how you can hold "unemployment and need" to be prevalent in Palestine of today or how you can see in residential and agricultural cooperatives—a witnessing to collectivity and sacrifice—communistic tendencies which reflect back into "lands of culture and which wish to penetrate and poison those countries." Finally, the growing reality of faith within Zionism is totally unknown to you. (MARTIN BUBER)

1. In a later reply to Kittel, Buber observed that the failure of emancipation was that Jews were emancipated individually but not collectively (F.E.T.)

PART II

MESSIAH AND CHRIST

From the outset, Christianity had marveled at the failure of the Jews to accept Jesus as the Messiah. He was, in the words of Paul, a "stumbling-block" (1 Cor. 1:23) with which the Jewish people could not come to terms. Yet if Jesus was the central fact in the lives of the early Jewish and Gentile Christians, he was, for the majority of his Jewish contemporaries only one among many "messiahs" who made their appearance in first and second century Palestine. From their own traditions, biblical and rabbinic-apocalyptic, the Jews had a certain conception of how the true Messiah would appear and what deeds he would accomplish. He was first of all to be a man of commanding presence; he was to restore the Kingdom to Israel. Only those figures who held some promise of fulfilling these conditions could get a hearing on the part of the Jews. Simon Bar Kokhba, at the time of the Hadrianic War in 135, could be declared a messianic figure even by the illustrious Rabbi Akiba. Jesus could not have been. Bar Kokhba's exploits on the battlefield gave hope that Israel might be liberated. Jesus' triumphal entry into Jerusalem could be seen at the very best as a simulation.

There have been two streams in Jewish messianism throughout post-biblical times. One is apocalyptic with the expectation of a great cataclysm which would change the order of nature or at least the order of society; the other is evolutionary and envisions a gradual progression, or indeed regression, to the primordial state of creation. Both functioned side by side and indeed at times might become fused. In the seventeenth century, a time of general world-wide messianic expectations, a new Jewish "messiah", Shabbetai Zevi, appeared in Turkey. With astonishing rapidity, his fame became known throughout world Jewry. It was indeed believed by many—if not most—that the redemption was at hand. Shabbetai Zevi's messianic career ended, however, not with his leading Israel to Zion but in his apostasizing to Islam. Many of his followers, of course, abandoned him. Others, however, were unable to believe that they had been living a lie. They developed a theology, or rather messialogy, in which they maintained that Zevi's apostasy was part of his messianic mission: In order for him to achieve total redemption, he had to descend into total evil. With the passage of time, these followers went underground and broke into several splinter sects. Some, indeed, developed a theory in which Zevi and his successors were considered to have been incarnations of the Divinity. Today, these crypto-Sabbatians, the Turkish Dönmeh, still survive but their numbers are rapidly diminishing. This then is a classical example of a Jewish messianism which failed because it did not fulfill the traditional conception of the role of the Messiah.

Of course, this classical Jewish conception is not absent from Christianity either. It is present in the concept of the *parousia,* the second coming, in which Christ is destined to come again in might as He came once in humility. Yet, in advancing the argument that the Messiah *had* come, the Church neglected the doctrine that He *will* come, thereby creating an ever greater gap between the Jewish and Christian conceptions.

For the Jew in all ages, there was a bitter, if not unbearable, irony in being told that the world had been redeemed as he witnessed a world so very far from redemption—and as he was told that the proof of the world's redemption was his own lack of it.

The fundamental differences between the Jewish and the Christian views on the Messiah are presented here in an essay by Joseph Klausner. David Kimhi elaborates on messianic passages in the Bible and Moses Nahmanides expresses his reaction to certain Christologically interpreted rabbinic passages in the 1263 Barcelona debate devoted to the question of whether the Messiah had come or not. Justin Martyr's *Dialogue with Trypho,* largely concerned with Christology, demonstrates how Jesus' life is related to texts from the Hebrew Bible. This is done too in a rather engaging fashion in a twelfth century religious play which has the prophets come forth in procession presenting their own Christological prophecies.

A SCHOLAR'S FORMULATION

Joseph Klausner (1878-1958), literary critic, historian, and philologist, received his early education in Odessa where he later became active in Zionist and Hebrew literary circles. After the Russian Revolution, he was offered a university lectureship but emigrated to Palestine in 1919. There, he became Professor of Hebrew Literature at the Hebrew University.

Among Klausner's many concerns was an interest in Christian origins. His classic *Jesus of Nazareth* (1922) was written in Hebrew with the intention of making it accessible to the *Yishuv* or Palestinian Jewish community. It was therefore a biography of Jesus written for Jewish nationalists from the Jewish nationalist point of view. In this, he broke with the liberal-apologetic tendency in appraisals of Jesus which sought to reclaim him in the context of a negative assessment of Christianity. Klausner, through a mastery of the contemporary rabbinic sources, placed Jesus in his Jewish setting and presented him as a Jew. For Klausner, Jesus saw himself less as a universal savior than as the Jewish Messiah—although his utopianism led him beyond the limits of the "normative" Jewish framework. Klausner maintained that the true break came with Paul. He developed this theme in a sequel, *From Jesus to Paul* (1933). A third volume, *The Messianic Idea in Israel,* traced the development of the Jewish conception of Messiah from the prophets through the apocrypha and the period of the Mishnah. To the third edition of this work, Klausner added an appendix which had originally appeared separately in Hebrew. This appendix, "The Jewish and the Christian Messiah," distinguishes between the Jewish and Christian conceptions of redemption. The former speaks of a Messiah who is a physical redeemer who comes for the sake of Israel; who is a human king who dies a natural death; and who, finally, is not really indispensable since the redemption of Israel can be conceived without him for God alone is the Redeemer. The Christian Messiah is a spiritual savior who has come to redeem mankind as a whole; who does so through vicarious atonement; and who, as son of God, is God Himself so that the Divinity and the Messiah are one.

As a piece of scholarship, Klausner's essay aspires to objectivity. Yet every scholar works from a particular set of preconceptions and the sought-for objectivity may be illusory. (Note his concluding sentence.) Yet this study is based entirely on classical sources and, as such, serves as an excellent introduction to the controversies on this question in the Middle Ages. It has been reprinted from *The Messianic Idea in Israel,* trans. W. F. Stinespring, New York: Macmillan, 1955, pp. 519-531.

8.

THE JEWISH AND THE CHRISTIAN MESSIAH

Joseph Klausner

REMARK ONE:

The subject of this article would require a whole book for its elucidation. Within the limits of a short article I can only indicate the general outlines of the problem and restrict myself to certain important principles. Also, for the sake of brevity, I shall be compelled to cite from the extensive literature on matters pertaining to this subject only what is most relevant.

REMARK TWO:

The conception both of the Jewish Messiah and of the Christian Messiah has changed from period to period. The Jewish Messiah of Isaiah and Jeremiah is not the same as that of Daniel or the Ethiopic Enoch; nor is the conception of the Jewish Messiah in all these like that in the early Talmudic Aggadah, the *Mishneh Torah* [law code] of Maimonides, or the Kabbalistic books. It is likewise with respect to the conception of the Christian Messiah: Jesus himself understood his Messiahship very differently from the way in which Paul understood it. The later Church Fathers greatly modified what Paul taught; and the

Catholics, Greek Orthodox, and Protestants differ greatly among themselves about how to conceive of the Messiah.

In this brief article I shall deal only with the conception of the Jewish Messiah as it has become crystallized in Biblical-Talmudic Judaism and accepted by most Jews; and with respect to the Christian conception of the Messiah I shall deal only with those features now shared by all three branches of the Christian faith. Then I shall attempt to present these two conceptions, the Jewish and the Christian, in contrast with each other, in order to show the difference between them.

I

The Jewish Messiah is a redeemer strong in physical power and in spirit, who in the final days will bring complete redemption, economic and spiritual, to the Jewish people—and along with this, eternal peace, material prosperity, and ethical perfection to the whole human race.

The Jewish Messiah is truly human in origin, of flesh and blood like all mortals. Justin Martyr in his time put this clearly into the mouth of Trypho the Jew, thus: "We Jews all expect that the Messiah will be a man of purely human origin." This human conception of the Messiah remains normative in Judaism to this day. To be sure, a Talmudic passage numbers the name of the Messiah among the seven things which "were created before the world was created"; there is also something of this sort in the "Parables" of the Ethiopic Enoch. But no doubt what is intended is the *idea* of the Messiah or the idea of redemption through the Messiah.

The Messiah is full of the spirit of wisdom and understanding, counsel and might, knowledge and the fear of the LORD. He has a special feeling for justice: he "smells and judges" [that is, he can almost tell a man's guilt or innocence by his sense of smell]. He "shall smite the land (or, the tyrant) with the rod of his mouth, and with the breath of his lips shall he slay the wicked." For "the war against Gog and Magog," who come to destroy Israel, there is a special Messiah— Messiah ben Joseph, who is slain in the war. But Messiah ben David is the king of peace:

> When the King-Messiah is revealed to Israel, he will not open his mouth except for peace, as it is written (Isa. 52:7), "How beautiful upon the mountains are the feet of the messenger of good tidings, that announceth peace."

Also, "the Messiah shall be peaceful in his very name, as it is written (Isa. 9:5), 'Everlasting father, prince of peace.' "

What in essence is the task of the King-Messiah?

He redeems Israel from exile and servitude, and he redeems the whole world from oppression, suffering, war, and above all from heathenism and everything which it involves: man's sins both against God and against his fellow man, and particularly the sins of nation against nation. For in the Messianic age all peoples will be converted to Judaism—some of them becoming "true proselytes" and some only "proselytes hanging on" (from self-interest). In the *Alenu* prayer, which is offered by Jews three times daily, we find the hope that speedily

> . . . the world will be perfected under the kingdom of the Almighty, and *all the children of flesh* will call upon Thy name, when Thou wilt turn unto Thyself all the wicked of the earth. Let *all the inhabitants of the world* perceive and know that unto Thee *every* knee must bow, *every* tongue must swear . . . and let them *all* accept the yoke of Thy kingdom.

And in the *Shemoneh Esreh* prayer for "Solemn Days" [New Year and Day of Atonement], Jews say: "And let all creatures prostrate themselves before Thee, that they may all form a single band to do Thy will with a perfect heart." In this prayer the Jew prays:

> Give then glory, O LORD, unto Thy people, . . . joy to Thy land (Palestine), gladness to Thy city (Jerusalem), a flourishing horn unto David Thy servant, and a clear shining light unto the son of Jesse, Thine anointed.

But at the same time he also prays that "all wickedness shall be wholly consumed like smoke, when Thou makest the dominion of arrogance to pass away from the (whole) earth."

Along with redemption from servitude, from evil, and from heathenism, that is to say, from the evil in man, the Messiah will save man from the evil in nature. No longer will poisonous reptiles and beasts of prey exist; or rather, they will exist, but will do no harm. There will be great material prosperity in the world: the earth will bring forth an abundance of grain and fruit, which man will be able to enjoy without excessive toil. As to the Jewish people, not only will they freely dwell in their own land, but there will also be an "ingathering of exiles," whereby all Jews scattered to the four corners of the earth will be returned to Palestine. All nations will acknowledge the God of Israel and accept His revelation of truth. Thus the King-Messiah, the king of righteousness, will be in a certain sense also the king of all nations, just as the God of Israel will be King over all the earth because He is the One and Only God.

Not every book of prophecy mentions an individual human Messiah. In the books of Nahum, Zephaniah, Habakkuk, Malachi, Joel, and Daniel, God alone is the redeemer. In the books of Amos, Ezekiel, Obadiah, and in the Book of Psalms, there is only a collective Messiah: "deliverers" and "saints" redeem the world by their righteousness and piety. In the books of Haggai and Zechariah, the Messiah is none other than Zerubbabel, a person who is not out of the ordinary except that he is of the house of David. In Deutero-Isaiah and Daniel, the Messiah is not a person at all, but is the whole Jewish people. Likewise, in the Apocryphal books (as distinguished from the Pseudepigrapha), there is no individual Messiah. In the Talmud, Rabbi Hillel (to be distinguished from Hillel the Elder) makes bold to say: "There shall be no Messiah for Israel, because they have already enjoyed him in the days of Hezekiah." To be sure, Rab Joseph rebelled against this opinion, saying: "May God forgive R. Hillel for saying this." But the fact remains that it was possible for a Jew faithful to his nation and his religion to conceive of redemption without an individual human redeemer: God Himself would be the redeemer.

This view did not prevail in Judaism. Belief in the coming of the Messiah is the twelfth in the thirteen "Articles of Faith" of Maimonides. But the fact that at one time Judaism could have conceived of redemption without a Messiah is not surprising. For redemption comes from God and through God. The Messiah is only an instrument in the hands of God. He is a human being, flesh and blood, like all mortals. He is but the finest of the human race and the chosen of his nation. And as the chosen of his nation, who is also the choicest of the human race, he must needs be crowned with all the highest virtues to which mortal man can attain.

As the Messiah, he exemplifies both physical and spiritual perfection. Even such an extremely spiritual and ethical person as Philo of Alexandria sees in the Messiah not only the spiritual and ethical side, but also finds in him "all-powerful strength of body" and "might;" for "leading his host to war he will subdue great and populous nations."

At the same time Philo finds in the Messiah "holiness and beneficence." Both with respect to holiness, righteousness, truth, and goodness, and with respect to might and authority, the Messiah is the "supreme man" of Judaism, which is very far from Nietzsche's "blond beast." But with all his superior qualities, the Messiah remains a human being. Within the limits of a constantly improving humanity, Judaism has devised the ideal man, or, if we may speak in the language of Kant, "the conception of the [upper] limit of man"—concerning whom we may say with the divinely inspired psalmist, "Thou hast made him but little lower than God" [Ps. 8:6]. But this "little" leaves the Messiah within the bounds of humanity and does not allow him to pass beyond. The kingdom of the Jewish Messiah is definitely "of this world."

Judaism is not only a religion, but is also the view of life of a single nation that holds to this religion alone, while the other religions include various nations. It is absolutely necessary, therefore, that Judaism's ideal for mankind should require first of all the realization of the yearning of its oppressed, suffering, exiled, and persecuted nation to return to its own land and recover its former status. But this ingathering of exiles and this national freedom are closely linked with the emancipation of all humanity—the destruction of evil and tyranny in the world, man's conquest of nature (material prosperity and the elimination of natural forces of destruction), the union of all peoples into "a single band" to fulfill God's purpose, that is, to do good and to seek perfection, righteousness, and brotherhood. This is the "kingdom of heaven" or the "kingdom of the Almighty"; it is the Messiah's reign or the "Days of the Messiah." But the Messiah is not the primary figure, although he occupies a central place in this "kingdom of heaven"; "heaven," that is, God, is the primary figure. (The word "heaven" is used here as a surrogate for God, to avoid blasphemy; hence "kingdom of heaven" and "kingdom of God," or "kingdom of the Almighty," are used interchangeably in the literature of the end of the period of the Second Temple and later.)

Finally, the "kingdom of heaven" will come only "in the end of days." The chief difference [on this point] between Judaism and Hellenism is that the Greeks and Romans saw the "Golden Age" *in the past,* at the beginning of history, while the Jews saw it *in the future,* at the end of history. Humanity is steeped in wickedness and injustice, and hence is incomplete, or lacking in fulfillment. This fulfillment will come "in the end of days," when wrongdoing, insolence, and conflict will pass from the earth, when "the wolf shall dwell with the lamb" and "the earth shall be full of the knowledge of the LORD as the waters cover the sea." Then those national achievements for which Israel longs in its exile and bondage will be realized: the return of the banished, the recovery of the homeland, the revival of the Hebrew language, and the restoration of the kingdom (the kingdom of the house of David or the kingdom of the Messiah).

This notion of perfection stems from the ardent progressivism that belongs to the very foundation of Judaism. Both present-day Judaism and present-day humanity require completion, that is, they demand and are prepared for development and progress. This completion, the fruition of improvement by means of repentance and good works, will be achieved in the Messianic age. To be sure, the Messiah is reckoned among "three things that come unexpectedly"; but among the "seven things hidden from men" is included also this: "when the kingdom of David will be restored to its former position." Therefore, "unexpectedly" is not to be interpreted to mean that the Messiah will come without preparation, but that it is impossible to know in advance when the preparation will be complete, so that the Messiah *will be able* to come. And therefore, "the advent of Messiah" is not to be contrasted with "the end of days": "the Messianic time of the end" and "the end of days" are one and the same. The elimination of imperialistic oppression, the cessation of wars, everlasting peace, the fraternity of nations in "a single band," the removal of evil in man and nature, economic abundance, the flowing of all peoples to "the mountain of the LORD's house"—this whole complex of material and spiritual well-being is the Messianic age or the "kingdom of heaven"; for "heaven" (God) will bring all these things to the world through the Messiah, the exalted instrument of the Divine Will.

This is the Jewish Messiah and these his characteristics and activities.

II

And now by contrast—the Christian Messiah.

Christianity is wholly based on the personality of the Messiah. This statement needs no proof. When the people of Antioch began to make a distinction between the believers in Jesus on the one hand, and Jews expecting the Messiah along with pagan Greeks on the other hand, they could find no more fitting name than "Christians"—a term derived from the Greek translation (*Christos*) of the Hebrew word "Messiah" (*Mashîaḥ*). For at first the only difference between Jews and Christians was that the former believed that the Messiah *was still to come,* and the latter that the Messiah *had already come.*

But because of the fact that the Messiah who had already come was crucified as an ordinary rebel after being scourged and humiliated, and thus was not successful in the political sense, having failed to redeem his people Israel; because of the lowly political status of the Jews at the end of the period of the Second Temple and after the Destruction; and because of the fear that the Romans would persecute believers in a political Messiah—for these reasons there perforce came about a development of ideas, which after centuries of controversy became crystallized in Christianity in the following form:

1. The Messiah did not come to redeem from political oppression and economic wrong, but to redeem from spiritual evil alone.

2. Political oppression is a special problem of the Jews, but spiritual evil is world-wide. Hence Jesus came to redeem the whole world; *not* to redeem the Jewish people and their land *first,* and *then as a consequence* to redeem the whole world, which will forsake idolatry and become like Israel in every respect. And hence the kingdom of the Christian Messiah is "not of this world."

3. Jesus was scourged and humiliated as a common rebel. But he was not a common rebel; he only preached repentance and good works. Therefore, he was a true Messiah and not a false Messiah. Then why did God allow His Chosen One, the Messiah, to undergo frightful suffering and even to be crucified—the most shameful death of all, according to Cicero and Tacitus—and not save him from all these things? The answer can only be that it was the will of God and the will of the Messiah himself that he should be scourged, humiliated, and crucified. But whence came a purpose like this, that would bring about suffering and death without sin? The answer can only be that the suffering was *vicarious* and the death was an *atoning death.* Jesus the Messiah suffered for others, for many, for all humanity. With his blood the Messiah redeemed humanity from sin, *inherited sin,* the sin of Adam, sin which became a part of Adam's nature, bringing death upon him and upon all his descendants. The Messiah went willingly to a disgraceful death in order that humanity might be redeemed from evil, from sin, from suffering, from death, and from the powers of Satan that prevail in the

world—that Satan who by his enticement to sin brought death to the world. Support for this belief that the Messiah suffers for the iniquity of others (vicarious suffering) was found in Isaiah 53, which was interpreted not as referring to the persecuted people Israel, but to the suffering Messiah: "Yet he bore the sin of many."

4. But the Messianic suffering which Jesus took upon himself by his own will and by the will of God cannot end in a shameful death. After the Messianic age comes the resurrection of the dead, according to Jewish doctrine. Therefore, of course, the Messiah rose from the dead—the first of men so to rise ("the firstfruits of them that slept," "the firstborn from the dead"). And therefore, Jesus is not mortal like other men. The will of God has been revealed in the will of the Messiah, and hence the Messiah is related to God *in a special way.*

5. God says to the Messiah, "Thou art My son, this day have I begotten thee" [Ps. 2:7]. And Jesus during his lifetime spoke much of "my Father who is in heaven." For Jews this was a common poetic-figurative expression. But the Gentiles, who asserted that certain of their eminent men—Alexander the Great, Plato, Pythagoras—had been fathered by gods who had visited mortal women, saw in this expression an actual genetic relationship of Jesus to God. Saul-Paul of Tarsus, who was a Jew, but one steeped in Greek culture, began to employ the concept "son of God" in a sense close to but not identical with the pagan concept: as Messiah, Jesus is "son of God" in the sense of a "heavenly man" not susceptible to sin nor even to death. By his *temporary* death he atoned for the sin of Adam, and in his resurrection for eternity he ascended into heaven and sits at the right hand of God because he is closer to God than are the angels. This was the first step toward deification. But Paul the Jew did not go so far as to call Jesus "God."

The second step was to identify Jesus with the "Word" by which the world was created according to Judaism, or with the "Logos," which is a sort of angelic being according to Philo of Alexandria. This identification we find in the Gospel of John. But it was natural that the Gentiles whom Paul brought into Christianity should take the third and final step and make Jesus a "God-man"—"one person with two natures"— God and man at one and the same time. Thus Jesus' Messiahship was gradually obscured: Jesus the Messiah gave way to "Jesus the God-man," or "the God Jesus"; and matters finally reached such a pass that the name "Christ" became the essential cognomen of Jesus ("Jesus

Christ" and not "Jesus the Messiah"). The Messiahship of Jesus became secondary to his deity.

6. Although Jesus has been elevated to a rank fully equal to that of "God the Father," he still remains "Redeemer," and hence is still Messiah also. He has already come once into the world in the form of a man and has redeemed the world from sin and evil and death and Satan. Yet sin and evil and death and Satan still prevail in the world; therefore we are to expect his second coming, his "Parousia," at which time the Day of Judgment will occur, and Jesus, having taken his seat at the right hand of "his Father," will judge all persons that have ever lived, and will deliver those who believe in him. Then will Satan be conquered, evil will come to an end, sin will cease, and death will pass away; all the powers of darkness will vanish, and the kingdom of heaven will be fully established, though it had already begun with the first appearance of Jesus in the world.

7. Meanwhile, in "this world," men may turn in prayer to Jesus *as* to God his Father *and instead of* God his Father. In this sense he is "mediator" and "Paraclete" between God and man, although actually he himself is God and the true mediator is none other than Mary his mother, the Holy Virgin, "the mother of God" by the Holy Spirit.

This is what happened in Christianity to the Jewish conception of the Messiah. The Christian Messiah ceased to be only a man, and passed beyond the limitations of mortality. Man cannot redeem himself from sin; but the Messiah-God, clothed in the form of a man, is the one who by his own freely shed blood has redeemed mankind. And he will come a second time to redeem humanity, since his first appearance, and even his death on the cross, did not suffice to eradicate evil from the world and to convert all men to belief in him. The first Christians expected this "Parousia" in their own time, and hence would pray, *Marana Tha*—"Our Lord, come!" (and not *Maran Atha*—"Our Lord has come"). When their prayer failed to be answered, and the Messiah-God did not again appear, they began to hope for the "thousand-year kingdom" or millennium (chiliasm); and finally they postponed the "Parousia" to an indefinite time.

III

The Christian Messiah is in essence only a further development of the Jewish Messiah. For from Judaism Christianity received the ideas of redemption, the redeemer-Messiah, the Day of Judgment, and the kingdom of heaven. And much of what was common to Judaism and Christianity with respect to Messianic thinking remained even after estrangement and separation between them took place. Nevertheless, the difference between the Jewish and the Christian Messiah is very great.

First of all, Jewish redemption can be conceived without any individual Messiah at all—something which is absolutely impossible in Christianity. Also, "the Redeemer of Israel" for Judaism can mean God alone; in Christianity the Redeemer is Jesus only. Without the Jewish Messiah, Judaism is defective; without the Christian Messiah, Christianity does not exist at all.

Second, there is an irrational side even in the Jewish Messianic conception: where there is no mysticism at all there is no faith. But the irrational and mystical element in the Jewish Messiah is only unnatural, but not anti-natural, not opposed to nature. The unity of God is not affected in any essential way by the Jewish Messiah. In the last analysis, the Jewish Messiah is only, as said above, the instrument of deity— although of course a choice and superb instrument. But in Christianity monotheism is obscured by the Messiah, who is "Son of God," the "Logos," "the Lord," a "God-man," and "one person with two natures." And from this spring the rest of the marked differences between the Jewish and Christian Messiahs: one cannot pray to the Jewish Messiah, he is not a mediator between God and man, he is not a "Paraclete" for man, and so on.

Third, the Jewish Messiah is the redeemer of his people and the redeemer of mankind. But he does not redeem them by his blood; instead, he lends aid to their redemption by his great abilities and deeds. Even Messiah ben Joseph, who is slain, affords no atonement by his blood and his sufferings are not vicarious. Judaism is familiar with "the sin of Adam," but the Jewish Messiah does not with his blood redeem from "original sin," nor from death, nor from Satan. To be sure, Satan will be vanquished in the Messianic age—not by the Messiah, but by God. Man must redeem himself from sin *not by faith alone,* but *by repentance and good works;* then God will redeem him from death and Satan. (Generally speaking, Satan does not occupy in Judaism the central place that he takes in Christianity; Satan in Christianity is almost like the God of Evil of the Persians.) Each man is responsible for himself, and through his good deeds he must find atonement for his sins. He cannot lean upon the Messiah or upon the Messiah's suffering and death.

Fourth and finally, since the Jewish Messiah is only "a righteous man ruling in the fear of God," and since he brings only ethical perfection to the world, the progress of humanity does not depend on him, but *on humanity itself*. Numberless times the Talmud returns to the idea that redemption depends on repentance and good works; well known is the interpretation of the verse "I the LORD will hasten it in its time" [Isa. 60:22]: "If they are worthy, I will hasten it [the redemption]; if not, it will come in its [own good] time." And the Hebrew people, who were the first to acknowledge faith in One God, the God of goodness, and to whom came prophets of truth and righteousness, can and will be the first to "hasten the redemption" by repentance and good works. In other words, the Jews can and must march at the head of humanity on the road of personal and social progress, on the road to ethical perfection. This will be possible only when they have returned to their own land, have gathered in their exiles, have reestablished their own state, and are no longer under the oppression of foreigners; but the "kingdom of heaven" is their goal and their highest aspiration, and without this goal Israel would never be freed from "bondage to foreign powers"—cessation of which will be the obvious external sign that the Days of the Messiah are near.

Therefore, we can say, without being suspected of undue bias toward Judaism, that the Jewish Messianic faith is the seed of progress, which has been planted by Judaism throughout the whole world.

THE CLASSICAL JEWISH VIEW

David Kimhi (1160?-1235?) was, like his father Joseph (see above, sel. 1.), a grammarian and biblical commentator. Kimhi's writings attained a high degree of popularity and are still studied and consulted by laymen and scholars. His commentaries are characterized by a concern for *peshat,* the plain meaning of the text, and a judicious use of midrash or rabbinic exegesis. Because of his lucidity and comprehensive knowledge of earlier exegetes, the younger Kimhi was avidly read by Christian Hebraists at the time of the Reformation. For this reason, the King James Version of the Bible bears the unmistakable stamp of his influence. Like his father, David Kimhi or Radak (from his initials *Ra*bbi *Da*vid *K*imhi) was an avowed rationalist. His devotion to the illustrious philosopher Moses Maimonides led him to defend Maimonides in the dispute over the latter's writings which broke out in thirteenth century France and Spain. In this controversy, Radak attempted to assume a mediating role.

Radak's polemical streak as expressed in his advocacy of rationalism *within* Judaism expressed itself as well in his role as an advocate *for* Judaism against Christianity. Unlike Joseph Kimhi, he never wrote a separate polemical treatise just as he never wrote a discursive treatise on any topic. His views on any one subject must be assembled from scattered statements in his biblical commentaries. Thus his anti-Christian remarks are found in his comments to classical biblical proof-texts cited in the Jewish-Christian debate. In the course of time, many of these passages were censored and are extant only in manuscript.

The medieval exegete attempted to convey to his contemporaries the meaning (or meanings!) of the sacred text as he understood it. Yet he could not prevent his own personal concerns and preoccupations from being reflected in his interpretations. One of Radak's overriding preoccupations was—as for so many others—the fact of Israel's exile from their land. For him, the national tragedy was very much a personal tragedy; through the mouths of biblical personalities and authors, he constantly lamented the "darkness" and "night" of exile. Radak found solace for Israel's predicament in a rationalistic mysticism in which he

71

sought to transcend the harsh realities of exile through metaphysical speculation. Nonetheless, his rationalism did not rule out a firm belief in an eventual concrete redemption of Israel. Nor did this rationalism—which colored his explanations of miracles and "supernatural" phenomena—restrain the enthusiasm of his description of the miraculous events decreed by the prophets as signs of the restoration of Israel. In the course of this description Radak, as Joseph Kimhi before him, vociferously rejected the possibility that the messianic age began with Jesus or that he was the Messiah.

Selection 9 is taken from my forthcoming *David Kimhi: The Man and the Commentaries* to be published by Harvard University Press.

Moses ben Nahman or Nahmanides (1195?-1270) was a younger contemporary of David Kimhi. A native of Gerona in Catalonia, he too was a biblical exegete. His commentaries, like many of his writings, were strongly influenced by the kabbalah, that stream of the Jewish mystical tradition that was then coming into maturity in Spain. His rationalism, although of a different stamp from that of Kimhi, led him to take a conciliating position also in the continuing Maimonidean controversy.

As the leading Spanish Jewish scholar of his day, Nahmanides was called upon to defend Judaism at the disputation held in 1263 under the royal patronage of James I of Aragon. Nahmanides' chief antagonist on the Christian side was Fra Pablo (Paulo) Cristiá, a convert to Christianity from Judaism. The principal issue in the debate was whether the Messiah had already come or not. It was to be understood that the veracity of the Christian faith was not to be impugned. Consequently, Nahmanides' role was more or less restricted to that of advocate for the defense with limited opportunity for cross-examination. He was, however, given more freedom of speech than was Rabbi Yehiel, the chief protagonist of the 1240 Paris disputation.

Among those present at the debate was the former general of the Dominican order, Ramón de Penyafort. Penyafort had established a system of colleges for the teaching of Hebrew and Arabic with the object of training missionaries to the Jews and Muslims. His student, Raymundus Martini (Ramón Martí), who was probably present at the disputation, composed a treatise entitled *Dagger of the Faith* which was written in Hebrew, Aramaic, Arabic, and Latin and which altered the course of Christian anti-Jewish polemics for several centuries. The chief innovation of this school of apologists was the use of rabbinic literature to prove the truth of Christianity in much the same way that Jewish polemicists used the New Testament to prove the truth of Judaism. (See, e.g., sel. 2.) Although Talmud and midrash had been used in this way before, never had there been such a thorough search for rabbinic passages which could be interpreted Christologically. Despite the fact that the Talmud had been burned in Paris only twenty-three years before, the underlying assumption that allowed its use as a witness for the Church was the notion that the rabbis knew the truth of Christianity but obdurately withheld it from the masses. Thus in the 1263 disputation, Fra Pablo invoked Talmud and midrash to prove that the Messiah had come, that he was God and man, etc.

Nahmanides, one of the leading talmudists of the time, was able to fault his opponent for misquoting, misinterpreting, and taking passages out of context. Yet his main line of defense was quite different. He maintained that whereas *halakhah* or rabbinic legal dicta are binding, the non-legal literature or *'aggadah* (also: *haggadah*) is not. This genre, which includes legend, homily, and ethics, is to be thought of as *derashot* or sermons. Thus if one finds value in them, he may accept them; if not, he should look for a deeper meaning or disregard them. While this attitude had been frequently expressed in rationalist circles within Judaism, it had not yet been heard in interreligious polemics.

Important too is Nahmanides' ironic remark to the king that he, the king, is more valuable than a Messiah. It is a greater challenge to serve God under conditions of exile than under messianic rule. The Jew is thus grateful to the king for freedom to practice his religion. This gratitude, however, does not prevent Nahmanides from informing the king that he believes in the dogmas of Christianity only because he was, to use contemporary language, "brainwashed" from the time of his youth.

Nahmanides, convinced that he had won the debate, published an account of the proceedings which provoked strong ecclesiastical censure. He was ultimately forced to leave Spain and left for Palestine where he spent the remainder of his days.

Selection 10 is taken from O. S. Rankin, *Jewish Religious Polemic of Earlier and Later Centuries,* Edinburgh: University Press, 1956, pp. 187-94.

9.

DAVID KIMHI ON THE MESSIANIC AGE

Frank Ephraim Talmage

Radak's literary enterprise was permeated with the consciousness of Israel's exile and the longing for her redemption. As for so many medievals, both punishment and reward were predicated upon the principle of measure for measure. In all contexts one finds that the consequence is always of the same nature as the cause: Jacob halted after his encounter with the angel because of his halting belief in God's promises. All of Joseph's tribulations ironically correspond in some way to his slanderous behavior against his brothers. Samson's eyes were gouged out because he allowed them to lead him into error. As for the nation as a whole:

> Because of all the idols of your abominations and as the blood of your children that you gave them (Ezekiel 16:36). [As the blood] with the prefix as (kaf). You have received punishment measure for measure in accordance with the sin. You had no compassion on the blood of your children when you slaughtered them to the idols. I have no compassion on your blood either and bring the vengeful sword . . . upon you.

Yet the principle of measure for measure could be positive as well as negative. Israel's rewards in the future would counterbalance, if not outweigh, her tribulations in the past. But just as the exile was of this

74

world, so must the redemption be of this world, of flesh and blood, of "wood and stones." Radak knew of a spiritual Jerusalem, of the supernal Sanctuary for the immortal intellect—but this was quite a different matter.

> *The soul that sins shall die* (Ezekiel 18:4). R. Saadia Gaon wrote that the life and death referred to here are of the next world. I say that this is true, for reward and punishment is mainly a matter of the next world. However, what is discussed *here* is *not* a matter of the next world. For this is a reply to those of that generation who said that the son bears the sins of the father, when they saw the great afflictions of the sons while the fathers had sinned and were no longer. They were not perturbed about the next world— *for they did not know what it is*—but about what they saw with their own eyes. The answer has to fit the question. . . .

No, the redemption of Israel must be a concrete redemption. The Messiah of Israel must redeem in a real, not a ghostly, sense. What Christianity was trying to perpetrate, he could not fathom.

> *Yea, he says: It is too light a thing that you should be My servant to raise up the tribes of Jacob, and to restore the offspring of Israel. I will also make you a light of the nations that My salvation may be unto the end of earth* (Isaiah 49:6). The Christians refer these verses to the Nazarene saying that he illuminated the eyes of the nations to the end of the earth. How did he illuminate the eyes of the Gentiles? By faith in him to the end of the earth? Most of the nations do not believe in him for Israel and Ishmael do not. . . . They say that God has become his strength (vs. 5) to save him from his enemies. He was not saved nor protected from his enemies who sought his soul and harmed him.

> Can it be Jesus that *will be exalted and lifted up and shall be very high* (Isaiah 52:13)? The only place "he was lifted up and exalted was the tree on which they hung him!" Can the "ruler of Israel" of Micah 5:1 refer to Jesus? "He did not govern Israel but they governed him." The Messiah will not be poor as they say. The biblical expression refers to humility. If he is to ride on a donkey, it is not for want. All the world is under his rule! He rides it to demonstrate that Israel will have no more need of horses and chariots.

Yet even granting this notion of a spiritual Messiah, Radak contends that the Christians cannot maintain their case consistently. They "halt between two opinions."

As had Joseph [Kimhi], David set forth Christianity as a web of inconsistencies.

> The very verse which they bring as a proof-text and a support for their error is their own stumbling block: *The Lord said to me, "You are My son"* (Psalms 2:7).
>
> When they tell you that he was the son of God, tell them that it is impossible to say that the horse is the son of Reuben. If so, he to whom God says *You are My son* must be of His nature and divine like Him. Scripture says further *I have begotten you this day* (*ibid.*) and the procreated is of the same species as the procreator.
>
> Tell them that there can be no father and son in the Divinity, for the Divinity is indivisible and is one in every aspect of unity unlike matter which is divisible.
>
> Tell them further that a father precedes a son in time and a son is born through the agency of a father. Now even though each of the terms "father" and "son" implies the other . . . he who is called the father must undoubtedly be prior in time. Therefore, with reference to this God whom you call Father, Son, and Holy Spirit, that part which you call Father must be prior to that which you call Son, for if they were always coexistent, they would have to be called twin brothers. . . .

This alleged inconsistency is nowhere more evident then in their Messiah concept.

> *He asked life of You* (Psalms 21:5). If it is to refer to [Jesus'] humanity, he cannot be said to have had a life. If to his divinity, why did Scripture say *You gave it to him* (*ibid.*)? It says further, *His glory is great through Your salvation* (vs. 6). If so, he is not divine. If it refers to his humanity, [he had no glory] for he was belittled and scorned.
>
> *For the king trusts in the Lord* (vs. 8). If it refers to his divinity, he should have no need to trust in another. Nor should he have need for the Most High that *he shall not be moved* (*ibid.*). If it refers to his humanity, he was certainly moved—in downfall.

How can they claim that Jesus established Jerusalem. Since he accomplished nothing in the terrestrial Jerusalem, Radak concludes, they must be thinking of the spiritual Jerusalem. Yet this cannot be, as long as they took the context of their proof-text literally. No matter which path they took, they came to an impasse.

God must be taken at His word. If His promises have not yet been fulfilled, we have every right to expect them to be realized in the future.

I will turn their captivity, the captivity of Sodom and her daughters (Ezekiel 16:53). This verse is a reply to the Christian heretics who say that the future consolations have already been fulfilled. Sodom is still overturned as it was and is still unsettled.

And what of Israel? Radak does "not know the mind" of Jonathan the Aramaic translator of the Prophets, whose translation of a prophecy seems to imply a reference to the second commonwealth. The Lord has *not* yet gone before Israel in redemption: the remnant of the flock has *not* yet been gathered; the Temple as envisioned by Ezekiel has *not* yet been built; the children of Judah and the children of Israel have *not* yet been united. The continued absence of Israel was Radak's trump card. The Church may refer the redemption of Judah to itself but the promise to Israel still awaits.

I will afflict the seed of David for this but not forever (I Kings 11:39). Here is an answer to those who say that we wait in vain for the days of the King Messiah. . . . The prophet says, *but not forever*. Since the kingdom of David was divided in the time of Rehoboam, it was never reunited. . . . When [the Jews of the] exile returned, the tribes did not return—only . . . Judah and Benjamin.

Christianity could claim that the ten tribes of Israel had been given a *bill of divorce* (Jeremiah 3:8); that *the daughter of Israel has fallen and is to rise no more* (Amos 5:2). Not quite, replies Radak. "It is *as if* He had given them a bill of divorce." "She is not to rise again—*for a long time.*" But in the time of the redemption, *all the house of Israel* (Ezekiel 11:15) will be included. They will all be restored to their former tribes and their former status. Joseph Kimhi was conservative with respect to the passage: *They shall bring all your brethren from*

all nations . . . and some of them I shall take for priests and for Levites
(Isaiah 66:20). He understood the *for* quite literally, "for the assistance
of the priests." Radak, however, claims that those who were originally
of priestly or levitical descent would be restored to their function even
though "they were immersed among the Gentiles on distant islands to
the point of oblivion. . . ."

The restoration of the land accompanies the restoration of the
nation. It represents a return to the natural order of things; to God's
original intention. Even though the Land today is closed to Israel, its
reopening is guaranteed, "for since He gave it to Abraham and his
sons, His truth is to maintain that gift . . . for He is a God of truth and
His good word will not be turned back." From the very beginning the
Land was reserved for Israel. The Canaanites were placed there only
to prepare it. When Abraham appeared, they did not lift a finger
against him for God placed His fear upon them.

Like Rashi in the remark which opens his Torah commentary,
Radak stressed that "the earth is the Lord's. . . . He takes from one
and gives to the other." For a millennium now, the Lord had been
taking from one and giving to the other. The interchange between
Edom and Ishmael was incessant.

> *The uncircumcised and the unclean* (Isaiah 52:1). *The uncircum-
> cised* are the kingdom of Edom . . . and the *unclean* are the king-
> dom of Ishmael who affect purity by washing their bodies but
> are . . . impure in their evil deeds. These two kingdoms have held
> Jerusalem from the day of the destruction. They fight over it end-
> lessly and one conquers it from the other. But from the day of the
> redemption, they will no longer pass through it.

Their attempts to gain effective control of Jerusalem are in vain.
Their building is no building: *"Our holy . . . house . . . is burned with
fire* (Isaiah 64:10). The place of the Temple was never built by the
Gentiles."

> *Your holy cities have become a wilderness. Zion is a wilder-
> ness, Jerusalem a desolation* (Isaiah 64:9). Even though the Gen-
> tiles came and built it after its destruction, it is desolate and devoid
> of . . . inhabitants because Israel is not there. . . . The Edomites

take it from the Ishmaelites and destroy it. . . . It was like this since the day Israel was exiled from it.

The association of the Land of Israel with the Gentiles is ludicrous: it is like the marriage of an old man with a maiden or of a young man with a matron. The Land of Israel is "allergic" to foreigners, it spews them out.

> *He planted it in a field of seed* (Ezekiel 17:5). In a field which is suitable for seed and makes that which is sown there flourish. Thus good men of integrity, the servants of God should be in Jerusalem. Their opposite are people alien to the land, as it says *alien gods of the land* (Deuteronomy 31:16), *that the land not vomit you out as it vomited out the nation that was before you* (Leviticus 18:28).

Thus shall the restoration begin with a purification of Jerusalem.

> *They shall come there and take away all the detestable things* (Ezekiel 11:18). The detestable things and the abominations which the Christians made: the detestable things of the crucified one— for it will be in their hands when the redemption comes. They will find the detestable thing in it—which is the pit (the sepulchre) of the crucified one, of which it says *to make the detestable thing desolate* (Daniel 12:11).

Jerusalem shall henceforth be the home of the righteous only. While this probably includes the righteous Gentile as well as the righteous Jew,

> it is possible that strangers will not enter Jerusalem at all because its sanctity will increase in the future. Just as no one, not even a priest, can enter the sanctuary, thus will the city be holy and no strangers from among the nations will enter it.

Thus, in "retaliation" for Israel's exile, Edom is to undergo herself a double exile—one from her own land, the Land of Esau, and from Jerusalem which she sought to dominate. On the other hand, Israel will undergo a double redemption. The exodus itself will startle the world.

"When will God's praise be great? At the ingathering of the exiles when the whole world sees the wonders he accomplishes with Israel." It is not only that

> He will take a nation out of the midst of many nations, [for] they were engulfed in exiles so many years that all the nations thought that they would never escape their control. . . . But he will bring them to the Land of Israel with great honor *upon horses and in chariots and litters* (Isaiah 66:20).

In return for their impoverishment in the exile, they will leave the exile with silver and gold and the spoil of the Gentiles. Their dominion will of course be securely established. They shall return to their former rank and be above the nations. The fears of the exile will cease. They will never again have to climb the walls and close the gates in the face of the enemy. They will never again have overseers above them. Since there will be no ruler but the Messiah, they shall not have to pay taxes to foreigners.

Yet glorious as this is in itself, Radak's dreams go farther than a mere political restoration. No longer the measure-for-measure moralist, he is now the proletarian who aspires to the bourgeoisie. Israel is not only to be compensated but compensated on a Jobian scale. A new era in the history of the world will be inaugurated. So great will be the grace of God that the interminable exile will appear as but an instant.

> *For as the earth brings forth her growth and as the garden causes the things that are sown in it to spring forth, so the Lord God will cause victory and glory to spring forth before all the nations* (Isaiah 61:11). He likened the salvation of Israel to a land which brings forth her growth. The seed in the ground was rotted and decayed but then it blossomed, revived and recovered, and was better and finer [than ever]. . . . This is Israel. For a long time, they were rotting and decaying in exile with their hope almost lost. Yet at the time of redemption, they shall blossom and grow and multiply and increase in number and glory and greatness many times over what they were. . . . [Also], since plants do not bloom at the same time but each in its own time, so one good thing will happen to Israel after another.

As we have seen, everything will be on a greater scale. The Land of Israel will be greater than it was. The dimensions of the rebuilt Temple will be increased. It will be of unprecedented beauty. It will have (as do the cathedrals) stained glass windows. The young men of Israel, like the Gentile aristocracy, will tour the world in their finery. But more than this. Nature herself will be forced to abdicate her authority in this world. When the Temple is built, it will be built without human labor but through the power and will of God! Abundance will stand in readiness without human exertion or effort as if the mountains were themselves dripping with sweet wine and the hills flowing with milk. *"Every tree for food whose leaf shall not wither nor shall its fruit fail . . . miraculously."*

Yet these miracles stop at the borders of the Land of Israel. The world's one disadvantaged nation now becomes the one that is advantaged. Radak objects to Ibn Ezra's interpretation of *for I create new heavens and a new earth* (Isaiah 65:17) as implying that all mankind will benefit from increased longevity. "If it is as he interprets it", argues Radak, "it would apply to all nations while Scripture says *for as the days of a tree shall be the days of My people* (Isaiah 65:22), not other peoples." Radak speaks of people who felt themselves dying before their time because they died without seeing the Messiah. They receive their lives now. This extraordinary longevity is mentioned often; three to five hundred year lifespans will not be unusual. People will live so long that it will no longer be felt necessary to weep for the dead.

As the life of the individual shall be extended several hundred years, so shall the life of the nation be extended indefinitely. Israel need never fear that the third Temple will go the way of the first and second. Man's wicked inclinations shall be miraculously transformed. Since sin will be abolished, there is no danger of another destruction. As Israel remembers her ways and is ashamed of them, so does God promise to maintain the covenant for ever. Never again will Israel know shame for *this* time they shall suffer no troubles upon their return. Never again shall the walls of Jerusalem fall for *"I have set watchmen* (divine providence) *upon them day and night. They shall never hold their peace* (Isaiah 62:6)."

10.

DEBATE

Moses Nahmanides

On the day appointed, the king came to a convent that was within the city bounds, where was assembled all the male population, both Gentiles and Jews. There were present the bishop, all the priests, the scholars of the Minorites [i.e. the Franciscans] and the Preaching Friars [i.e. the Dominicans]. Fra Paulo, my opponent, stood up to speak, when I, intervening, requested our lord the king that I should now be heard. The king replied that Fra Paulo should speak first because he was the petitioner. But I urged that I should now be allowed to express my opinion on the subject of the Messiah and then afterwards he, Fra Paulo, could reply on the question of accuracy.

I then rose and calling upon all the people to attend said: 'Fra Paulo has asked me if the Messiah of whom the prophets have spoken has already come and I have asserted that he has not come. Also a Haggadic work, in which someone states that on the very day on which the temple was destroyed the Messiah was born, was brought by Fra Paulo as evidence on his behalf. I then stated that I gave no credence to this pronouncement of the Haggadah but that it lent support to my contention. And now I am going to explain to you why I said that I do not believe it. I would have you know that we Jews have three kinds of writings—first, the *Bible* in which we all believe with perfect faith. The second kind is that which is called *Talmud* which provides a commentary to the commandments of the Law, for in the Law there are six hundred and thirteen commandments and there is not a single one of them which is not expounded in the Talmud and we believe in it in regard to the exposition of the commandments. Further, there is a third kind of writing, which we have, called *Midrash,* that is to say sermonic literature [*sermones*] of the sort that would be produced if the bishop here should stand up and deliver a sermon which someone in the audience who liked it should write down. To a document of this sort, should any of us extend belief, then well and good, but if he refuses to do so no one will do him any harm. For we have scholars who in their writings say that the Messiah will not be born until the approach of the End-time when he will come to deliver us from exile. For this reason I do not believe in this book (which Fra Paulo cites) when it makes the assertion that the Messiah was born on the day of the destruction of the temple.'

'Furthermore, this (third kind of) literature is given by us the title *Haggadah* which is the equivalent of *razionamiento* in the current speech, that is to say that it is purely conversational in character. Nevertheless, as you wish, I shall accept in its literal sense that Haggadic narrative which Fra Paulo has quoted, because, as I have already remarked to you, it supplies manifest proof that your Jesus is not Messiah, in as much as he was not born on the day mentioned, the day of the destruction of the temple. In fact his whole career was already over long before. But you, our lord the king, more fittingly than the others put a question to me raising the objection that it was not customary for man to live a thousand years. And now I shall give you a plain answer to your question. You will observe that the first man lived for a thousand years all but seventy and it is made clear in the Scripture that it was through his transgression that he died and, had he not sinned, he would have lived much longer or even for ever. Also, Gentiles and Jews alike all confess that the sin and punishment of the first man will be rendered ineffective in the days of the Messiah. If this be so, then, after the Messiah shall come, transgression and its penalty will cease in all of us, but (especially) in the Messiah himself will they be entirely absent. Consequently it is appropriate that he who is the Messiah should live for thousands of years or for ever, as is said in Psalm 21:4: "He asked life of you, you gave it him; even length of days for ever and ever." That point then has been explained. But our lord the king further has raised the question: Where then does the Messiah (meanwhile) reside? It is manifest from Scripture that the abode of the first

man was in the garden of Eden which is upon earth; and after he had
sinned, as is said in Genesis 3:23, "the Lord God sent him forth from
the garden of Eden." That being the case, the Messiah, he who is
exempt from the penalty incurred by Adam, has his abode in the garden
of Eden, and so affirmed the scholars in the Haggadic writings to which
I have referred.'

Hereupon the king remarked: 'But in that Haggadic book have
not you Jews asserted that the Messiah was in Rome?' I replied to him
that I had not asserted that the Messiah's abode was in Rome but that
he had appeared there on a certain day, for Elijah had told the scholar
Jehoshua ben Levi that the latter would find the Messiah there on that
day and there he did appear. Moreover the reason for the Messiah
being seen in Rome was recorded in the Haggadic traditions but I was
unwilling to communicate it before so many people as those here assembled—the matter of which I did not wish to speak to the people was
that which is spoken of in the Haggadah, namely, that the Messiah
will remain [or abide, lit. stand] in Rome until he has destroyed the
city. Just as in the case of Moses our teacher, upon whom be blessing,
we find that he grew up in the palace of Pharaoh until he, Moses, had
called Pharaoh to account and had drowned all Pharaoh's people in the
sea. As also is said of Hiram king of Tyre (in Ezek. 28:18): 'Therefore
have I [the Lord] brought forth a fire from the midst of you, it has
devoured you;' and in Isaiah 27:10: 'There shall the calf feed and there
shall he lie down and consume the branches thereof.' And as is said in
the chapters of the Hekhalot Rabbati [a rabbinic mystical work] (5:21):
'When a man shall say to his neighbor: Here you are, here you are!
Rome and all that is in it for a farthing! And his neighbors shall reply:
It is not going to be bid for by me.' All this I said to the king in private.

Continuing the discussion, I asked the question: 'You will agree,
would you not, with my statement that in the Messianic age the sin of
Adam is made of no effect?' Our lord the king and also Fra Paulo
answered: 'Yes, we agree upon that but think otherwise than you upon
the manner of its happening, for the fact is that, in virtue of that penalty
which the sin of Adam incurred, all mankind had to enter Gehenna,
but in the days of Jesus the Messiah this penalty was brought to naught,
for he led them forth from that place.' My reply to this claim was: 'In
our home-land we Jews have a saying that he who intends to tell a
falsehood must get rid of the witnesses who testify against him. And,
in Genesis chapter 3, many are the penalties which Scripture records

as falling upon Adam and Eve, such as: "Cursed is the ground for your sake . . . thorns also and thistles shall it bring forth to you . . . in the sweat of your face shall you eat bread . . . for dust you are." And so also upon the woman does punishment fall: "in sorrow you shall bring forth children." Now, all these conditions endure even up to the present day and nothing of what is seen and experienced of them was cancelled by expiatory action in the time of your Messiah. But of the penalty of Gehenna, of which the scripture says nothing, you affirm that this has been thus cancelled. In order then that no one may be able to contradict you on this point send one of your number to Gehenna that he may come back and report to you! But far be it from God that He should do as you say! For the righteous suffer no penalty of Gehenna imposed on account of the sin of Adam their first parent. For my soul is related to the soul of my father (Adam) in as equal a degree as it is related to the soul of Pharaoh and it cannot be that on account of Pharaoh's sin my soul will enter Gehenna. But the penalties of sin are inflicted *on the body,* because my body is derived from my father (Adam) and my mother (Eve) and when judgment was made upon both of them (in the Garden of Eden) and they became subject to death, their descendants also for ever became by nature subject to death.'

My opponent now stood up and said: 'I shall bring further evidence that the Messianic age has already been.' But I craved my lord the king to be allowed to speak a little longer and spoke as follows: 'Religion and truth, and justice which for us Jews is the substance of religion, does not depend upon a Messiah. For you, our lord the king, are, in my view, more profitable than a Messiah. You are a king and he is a king, you a Gentile, and he (to be) king of Israel—for a Messiah is but a human monarch as you are. And when I, in exile and in affliction and servitude, under the reproach of the peoples who reproach us continually, can yet worship my Creator with your permission, my gain is great. For now I make of my body a whole-burnt offering to God and thus become more and more worthy of the life of the world to come. But when there shall be a king of Israel of my own religion ruling over all peoples then I would be forced to abide in the law of the Jews, and my gain would not be so much increased. But the core of the contention and the disagreement between Jews and Christians lies in what you Christians assert in regard to the chief topic of faith, namely the deity, for here you make an assertion that is exceedingly distasteful. And you, our lord the king, are a Christian born of a Christian [man and of a Christian woman] and all your days you have listened to priests [and Minorites and Preaching Friars talking of the nativity of Jesus] and they have filled your brain and the marrow of your bones with this doctrine and I would set you free again from that realm of habit and custom. Of a certainty the doctrine which you believe and which is a dogma of your faith cannot be accepted by reason. Nature does not admit of it. The prophets have never said anything that would support it. Also the miracle itself cannot be made intelligible by the doctrine in question as I shall make clear with ample proofs at the proper time and place. That the Creator of heaven and earth and all that in them is should withdraw into and pass through the womb of a certain Jewess and should grow there for seven months and be born a small child and after this grow up to be handed over to his enemies who condemn him to death and kill him, after which, you say, he came to life and returned to his former abode—neither the mind of Jew nor of any man will sustain this. Hence vain and fruitless is your arguing with us, for here lies the root of our disagreement. However, as it is your wish, let us further discuss the question of the Messiah.'

Fra Paulo then said to me: 'Then you do believe that the Messiah has come?' I replied: 'No, but I believe and am convinced that he has not come and there never has been anyone who has said concerning himself that he was Messiah—nor will there ever be such who will say so [viz. concerning themselves]—except Jesus. And it is impossible for me to believe in the Messiahship of Jesus, because the prophet says of the Messiah (in Ps. 72:8) that "he shall have dominion from sea to sea and from the River until the ends of the earth". Jesus, on the other hand, never had dominion, but in his lifetime he was pursued by his enemies and hid himself from them, falling finally into their power whence he was not able to liberate himself. How then could he save all Israel? Moreover, after his death dominion was not his. For in regard to the Empire of Rome, he had no part in the growth of that. Since, before men believed in him the city of Rome ruled over most of the world and after faith in him had spread, Rome lost many lands over which it once held sovereign power. And now the followers of Muhammad possess a larger empire than Rome has. In like manner the prophet Jeremiah (31:34) says that in the Messianic age "they shall teach no more every man his neighbor, and every man his brother, saying, Know the Lord: for they shall all know Me", while in Isaiah (11:9) it is written, that "the earth shall be full of the knowledge of the Lord, as the waters cover the sea". Moreover the latter prophet states (2:4) that, in this time, "they shall beat their swords into ploughshares . . . nation shall not lift up sword against nation, neither shall they learn war any more". But since the days of Jesus up to the present the whole world has been full of violence and rapine, the Christians more than other peoples being shedders of blood and revealers likewise of indecencies. And how hard it would be for you, my lord the king, and for those knights of yours, if they should learn war no more! And yet another oracle of the prophet Isaiah (11:4) is to this effect: "He shall smite the earth with the rod of his mouth." In the Haggadic work in the hands of Fra Paulo this verse receives the following commentary: "It was reported to the king Messiah that a certain province had rebelled against him. The king Messiah commanded the locusts to come and destroy the province. He was told that such and such an eparchy had rebelled against him. He commanded a swarm of insects to come and consume it." But it was not thus in the case of Jesus. And you his servants deem to be better for your purposes horses that are clad in armor; and sometimes even all this proves to be of no avail for you. But I would yet submit for your attention many other arguments drawn from what the prophets have said.' At this juncture my opponent called out: 'Such is always his method —to make a long speech when I have a question to put to him.' The king thereupon told me to cease speaking on the ground that he, Fra Paulo, was asking a question. So I was silent.

Fra Paulo said: 'The Jewish scholars say of the Messiah that he is to be more honored than the angels. This cannot apply to any but Jesus who in his one person was both the Messiah and God.' Then he adduced the Haggadic interpretation of the words 'My servant shall be exalted and lifted up and shall be very high' (Isa. 52:13), namely, that the Messiah is exalted above Abraham, lifted up above Moses and higher than the ministering angels. My answer to him on this point was: 'Our scholars constantly speak in this manner of all the eminently righteous, saying that they are more righteous than the ministering angels. Our teacher Moses said to an angel: "In the place where I have my dwelling, you have not authority to stand." And, in general, Israel avers that Israel is more beloved of God than are the angelic ministrants. But what the author of this Haggadic passage on the Messiah proposes to say is that Abraham, our father, on whom be blessing, wrought the conversion of Gentiles, explained to the peoples his faith in the Holy One, and in debate opposed Nimrod without fear. Yet,

Moses did more than he. For Moses in his meekness stood before the great and wicked king Pharaoh and did not spare him in the mighty plagues with which he smote him, and brought Israel out beyond the range of Pharaoh's power. But exceedingly zealous were the ministering angels in the task of redemption. As is written in the Book of Daniel (10:21): "And now will I return to fight with the prince of Persia." Yet more than these all will the Messiah do. For his courage will be high in the performance of the purposes of the Lord. For he will come and command the Pope and all the kings of the nations in the name of God, saying: "Let my people go that they may serve me." And he will do among them many mighty signs and wonders and in no wise will he be afraid of them. He will make his abode (will stand) in their city of Rome until he has destroyed it. Having spoken thus, I said to Fra Paulo that I would give an exposition of the whole of the Haggadic passage if he cared to have it; but he did not so desire.

Fra Paulo now submitted another Haggadic passage where it is said about the Messiah that he prays for Israel that the Holy One may pardon their iniquities and undertakes to endure sufferings in behalf of others. In his prayer he says to God: 'I undertake to endure sufferings on condition that the resurrection of the dead be in my days, and I undertake this not only on account of the dead of my generation but for all the dead who have died from the days of the first men up to the present, and not only those who died [and whom the earth received] but even those who were cast into the sea and drowned or who were devoured by wolves and wild beasts.' 'Now,' claimed Fra Paulo, 'the suffering which the Messiah took upon himself to endure refers to the death of Jesus which Jesus willingly bore.'

To that argument I replied: "Woe be to him who is shameless! All that is spoken of in the prayer of the Messiah was not performed by Jesus. Jesus has not raised to life those who have died from the time of Adam up till now, nor has he done anything at all of this sort. Furthermore that a prayer is spoken of in the passage shows that he, the Messiah, is human and not divine and that he has not power to raise from the dead. Moreover those so-named sufferings of the Messiah signify nothing other than the grief he endures because his advent is exceeding long delayed and he sees his people in exile and he has not power (to deliver them). Also he beholds brought to honor above his own people them that worship that which is not God and who have denied him and make for themselves a Messiah other than himself.'

"THE STUMBLING BLOCK"

One of the best known and most significant of all anti-Jewish polemical treatises is the *Dialogue with Trypho* of St. Justin Martyr (100-165). This Greek disputation is written as the protocol of an actual discussion between a Jew and a Christian. However, like the *Book of the Covenant* or most other works in this genre, the form is probably only a literary device used to bring unity to a composite of many such discussions held over a period of time. Similarly, the attempted identification of the Jew, Trypho, with Rabbi Tarphon, a leading scholar of the mishnaic period, is unlikely.

The reputation that the *Dialogue* has for being a sort of gentlemen's disagreement is largely based on its conclusion, where both discussants part amicably and promise to offer prayers for each other. To be sure, it is free of harsh invective. Yet, by modern standards, it oversteps the bounds of courtesy. Trypho accuses his interlocutor of madness; Justin accuses the Jews of unmitigated hatred for Christ and Christians. Indeed, it is here for the first time that we hear that the Jews undergo their tribulations because they "have murdered the Just One."

The *Dialogue* was written at a time when Christianity was still a persecuted religion and Justin numbers Jews among the persecutors. It is this experience of Christian martyrdom, however, that helps Justin explain to himself why the Jews remain in their blindness regarding Christianity. As with many a true believer, it was inconceivable to Justin how anyone could understand Scripture except in the way that he understood it. If then the Jews will not confess the Christological interpretation of the Bible, it is because of the "fear of the death which awaits every Christian."

Like Aphrahat (See sel. 3), Justin based his arguments primarily on Scripture from which he cites relatively lengthy sections. Justin, however, makes liberal use of allegorical exegesis. Trypho insists on proof that Jesus was the Messiah. Justin answers with a discourse on the Passover sacrifice and other aspects of biblical ritual which are taken to be types, i.e. prefigurings, of Christ's passion and of Christian symbols and rites. This mode of interpretation, when used in a Christo-logical context, was of course rejected *a priori* by Jews. (See below, sel. 13.)

The argument is not confined, however, to a dispute over letter and spirit. In the discussion of Isaiah 7:14, the classic proof-text of the virgin birth, philological arguments are employed. Here the controversy centers on whether the Hebrew *'almah* means "virgin" as Christian tradition maintained or simply "young woman" as the Jews interpreted.

Selection 11 is reprinted with minor adaptations from the *Writings of St. Justin Martyr,* ed. Thomas B. Falls, New York: Christian Heritage, 1948, pp. 202-210, 212-214. Biblical references are according to the Vulgate.

Religious polemics in the Middle Ages were not confined to formal theological treatises and protocols of actual or simulated disputations. Since the tension between Church and Synagogue permeated almost every facet of life, it is no surprise that polemical motifs may be found in virtually every literary genre. We have gained some notion of how the biblical commentaries of David Kimhi are imbued with implicit and explicit polemical remarks. In quite a different vein, one may easily discern the anti-Jewish element in popular medieval drama. The *Mystère d'Adam* ("Mystery of Adam"), written in twelfth-century France, is the first medieval religious drama to have been presented outside the precincts of a church and the first to make exclusive use of the vernacular. In the opinion of its translator, E. N. Stone, it is, in terms of style, "one of the finest monuments of mediaeval poetry." The play is largely concerned with events in the lives of Adam, Eve, Cain, and Abel. It concludes, however, with a "procession of the prophets" in which a number of the Old Testament saints set forth their prophecies of Christ, elaborate on them, and berate the Jews for their failure to believe. This portion of the play is based on a pseudo-Augustinian sermon written in the sixth century. The play cites the conflation of Dan. 9:24 and 9:26 which is found in that sermon and with which Joseph Kimhi was familiar (sel. 21). Indeed it is not unlikely that Kimhi might have witnessed this or a similar production.

Both the play and the sermon begin with the solemn invocation: "Vos, inquam, convenio, O Judei"—"You, I say, do I challenge, O Jews." The Jews, representatives of the Synagogue, are assigned a special place on stage to the left of the prophets. The dialogue between

Isaiah and the Jew, in which the Jew is roundly denounced for his faith-lessness, is the dramatic climax of the piece. The stage directions, written in Latin, possess a good deal of charm in themselves. The prophets' descent into hell does not represent permanent damnation but a sojourn in the *limbus patrum* where the souls of the righteous wait for Jesus to redeem them.

This very felicitous verse translation by E. N. Stone was originally published in "Adam: A Religious Play of the Twelfth Century," *University of Washington Publications in Language and Literature* IV (1926), 184-93.

11.

DIALOGUE WITH TRYPHO

Justin Martyr

Trypho then said . . . 'Prove to us that Jesus Christ is the one about whom these prophecies were spoken.'

'At the proper time,' I replied, 'I will supply the proofs you wish, but for the present permit me to quote the following prophecies to show that the Holy Spirit by parable called Christ God, and Lord of hosts and of Jacob. God Himself calls your interpreters stupid [Jer. 4:22] because they claim that these prophecies were not spoken of Christ, but of Solomon, when he transported the ark of testimony into the temple built by himself. Listen to these words of David's Psalm: "The earth is the Lord's and the fulness thereof; the world, and all they that dwell therein. For He has founded it upon the seas, and has prepared it upon the rivers. Who shall ascend into the mountain of the Lord; or who shall stand in His holy place? The innocent in hands, and clean of heart, who has not taken his soul in vain, nor sworn deceitfully to his neighbor. He shall receive a blessing from the Lord, and mercy from God his Savior. This is the generation of them that seek Him, of them that seek the face of the God of Jacob. Lift up your gates, O you princes, and be you lifted up, O eternal gates, and the King of Glory shall enter in. Who is this King of Glory? The Lord who is strong and mighty in battle. Lift up your gates, O you princes, and be you lifted up, O eternal gates, and the King of Glory shall enter in. Who is this

King of Glory? The Lord of hosts, He is the king of Glory" [Ps. 23:1-
10]. This proves that Solomon was not the Lord of hosts. But, when
our Christ arose from the dead and ascended into Heaven, the heavenly
princes chosen by God were ordered to open the gates of Heaven that
the King of Glory might enter and sit at the right hand of the Father
until He makes His enemies His footstool. . . . Now, when these heavenly princes saw that He was in appearance without beauty, honor, or
glory, and not recognizing Him, they asked: "Who is this King of
Glory?" And the Holy Spirit, either in His own name or in the Father's,
answered: "The Lord of Hosts. He is the King of Glory." But I am
sure that everyone will admit that none of the gate-keepers of the
Temple at Jerusalem ever said of Solomon (though he was ever so
glorious a king), or of the ark of testimony, "Who is this King of
Glory?" '

'Christ is thus further described,' I continued, 'in the diapsalm of
the forty-sixth Psalm, "God is ascended with jubilee, and the Lord with
the sound of a trumpet. Sing praises to our God, sing; sing praises to
our king, sing. For God is the king of all the earth, sing wisely. God
has reigned over the Gentiles; God sits on His holy throne. The princes
of the people are gathered together with the God of Abraham, for the
strong ones of the earth are of God, and have been exceedingly exalted"
[Ps. 46:6-10]. And in Psalm ninety-eight the Holy Spirit reprimands
you, and announces that He whom you refuse to recognize as your
king is the King and Lord of Samuel, Aaron, Moses, and of every other
man. Here are the words of that Psalm: "The Lord has reigned, let
the people be angry. He that sits on the cherubim; let the earth be
moved. The Lord is great in Sion, and high above all people. Let them
give praise to Your great name, for it is terrible, and holy; and the
King's honor loves judgment. You have prepared directions; You have
done judgment and justice in Jacob. Exalt the Lord our God, and adore
His footstool, for He is holy. Moses and Aaron among His priests, and
Samuel among them that call upon His name. They called upon the
Lord (say the Scriptures), and He heard them. He spoke to them in
the pillar of the cloud. They kept His testimonies, and the commandment which He gave them. You did hear them, O Lord our God. You
were merciful to them, O God, and [yet] taking vengeance on all their
inventions. Exalt the Lord our God, and adore at His holy mountain;
for the Lord our God is holy" [Ps. 98:1-9].

'It would be better for us,' Trypho concluded, 'to have obeyed our teachers who warned us not to listen to you Christians, nor to converse with you on these subjects, for you have blasphemed many times in your attempt to convince us that this crucified man was with Moses and Aaron, and spoke with them in the pillar of the cloud; that He became man, was crucified, and ascended into Heaven, and will return again to this earth; and that He should be worshipped.'

'I am aware,' I replied, 'that, as the Word of God testifies, this great wisdom of Almighty God, the Creator of all, is concealed from you. It is, therefore, with feelings of pity that I exert every possible effort to help you understand our teachings, which to you seem paradoxical. If I fail, then I shall not be held accountable on judgment day. I shall recount to you other doctrines which may seem even more paradoxical to you, but don't be disturbed; instead of leaving me, become more zealous and inquisitive listeners. At the same time, forsake the tradition of your teachers, for they are convicted by the Prophetic Spirit of being incapable of understanding the truths spoken by God, and of preferring to spread their own opinions. The forty-fourth Psalm speaks thus of Christ: "My heart has uttered a good word; I speak my works to the King. My tongue is the pen of a scrivener that writes swiftly. You are beautiful above the sons of men; grace is poured abroad in Your lips; therefore has God blessed you forever. Gird Your sword upon Your thigh, O You most mighty. With Your comeliness and Your beauty set out, proceed prosperously, and reign, because of truth and meekness and justice; and Your right hand shall conduct You wonderfully. Your arrows are sharp, O Mighty One; under You shall people fall; in the heart of the King's enemies. Your throne, O God, is forever and ever; the scepter of Your kingdom is a scepter of uprightness. You have loved justice, and hated iniquity; therefore God, Your God, has anointed You with the oil of gladness above Your fellows. Myrrh and stacte and cassia perfume Your garments, from the ivory houses, whereby they have made You glad. King's daughters are in Your honor. The queen stood at Your right hand, in gilded clothing, surrounded with variety. Hearken, O daughter, and see, and incline your ear, and forget your people and your father's house. And the king shall greatly desire your beauty, for He is the Lord your God, and Him they shall adore. And the daughter of Tyre shall be there with gifts; the rich among the people shall entreat Your countenance. All the glory of the king's daughter is within in golden borders, clothed round about with varieties. After her shall virgins be brought to the King; her neighbors shall be brought to You. They shall be brought with gladness and rejoicing; they shall be brought into the temple of the King. Instead of Your fathers, sons are born to You. You shall make them princes over all the earth. I will remember Your name throughout all generations. Therefore shall people praise You forever, and forever and ever" [Ps. 44:1-18].

'It is small wonder,' I continued, 'that you Jews hate us Christians who have grasped the meaning of these truths, and take you to task for your stubborn prejudice. Indeed, Elijah, when interceding for you before God, spoke thus: "Lord, they have slain Your prophets, and have destroyed Your altars; and I am left alone, and they seek my life." And God answered: "I still have seven thousand men, whose knees have not been bowed before Baal" [I Kings 19:18]. Therefore, just as God did not show His anger on account of those seven thousand men, so now He has not yet exacted judgment of you, because He knows that every day some of you are forsaking your erroneous ways to become disciples in the name of Christ, and this same name of Christ enlightens you to receive all the graces and gifts according to your merits. One receives the spirit of wisdom, another of counsel, another of fortitude, another of healing, another of foreknowledge, another of teaching, and another of the fear of God.'

'Don't you realize,' interposed Trypho, 'that you are out of your mind to say such things?'

'Listen to me, my friend,' I retorted, 'and I'll prove that I'm not out of my mind when I mention these special gifts. For it was predicted that, after His Ascension into Heaven, Christ would free us from the captivity of error and endow us with gifts. Here are the words of the prophecy: "He ascended on high; He led captivity captive; He gave gifts to men" [Ps. 67:19]. Thus, having received gifts from Christ, who ascended into Heaven, we can show from the prophecies that you "who are wise in your own eyes and prudent in your own sight" [Isa. 5:21], are in reality stupid, for you honor God and His Christ only with your lips. We, on the other hand, who have been well instructed in His whole truth, honor Them with our actions, our knowledge, and our hearts, even unto death. The reason why you hesitate to acknowledge that Jesus is the Christ (which is proved by the Scriptures, the events which you yourselves witnessed, and the miracles wrought in His name) is, perhaps, to avoid the harsh persecution of the officials, who, influenced by the serpent (that evil and treacherous spirit), will not cease to perse-

cute and slaughter those who acknowledge the name of Christ until He
shall come again to destroy them all and to distribute rewards according
to merit.'

'Prove to us,' interrupted Trypho, 'that this man who you claim
was crucified, and ascended into Heaven, is the Christ of God. It has
indeed been proved sufficiently by your Scriptural quotations that it was
predicted in the Scriptures that Christ should suffer, and that He should
come again in glory to accept the eternal kingdom over all nations, and
that every kingdom should be made subject to Him. But what we want
you to prove is that this Jesus is the Christ spoken of in the Scriptures.'

'My dear friends,' I replied, 'anyone with ears would know that I
have already proved that very point, and it can be shown also from the
facts which you yourselves have admitted. But, lest you think that I am
not able to furnish further proof that Jesus is the Messiah, I renew my
promise to produce additional arguments in their proper place. For the
present, however, I would like to continue on the same subject we were
discussing.'

'The mystery of the lamb which God ordered you to sacrifice as
the Passover was truly a type of Christ, with whose Blood the believers,
in proportion to the strength of their faith, anoint their homes, that is,
themselves. You are all aware that Adam, the result of God's creative
act, was the abode of His inspiration. In the following fashion I can
show that God's precept concerning the paschal lamb was only temporary. God does not allow the paschal lamb to be sacrificed in any
other place than where His name is invoked (that is, in the Temple at
Jerusalem), for He knew that there would come a time, after Christ's
Passion, when the place in Jerusalem (where you sacrificed the paschal
lamb) would be taken from you by your enemies, and then all sacrifices
would be stopped. Moreover, that lamb which you were ordered to
roast whole was a symbol of Christ's Passion on the Cross. Indeed, the
lamb, while being roasted, resembles the figure of the cross, for one
spit transfixes it horizontally from the lower parts up to the head, and
another pierces it across the back, and holds up its forelegs. Likewise,
the two identical goats which had to be offered during the fast (one of
which was to be the scapegoat and the other the sacrificial goat) were
an announcement of the two advents of Christ: of the first Advent, in
which your priests and elders sent Him away as a scapegoat, seizing
Him and putting Him to death; of the second Advent, because in that
same place of Jerusalem you shall recognize Him whom you had sub-

jected to shame, and who was a sacrificial offering for all sinners who are willing to repent and to comply with that fast which Isaiah prescribed when he said "loosing the knot of violent contracts" [Isa. 58:6], and to observe likewise all the other precepts laid down by him. . . . You also know very well that the offering of the two goats, which had to take place during the fast, could not take place anywhere else outside of Jerusalem.'

'Likewise,' I continued, 'the offering of flour' [cf. Lev. 14:10], my friends, which was ordered to be presented for those cleansed from leprosy, was a prototype of the Eucharistic Bread, which our Lord Jesus Christ commanded us to offer in remembrance of the Passion He endured for all those souls who are cleansed from sin, and that at the same time we should thank God for having created the world, and everything in it, for the sake of mankind, and for having saved us from the sin in which we were born, and for the total destruction of the powers and principalities of evil through Him who suffered in accordance with His will. Thus, as I already stated, God speaks through Malachi, one of the twelve Prophets, concerning the sacrifices you then offered up to Him: "I have no pleasure in you, says the Lord, and I will not receive your sacrifices at your hands. For from the rising of the sun even to the going down, My name is great among the Gentiles, and in every place incense is offered to My name, and a clean oblation; for My name is great among the Gentiles, says the Lord, but you profane it" [Mal. 1:10-12]. By making reference to the sacrifices which we Gentiles offer to Him everywhere, the Eucharistic Bread and the Eucharistic Chalice, He predicted that we should glorify His name, but that you should profane it. Furthermore, the precept of circumcision, obliging you without fail to circumcise your sons on the eighth day, was a type of the true circumcision by which we are circumcised from error and wickedness through our Lord Jesus Christ who arose from the dead on the first day of the week. For the first day of the week, while it remains the first of all the days, yet is called the eighth, according to the number of all the days of the cycle, and still it remains the first. . . .'

'As circumcision originated with Abraham, and the Sabbath, sacrifices, oblations, and festivals with Moses (and it has already been shown that your people were commanded to observe these things because of their hardness of heart), so it was expedient that, in accordance with the will of the Father, these things should have their end in Him who was born of the Virgin, of the race of Abraham, of the tribe of

Judah, and of the family of David: namely, in Christ, the Son of God, who was proclaimed as the future Eternal Law and New Testament for the whole world (as the above-quoted prophecies clearly show). We, indeed, who have come to God through Jesus Christ, have received not a carnal, but a spiritual, circumcision, as did Enoch and those like him. Through God's mercy we received this by means of baptism, since we had become sinners, and all men should likewise receive it. But the topic to which we must now direct our attention is the mystery of the Birth of Christ. Isaiah already stated that man cannot describe it, when he exclaimed: "Who shall declare His generation? Because He is cut off out of the land of the living; for the wickedness of My people He was led to death" [Isa. 53:8]. The Prophetic Spirit thus declared that the Birth of Him who was to die in order to save us sinners by His stripes was inexpressible. Furthermore, the same Prophetic Spirit, through the same Isaiah, informed the faithful how Christ was to be born and how He was to come into this world. The words of the prophecy are: "And the Lord spoke again to Ahaz saying: Ask a sign of the Lord your God, in the depth, or in the height above. And Ahaz said: I will not ask, and I will not tempt the Lord. And Isaiah said: Hear therefore, O house of David; Is it a small thing for you to contend with men, that you are to contend with God also? Therefore the Lord Himself shall give you a sign. Behold a Virgin shall conceive, and bear a Son, and His name shall be called Emmanuel. He shall eat butter and honey before He knows to refuse the evil, and to choose the good. For before the Child shall know good or evil, He refuses evil to choose the good. For before the Child knows how to call father or mother, He shall receive the power of Damascus and the spoil of Samaria in the presence of the king of Assyria. And the land shall be forsaken, which you shall hardly endure on account of the presence of the two kings. But God shall bring upon you, and upon your people, and upon the house of your father, days that have not yet come upon you, since the day that He took away Ephraim from Judah the king of the Assyrians" [Isa. 7:10-16]. Now, it is clear to all that no one of the race of Abraham was ever born, or even said to be born, of a virgin, except of our Christ. But, since you and your teachers venture to assert that the real words of Isaiah are not "Behold, a virgin shall conceive," but "Behold a young woman shall conceive, and bear a son;" and since you refer this prophecy to your king Hezekiah, I will attempt to answer you and show that this prophecy applies to Him whom we profess as our Christ.'

'I will be absolutely without blame in my obligations to you, if I endeavor to convince you with every possible proof. But, if you persist in your obstinacy of heart and feebleness of mind, or if you refuse to agree to the truth through fear of the death which awaits every Christian [i.e. the death penalty for being a Christian], you will have only yourselves to blame. And you are sadly mistaken if you think that, just because you are descendants of Abraham according to the flesh, you will share in the legacy of benefits which God promised would be distributed by Christ. No one can by any means participate in any of these gifts, except those who have the same ardent faith as Abraham, and who approve of all the mysteries. For I say that some precepts were given for the worship of God and the practice of virtue, whereas other commandments and customs were arranged either in respect to the mystery of Christ [or] the hardness of your people's hearts. To prove this, God thus says through the mouth of Ezekiel: "If Noah and Jacob and Daniel should ask for either sons or daughters, it will not be given unto them" [Ezek. 4:20]. And the same is stated in Isaiah: "The Lord God said: And they shall go out and see the carcasses of the men that have transgressed against Me: for their worm shall not die, and their fire shall not be quenched, and they shall be a loathsome sight to all flesh" [Isa. 66:24]. As men who have cut your souls off from this hope, it is necessary that you know how to obtain pardon of your sins and a hope of sharing in the promised blessings. There is no other way than this, that you come to know our Christ, be baptized with the baptism which cleanses you of sin (as Isaiah testified), and thus live a life free of sin.'

12.

THE MYSTERY OF ADAM

A Twelfth Century Religious Drama

Then shall the Prophets be made ready, one by one, in a secret place, as their order is.
   Let the Lesson be read in the choir.

"YOU, I SAY, DO I CHALLENGE, O JEWS."

And let the Prophets be summoned by name; and when they shall come forward, let them advance with dignity and utter their prophecies loudly and distinctly. So shall ABRAHAM *come first, an old man with an exceeding long beard, arrayed in ample robes; and when he shall have sat for a brief season upon the bench, let him begin his prophecy in a loud voice:*

"*Thy seed shall possess the gates of their enemies, and in thy seed shall all the nations of the earth be blessed*" [Gen. 22:17f.].

> Abraham, I; such is my name.
> Hear, now, the message I proclaim:
> Whose hope is on God's promise stayed,
> Let him keep faith and trust unswayed;
> Whose faith is fixed in God, for aye
> Will God be with him. This I say
> Through knowledge; God my faith did test;

100

I did his will, obeyed his hest;
For him, mine own son had I slain,
But God's hand did my hand restrain.
The unfinished offering did he bless,
'T was counted me for righteousness.
God promised me—'t is truth, indeed,—
An heir shall issue from my seed
Who shall subdue his every foe,
And strong and mighty shall he grow;
Their gates possessing, ne'er shall he
A menial in their castles be.
E'en such an one, sprung from my root,
Shall all our punishment commute;
By him the world shall ransomed be,
And Adam from his pain set free;
And men, of every race and kind
On earth, through him shall blessing find.

After these words have been said, and a little time hath intervened, the devils shall lead Abraham to hell.

Then shall come MOSES, *bearing in his right hand a rod, and in his left the tables [of stone.] After he hath seated himself, let him utter his prophecy:*

"God shall raise up a prophet from among your brethren; to him shall ye hearken as to me" [Deut. 18:15].

That which I speak, through God I saw:
From our own brethren, from our law,
God shall raise up a man who'll be
Prophet and sum of prophecy.
Heaven's secrets all shall he receive;
Him, more than me, shall ye believe.

Thereafter shall he be led away by the Devil into hell. In like manner shall it be done with all the prophets.

Then shall come AARON, *in the vestments of a bishop, bearing in his hand a rod having flowers and fruit; and being seated, let him say:*

*"From this rod the flower that springeth
Perfume of salvation bringeth;*

Sweet its fruit, 't will end all crying
And all sorrow for our dying."

> This rod—unplanted, without root,—
> Can bud, and blossom, and bear fruit;
> Such Rod from mine own line shall spring
> And deadly hurt to Satan bring.
> No taint of fleshly birth he'll bear,
> Yet man's own nature shall he wear.
> This is salvation's fruit, 't will free
> Adam from his captivity.

After him, let DAVID *draw nigh, arrayed in royal robes and wearing a crown; and let him say:*

"Truth is sprung out of the earth; and justice hath looked down from heaven. For the Lord will give goodness; and our earth shall yield her fruit" [Ps. 85:11f.].

> Out of the earth shall truth arise,
> And justice watch us from the skies;
> Yea, God shall give us all things good;
> Our land shall richly bring us food,
> Her increase yield that saving Bread
> Whereby Eve's sons shall all be fed;
> O'er all the earth shall he hold sway,
> Shall stablish peace, drive war away.

Thereafter let SOLOMON *come forth, with the same adornments as David, yet in such a manner that he shall seem to be younger; and sitting down, let him say:*

"Being ministers of God's kingdom, you have not judged rightly, nor kept the law of justice, nor walked according to the will of God; horribly and speedily will he appear to you; for a most severe judgment shall be for them that bear rule. For to him that is little, mercy is granted" [Wisdom of Solomon, 6:5-7].

> God gave to you his law, O Jews,
> But faith with him ye would not use;
> Wardens of his domain were ye,
> He stablished you right royally;

Ye would not render judgment right,
Your verdicts were in God's despite;
His will ye would perform no more,
And your iniquity waxed sore.
Your deeds shall all to light be brought;
Most grievous vengeance shall be wrought
On those that highest sat of all.
And they shall suffer fearful fall.
But God shall set the lowly free
And raise him to felicity.
This saying shall be verified
When God's own Son for us hath died.
The masters of the law 't will be
That slay him, most unlawfully;
Against all justice, all belief,
They'll crucify him, like a thief.
But they shall lose their lordly seat,
Who envy him, and ill entreat.
Low down they'll come, from a great height,
Well may they mourn their woeful plight.
Howbeit, poor Adam shall he see
And pity, and from sin set free.

After him shall come BALAAM, *an old man arrayed in ample robes, sitting upon an ass: and he shall come into the midst, and still sitting upon his beast, he shall speak his prophecy:*

"A Star shall rise out of Jacob, and a Scepter shall spring up from Israel, and shall strike the chiefs of Moab, and shall waste all the children of Seth" [Num. 24:17].

From Jacob shall a Star arise,
Reddening with heaven's own fire the skies,
A Scepter spring from Israel
That shall 'gainst Moab's rule rebel,
Their haughtiness diminishing;
For out of Israel Christ shall spring,
And he shall be that glorious Star
Whereby all things illumined are.
His faithful ones he'll lead to joy,
But all his enemies destroy.

Thereafter shall DANIEL *draw nigh, in years a youth, but in his demeanor like unto an old man; and when he shall have seated himself, let him speak his prophecy, stretching forth his hand against those whom he addresseth:*

"When the Most Holy One shall have come, your anointing shall cease" [Dan. 9:24, 26].

> You, O ye Jews, do I address,
> Who use toward God great wickedness.
> When he, the Chief of Saints, draws near,
> Then your confusion shall appear,
> For then shall your anointing cease;
> All claim thereto must ye release.
> This Holy One is Christ, 't is plain;
> Through him the faithful life shall gain.
> To earth come, for his people's sake,
> On him your race great war shall make,
> Shall drive him to his Passion; so
> Shall they their unction's grace forego,
> Thenceforth nor priest nor king shall own,
> Their Law lost through themselves alone.

After him shall come HABAKKUK, *an old man; and sitting down, when he beginneth his prophecy, he shall lift up his hands toward the church, manifesting wonder and fear. Let him say:*

"O Lord, I have heard thy speech and was afraid. In the midst of the two beasts shalt thou be recognized" [Hab. 3:2].

> From God strange tidings have I heard,
> Whereby my mind is greatly stirred;
> So long did I this sign explore
> My heart thereat is trouble sore:
> Between two beasts shall he be shown,
> By all the world he shall be known.
> To him of whom this thing I say,
> Behold, a star shall point the way;
> Shepherds shall find him, thither brought,
> Within a crib in dry stone wrought
> Wherefrom the beasts shall eat their hay;

> To kings he'll be declared straightway;
> Thither the star shall lead the kings,
> All three shall bring their offerings.

Then shall JEREMIAH *enter, bearing a scroll in his hand; and let him say:*

"Hear ye the word of the Lord, all ye men of Judah, that enter in at these gates to adore the Lord. Thus saith the Lord of Hosts, the God of Israel: Make your ways and your doings good, and I will dwell with you in this place" [Jer. 7:2f.].

> The holy word of God now hear,
> All who are of his school, give ear,
> All righteous Judah's mighty race,
> Who in his household have a place:
> Ye all shall enter by this door,
> Our Lord to worship, evermore;
> The Lord of Hosts to you doth cry,
> The God of Israel, from on high:
> Make good your ways, amend each one,
> Let them be straight as furrows run,
> And let your hearts be clean, withal,
> Lest any evil you befall;
> Let all your thoughts in good abound,
> Nor wickedness therein be found.
> If thus ye do, then God will come
> And in your dwellings make his home,
> The Son of God, the glorious,
> For you come down to earth, and thus,
> As mortal man, with you shall be—
> The Lord of heavenly majesty!
> Adam he shall from prison bring,
> Himself as ransom offering.

After him shall come ISAIAS, *bearing a book in his hand, and wrapped in a large mantle; and let him speak his prophecy:*

"And there shall come forth a rod out of the root of Jesse, and a flower shall rise up out of his root, and the Spirit of the Lord shall rest upon it" [Isa. 11:1f.].

Now will I tell a wondrous thing:
From Jesse's root a Rod shall spring,
Shall burgeon and bear flower withal,
Whereto great honor shall befall;
The Holy Spirit shall enclose
This flower, and shall thereon repose.

Then shall there stand up a certain one of the synagogue, disputing
with Isaias; and he shall say unto him:

[JEW.]   Now, Sir Isaias, answer me:
           Is this a tale, or prophecy?
           This thing thou'st told—pray, what is it?
           Didst it invent, or is it writ?
           Thou'st been asleep—didst dream the rest?
           Speak'st thou in earnest, or in jest?

ISAIAS.   This is no tale, 't is very truth!

JEW.   Then, let's know all of it, forsooth!

ISAIAS.   What I have spoke is prophecy.

JEW.   Writ in a book?

ISAIAS.   Yea, verily,
           —In Life's!   I've dreamed it not, but seen!

JEW.   And how?

ISAIAS.   Through grace of God, I ween.

JEW.   Thou seem'st to me a dotard grey,
           Thy mind and sense all gone astray!
           A soothsayer thou seem'st, indeed,
           Skilled in the glass, perchance, to read;
           Come, read me now this hand, and tell

(Then shall he shew him his hand:)

           Whether my heart be sick or well.

ISAIAS.   Thou hast sin's murrain in thy soul,
           Ne'er in thy life shalt thou be whole!

JEW.   Am I, then, sick?

ISAIAS.   With error sore.

JEW.   When shall I mend me?

ISAIAS.   Never more!

JEW.   Begin thy soothsaying, I pray.

ISAIAS.   There'll be no lie in what I say.

JEW.   Come now, re-tell thy vision, quick!
If 't was a rod, or but a stick,
And what its blossom shall engender;
Then due respect to thee we'll render,
And all the present generation
Will listen to thy dissertation.

ISAIAS.   Then, this great marvel shall ye hear;
—Such ne'er was told to mortal ear,
To such a marvel never man
Hath listened since the world began:

"Behold, a virgin shall conceive and bear a son, and his name shall be called Immanuel" [Isa. 7:14].

The time is near, within your ken,
Not tarrying or distant, when
A virgin shall conceive, most fair,
And, virgin still, a son shall bear;
His name shall be Emmanuel.
Saint Gabriel shall the message tell;
The maid shall Virgin Mary be,
She'll bear the fruit of Life's own tree,
Jesus, our Savior, who shall bring
Adam from dole and suffering,
And him to Paradise return.
That which I speak from God I learn;
All this shall surely be fulfilled,
And ye thereon your hope shall build.

Then shall come NEBUCHADNEZZAR, *adorned as befitteth a king.* [*And he shall say:*]

"Did we not cast three youths, bound, into the fire?"
HIS MINISTERS. *"True, O King."*

[NEBUCHADNEZZAR.] *"Lo, I see four men loose, walking in the midst of the fire, and they have no hurt, and the form of the fourth is like the Son of God"* [Dan. 3:91f.].

Hear now a wondrous prodigy,
Unheard-of by all men that be!
This saw I with the children three

Cast in the blazing fire by me:
The fire was hot and fierce to dree,
The bright flame glowed exceedingly;
The three rejoiced and made great glee,
Within the furnace walking free.
But when I came the fourth to see,
(Great comfort to the rest gave he,)
His face shone, full of majesty,
The Son of God he seemed to be!

PART III

LAW AND GOSPEL—
LETTER AND SPIRIT

Allegorization of Scripture, the "reading of another" meaning for the literal meaning of the text, did not originate with Christianity. It began within Judaism itself. Philo of Alexandria (25 B.C.E. to before 50 C.E.) interpreted the creation of the world, the wanderings of Abraham, the life of Moses, and the commandments of the Torah in terms of Platonic philosophy. Philo's inner meaning, however, was not intended to supplant the outer. It was meant rather as an explanation and a reinforcement. Philo never directly entered the mainstream of Jewish thought. As a general rule, it may be said that only those works written in Hebrew (or the cognate Aramaic) or translated into Hebrew have had an enduring influence in Judaism. The Greek writings of Philo the Alexandrian never became determinative for Jews; the Hebrew midrash of the Palestinian schools did.

Philonic allegory did take hold in Christianity however. Here, in its own midrash, the Church used Alexandrian exegesis not to show

109

the interdependence of spirit and letter but the liberation of spirit from letter. Now the two were seen as diametrically opposed—to reach for the one meant to cast off the other. The value of the Jewish Bible, or Old Testament, lay not in its apparent message but in its foreshadowing of the New Covenant. Persons and events of the Torah and the Prophets were "types" or prefigurations of those of the gospels. The Psalms speak of Christ or are the very words of the Father to the Son.

The one facet of the Jewish Scriptures that was most heavily subjected to allegorization was the commandments of the Torah. According to certain marginal Jewish traditions, the observance of some or all of the commandments would be suspended at the advent of the Messiah. Paul simply drew the logical conclusion. Understanding *Torah* as *nomos* (law), Paul viewed the latter not only as dead but as deadening—a "dispensation of death" (2 Cor. 3:7). Those who observe the law are "like Moses, who put a veil over his face [an inversion of Exod. 29:35f.] so that the Israelites might not see the end of the fading splendor. But their minds were hardened; for to this day, when they read the old covenant, that same veil remains unlifted, because only through Christ is it taken away. Yes, to this day whenever Moses is read, a veil lies over their minds. . . ." (2 Cor. 3:13-16). Hence, the contrast between the law of the old covenant and the grace—liberating and saving—of the new dispensation.

The Law-Gospel dichotomy was given renewed impetus in Lutheranism. Lutherans in a sense approached the doctrines of Marcion, the second century gnostic who had established a radical break between the law, revealed by the demonic creator-god (cf. 2 Cor. 4:4 ". . . the god of this world has blinded the minds of the unbelievers, to keep them from seeing the light of the gospel . . ."), and the grace of the dispensation of the God of Love. While not, of course, espousing Marcionite dualism, Lutheranism became a true bearer of the Torah-Gospel antithesis. (Roman Catholicism had, as it were, developed its own halakhah, while Calvin's attraction to biblical law earned him the title "Calvin the Judaizer" in Lutheran circles.) The legacy of Lutheranism made itself felt in Germany in several ways—notably in the development of biblical criticism. Literary-historical analysis defined several strata in the Pentateuch which were said to have stemmed from various stages of development of Israelite religion. The priestly-levitical-legalistic material was contrasted with those texts demonstrating a greater degree of spirituality and composed in the post-exilic period. In this manner, they discerned an evolutionary process which was to culminate in Christianity. Such analysis did not necessarily have to lead to such conclusions. One might compare Y. Kaufmann's *The Religion of Israel* (trans. M. Greenberg, Chicago: U. of Chicago Press, 1960) for an alternative approach. Yet these conclusions still pervade the thinking of many—especially Protestant—biblical scholars.

This point was made rather dramatically to an instructor in a course on Jewish religious literature. Confronted with a passage which identified the high priest Aaron with divine grace, the students were quite at a loss to explain it. No one in the class, which consisted of both non-Jews and Jews (among them yeshiva-trained students steeped in traditional literature) knew how to come to terms with the fact that Judaism saw the priesthood as an instrument of love and grace and not of wrath and punishment. So deeply had they internalized the ideology of the dominant culture (cf. Baum) and the lessons learned in Old Testament courses! For this reason, Solomon Schechter's essay "The 'Law' " is no less relevant today than it was seventy years ago.

Another instance of the persistence of the Law-Gospel dichotomy in "post-Christian" thinking is found in Harvey Cox's argument for a secularized Christianity in *The Secular City*. Cox, of course, has no particular argument with Judaism; his concern is with the Church. Yet in setting forth his argument, he inevitably falls back on the old Christian prejudices.

These pieces of contemporary interest are introduced by some classical views—Joseph Kimhi and Profiat Duran for the Jewish point of view; St. John of Damascus and Francisco Machado for the Christian.

THE TORAH AFFIRMED

Joseph Kimhi's claim that the Jews are still the true Israel was based, we recall, on the fact of their adherence to the commandments, the symbol of the covenant. (See above, sel. 1.) Christians, no less than Jews, claimed that they too observed the commandments but not in their literal, "carnal" sense, i.e. their "Jewish sense" (*sensus Judaicus*). In this way, Christianity was able at the same time to preserve the Hebrew Scriptures and to declare them superseded through the use of allegorical or "spiritual" exegesis. Kimhi's "Christian" gives expression to this in his statement that the Jews "resemble him who gnaws at the bone, while we [suck at] the marrow within." Kimhi, it must be remembered, allots relatively few words to his Christian antagonist. Had he been more generous, we perhaps might have heard something of the sort expressed by his contemporary, Bartholomew, bishop of Exeter (d. 1184):

> The chief cause of disagreement between ourselves and the Jews seems to me to be this: they take all the Old Testament literally, wherever they can find a literal sense, unless it gives a manifest witness to Christ. Then they repudiate it, saying that it is not in the Hebrew Truth, that is in their books, or they refer it to some fable, as that they are still awaiting its fulfilment, or they escape by some other serpentine wile, when they feel themselves pressed. They will never accept allegory, except when they have no other way out. *We* interpret not only the words of Scripture, but the things done, and the deeds themselves in a mystical sense, yet in such a way that the freedom of allegory may in no wise nullify, either history in the events, or proper understanding of the words, of Scripture. (From the *Dialogue against the Jews,* cited from B. Smalley, *The Study of the Bible in the Middle Ages,* Oxford: Blackwell, 1952, pp. 170-71)

Kimhi agreed with Bartholomew that "they will never accept allegory, except when they have no way out." Thus he argues that Moses and the prophets, who above all should have known God's true intention, understood the Torah literally. Figurative interpretation is to be allowed only when the literal meaning is absurd. Surely, he contends, "Take away the foreskins of your hearts" is absurd in its literal sense, since it would be an order to commit suicide; but "circumcise yourselves to the Lord" is quite within the realm of possibility.

Kimhi closes with the common presentation of a proof-text to show that God gave the Torah for all times never to be abrogated.

Selection 13 is reprinted from *Book of the Covenant*, Toronto: Pontifical Institute for Mediaeval Studies, 1972, pp. 46-49.

The wave of anti-Jewish massacres in Spain in the year 1391 created a class of converts baptized by force who eventually came to be known as "New Christians" or "Marranos." Among these were the two friends, Isaac Profiat Duran and David Bonet Bonjorn. Finding their predicament intolerable, they agreed to emigrate to Palestine where they could return openly to Judaism. Duran went to the appointed departure point only to learn that his friend had changed his mind. Bonjorn informed Duran in a letter that he had been convinced of the truth of Christianity by his apostate teacher, Paul of Burgos (formerly Solomon Halevi). Paul's achievements in science and theology had impressed both secular and ecclesiastical officials and Bonjorn saw him as a worthy model. Duran's reaction took the form of a letter, known as the "Be Not like unto Thy Fathers" (*'Al Tehi ka-'Avotekha*), which became one of the classic texts of Jewish polemical literature. Satire and irony were frequent weapons in religious polemics but seldom were they so artfully developed. Ostensibly, Duran praises his friend for having embraced Christianity and for having turned from the ways of his fathers. In fact, however, his praise is damnation. Admittedly, the satire is fairly transparent. Yet, when it was first published, some Christian clergy took it as a genuine confession of faith and put their seal of approval on it. They soon realized, however, what this composition, which they called the *Alteca Boteca*, was.

Duran's critique centers on the fideistic conception of religion advocated by Paul and Bonjorn. He grants that "the just shall live by his faith" but does not agree with the Christian definition of faith. For Duran, faith, i.e. the faithful observance of the covenant, consists of a combination of rational belief and observance of the commandments. At the same time, he criticizes Christian abrogation of the precepts (stressing that Jesus and the disciples themselves observed them) while mocking what he felt were the irrational doctrines of the Trinity, the incarnation, and the virgin birth.

It had generally been thought that Duran openly returned to Judaism as he had planned. However, recently discovered evidence has shown that until as late as 1403 he continued to live as a Christian in Perpignan under the eyes of the Inquisition. Never losing his sense of irony, he assumed the name Honoratus de Bona Fide and proceeded to write a more ambitious polemical treatise, the *Reproach of the Nations*. Its philosophical arguments against Christian doctrine were quoted and copied for centuries. It was during this period too that he compiled the important grammar, *Ma'aseh 'Efod,* in which he expounds his views on the cultural values of the Judaism of the time.

Duran's letter has been reprinted from F. Kobler, *Letters of Jews through the Ages from Biblical Times to the Middle of the Eighteenth Century,* London: Ararat and East & West Library, 1953, I, 276-82.

Solomon Schechter (1847-1915) was one of the great forces in the shaping of American Judaism. Born in eastern Europe, he studied in Germany and later received the opportunity to go to England. Schechter's scholarship won him the position of reader in rabbinics at Cambridge and professor at the University of London. He gained distinction through his editions of Hebrew texts and in his role in making the Cairo Geniza accessible to scholars. This great depository of records and documents found in the attic of an Old Cairo synagogue has been a bountiful source of information for historians of medieval civilization. In 1901, Schechter was invited to America to assume the presidency of the Jewish Theological Seminary of America where he advocated his conception of Conservative Judaism, loyal to tradition yet comfortable in the modern world. One of the most literate of scholars, his *Some Aspects of Rabbinic Theology* and three volumes of *Studies in Judaism* remain among the most readable essays in Jewish scholarship.

In his contacts with German and British scholars, Schechter militantly opposed Christian prejudices against Jews and Judaism which permeated biblical and Hebrew studies. Schechter was a vociferous critic of "higher criticism" or source analysis of the Pentateuch. This was not due to fear of scientific inquiry but to animosity towards the inevitable denigration of Judaism which resulted from the researches of these scholars. In his opinion: "Higher criticism—higher antisemitism." Schechter was concerned with demonstrating the simplistic quality of the distinction between law-legalism-leviticalism, seen as a primitive stage in the development of Israelite religion, and prophetism, seen as a more sophisticated stage and the precursor of Christianity. In his essay, "The Law," Schechter shows how the word "law" is an inadequate translation for *Torah* and how the facile dichotomies of the critics rest on weak grounds.

"The Law" was originally published in *Some Aspects of Rabbinic Theology,* New York: Macmillan, 1909, pp. 116-126.

13.

THE BOOK OF THE COVENANT

Joseph Kimhi

The [Christian] said: You understand most of the Torah literally while we understand it figuratively. Your whole reading of the Bible is erroneous for you resemble him who gnaws at the bone, while we [suck at] the marrow within. You are like the beast that eats the chaff, while we [eat] the wheat.

The [Jew] said: Tell me. When the Holy One, blessed be He, gave the Torah to Moses who taught it to Israel, did he understand it figuratively or not? If you say that he did not understand it figuratively but literally and taught it so to Israel, then Israel is not to be held accountable in this matter. How is it that the Creator did not teach it to Moses figuratively so that he might have taught it [so] to Israel? If you say that he understood it figuratively, why did he not teach it to Israel figuratively? For that matter, why did the prophets who came after him not do so? Indeed the prophets understood [the laws] according to the intention of Moses. Joshua circumcised the people and celebrated the Passover, as did Hezekiah and Josiah, according to the command of Moses. It was so with other commandments. What will you say of the Sabbath? Did Moses not try the one who gathered sticks [on the Sabbath] and did not Ezra exhort the people concerning the Sabbath? Further, if the cessation of [immoral] activities is not dependent on the seventh day since they are forbidden the entire week, why did the Torah not teach it allegorically as you say?

117

Know that the fact is that the Torah is not [to be taken] altogether literally or altogether figuratively. If one says to his servant, "Take the horse and ride it on the sea," we must try to interpret this figuratively; likewise, if he says to him, "Board the ship and go in it on dry land." There is no need for figurative interpretation if he says to him, "Board the ship and go on the sea in it." Some commandments may be understood both literally and figuratively. *Circumcise yourselves to the Lord and take away the foreskins of your heart* (Jer. 4:4) is to be taken figuratively, but *at the age of eight days, every male among you shall be circumcised* (Gen. 17:12) is to be taken literally. Both the circumcision of the flesh, i.e. the flesh of the foreskin and of the heart are obligatory, (i.e. we must circumcise our flesh and our hearts.) The prophet Ezekiel said *No uncircumcised in heart nor uncircumcised in flesh shall enter My sanctuary* (Ezek. 44:9). Now you are uncircumcised in flesh—which you cannot deny. If you are prevented from [entering] His sanctuary on one count, you are most certainly prevented [from doing so] on two. Now you cannot claim that you are not uncircumcised in heart, for whoever transgresses the commandments and murders, fornicates, steals, oppresses, speaks abusively to people, and mocks and robs them is uncircumcised in heart. You are uncircumcised in heart and uncircumcised in flesh while Israel are circumcised in heart and circumcised in flesh. You will not find a Jew who has been hanged or who has had his eyes gouged or who has one of his limbs cut off on account of crimes he has committed. Now if you say that the Torah was [to be understood] literally but that Jesus came afterward and commanded us a law of grace and explained it figuratively and introduced baptism, known as *batisme,* instead of circumcision and Sunday instead of the Sabbath, then the Creator changed His mind, for He gave the Torah for a limited time only. Is it not said *This is My covenant with them, says the Lord, My spirit that is upon you and My words which I have put in your mouth will not depart from your mouth* (Isa. 59:21). How can we say that He would change this Torah which he said would never depart from our mouths?

14.

"BE NOT LIKE UNTO THY FATHERS"

Profiat Duran

PROFIAT DURAN TO DAVID BONET BONGORON

*'I should like to ask thee one thing, this only thing, please, do for my
sake: do not call thyself any longer after the honored
name of thy wise father'*

[A port in Southern France, about 1396]

To David, when he changed his mind, before the Ruler of the world,
and sang of the death of the son who suffered for him and carried the
burden for him. He said to his father: 'I do not know thee,' and does
not ask after the forefathers any more. I called him once my brother.
Maestro Bonet Bonjorn, the new Christian, is his name. In Israel he
was called once: David Bonet ben Goron.

I received a letter. . . . I read it with aching head and tired lips,
because it was full of hidden meaning, of dark and secret wisdom, as
if it were a book sealed with seven seals. I understood little, but *one*
thing became clear to me: that the heritage of the ancestors was a
deplorable mistake. . . . They missed the light in spite of their learning,
they believed they ascended to heaven and went, instead, down to obscure graves. . . . Woe to them for all their labors, for they were in
vain! I redoubled my efforts and perceived at last: The holy spirit has
awakened thee, blessed be the Messiah who gave thee a willing heart

119

and listening ear! Human Reason will seduce thee never more to dwell with her in dark chambers, thou recognizest her as an enemy, pernicious like vipers. For she was always an adversary of Faith and ever ready to wound Faith time and again. He is a fool who said: 'Reason and Torah are two lights in the heaven of life.' We have nothing to do with Reason, her syllogisms and evidences, any more. . . . Faith alone goes up to heaven. Those who deny this go to hell. Also Scripture says therefore: 'The just shall live by his faith' [Hab. 2:4], if the Hebrew word does mean indeed that which thou and thy teachers wish to understand by it.

Now, my brother, I became aware of thy good intentions, and that all thou dost is for the sake of the Lord. Faith is for thee a girdle round the loins, and Reason with all her lies is unable to entice thee and divert thy paths. Therefore I made up my mind to show thee clearly the ways of the faith which thou hast chosen as thy compass in the light of the Messiah.

Be not like unto thy fathers, who believed in one God from whose unity they removed any plurality. They have erred indeed, when they said, 'Hear Israel, the Lord is One!', when they understood this unity in the purest sense without inclusion of species, kind or number. *Not so thou!* Thou shalt believe that one can become three, and that three united make one. Lips will never tell it, ears never take it in.

Be not like unto thy fathers, who conceived by deep meditations the eternal Ruler beyond change and body, as expressed in the words 'I change not' [Mal. 3:6], and who explained in this sense even those passages which, when interpreted unskilfully, perplex simple souls. *Not so thou!* Heaven forbid that thou shouldst deny His corporeal embodiment, but believe rather that one of His three persons became flesh, when He wanted to shed blood for the atonement of mankind. Offer Him thanks that He suffered death in order to redeem thee. . . . For this was surely the only way which could be found by the wisdom of the Almighty! Believe that He became flesh in the womb of a virgin, of an ''Almah' as the Hebrew word reads [The Vulgate translates *'almah*, "young woman," in Isa. 7:14 as "virgin"], it occurs also in the passage 'the way of the man with a young woman' [Prov. 30:19]. This miracle was able to encourage the faint-hearted Ahaz, although he had lived five hundred years earlier. . . . [See Isa. 7:1ff.]

Be not like unto thy fathers, who by close scrutiny tried to find a deep philosophical meaning in the account of creation, and who had much to disclose about the first human couple, about the four rivers, the tree of knowledge, the serpent, and the coats of skin which the Lord made them for clothing. *Not so thou!* Conceive all this literally! Add, however, yet an inner punishment to Adam's misfortune, increase through it the burden of his bitter fate that he has to carry on his back. He will never get rid of it, and is entirely in the grip of Satan, until the Redeemer comes and purifies him by his death. Now that sin is abolished, although it is not mentioned in our holy Scripture, while the other curses, the punishments of hell, remain for ever. . . . Stick to the mystery of hereditary sin which the head of the Apostles proclaimed, he whose name is identical with that of thy teacher [Paul of Burgos]. Thy reward will grow immensely like thy faith.

Be not like unto thy fathers, who were continuously engaged in sciences of all kinds, in mathematics, metaphysics and logic, and tried to penetrate to the foundations of truth. *Not so thou!* Far be it from thee to recognize the first fundamental rule of reasoning in logic. For this would entice thee to deny thy faith by saying: God is Father; the Son, too, is God truly: the Son is therefore the Father. Brother, stick to this belief! It will lead thee to eternal life, and God will be with thee. . . . Alas, thy fathers ate the bread of affliction, suffered thirst and hunger; thou, however, hast saved thy soul, thou eatest and becomest satisfied, thou rejoicest in the Lord and praisest the Holy One of Israel. . . .

But above all believe sincerely in the almighty Redeemer. He is the root . . . of thy faith. . . . But do not believe in the metaphysical principle that affirmation and negation cannot exist at the same time, further that transformation of an accident into essence is impossible, and also that the being of a thing consists in its essence, but that the being of an accident depends on the object which carries it. For the body of the Messiah who sits on the throne in heaven does not move while that on the altar moves in every direction. The wafer is, before the utterance of the priest, nothing else than bread, but by this utterance the essence of the bread becomes an accidental quality or disappears entirely, and the previous accidental qualities become independent and enter the stomach of the priest who eats the wafer. None of the believers denies this. . . . In general, brother, do not accept the principle, 'What is impossible in itself remains impossible', but, on the contrary, accept faithfully all those impossibilities, for the almighty Messiah dominates all things, near or far, possible or impossible. . . .

Be not like unto thy fathers, upon whom the holy Torah of Moses was bestowed as heritage and possession, when they strove after spiritual perfection in thought and deed, when they called that godly doctrine the crown of their head, and kept faithfully the commandments and prohibitions, according to the saying, 'The secret things belong unto the Lord our God; but those things which are revealed belong unto us and to our children for ever' [Deut. 29:29]. Every prophet points to this, even the last one declares it through his last word [Mal. 4:4ff.]. *Not so thou!* For this would be shameful. If thou beget sons, do not introduce them into the covenant of the fathers! Take no heed of the multitude of those ancient laws of marriage. Neither change thy garb to sanctify the Sabbaths and Festivals. When the great, the only day of the long fast approaches, tell thyself: 'Now, eat and drink, for thou art without any guilt!' Eat leavened bread on the Passover; eat also meat and milk together! Where penalties threaten, believe that it is always better to permit. Eat of pork, of all animals in the water, on the earth and in the air, which have been interdicted thee once.

To be sure, have not the disciples of the Messiah themselves forbidden this to the faithful people, in the book of their teaching called 'The Acts of the Apostles'? [Chapter 15] . . . Did not those men as descendants of Abraham keep rigidly the Law? Even after the death of their leader? Even after their baptism? But why should I mention them, seeing that the Messiah himself confirmed the permanence of the Law! [Matt. 5:17] . . .

Behold! I should like to come to thee, my brother, and to thy new teacher, with all these and many other scruples, because I know that the holy spirit speaks through you, elected men! No secret exists for you, thanks to the Lord, who has chosen you. . . . There is one thing, however, which I want to tell thee. . . . Do not care for the shame in thy soul, or the mark on thy forehead, when the enemies will perhaps offend thee in future, for some of them will say 'Apostate' and others 'circumcised Jew': as a reward thy soul will share the eternal pleasures, and thou wilt see the faces of the king and of the queen[-mother] beside him.

As to the excellence of thy teacher, whom thou praisest so highly for his enormous wisdom, his dignity and ingenuity, that thou considerest him as created in the image of God and wouldst almost elect him Pope—although thou art not sure whether he should go to Rome or remain in Avignon [an allusion to the Great Schism in the papacy] —I am quite aware of the proficiency which this man acquired in astronomy and philosophy. Offer thanks to the Messiah that such a man is in his world. Not without reason our king bestowed upon him rich treasures in recognition of his piety. Thou tellest me also, my brother, that his mighty influence was instrumental for the important decision of the king that 'women and minor children—under fifteen years—are not allowed to [be seen in public without discriminatory clothing.] Thus it was published. This is a big thing indeed and very useful for the masses. Now, haste and show it to thy parents! Tell it also to the smart ladies!

There is a rumor that he was about to speak evil things against the Jews in Avignon. But his Excellency the Lord Cardinal of Pampeluna and also other princes protested against this strongly in secret. In addition the Jewish community gave him a lot of money in gold and silver. Then he was silent. The Pope, however, and his friends have the intention of bestowing upon him a bishopric or even appointing him a cardinal. Rejoice then, dear brother: his honor honors thee too. He will certainly not fail to establish many houses of priests and Levites for thy benefit.

I wonder that thou—methinks, just as it is the way of fools—warnest me writing that my friends try to perplex me. For ever and anon I strove seriously after truth, in thought and deed. Thou knowest this very well. I live entirely for my Lord, with all my heart, and with all my soul, today and always. It is my hope and my profound trust that *that* Messiah will come who carries His name. Behold, this is my song and praise, my pleasure, strength and power. To this faith I have clung for many years, without change, without apostasy, and I shall cling for ever.

I should like, however, to ask thee one thing, this thing only, please, do it for my sake: do not call thyself any longer after the honored name of thy wise father, may his memory be blessed! For his advice does not suit thee any more, and his merit does not shine upon thee. For if he were alive he would say today: 'Better no son than such a son!' And his soul in its resting place laments now, too, over thee and thy way. May the Messiah, he to whom thou adherest, he alone and nobody else, give thee light and peace for ever!

He who is writing this loves thee with all his heart. And if thou wilt choose the right way and listen to the voice of the Lord, He will always be with thee. As it is said, 'In all places where I record my name, I will bless thee' [Exod. 20:24]. And then thou wilt again be to me a brother and darling son.

He who wrote this is thy brother

Efodi

15.

THE "LAW"

Solomon Schechter

The Law derives its authority from the kingdom. For this, according to the Rabbis, is the meaning of the scriptural words, "I am the Lord your God," or "The Lord your God," with which certain groups of laws are introduced (*e.g.* Exod. 22:2 and Lev. 18:2); that is, God makes his people conscious of the fact of his claims on them because of their having received his kingdom, saying unto them, "You have received my kingdom in love." "Aye" and "Aye" answers Israel, wherefore God says, "If you have received my kingdom, you receive now my decrees."

Now the current notions about the Law or Torah are still so misleading that before entering upon the meaning and theological significance of the "decrees," a brief analysis of the term *Torah* seems most advisable. Even the hypothesis advanced by higher criticism, according to which it was just under the predominance of the Law that the Wisdom Literature was composed and most of the Psalms were written, had no effect on the general prejudice of theologians against the Torah. With a few exceptions our theologians still enlarge upon the "Night of Legalism," from the darkness of which religion only emerges by a miracle supposed to have taken place about the year 30 of our era.

An examination of the meaning of *Torah* and *Mizvot* to the Jew will show that Legalism was neither the evil thing commonly imagined nor did it lead to the evil consequences assumed by our theologians.

124

Nor has it ever constituted the whole religion of the Jew, as declared by most modern critics.

It must first be stated that the term *Law* or *Nomos* is not a correct rendering of the Hebrew word *Torah*. The legalistic element, which might rightly be called the Law, represents only one side of the Torah. To the Jew the word *Torah* means a teaching or an instruction of any kind. It may be either a general principle or a specific injunction, whether it be found in the Pentateuch or in other parts of the Scriptures, or even outside of the canon. The juxtaposition in which *Torah* and *Mizvot,* Teaching and Commandments, are to be found in the Rabbinic literature, implies already that the former means something more than merely the Law. Torah and Mizvot are a complement to each other, or, as a Rabbi expressed it, "they borrow from each other, as wisdom and understanding—charity and lovingkindness—the moon and the stars," but they are not identical. To use the modern phraseology, to the rabbinic Jew, Torah was both an institution and a faith. We shall treat them separately: first Torah, and then the Mizvot.

It is true that in rabbinic literature the term *Torah* is often applied to the Pentateuch to the exclusion of the Prophets and the Hagiographa. But this is chiefly for the purpose of classification. It is also true that to a certain extent the Pentateuch is put on a higher level than the Prophets—the prophetic vision of Moses having been, as the Rabbis avow, much clearer than that of his successors. But we must not forget that for the superiority of the Torah, they had the scriptural authority of the Torah itself (Num. 12:6-8, Deut. 34:10), whilst on the other hand *they* could not find in the Prophets anything deprecatory of Moses' superior authority. They may, occasionally, have felt some contradictions between the Prophets and the Torah, but only in matters of detail, not in matters of principle.

Of any real antagonism between Mosaism and "Leviticalism" and Prophetism, which modern criticism asserts to have brought to light, the Rabbis were absolutely unconscious. With the Rabbis, the Prophets formed only a complement or even a commentary to the Torah (a species of Agadah), which, indeed, needed explanation, as we shall see. Hence the *naïveté,* as we may almost call it, with which the Rabbis chose, for reading on the Day of Atonement, the 58th chapter of Isaiah —one of the most prophetic pieces of prophetism—as the accompanying lesson for the portion from the Pentateuch, Leviticus 16—the most Levitical piece in Leviticalism.

But even the Pentateuch is no mere legal code, without edifying elements in it. The Book of Genesis, the greater part of Exodus, and even a part of Numbers are simple history, recording the past of humanity on its way to the kingdom, culminating in Israel's entering it on Mount Sinai, and their subsequent relapses. The Book of Deuteronomy, as the "Book containing the words of exhortation" (Tokhahot), forms Israel's *Imitatio Dei,* consisting chiefly in goodness, and supplying to Israel its confession of faith (in the *Shema*); whilst the Book of Leviticus —marvel upon marvel—first proclaims that principle of loving one's neighbor as oneself (Lev. 19:18) which believers call Christianity, unbelievers, Humanity.

The language of the Midrash would seem to imply that at a certain period there were people who held the narratives of the Bible in slight estimation, looking upon them as fictions and useless stories. The Rabbis, however, reject such a thought with indignation. To them the whole of the Torah represented the word of God, dictated by the holy spirit, suggesting edifying lessons everywhere, and embodying even while it speaks of the past, a history of humanity written in advance. "The Book of Generations of Adam," that is, the history of the Genesis, in which the dignity of man is indicated by the fact of his having been created in the image of God, teaches, according to Ben Azai, even a greater principle than that of Lev. 19, in which the law of loving one's neighbor as oneself is contained. Another Rabbi deduces from the repetitions in Gen. 24 the theory that the conversation of the servants of the patriarchs is more beautiful than the laws even of later generations. Another Rabbi remarks that the Torah as a legal code would only have commenced with Exod. 12, where the first (larger) group of laws is set forth, but God's object was to show his people the power of his work, "that he may give them the inheritance of the heathen" (Ps. 111:6), and thus, in the end, justify the later history of their conquests.

The Book of Genesis, which contains the history of this manifestation of God's powers, as revealed in the act of creation as well as in the history of the patriarchs, and leads up to the story of the Exodus from Egypt, is, according to some Rabbis, the book of the covenant which Moses read to the people (Exod. 24:7) even before the act of revelation. To come into the possession of this book (the Book of Genesis), which unlocked before them one of the inner chambers of the king (or revealed to them the holy mysteries of God's working in the world), was considered by the Rabbis one of the greatest privileges of Israel, given to them as a reward for their submission to God's will.

Thus *Torah,* even as represented by the Pentateuch, is not mere Law, the Rabbis having discerned and appreciated in it other than merely legal elements. Moreover, the term *Torah* is not always confined to the Pentateuch. It also extends, as already indicated, to the whole of the Scriptures on which the Rabbis "labored" with the same spirit and devotion as on the Pentateuch. For indeed "the Torah is a *triad,* composed of Pentateuch, Prophets, and Hagiographa." "Have I not written to thee the three things in counsels and in knowledge?" That lessons from the Prophets almost always accompanied those taken from the Pentateuch is a well-known fact, as likewise that the Talmid Hakham, or the student, had to beautify himself with the knowledge of the twenty-four books of which the Bible consists, even as a bride adorns herself with twenty-four different kinds of ornaments. That this injunction was strictly fulfilled by the student is clear from the facility and frequency with which the Rabbis quoted the Prophets and the Hagiographa. A striking instance may be seen in the *Mekhilta,* a small work of not more than about seventy octavo pages when stripped from its commentaries; it has about one thousand citations from the Prophets and the Hagiographa.

"The sinners in Israel" (probably referring to the Samaritans), the Rabbis complain, "contend that the Prophets and the Hagiographa are not Torah, but are they not already refuted by Daniel (9:10), who said, 'Neither have we obeyed the voice of the Lord our God, to walk in his Torot which he set before us by his servants the prophets.'" Hence, the Rabbis proceed to say, Asaph's exclamation in Ps. 78, "Give ear, O my people, to my Torot." Note, in passing, that this Psalm, which claims to be Torah, is nothing but a *résumé* of Israel's history. With the rabbinic Jews, the Hagiographa formed an integral part of their holy Scriptures. "The prophets of truth and righteousness" were, as can be seen from the benediction preceding the weekly lesson from the Prophets, God's chosen ones, in the same way as the Torah, as his servant Moses, and his people Israel—the depository of revelation. In olden times they had even a special benediction before they began to read either the Prophets or the Hagiographa, running thus, "Blessed are You, O Lord our God, who have commanded us to read the holy writings." This was quite in accordance with their principle regarding prophecy as "the word of God," and the continuation of his voice heard on

Mount Sinai, a voice which will cease only with the messianic times,—perhaps for the reason that the earth will be full of the knowledge of God and all the people of the Lord will be prophets. Says R. Isaac, "All that the Prophets will reveal in (succeeding) generations had been received by them on Mount Sinai." "And so he says, 'The burden of the word of the Lord to Israel by *the hand* of Malachi.' It is not said '*In the days of Malachi*,' for the prophecy was already in his hands (since the revelation) on Mount Sinai." And so Isaiah, "From the time that it (the Torah) was (revealed) I was there," and received this prophecy, "but it is now that the Lord God and his spirit has sent me."

It is in harmony with this spirit—the Prophets and the Hagiographa being a part of Israel's Torah—that the former are cited in rabbinic literature with the terms "for it is said" or "it is written" in the same ways as the Pentateuch. Again, in the well-known controversy about the scriptural authority for the belief in resurrection, both the Prophets and the Hagiographa are quoted under the name of Torah; and the evidence brought forward by them seems to be of as much weight as that derived from the Pentateuch. In the New Testament they also occasionally appear under the title of Nomos or Law. To the Jew, as already pointed out, the term *Torah* implied a teaching or instruction, and was therefore wide enough to embrace the whole of the Scriptures.

In a certain manner it is extended even beyond the limits of the Scriptures. When certain Jewish Boswells apologized for observing the private life of their masters too closely, they said, "It is a Torah, which we are desirous of learning." In this sense it is used by another Rabbi, who maintained that even the everyday talk of the people in the Holy Land is a Torah (that is, it conveys an object lesson). For the poor man in Palestine, when applying to his neighbor for relief, was wont to say, "Acquire for yourself merit, or strengthen and purify yourself" (by helping me); thus implying the adage—that the man in want is just as much performing an act of charity in receiving as his benefactor in giving. In the east of Europe we can, even today, hear a member of the congregation addressing his minister, "Pray, tell me some Torah." The Rabbi would never answer him by reciting verses from the Bible, but would feel it incumbent on him to give him some spiritual or allegorical explanation of a verse from the Scriptures, or would treat him to some general remarks bearing upon morals and conduct.

THE LAW ABROGATED

St. John of Damascus (c. 645-c. 750) was a monk who taught and preached in the vicinity of Jerusalem and composed a number of theological treatises. His writings, in Greek, were highly influential in the East where they were translated into several languages. John's influence in the West was less pronounced but he was nonetheless considered the principal exponent of Greek theology in the Latin world. Among his works is *The Exposition of the Orthodox Faith* which treats of the basic principles of the Christian faith. In one short chapter (IV:23) on the Sabbath, John presents a critique of the Jewish understanding of the Mosaic precepts.

Patristic interpretations of the commandments had been varied. Aphrahat, for example, did not allegorize or "spiritualize" them. He thus did not claim that the literal meaning of a precept has no validity in itself, being only the husk which envelops a kernel of moral or doctrinal truth. Aphrahat allowed that commandments had (and in a sense may still have) practical value. In this he was at one with Judaism which perennially sought "reasons" for the commandments. Yet, Aphrahat maintained, they do not lead to salvation for man is justified through faith alone. It was on this point that he parted company with the Jews. For, although the rabbis would not speak in terms of salvation or salvific value, they would contend that the commandments, as the everbinding expression of the covenant, are eternally valid.

John's approach was the more radical and the more common. Not only did the literal meaning of the precepts have no validity in this, the messianic, age; they *never* had been a true means of pleasing God. The Jews may glory in their Sabbath and speak of how they set aside a day for sanctity and meditation. Yet only "unfeeling servants" who allot only a small portion of their lives to God from fear of punishment have need of such a Sabbath. Christians, especially the monastics, who "dedicate the whole space of our life to Him" do not.

In this, John proceeds from ascribing carnality to the precepts to ascribing carnality to the Jews. As the ox must rest, so must the Jews: It was only because of their bestial temperament that God demanded

129

such things. For the Christian, "the Sabbath . . . is the desisting from sin . . . at all times." (Cf. Joseph Kimhi's reaction to this argument above.)

As is often heard in later works, John claims that biblical figures themselves broke the commandments—an indication that they were dispensable. Likewise, he argued that Jews would break the Sabbath by circumcising an eight-day old boy or saving a life. (It is the saving of a human life that takes unqualified precedence over the Sabbath. John's remarks about removing an animal from a pit are based on Luke 14:5 and are not accurate as formulated. Cf. Maimonides, *Mishneh Torah,* Laws of the Sabbath 25:26.) In this, he ignores the Jewish explanation that if two commandments conflict with each other, it stands to reason that one must override the other on that particular occasion.

Selection 16 has been reprinted from John of Damascus, *Orthodox Faith,* trans. Frederic H. Chase, Jr., New York: Fathers of the Church, 1959, pp. 389-93.

In the year 1492, the Jews were expelled from the recently united Kingdom of Spain. Many of those who would not convert to Christianity turned to the East—Italy, Turkey, Palestine. Others sought what seemed to be a convenient place of asylum—Portugal. This country had been known for centuries for its favorable treatment of the Jews and thus a likely place of settlement. However, because of the Portuguese king's desire to establish an alliance with Spain, he too agreed to expel the Jews from his realm. Reluctant, however, to lose the economic advantages that the Jewish presence implied, he struck upon a unique plan. In 1497, rather than actually expelling the Jews, he forcibly baptized the entire community. There thus came into being a class of newly baptized Jews or "New Christians" alongside the "Old Christians" who had been Christian for centuries. It was because of these New Christians that the Portuguese Inquisition was established in 1536.

The nature of these converts has been the subject of considerable scholarly debate. Some maintain that the New Christians remained loyal Jews at heart. According to this, the Inquisition was sincerely trying to purge heretics from the Church. Others claim that the New Christians assimilated rapidly, losing all essential features of their Judaism. Thus the charges of the Inquisition are to be considered as contrived and intended only to dispossess the New Christians of their wealth.

To be sure, this is a complicated question to which no simplistic answers can be given. The fact remains, however, that in sixteenth-century Portugal there were certainly those who believed that New Christians were "judaizing," i.e. practicing Judaism in secret. Such a one was Francisco Machado, the author of the *Mirror of the New Christians*. Machado, a Cistercian monk, had gone to Paris to obtain the doctorate. Upon his return, he was assigned to the Monastery of Alcobaça, north of Lisbon. It was there that he learned, apparently indirectly, of the New Christians. With zeal for the faith and concern that no one was ministering to the spiritual needs of the New Christians, he wrote the *Mirror* in the summer of 1541 in order to bring the former Jews securely within the fold of the Catholic Church. Machado wrote the work in the form of a medieval theological treatise in which he attempted to demonstrate the "properties" or characteristics of the Messiah and how they were fulfilled in Jesus. Among these was that he would abrogate the old law and institute a new law. This is promised by Jeremiah, among others, who speaks of a "new covenant" (*berit ḥadashah*) that will ultimately be made with the House of Israel. For Christianity, this New Covenant was the new dispensation, the New Testament, of which one of the Hebrew names is *berit ḥadashah*. Jewish polemicists maintained that the verse referred not to a totally new covenant but to a renewal (*ḥiddushah*) of the old. In reply to this, Christians —with Machado among them—adduced further biblical passages. However, from the discussion of Nahmanides' *Debate* (sel. 10), it will be recalled that Christian polemicists had another weapon in their arsenal: the Talmud itself and related Jewish writings. From the thirteenth century, Raymundus Martini's *Dagger of the Faith* had fathered a whole series of writings which quoted rabbinic literature to show that the rabbis themselves believed in Christianity (but were too obdurate to reveal the truth to the people). Machado's *Mirror* was one of these works. There are, however, certain difficulties in his use of the material. Passages are seldom quoted accurately and at times are distorted almost beyond recognition. Furthermore, Machado was under the impression that certain tractates of the Talmud and other literary works were people. Thus, he speaks of "Midrash, your doctor" and "Rabbi Bereshit," i.e. Rabbi Genesis (Midrash Genesis Rabbah). It would seem then that Machado, who knew no Hebrew, had no direct access to any of the older, more sophisticated writings which employed rabbinic literature.

He probably obtained his information by word of mouth and proceeded to confuse it even further.

In the chapter printed here, Machado draws from or refers to a) *Targum*, the Aramaic translation of the Bible, and Jonathan, to whom the *Targum* on Prophets is attributed; b) *Midrash Rabbah*, a midrash on the Pentateuch and the Five Scrolls; c) *Sifra*, a tannaitic (i.e. of the mishnaic period) midrash on Leviticus; d) *Sifre*, a tannaitic midrash on Numbers and Deuteronomy; d) the *Grão Grande*, literally the "Great Great." This last is Machado's name for the *Genesis Rabbah of Moses the Preacher*, an eleventh-century midrashic compilation. This midrash, used liberally by Martini, was a favorite of Christian polemicists. Many of the passages cited are no longer extant in Hebrew literature and this has given rise to scholarly discussion of their authenticity.

Rabbinic literature is a repository of the most diverse points of view and the Christian Hebraists knew how to find those most suitable to their purposes. Machado draws upon a midrashic tradition that the Torah will be abrogated when the Messiah comes. In a remarkable play on words, one of the passages in this tradition asserts: "Why was the pig called *ḥazir*? For the Holy One, blessed be He, will return it (*le-haḥaziro*) to Israel." Since the Messiah has come, Machado concludes—as had Paul—that "the old Law has been replaced by the new."

Selection 17 is accompanied by notes which provide the original versions of the passages quoted by Machado. The translation is from a forthcoming edition of the *Mirror* by the late M. E. Vieira and myself.

When Harvey Cox's *The Secular City* appeared in 1965, it provoked a theological discussion far more extensive than had been anticipated. The variety of responses resulted in a companion volume, *The Secular City Debate*, which was published the following year and which consisted of various reviews and criticisms.

In *The Secular City*, Cox's central concern is the fact of modern urbanization and secularization—"the liberation of man from religious and metaphysical tutelage, the turning of his attention away from other worlds and toward this one." Rather than bemoan social change, Cox, who teaches at Harvard Divinity School, sees the process of secularization as a natural outgrowth of biblical faith which the Christian should accept and celebrate. Cox understood this process as a development from the myth-bound tribe through the metaphysics-bound town, to the megalo- and technopolis, freed from myth and metaphysics together.

The features of the city represent that freedom: anonymity—freedom from social convention; mobility—freedom from provincialism; bureaucracy—an organization with a *limited* end which provides freedom from enslavement to an absolute order.

Among the criticisms leveled at Cox was that of Steven S. Schwarzschild in an invited essay for *The Secular City Debate*. Schwarzschild, who teaches philosophy at Washington University in St. Louis, does not appear to be antiurban as such. Rather, his critique demonstrates vividly how time-venerated Christian typologies (old-new Israel, Law-Gospel) persist in "post-Christian" thinking. Schwarzschild's comments are based on *The Secular City* in its entirety. In all fairness, one would have to read the whole book before reading Schwarzschild's remarks. Here, because of limitations of space, one short section is reprinted (H. Cox, *The Secular City,* New York: Macmillan, 1965, pp. 46-49). Schwarzschild's essay is reprinted from D. Callahan, ed., *The Secular City Debate,* New York: Macmillan, 1966, pp. 145-155 as is Cox's rejoinder in the same volume, pp. 183-185.

16.

ON THE SABBATH

John of Damascus

The seventh day was called the Sabbath and it means rest, for on it God 'rested from all his work' [Gen. 2:2], as sacred Scripture has it. And it is for this reason that the numbering of the days goes up as far as seven and then starts over again from one. This number is held in honor by the Jews, because God prescribed that it be honored—not in any casual way, but under the most severe sanctions in case of violation. What is more, He did not prescribe this arbitrarily, but for certain reasons which are perceptible in a mystic sense to spiritual and discerning men.

At any rate, to start with the inferior and grosser things, as my unlearned self understands it, when God saw the grossness and sensuality of the people of Israel and their absolute propensity for material things, as well as their indiscretion, then first of all He prescribed that 'the manservant and the ox should rest' [Deut. 5:14], as it is written. This was because 'the just regards the lives of his beasts' [Prov. 12:10], but at the same time it was in order that they might rest from the distraction of material things and congregate to God to spend the entire seventh day 'in psalms, hymns and spiritual canticles' [Col. 3:16], in the study of sacred Scripture, and in taking rest in God. For, when there was no law or divinely inspired Scripture, neither was the Sabbath consecrated to God; but when the divinely inspired Scripture was given through Moses, then the Sabbath was consecrated to God, so that on that day such might have leisure to study it as do not consecrate their entire lives to God nor with longing serve the Lord as Father but like unfeeling servants—the kind who, if ever they do allot some short and very small part of their lives to God, do so from fear of the punishment and chastisement attendant upon its violation. For 'the law is not made for the just man but for the unjust' [I Tim. 1:9]. Moses was the first to wait upon God for forty days fasting, and again for another forty days, and, when he did so, he most certainly mortified himself with fasting on the Sabbaths, although the law prescribed that they should not mortify themselves on the Sabbath day. However, should they say that this happened before the Law, then what will they have to say about Elias the Thesbite who made a forty-day journey on one meal? For this man broke the Sabbath by afflicting himself on the Sabbaths of those forty days not only with fasting, but with traveling, and God, who had given the Law, was not angry with him, but on the contrary appeared to him on Horeb as a reward for virtue. And what will they say about Daniel? Did he not go for three weeks without food? And what about all Israel? Do they not circumcise a child on the Sabbath, if the eighth day happens to fall on it? And also, do they not keep the great fast, which is ordained by law, if it comes on the Sabbath? And also, do not the priests and levites profane the Sabbath in the works of the tabernacle, yet remain without blame? More than that, should a beast fall into a pit on the Sabbath, he who pulls it out is without blame, while he who neglects it is condemned. And what about all Israel? Did they not circle about the walls of Jericho carrying the ark for seven days, on one of which the Sabbath most certainly fell?

And so, as I said, for the sake of leisure time for God, in order that they might devote at least a minimum portion to Him and that their man-servant and beast might rest, the observance of the Sabbath was imposed upon them while still 'children and serving under the elements of the world' [Gal. 4:3], carnal and unable to understand anything beyond the body and the letter. 'But when the fulness of time was come, God sent His only-begotten Son, made man of a woman, made under the law; that he might redeem them who are under the law: that we might receive the adoption of sons' [Gal. 4:4f.]. For as many of us as received Him, He gave power to be made the sons of God, to those that believe in Him. And so we are no longer servants, but sons. We are no longer under the Law, but under grace. We no longer give the Lord just partial service out of fear, but we are bound to dedicate the whole space of our life to Him and constantly to make the man-servant, by which I mean anger and desire, desist from sin, while at the same time turning him to the service of God. And while we constantly raise up all our desire to God, our anger we arm against His enemies. And the beast of burden, that is to say, our body, we release from the servitude of sin, while at the same time we urge it onto the fullest ob-servance of the divine commandments.

These things the spiritual law of Christ enjoins upon us, and they who keep this law are become superior to the Law of Moses. For, since 'that which is perfect is come, that which is in part is done away,' and since the covering of the Law, the veil, that is to say, was rent because of the crucifixion of the Savior and the Spirit was radiant with tongues of fire, the letter is done away, the things of the body have ceased, the law of servitude has been fulfilled, and the law of freedom has been given us. And we celebrate the complete adjustment of human nature, by which I mean the day of the resurrection upon which the Lord Jesus, the Author of life and Savior, admitted us to the portion promised them that worship God in the spirit, into which He entered as our precursor when He rose from the dead and, with the gates of heaven opened to Him, sat down corporeally at the right hand of the Father, where they also shall enter who keep the law of the Spirit.

We, then, who follow the spirit and not the letter must put aside all things of the flesh and worship in the spirit and be joined with God. For circumcision is really the putting aside of bodily pleasure and super-fluous unnecessary things, since the foreskin is nothing more than a piece of skin, a superfluous part of the pleasurable member. Moreover, any pleasure which is not from God and in God is a pleasure, the figure of which is the foreskin. The Sabbath, moreover, is the desisting from sin. Hence, both amount to the same thing, and when both are observed together in this way by those who are spiritual, they induce no violation of the law whatsoever.

One must furthermore know that the number seven signifies all the present time, as the most wise Solomon says: 'Give a portion to seven, and also to eight' [Eccl. 11:2]. Also, when the inspired David was singing a psalm for the octave, he sang of the state of things to be after the resurrection from the dead. Therefore, when the Law pre-scribed that bodily things be refrained from on the seventh day and time devoted to the spiritual, it intimated to the true Israel, the Israel which has a mind that sees God, that it should devote itself to God at all times and rise up above the things of the body.

17.

THE MIRROR OF THE NEW CHRISTIANS

Francisco Machado

HOW THE MESSIAH WOULD GIVE A NEW LAW TO HIS PEOPLE.

The fifteenth characteristic written of the Messiah was that He would give a new Law to His people when He came. The old Law was to be rejected and abrogated. This is what Christ did, as we shall prove through the prophets and through your doctors.

The prophet Isaiah testifies to this in the second chapter: *In the last days the mountain of God's house shall be established above the mountains, and all the nations shall hasten to it, because the Law shall come forth from Zion, and the word from Jerusalem* (Isa. 2:2f.). This cannot be taken to mean the Law of Moses which had been given so many years before. For this Law was given on Mount Sinai (Exodus 20), and the prophet says that the other Law would come forth from Mount Zion, from Jerusalem. Thus, this Law can only refer to the new Law which the Messiah would give, as He in fact gave it to His disciples on Mount Zion. They received confirmation of it when the Holy Spirit descended upon them, as Joel had prophesied in chapter 2: *And in the last days I will pour out My spirit upon all flesh; your sons and daughters shall prophesy, your old men shall dream and your young men shall see visions* (Joel 2:28). Everything here written of the Messiah was fulfilled during the time of Christ. Therefore, do not be in doubt nor debate, because this was foretold and this has been fulfilled.

The prophet Jeremiah confirms all this in chapter 31 where he speaks of the new Law that the Messiah would give: *Know that days shall come, and I will make a new agreement and covenant with the house of Judah, unlike the one I made with your predecessors on that day when I delivered them from Egypt; a covenant they corrupted and broke. This, then, is the covenant and pact or agreement which I will make with the house of Israel, because after those days I will give them a Law, in their inward parts and in their hearts I will write it; and I will be their God, and they shall be My people* (Jer. 31:31ff.). What clearer proof do you want than this, esteemed Jews, to show that the Messiah would place a new Law in the hearts of men; one that is new, lenient, merciful, [and] acceptable to all, not written on stones, as was the first, but engraved with gold letters in the human heart.

Your old Law thus became invalid for it had limited duration and was not to function in perpetuity. The new one was placed in the bellies of the righteous and will endure until the end of the world. It is more perfect than yours because your old Law was given to Moses through the ministry and work of the angels (Exodus 19) while our [Law] was preached and promulgated through the mouth of the Messiah—God and man. For this reason, we infer that [our Law] was much more perfect than yours.

Your Talmud lends authority to this for it says that all of the Law that man learns in this world is nothing compared to the Law of the Messiah which shall be total perfection.[1] There is a verse in Isaiah, chapter 12, in which it says that *you shall draw and take out water with joy from the fountains of the Savior* (Isa. 12:3).[2] In the Chaldean [translation] there is a version based on this which reads: "You shall receive a new law with joy from the chosen of the righteous." In chapter 44 Isaiah adds: *Living waters shall go forth from Jerusalem* [not Isa. but Zech. 14:8]. In reference to this verse, Jonathan says: "And on that day a teaching of the law shall go forth like a fountain of water." [3] All these words of your doctors which are based on the sayings of the prophets conclude that when the Messiah comes He would give a new Law to His new people. This He did do and at that time all these things were fulfilled and accomplished.

In the book *Sifre*, which bears much authority among you, it is said that there shall be days in which living waters shall flow through Jerusalem, and these shall extinguish the old Law at the time the

Messiah is in the city of Jerusalem.[4] Rabbi Joshua confirms this: "Days shall come when foods [prohibited] under the Law of Moses, shall be allowed under the [new] Law." The Talmud affirms this where it says that the Law of Moses shall soon be forgotten; but in the days of the Messiah the Law that He shall give, the Law of grace, shall permit [the eating of] foods prohibited in the Law of Moses.[5]

I firmly believe that you maintain that when the Messiah comes He will give a new Law, for this is what your authors and doctors assert. But it grieves me that you refuse to believe that this has already taken place. Everything written about the Messiah took place during the time of Christ. This is important evidence that He was the Messiah promised in your Law.

In relation to what David says in Psalm 33: *Children, come, hear me; I will teach you the fear of the Lord* (Ps. 33:12), it says in the Talmud that God said to Abraham: "You taught your children [the] Law during your lifetime; however, during the Messiah's time I myself shall give the Law and teach it." [6] This certainly did happen, for the Messiah Himself—God and man—gave the new Law and taught it to His disciples. They [in turn] taught the new people of the Messiah the new Law which was given by Him. We can further prove this with the last chapter of Isaiah where he speaks of the gentiles assembling together in the faith of the Messiah: *I will take priests and Levites from among these, says the Lord. And as the heavens and the earth, I shall make them stand before Me* (Isa. 66:21f.). I tell you that these words of God related by the prophet were not directed at your forefathers nor were they said of them. They were declared only of Christian priests who would convert from paganism to the faith of the Messiah who determined to select His priests from among their numbers, as He did. He first chose the apostles whom he ordained as priests on the day of the Supper. The priests of the Temple and the [old] Law were rejected and He did not want to ordain any one of them on the day of the Supper as priest of the new Law. However, some from the tribe of Levi would be so ordained.

It says in the book *Sifre* that "the time will come when the Law will be changed along with everything commanded in it." [7] It is written explicitly in the Talmud in the chapter that discusses the advent of the Messiah that when He came He would put to an end the [celebration of] the Passover and the Sabbath and the period of that menstruous woman, and that he would make all things anew, rejecting the old.[8] He did that which it was written that the Messiah would do; He terminated the Passover and other feasts and ceremonies of the old Law and gave a new Law which He placed in the hearts of men. Rabbi Bereshit gives evidence of this in expounding David's words in Psalm 145: *God untied those who were bound* (Ps. 145:7). He says that all quadrupeds sent to this world will be pronounced clean by God at the time the Messiah comes as He gave them to the children of Noah [gentiles]. This is shown in the *Grão Grande* in accord with that written in chapter 9 of Genesis: God permitted the children of Noah to eat all things whereas before the Flood they ate no meat [Gen. 9:1, 3f.]. Thus it says in the *Grão Grande*: "As the deer[9] of the field, I permit it all to you" (Gen. 9:3). So will all things [prohibited by] Moses be permitted when the Messiah comes.[10]

Rabbi Solomon asks what it means in the *Grão Grande* when it says that God had released those who were bound, save the quadrupeds. He answers that those who were bound by the law would be released by the Messiah from [restrictions concerning] quadrupeds. These are the swine which will then be eaten with all the other meats that were forbidden. Now swine in Hebrew means "returned," [11] since, at the time of the Messiah, the Jews shall return to eating pork. They shall eat of the *herrod*,[12] the best animal in the world. In the Talmud, it says that God created them male and female. He castrated the male and killed the female to feed the righteous at the time of the Messiah. They shall also eat the fish Leviathan which represents all fish.[13]

In conclusion, we declare that all these sayings mean that when the Messiah comes, the Jews will be able to eat and use all the meats and fish prohibited in the Law. Therefore, accept the fact that this has all been granted you, since the old Law has been replaced by the new, which was given by the Messiah.

This is our faith and belief. May it be yours. Amen.

NOTES

1. Ecclesiastes Rabbah to Eccl. 11:8: "The Torah which a man learns in this world is vanity in comparison with the Torah [which will be learnt in the days] of the Messiah."

2. Machado follows the version of the Vulgate, the Latin Bible.

3. *Targum* to Zech. 13:1.

4. There is no such passage in the *Sifre* as that mentioned by Machado. He might, however, be referring to a passage from Ecclesiastes Rabbah to Eccl. 1:9 which follows a passage from *Sifre* in the *Dagger of the Faith:* "As the former redeemer [Moses] made a well to rise, so will the latter Redeemer [the Messiah] bring up water, as it is stated, *And a fountain shall come forth of the house of the Lord, and shall water the valley of Shittim"* (Joel 4:18).

5. Apparently a corruption of Ecclesiastes Rabbah to Eccl. 2:1: ". . . In this world a man learns Torah and forgets it, but with reference to the World to Come, what is written there? *I will put My law in their inward parts"* (Jer. 31:33).

6. An apparent reference to Song of Songs Rabbah to Song of Songs 1:2: *"Let him kiss me with the kisses of his mouth. . . .* When Israel heard the words, *I am the Lord your God,* the knowledge of the Torah was fixed in their heart and they learnt and forgot not. They came to Moses and said, Our master, Moses, become an intermediary between us, as it says, *Speak with us and we will hear . . . now therefore why should we die* (Exod. 20:16, Deut. 5:22). What profit is there in our perishing? They then became liable to forget what they learnt. They said: Just as Moses, being flesh and blood, is transitory, so his teaching is transitory. Forthwith, they came a second time to Moses and said: Our master Moses, would that God might be revealed to us a second time . . . ! He replied to them: This cannot be now, but it will be in the days to come; as it says, *I will put My law in their inward parts and in their heart will I write it"* (Jer. 31:33).

7. The reference is probably not to *Sifre* but to *Sifra* (*Beḥuqqotai,* II, end): *"I will confirm My covenant with you* (Lev. 26:9)—not like the first covenant which you violated . . . but a new covenant which will never be abrogated . . . ."

8. A passage from the *Genesis Rabbah of Moses the Preacher* preserved in the Midrash to Psalms on Ps. 146:7: "It is written: *The Lord releases the bound* (Ps. 146:7). Every beast considered unclean in this world will be declared by the Holy One, blessed be He, to be pure in the future . . . . What is *the Lord releases the bound?* There is no greater prohibition (binding) than the menstruous woman for a woman menstruates and [God] prohibits her to her husband. But in the future, He shall permit her . . . ."

9. The Portuguese *cerva* (deer) should be *herva* (grass).

10. Based on a continuation of the passage cited in note 8.

11. The Hebrew for "pig" is *ḥazir* while the verb *ḥazar* means "to return" or "turn." On the midrashic passage, see J. Rosenthal, "The Concept of the Abrogation of the Commandments in Jewish Eschatology (Hebrew), *Meyer Waxman Jubilee Volume* (Jerusalem: Newman, 1960), p. 221.

12. Machado's "of herrod" (*de herrod*) is a corruption of a probable original *behemod,* i.e. *behemoth,* the mythical animal reserved for the righteous in the world to come. See Leviticus Rabbah 13:3, 22:10.

13. On the creation of Leviathan as male and female and the future banquet for the righteous, see Babylonian Talmud Bava Batra 74a.

18.

ANONYMITY AS DELIVERANCE FROM THE LAW

Harvey Cox

How can urban anonymity be understood theologically? Here the traditional distinction between Law and Gospel comes to mind. In using these terms we refer not to religious rules or to fiery preaching, but to the tension between bondage to the past and freedom for the future. In this sense Law means anything that binds us uncritically to inherited conventions, and Gospel is that which frees us to decide for ourselves.

As the contemporary German theologian Rudolf Bultmann once wrote, Law means the "standards of this world." It is what Riesman calls the power of "other-direction" driving us toward conformity to the expectations and customs of the culture, enforced in a thousand small, nearly unnoticeable ways by the people who make our choices for us. When Law rather than Gospel becomes the basis for our lives, it militates against choice and freedom. It decides for us, thus sapping our powers of responsibility. Similarly, Gospel in a broader sense means a summons to choice and answerability. It designates not merely the verbal message of the church, but also the call which comes to any man when he is confronted with the privilege and necessity of making a free and responsible decision, not determined by cultural background or social convention. Our use of the Law-Gospel dialectic here suggests that it has a broader relevance than is ordinarily accorded it in theology. It suggests that in the historical process itself man meets the One who calls him into being as a free deciding self, and knows that neither his past history nor his environment determines what he does. In the anony-

142

mity of urban culture, far from the fishbowl of town life, modern man experiences both the terror and the delight of human freedom more acutely. The biblical God is perceived in the whole of social reality, and Law and Gospel provide us an angle of vision by which to understand secular events, including urbanization. The God of the Gospel is the One who wills freedom and responsibility, who points toward the future in hope. The Law, on the other hand, includes any cultural phenomenon which holds men in immaturity, in captivity to convention and tradition. The Law is enforced by the weight of human opinion; the Gospel is the activity of God creating new possibilities in history. Law signifies the fact that man does live in society; Gospel points to the equally important fact that he is more than the intersection of social forces. He feels himself summoned to choose, to actualize a potential selfhood which is more than the sum of genes plus glands plus class. Man cannot live without Law, but when Law becomes wholly determinative, he is no longer really man.

From this perspective, urbanization can be seen as a liberation from some of the cloying bondages of preurban society. It is the chance to be free. Urban man's deliverance from enforced conventions makes it necessary to choose for himself. His being anonymous to most people permits him to have a face and a name for others.

This is not an easy thing to accomplish. The challenge of living responsibly within segmental relationships is formidable, especially for those who have been reared in small-town or traditional cultures. Often a nagging sense of guilt plagues the urban man with rural roots because he cannot possibly cultivate an I-Thou relationship with everyone. Unfortunately the church, largely bound to a preurban ethos, often exacerbates his difficulty by seeking to promote small-town intimacy among urban people and by preaching the necessity of I-Thou relationships as the only ones that are really human. But this represents a misreading of the Gospel and a disservice to urban man. Relationships among urbanites do not have to be lifeless or heartless just because they are impersonal. Jane Jacobs in her *Death and Life of Great American Cities* has caught the flavor of urban neighborliness exceptionally well. It necessitates learning how to enjoy public relationships without allowing them to become private:

Nobody can keep open house in a great city. Nobody wants to. And yet if interesting useful and significant contacts among the people of cities are confined to acquaintanceships suitable for pri-

vate life, the city becomes stultified. Cities are full of people with
whom, from your viewpoint, or mine, or any other individual's, a
certain degree of contact is useful or enjoyable; but you do not
want them in your hair. And they do not want you in theirs either.

Theologians would do well to appreciate this characteristically urban
"togetherness" so aptly described by Jane Jacobs and to see in its impersonal, even anonymous, interrelatedness an authentic form of cor-
porate human existence in the urban epoch.

We need to develop a viable theology of anonymity. In doing so,
it might be useful to add another type of human relationship to Buber's
famous pair. Besides "I-It" relationships, in which the other person is
reduced to the status of an object, and in addition to the profound,
personally formative "I-Thou" encounter, why could we not evolve a
theology of the "*I-You*" relationship? Buber's philosophy suffers from
an unnecessary dichotomy. Perhaps between the poles of the two types
of human relationship he has elaborated we could designate a third. It
would include all those public relationships we so enjoy in the city but
which we do not allow to develop into private ones. These contacts
can be decidedly human even though they remain somewhat distant. We
like and enjoy these people, but as Jane Jacobs says, we "don't want
them in our hair, and they don't want us in theirs either."

The danger with an I-Thou typology is that all relationships which
are not deeply personal and significant tend to be swept or shoved into
the I-It category. But they need not be. The development of an I-You
theology would greatly clarify the human possibilities of urban life, and
would help stall attempts to lure urban people back into preurban con-
viviality under the color of saving their souls.

The development of such a theology would help expose the *real*
dangers inherent in urban anonymity, as opposed to the pseudodangers.
Technopolitan possibilities *can* harden into rigid new conventions. Freedom can always be used for antihuman purposes. The Gospel can ossify
into a new legalism. But none of these hazards can be exposed if we
continue to insist on judging urban life by preurban norms. Despite its
pitfalls, the anonymous shape of urban life helps free man from the
Law. For many people it is a glorious liberation, a deliverance from the
saddling traditions and burdensome expectations of town life and an
entry into the exciting new possibilities of choice which pervade the
secular metropolis.

19.

A LITTLE BIT OF A REVOLUTION?

Steven S. Schwarzschild

John Cogley has described Vatican Council II as the advance of the
Roman Catholic Church into the seventeenth century. Paul Van Buren,
after he has finished being very shocking, favors all the virtues of orthodox theology and the Boy Scout Code. Harvey Cox proclaims that the
pragmatic hero of his secularized Gospel is John F. Kennedy. I suppose
we ought to be grateful for little favors: it could have been Richard
Nixon—and in the past it often was. But we also have to realize that
these favors are, indeed, little. And to use such grandiloquent phrases
as "a theology of revolution" is at best pretentious. Real revolutionaries,
in Afro-Asia, Warsaw, and Berkeley will, optimally, shrug their shoul-
ders. Which Kennedy is Cox talking about? The Kennedy of the Bay of
Pigs, the hereditary prince of a ruthless and opportunistic political
family-empire, the advocate of rabidly racist Federal judges, and the
patron of the arts whose idea of culture is *Camelot*?

But our argument is not primarily political. It is essentially theological. Cox, like so many other contemporary Christian theological
"radicals"—including the "God-is-dead" theologians—is paying the
price of having to be the antithesis of a meretricious basis. The thesis
of historical Christianity has been "otherworldliness." This has now
become, if it was not always, irrelevant. The "radicals" are right in
wanting to regain relevance; against the earlier otherworldliness they,

therefore, pit their worldliness. Their technical term for worldliness is "secularity"; a philosophical term for it is "immanentism."

These "radical" theologians are, however, merely perpetuating the ancient error which they think they are combating. The old metaphysic said in effect: God is outside of this world; therefore, let the world be as it is. The new immanentism is saying in effect: the world is God; therefore, let the world become as it will.

This is an improvement. At least some possibility of change is envisioned. Thus, Cox speaks of the church as the avant-garde of God's Kingdom, and he realizes that the Kingdom is always ahead of where the world is and demands that the latter catch up with it. But he is taking, as I say, a very small step. The Kingdom is always only one little step ahead of the world, never two steps, and certainly not an infinite distance—and the direction which the Kingdom urges is always the one in which the world is going already. To call "revolution" what is really an extremely gradual development in a direction already determined by the present situation is to misuse the English language. The world is still essentially being left where it is, or let go where it is going (*sich realisierende Eschatologie*). The proper word for this is "conservatism."

The reason for this built-in Christian conservatism is, as Cox is perfectly aware, the doctrine of the Incarnation. What this doctrine minimally means is that at least one person, at one time and in one place, has been divine. That is to say, the world as it now is, and indeed as it once was, has been at least partly redeemed—and therefore the whole world as it now is is in principle capable of redemption. Cox's only argument with the reactionaries is that they think the entire world is already completely redeemed. The issue between them is one of degree, not of principle.

Corruptio optimi pessima. Even though Cox is fully aware of the need for "Hebraizing" the pagan metaphysics of classic Christian theology, I fear that he is caught up in something that he surely hates profoundly: the ideological bias of cultural, ethnic, political, and religious egocentrism—Christian egocentrism. The catalogue of Cox's fantastic historical falsifications and profound misunderstandings of Judaism, "Pharisaic Judaism," includes legalistic psychoneurosis, sexual hypocrisy, tribal chauvinism, demonism, etc.

What is it about his theology that forces him into this position, and in what relationship does this stand to his fundamental conservatism?

Judaism is not immanentist. It is not solely transcendentalist either, because that would imply that God has no relationship to the world. Perhaps the best way to put it is that the God of Israel is totally concerned with the world precisely because He is entirely beyond it. Among other things, this means that the Kingdom is not here in any fashion and to any degree; the Messiah has not yet arrived. Cox is entirely right when he says that genuine biblical faith is truly revolutionary: it demands the complete overthrow of the present world because this world is totally different from what God wants it to be. The Law of Revelation is the exact opposite of what Cox—in his perhaps most objectionably anti-Judaic misrepresentation—defines it as being; it is not the dead hand of past social institutions but the commands of the future Kingdom upon present man.

One specific example: A Marxist would be wryly amused by Cox's squirmings on the question of private property. Cox states correctly and with apparent sympathy that, according to Marxist doctrine, only a rearrangement of property relations can correct the "false consciousness" of an immoral culture. That would be a pretty daring and genuinely revolutionary theologumenon. Cox does not have such daring and quickly hides behind such spiritualistic categories as "message," "service," and "fellowship." In activist circles these pretty phrases are recognized as soft soap. You do not change the basic realities of our society with them—indeed, they are evidence that you do not really want to.

On the other hand, Cox quotes Luke 4:18f. I claim no competence as a New Testament theologian, but it seems perfectly clear to me that, if Jesus there spoke as a Jew, he was actually doing what Jeremiah had done before him in besieged Jerusalem—demanding the fulfillment of the Levitical law (!) of the Sabbath and of the Sabbatical and Jubilee years. Never mind such fancy terms as *"kerygma," "diakonia,"* and *"koinonia"* [proclamation, service, fellowship]—return the land to the proprietorship of the sanctified community! This is real, even as Cox correctly recognizes that the Negro is not primarily concerned with whether you love him but with a job, a decent home, a doctor, a teacher for his children, and an effective vote. Furthermore, in Judaism the Sabbath law (and, indeed, the law of "the eternal Sabbath," which is the Messianic Kingdom) long ago broke the employment-income nexus not only in theory but also in practice. (See my "The Necessity of the Lone Man," *Fellowship,* May, 1965.)

The doctrine of the Incarnation, which says that redemption already exists in this world, has always tempted Christians to make their peace with whatever this world has been at any given time. Under the Nazis it called itself "German Christianity." Now Cox sympathizes with the Christians behind "the Iron Curtain" who give their political loyalty to the Communist states while retaining their ideological aloofness. I agree with him that Karl Barth's positive though critical stance toward Communism (unblemished as it is, on the whole, by previous political betrayals) is preferable to Bishop Dibelius' sacred crusade against Marxist atheism (laden down, as *it* is, with a history of collaboration with German archconservative nationalism and postwar apologetics). But one has reason to think that Cox's understanding for Communist Christians is due not to an appreciation of the ethical difference between Nazism and Communism but to the fact that Communism in fact exists at the present historical juncture—and, incarnationally, pantheistically, "all that is is rational." After all, the "organization man" also is—whatever is is "the wave of the future"—and thus Cox welcomes the organization man as the new Christian.

The only thing that he objects to in the organization is that it is not sufficiently organizational: there are still tribal or familial elements left in the bureaucracy. He holds that the completion of the organization in economic life will give us a chance for what Goethe called *"Wahlverwandschaften,"* i.e., the opportunity to choose our own spiritual family and friends. (Compare this to what Benjamin F. Payton rightly analyzes as the causal relationship between Negro misery in the North and the megalopolis which Cox so welcomes: "New Trends in Civil Rights," *Christianity and Crisis,* Dec. 13, 1965.) Knowing what we do about the dynamics of modern organization and what Cox himself alludes to as its imperfections, it is very difficult, if not impossible, to avoid the conclusion that the organization by its very nature will usurp the place and the power of the sanctified family. In my last community the General Electric Company was well-known for shifting its executive personnel around the country sufficiently often so that they and their families would end up having only one community, the organization, its country clubs and other appurtenances. In my present community the workers at McDonnell Aircraft are out on strike as I write. This is the first such episode in decades, and it is the more remarkable in that no financial issues divide the parties; but Mr. McDonnell frequently gives mawkish speeches over the plant loudspeaker system in which he addresses everybody as a "teammate" and a member of one big, happy family of equals.

Cox suggests that Buber's distinction between I-Thou and I-It relationships ought to be supplemented with the category of I-You relationships, *i.e.,* limitedly, functionally personal relations of the secular city. Buber would have regarded this as a *contradictio in adjecto*: functional relations are the precise opposite of personal relations.

Be that as it may, in his climactic last, theological chapter, Cox applies this I-You category to God Himself. He realizes, of course, that a completely immanent God can hardly be a God of revolution. God has to be at least somewhat outside of what is, in order to open the way for what is not yet. But since Cox is less interested in revolution than in gradual change along lines which have already been projected, a God is needed who is a tiny little bit transcendent. And that is precisely the God he gives us. It is a God with whom men do not have an I-Thou but an I-You relationship. He defines this not so much as confrontation but as "alongsidedness" and compares it to the way men work together as equals on a modern technical team.

At this point the tendentious falsehood of Cox's biblical theology needs to be explicated. Cox begins by claiming that the YHWH of the Bible has usually been translated as *deus, theos,* or God. This is simply false. The usual translation of YHWH has in fact been *kyrios, dominus,* or Lord. The point is important, because Cox rightly insists that God ought to be a name, not a word of meaning. *Deus* is a generic term, not a name, corresponding more to the Hebrew *'elohim.* By means of this error Cox degrades the biblical God into the class of ancient deities—in the best tradition of German anti-Semitic "scholarship." Thus he goes on to the statement "Tribal man experienced God as one of the 'gods.' The Old Testament, incorporating elements of this tribal mentality, is in no sense 'monotheistic.' Yahweh is the ruler of the gods." Now, this is either so incredibly and frightfully subtle that it completely escapes my understanding, or it is so horrible that no sophomore could get away with it. I have gone through all the usual claptrap of modern biblical scholarship, but at its very worst I have never before seen even an intimation of this claim. The God of all of the Bible is really "in no sense" monotheistic?—Cox ends by translating the famous theophanic pronouncement in Exodus 3:14 as "I will do what I will do." Perhaps Professor Cox's Hebrew is better than mine and everybody else's, but, whatever divergencies of view on this *crux interpretationis* [classically obscure passage] may exist, this is an entirely new version. Where *do* our self-proclaimed scientific academicians get the absolute confidence of their willfulness?

Why then does Cox propound such nonsense? Because he has to justify the thesis that the God of the Bible is the God of Christianity, and that He is a little bit transcendent—but not too much. (I do not wish to sound either blasphemous or disrespectful, but I am irrepressibly reminded of the girl who was "a little bit pregnant.") The God of the Hebrew Bible, therefore, has to be tribalized, and the God of Christianity has to be de-immanentized in just the right measure. . . .

Another important criticism must be leveled at the proposed concept of an I-You relationship. The Jewish theologian E. Berkovits has rightly observed that the I-Thou and I-It dichotomy leaves little room for a very special human relationship which is enshrined in the Bible and the covenantal life, the I-We relationship. To such a critique Cox does not, and cannot, rise. The social, more-than-individual dimension of human existence has always lain outside the universe of normative Christian discourse. Despite his political interests, Cox remains within this historic Christian limit, by welcoming the atomization of the sanctified family by modern, mobile technology.

Cox's section on the organization man turns one's mind to the *kibbutzim,* on which Buber exerted great intellectual and moral influence. Whatever the theoretical limitations of the I-Thou concept, in practice Buber was an utopian socialist. The *kibbutzim* try very hard to humanize modern social organization and economics; they abhor the organization man—and it seems that lots of people in Africa and Asia, and Christian utopians (whom Cox undoubtedly regards as well-meaning atavists), are eager to learn from them. We are back with the law of the Sabbatical year: the *kibbutzim* do not even own their own land—it belongs to the community as a whole. The religious *kibbutzim* are wrestling this very year with the technicalities (I believe the Christian term for this is "casuistry," and *Time* magazine has headlines about "Shmittah [Sabbatical year] and Sham") of having to let the land lie fallow for God.

The theological principle in all this, I submit, is that only radical transcendentalism, in the Jewish sense, and devout concern with divine law can lead to an authentic revolutionary stance in the modern world. God is beyond the world, not in it—and so is His Kingdom. The man of believing action feels under the ineluctable command to understand and to carry out the law which is to bring about the total revolution from "this world" to "the world-to-come." The Kingdom is a total, ultimate, unified vision; and it is, therefore, conducive to total, ultimate, and unified Messianic action. But of such total demands the men of little revolutions—not so much "of little faith"—are afraid, and their fear takes the form of a barbaric misreading of the (Hebrew) Bible. Christians are still shrinking from the imperatives of the law and in its stead put their faith in the present.

Let it be clear: The man of believing action is not laboring under the idolatrous illusion that he is bringing about the Kingdom; he is only trying to do God's will, so that He may, in His grace, bring it about. This unified vision cannot deteriorate into utopian totalitarianism (as Reinhold Niebuhr has made us constantly, bogeyman-like, worry), because the action program always knows itself to be human—and, therefore, under the judgment and in the need of divine consummation. But this man is also not engaging in any hand-to-mouth "pragmatic" meliorism. He knows that there will always be enough politicians around to compromise between the stand-pat reactionaries who proclaim that their world is the Kingdom of Heaven and his own genuinely eschatological demands. . . . But without religious or atheistic "extremists" the politicians would make their compromises far more to the "right."

To revert finally to my Jewish apologetic argument: This is a theology of the revolutionary, divine law. It may still strike some as casuistic and legalistic. I wonder whether there is a revolutionary on earth who would not prefer it to Cox's theology of punctuation marks (he calls it "the grammar of the Gospel"); for Cox, the Kingdom of God resides in the semicolon of Mark 1:15! Speaking of casuistry, my edition of the King James version has no semicolon there. Did the Septuagint? Or did divine revelation come only with the [Revised Standard Version]?

I suppose I sound angry. To tell the truth, I am angry. Once the bandwagon has begun to roll, Christian theologians persist in arrogating to themselves, or to Christianity, the titles of everything that Divine Revelation at Sinai, in Bible and Talmud, lays down to Jews—everything that conscientious Jews have worked hard through the centuries to enact in their personal and social lives—everything that Christian civilization with all its power has consistently tried to frustrate and everything that Christian and Jewish heretics have made operative in modern times. This is the more provoking as these same Christian theologians at the same time perpetuate the vicious myths of Jewish tribalism, *Werkheiligkeit,* and vengeful justice. I can put this more anecdotally: I like a record of folk songs by the Weavers which was recorded live at a Christmas night concert in New York; on it they sing a medley of the Hebrew song "Shalom chaverim" ("Peace, comrades") and a Christmas carol. Normally I would dislike intensely such eclecticism. In this case I find myself liking it for two reasons: I know that the crowds present at this concert "voted with their feet" by absenting themselves from midnight church services; and I know that, though the religious eclecticism may be shoddy, the social passion is genuine.

Let this bitter complaint be a contribution to honest "dialogue" as well as to a renewed understanding of the authentic revolutionary import of biblical actions of faith.

20.

REJOINDER TO STEVEN SCHWARZSCHILD

Harvey Cox

[It seems that Steven] Schwarzschild found it necessary to compose such a polemical tirade that I am sure he himself will be embarrassed when he reads it in a quieter moment. The purple hue of Schwarzschild's words and the obvious disproportion between the intensity of emotion he displays and the question at issue suggest that he is not really attacking me but is using this occasion to vent his feelings about many things, feelings that have been accumulating for a long time. I will content myself, therefore, with pointing out that I have seldom encountered such a grotesque misreading of *The Secular City*. By lumping me with some vague thing he labels "the new immanentism," Schwarzschild makes me say that "the world is God; therefore let the world become as it will." Even the most casual reader of *The Secular City* knows that this is the exact opposite of my thesis. What I said was that since the world is *not* God (desacralization, deconsecration), it is our responsibility to shape and steer it. Schwarzschild shows this low regard for accuracy throughout his philippic. He is so angry that what I actually say about something has only casual interest. For example, if he had read my sharp criticism of those business organizations which try to make themselves over into pseudofamilies he would know that I share his disgust with the "familial" rhetoric and "big-brother" policies he rightly assails in General Electric and McDonnell Aircraft. But he seems to believe that by slugging them he is bashing me too. The only safe

153

thing to do when someone is acting this way is to step aside until he
has triumphed over all the things he is against and then hope that a
conversation can begin.

If a conversation could begin, I would agree with Schwarzschild
that Christian theologians have been wrong in confusing the YHWH of
the Bible with a *deus* or *theos*. In fact this is what I thought I said in
The Secular City. If he could stop shouting, we might quietly discuss
the translation of Exodus 3:14. Though my interpretation of the text
may not be to Schwarzschild's liking, it is in no sense "an entirely new
version." The Hebrew verb in question can mean "to be," or "cause to
be, perform, do." I got the idea he refers to from Bernhard Anderson's
Understanding the Old Testament (Englewood Cliffs: Prentice-Hall,
Inc., 1959, p. 34). I would refer interested readers to W. F. Albright's
discussion in *From the Stone Age to Christianity* (Garden City: Double-
day & Company, Inc., 1957, pp. 196-199). If he could sit still, Schwarzschild and I might talk together about whether the whole Old Testament
can really be called monotheistic. It is hard to read about Elijah's con-
test with the prophets of Baal without seeing some evidence that the
existence of other deities is not denied. Perhaps the very idea of monotheism represents a projection of later philosophical categories into a
Bible interested in something different, a practice we moderns have in-
dulged in too often.

Still, I am afraid that even in the calmest atmosphere, Schwarzschild and I would finally disagree, for he goes on to say: "Why then
does Cox propound such nonsense? Because he has to justify the thesis
that the God of the Bible is the God of Christianity . . ." If Schwarzschild rightly locates the real nub of my error then I must plead guilty.
I *do* believe that the God of the Hebrew Bible, the God of Abraham,
Isaac and Jacob is indeed the God and Father of Jesus of Nazareth.
But here my perversity is not mine alone. It has been shared by almost
all Christians (except the Montanists) and by many Jews for two thousand years.

I look forward intensely to the coming dialogue between Christians
and Jews. I rejoice that very few Jews will exact as a precondition of the
conversation my accepting Schwarzschild's definition of my reprobacy.
To do so would be to surrender the whole faith before the dialogue
begins, which no conversation partner can justifiably expect.

PART IV

THE SCEPTER OF JUDAH

The Christian legend of the wandering Jew became an integral part of patristic and medieval theology. However, the curse of Cain upon the Jews was not seen merely as a punishment for their guilt in the crucifixion and for their perfidy. It was taken as evidence for the very truth of Christianity. So it was that when Frederick the Great asked for a proof of his faith, he was answered with the Augustinian teaching: "Your Majesty, the Jews." In the context of such thinking, it is no wonder that the Zionist movement and the establishment of the State of Israel might come as an affront to certain Christians who remained loyal to these beliefs. As phrased by A. Roy Eckardt, they ask: "After all, are not we Christians the *real* Israel? And is not original Israel barred from Zion until or unless it accepts Christ?" He continues:

> The entire movement to re-establish the Jewish people in their ancient homeland, culminating in the reconstituting of the State of Israel in 1948, has been a traumatic experience from which the collective Christian psyche has never recovered. The reaction is revealed, on the one hand, in the inability of many representatives

of the churches to find any theological meaning in the drama, together with their attempted reduction of Israel to a purely "political" or "secular" phenomenon, and, on the other hand, in the contention of many that something has gone awry religiously. God could not very well have made a historical-theological miscalculation by sanctioning the "return" of the Jews before the proper time. So perhaps the whole operation was the work either of the devil or of human idolatry, or both. How presumptuous for Israel to be "reborn" in clear violation of Christian eschatology! (*Elder and Younger Brothers,* p. 171)

Yet often even those Christians who do not share these ideological reservations concerning the return of the Jewish people to Palestine encounter another, more subtle difficulty: the religious significance for the Jewish people of what appears to Christians to be a secular phenomenon. This is further obfuscated by the fact that the State of Israel —although branded by her enemies as a theocracy—is largely populated with "secularized" Jews. The core of the misunderstanding is the introduction of distinctions—"sacred" and "secular," "religion" and "nationalism" (cf. Fackenheim)—which are foreign to Judaism.

The Christian dichotomy between letter and spirit was applied to the concept of the promised land as it was to many biblical concepts. Since "spiritual" meant "not of this world," the promised land was not a place on earth but a metaphor for the Kingdom of Heaven. The Jewish desire for their land "flowing with milk and honey" once again showed their "carnal" blind misinterpretation of the Divine Word. Hence, how can political Zionism represent a spiritual reality?

To understand this one must know something of the composition of modern Judaism. Judaism's Palestinian origins are not confined to the centuries of the biblical and rabbinic periods. In the sixteenth century, on the eve of the modern era, the influence of the remarkable Galilean community of Safed made itself felt throughout the entire Jewish world. The achievements of this kabbalistic community in theology, halakhah, liturgy, and homiletics were adopted by virtually all currents of Judaism in the subsequent centuries—by the European Hasidim and their opponents, the Mitnagdim, as well as by Oriental Jewry. The fruits of this community's theological thinking were a response to the great trauma of the close of the fifteenth century—the expulsion from Spain. Drawing on older Jewish tradition and on classical

Spanish kabbalism, they elaborated a veritable theology of exile. According to it, the tripartite exile—Israel from the Land, Israel from God, God from the Land—is paralleled, as it were, by an exile within God Himself. The restoration of unity within God is a correlative of the restoration of the primordial unity here on earth. Both man and God are partners in redemption. It is the task of man to observe the commandments faithfully with the proper mystical intention "for the sake of the unification of the Holy One, blessed be He. . . ." Thus the fulfillment of these "carnal" precepts is seen by the Jews as having cosmic significance, for nothing happens above which does not happen below and nothing is ordained below which is not ordained above. Thus there is no dichotomy between letter and spirit because the one nourishes and gives life to the other.

S. Y. Agnon's *In the Heart of the Seas* is a tale, replete with kabbalistic motifs, of a group of pious Jews from Polish Galicia who sought the unity of redemption through migration to the Land of Israel. As the story opens, the hero Hananiah tells of his wandering in a strange, mythical land. Ironically, the inhabitants of this land of unreality doubted reality. For when Hananiah told them of his wishes, they did not believe him "because they had never in all their days heard of any man who really and truly went up to the Land of Israel. By that time I myself," relates Hananiah, "was beginning to doubt whether the Land of Israel actually existed; so I decided that I had better leave them to themselves and went away. Better, said I to myself, that I should perish on the way and *not lose my faith in the Land of Israel*." Hananiah's plight was not excessive literalism; it was excessive spiritualism.

Modern political Zionism began among religious Jews. (Cf. Samuel.) Today's Zionists—"religious" and "secular"—are their heirs. Traditional religious Zionist concepts permeate the thinking of both observant and secularized Jews just as traditional religious anti-Zionist concepts permeate the thinking of some observant and secularized Christians.

These issues are discussed in the readings and essays that follow. Joseph Kimhi argues that Jewish self-government is to be restored in the future and Jerome presents his allegorization of the promised land as the Kingdom of Heaven. This provides the setting for the presentation of various Christian attitudes toward the State of Israel and some Jewish defenses of Zionism on various grounds.

THE PROMISE OF THE LAND

In Joseph Kimhi's *Book of the Covenant* (see above, sels. 1, 13.), the arguments concerning the question of the permanent loss of Jewish sovereignty center on certain classical biblical proof-texts, Genesis 49:10 and Daniel 9:24ff. In the Christian tradition, these verses speak of the cessation of Jewish dominion with the coming of Jesus. It so happens, however, that Kimhi is confronted with versions of these biblical passages which are not in conformity with the masoretic or standard Hebrew text. This is due to the fact that these versions stemmed from different textual traditions. To begin with, Genesis 49:10 is ambiguous in the Hebrew, reading "The scepter shall not depart from Judah, nor the ruler's staff from between his feet, until Shiloh [*sylh*] comes" or ". . . until he comes to Shiloh." This passage has been variously interpreted as referring to King David, the future Messiah, etc. Indeed, the history of the interpretation of this verse alone has filled the two volumes of A. Posnanski's *Schiloh* published in Leipzig in 1904. The Vulgate, as reflected in the version of Kimhi's "Christian," follows a different text. Apparently reading *slyh* (*shaliah*) instead of *sylh* (*shiloh*), it translates "he who is to be sent" (*qui mittendus est*), i.e. Jesus.

In the case of Daniel 9:24ff. the situation is different. On these verses the Vulgate and the Masoretic Text basically concur. There was, however, another version which originated in a sixth-century sermon attributed to St. Augustine and which is cited above in sel. 12. This version, which circulated in various writings and polemical treatises including the *Book of the Covenant,* conflates two verses (9:24 and 9:26) and alters the Hebrew so as to yield: "When the Most Holy comes, your anointing shall cease." According to this, the monarchy (anointing) of the Jews shall cease when the Most Holy (Jesus) comes.

The textual variations between the Jewish and Christian biblical versions led to charges of falsification and error in translation. Jewish polemicists referred to Jerome, translator of the Vulgate, as the "confounder" who deliberately misled his readers or erred through ignorance. This was the first stage of Joseph Kimhi's argument in these passages. The second involved the actual reinterpretation of the verses themselves

159

to show that they could not refer to Jesus. On the "Shiloh" passage, Kimhi argues that the verse can refer only to David. On the Daniel passage, he redivides the seventy "weeks" so that no connection between Jewish loss of political independence and Jesus' advent can be alleged.

The passages are reprinted from *Book of the Covenant,* Toronto: Pontifical Institute of Mediaeval Studies, 1972, pp. 43-45, 49-53.

Although Zionism as a broadly based political movement is a relatively recent phenomenon in Jewish history, the longing for the return was echoed by countless generations of Jewish exiles throughout the ages. The yearning for redemption—the triumphant restoration to the ancestral homeland—resounded not only in the prayer for the return uttered thrice daily but in the philosophical, homiletical, polemical, and poetic writings of the Middle Ages as well. No better expression of the religious meaning of Zion for the medieval Jew can be found than the writings of the twelfth century poet and philosopher, Judah Halevi. His masterpiece, the *Kuzari,* is a romanticized account of the conversion of the king of the Khazar nation in southern Russia to Judaism several centuries earlier. In his artful manner, Halevi has the king convert at the initial stages of his indoctrination. In this way, the latter maintains a certain ambivalence throughout the dialogue; for while he has accepted Judaism in principle, he is often puzzled by it and even antagonistic. One of the moments of greatest tension in the book is the discussion of the Land of Israel. In the midst of a technical philosophical discourse, the Rabbi (Halevi) refers, almost casually, to Eretz Israel as God's country. The king is taken aback! He had, Heaven knows, enough trouble with the concept of God's people. Must he contend with God's country as well? The Rabbi explains the special qualities of the Land in great detail. Just as one needs both fine plants and fine soil to produce the best grapes, so can God's elect be truly fulfilled only in that Land that was especially ordained for them. Numerous biblical texts are cited to show the epithets of love and esteem which God and Israel have applied to Eretz Israel. Above all, Sabbaths, festivals, and numerous other commandments can be observed perfectly only in the Holy Land. Suddenly, the king waxes indignant. He turns the arguments of the Rabbi back upon him and accuses him of "armchair Zionism":

> If this be so, thou fallest short of thy religious duty by not endeavoring to reach that place, and making it thy abode in life

and death, although thou sayest: 'Have mercy on Zion, for it is the house of our life'; and thou believest that the Shekinah will return thither . . . [Even the Gentiles] turn to it in prayer and visit it in pilgrimage. Thus, thy bowing and kneeling in the direction of it is either hypocrisy or thoughtless practice.

The king's zeal is not difficult to fathom. Having his own kingdom, his own vested interest, he is not keen on hearing about any obligation to remove himself to an unknown Mediterranean outpost. He sees, moreover, that the Rabbi appears to be in no hurry to leave Khazarstan either and he therefore goads him on expecting to hear some justification for this. Unfortunately, this is not what he hears:

> That is a justified reproach, O King of the Khazars! . . . Were we prepared to meet the God of our forefathers with a pure mind, we should find the same salvation as our fathers did in Egypt. But when we only say: "Bow to His holy hill, bow to His footstool" . . . this is but as the chattering of the starling and the nightingale. We do not realize what we are saying through these and other words as thou observest, O Prince of the Khazars.

This, of course, is the last thing that the king had hoped to hear and he dismisses the issue with an abrupt "Enough on this subject!" The king, naturally, represents none other than the average well-to-do Spanish Jew of the twelfth century, reluctant to leave his comforts and familiar surroundings for the duty of living in the Land of Israel. But Judah Halevi was not average. In some of the most stirring poetry ever written in the Hebrew language, he sings of his longing:

Prostrate upon thine earth, I fain would thrust
Myself, delighting in thy stones, and lay
Exceeding tender hold upon thy dust.

At the end of the *Kuzari,* the Rabbi, to the disappointment of the king, expresses his intent to go on pilgrimage to Eretz Israel. It was this in fact that Judah Halevi did toward the end of his lifetime. For centuries, this journey was shrouded in legend until the famous Cairo Geniza revealed the actual details and circumstances of the voyage. Of Halevi's experience in the Land we know little. Of this, however, we can be certain: His "exceeding tender hold upon the dust" of Eretz Israel brought him more joy than all the gilded castles of Spain.

The selection from the *Kuzari* is taken from I. Heinemann, ed., *Kuzari,* London: East & West Library, 1947, pp. 64-70.

No Church father was better acquainted with the Land of Israel than was St. Jerome (345?-420?). Born in Stridon in Dalmatia, he studied in Rome and traveled extensively in both Europe and the East. During a sojourn in Syria, he learned the Syriac language which served as an introduction to his later acquisition of Hebrew and Aramaic. Jerome was primarily a biblical scholar who made great efforts to gain access to the Hebrew and Greek versions of the Bible in order to correct the Old Latin (Itala) version then current in the Latin Church. Jerome's knowledge of Hebrew was acquired in Palestine. After traveling the length and breadth of the land in the company of his friend Paula and her nuns, he settled in Bethlehem where he spent the remainder of his days. His final translation of the major part of the Bible was completed there. This Vulgate, as it later came to be known, was based on Jerome's knowledge of Origen's *Hexapla,* a Hebrew-Greek "polyglot" Bible, and his acquaintance with Hebrew and Aramaic. As a Semitist, Jerome also wrote the *Book of Hebrew Questions on Genesis* and the *Book of the Interpretation of Hebrew Names.* Jerome acquired his knowledge of Hebrew with the assistance of several Jewish teachers. Among them he mentions one from Lydda, a Bar Hanina from Tiberias, and a third who taught him Aramaic. Jerome eagerly absorbed their linguistic and critical-exegetical information but had little use for the midrashic or homiletical material that came with it, even though much of it would be incorporated into his biblical commentaries. Nor did he hold his teachers —or Jews in general—in any great esteem. He wondered how much he really had gained from his teacher from Lydda; yet he admitted that without him he could not really have made a start. Some Christians opposed Jerome's absorption in Jewish learning out of a fear that he might judaize Christian teaching. On the contrary, he replied, "why should I not be permitted, . . . for the purpose of confuting the Jews, to use those copies of the Bible which they themselves admit to be genuine? Then when the Christians dispute with them, they shall have no excuse."

Jerome wrote no formal treatises against the Jews or Judaism. Yet his writings are full of criticisms of Jewish belief. They contain as well a mine of information on the Jews of Palestine in that period. Jerome's letter (Letter 129) to Dardanus, a noble of Gaul, concerns itself with the question of the Promised Land. Jerome is not content with merely restating that the Jews are condemned to wander the earth for their crimes (although, to be sure, he does not pass over this point in silence). Rather, we see the master exegete at work, skillfully interweaving verses in a demonstration that the land truly promised is not on earth but in heaven. Here then is a classic example of the allegorization of that which in Judaism is a concrete reality. Note, however, how careful Jerome is to assert that he has no intention of destroying the literal meaning altogether, since to do so would border on heresy. The delicate relationship between letter and spirit would preoccupy exegetes ever after and a wide variety of resolutions of this problem would be sought. Jerome's argument is based on a repeated play on the word *terra* which may mean "land" or "earth" in English. In order to retain the effect of the original, the translation "land" has been used throughout. Biblical references are according to the Vulgate.

21.

THE BOOK OF THE COVENANT

Joseph Kimhi

The [Christian] said: What can you say of the passage in the Torah: *The scepter shall not be taken from Judah, nor the ruler (dux) from his thigh until he comes who is to be sent* (Gen. 49:10)? This is Jesus, for when He came, you lost your kingdom and you have neither sovereignty nor king because of what you did to the Messiah.

The [Jew] said: Do you not know that this blessing is in the benediction with which Jacob blessed his sons! He blessed each one of them with his own blessing. In blessing Judah, he gave him the kingship, i.e. the king who would reign over Israel, along with his progeny, would come forth from him. This was David, the first king who ruled over Israel (he and his progeny). This is [the meaning of] *the scepter [shall not depart] from Judah.* From the time that he blessed him, he gave him dominion over his brothers. Thus we have found concerning the [location of the] standards in the desert that it says that the standard of the division of Judah was on the east side [Num. 2:3] and that Moses and Aaron camped near their standard, as it says *Those who were to camp before the Tabernacle, in front—before the Tent of Meeting, on the east—were Moses and Aaron and his sons* (Num. 3:38). *Now the chieftain of the tribe of Judah, Nahshon the son of Aminadab* (Num. 3:2) entered the [red] sea first, for it is written in connection with the war against Canaan *Who will go up for us first against the Canaanites*

164

to fight against them? The Lord said: Judah shall go up, for I have delivered the land into his hand (Jud. 1:1f.). Also in the account [of the events] of Gibeah of Benjamin, Judah was first (Jud. 20:18). Therefore, Jacob blessed him, saying that dominion and rulership would not depart from him until David his son comes to receive the kingship. This is [the meaning of] *the scepter shall not depart from Judah, nor the ruler's staff between his feet, until Shiloh comes, and to him shall be the obedience of peoples* (Gen. 49:10). It is known that *shevet* (scepter) and *mehoqeq* (ruler's staff) represent ranks lower than kingship. Indeed, you translate [*mehoqeq* by] *duc* and the duke is a governor lower in rank than the king. This was [the status of] Nahshon the chieftain and the chieftains after him until David came. They continued to be rulers over the rest of the tribes until David, who received the kingship, was born. This may be likened to a king who deigned to grant a patent of nobility to one of his servants for a limited period. In the interim, until the termination of that period, he says, "You shall have authority and this province shall be under your jurisdiction." Thus Judah was told that dominion would not pass from his sons until David came to receive his kingship.

How can you! Do you not see the prophecies? For more than four hundred years before the coming of Jesus, the kingship had passed from the house of David. The last king from the house of David was Zedekiah whom Nebuchadnezzar king of Babylon blinded and led into exile. After him there arose no king from the House of David, for all the kings in the time of the Second Temple were priests. Likewise Herod was a slave and also was not of the House of David. Now the number of years from the Babylonian exile, until the [destruction of the] Second Temple, was four hundred and twenty, and Jesus lived towards [the time of] the destruction of the Second Temple when Jerusalem was destroyed. How then can you say that the kingship of the House of David did not pass until Jesus came. I shall show that it had passed four hundred and twenty years before the coming of Jesus. Your words are false and your belief is untrue. This is clear and evident . . . .

The [Christian] said: Daniel said *When the Most Holy comes, your anointing shall cease.* This refers to Jesus, for when Jesus came, your dominion and Messiah were lost.

The [Jew] said: See how you are wrong on several counts. Firstly, in the Book of Daniel there is no verse such as you have quoted *when the Most Holy comes, your anointing shall cease.* Scripture says *to anoint the most holy* (Dan. 9:24) and in another place *the anointed one shall be cut off and be no more* (vs. 26). You do not understand this passage. At the beginning of the passage, it says *Seventy weeks are decreed upon your people and upon your holy city, to finish the transgression and to make an end of sin, and to forgive iniquity, and to bring in everlasting righteousness, and to seal vision and prophet, and to anoint the most holy* (vs. 24). Afterwards, it says: *Know therefore and discern that from the going forth of the word to restore and build Jerusalem unto one anointed, a prince, shall be seven weeks; and for sixty-two weeks it shall be built again with broad place and moat, but in troublous times* (vs. 25). Then it says *After the sixty-two weeks an anointed one will be cut off and be no more; and the people of a prince that shall come shall destroy the sanctuary; but his end shall be with a flood; and unto the end of the war desolations are determined* (vs. 26). If you know how to explain this passage, I shall listen to what you have to say. Yet if you do not know how to explain it, be still and listen to me, and I shall teach you wisdom. Daniel said *I pondered the books, over the number of years, whereof the word of the Lord came to Jeremiah the prophet, that He would accomplish for the desolation of Jerusalem seventy years* (vs. 2). Now I ask you what these, concerning which he said *I pondered the books,* were. If you can, answer me, and if not, hear me out. These books were the *Sefer ha-galui* and the *Sefer ha-miqnah* which the prophet Jeremiah acquired from his uncle along with the field [Jer. 32:12ff.]. Concerning these he was commanded *Take these books,* etc. (Jer. 32:14) and it is written *And put them in an earthen vessel that they may last a long time (ibid.).* He studied those books and saw that they were fulfilled and then he fasted. Then the angel came and said: *or from the first day that you began to understand and fast before God, your words were heard and I came because of your words* (Dan. 10:12). The angel came to reveal to him the mysterious prophecies and stated explicitly *Seventy weeks, etc.* These seventy weeks are seventy weeks of years, *viz.* four hundred and ninety years—seventy of the Babylonian exile and four hundred and twenty years of the existence of the second Temple. These figures are well known. Now he divided this period and said that from the beginning of the period . . ., *from the going forth of the word to restore and rebuild Jerusalem unto one anointed, a prince, shall be seven weeks, and for sixty-two weeks, it shall be built again with broad place and moat and in troublous times* (Dan. 9:25). *Unto one anointed, a prince* refers to Cyrus of whom it is said *To His anointed, to Cyrus, whose right hand I have held* (Isa. 45:1) and of whom it is said *He shall build My city and set free My exiles, not for price nor reward* (*ibid.*, vs. 13). The sixty-two weeks were from the time they left Babylon to the time when the anointed one was cut off, as it is said *And after the sixty-two weeks shall an anointed one be cut off and be no more.* Now the phrase, *your anointed one shall be cut off,* which you cited is not in the book. The truth is that this anointed one of yours is King Agrippa whom the wicked Titus killed, for in his days Jerusalem and the Temple, may it be rebuilt speedily and in our days, were destroyed. The phrase *and be no more* means that he has no one to replace him, for no king of Israel rose after him until this day. Now there is one week remaining from the figure of seventy weeks, for first he counted seven weeks and then sixty-two making sixty-nine. Afterwards he said *He shall make a firm covenant with many for one week* (Dan. 9:27), thereby making seventy weeks. One of the commentators said that the half week [of which it is said], *And for half a week he shall cause the sacrifice and offering to cease* (*ibid.*) is part of that week of which he said that he would make a firm covenant with many for one week. That half week is three and a half years. I have thus clarified your first error.

Now as for your second error according to which you said that [the expression] "most holy" could refer only to God. With reference to the altar, does it not say *The altar shall become most holy* (Exod. 29:37, 40:10). So was all the apparatus of the Temple which was anointed with the anointing oil most holy. The meaning of *decreed upon your people and upon your holy city* is this: It says: *Seventy weeks are decreed upon your people, etc.* until the sixty weeks in Jerusalem are completed [until the destruction of the Temple]. After this it was decreed that they be exiled and remain in exile for a long period *to finish the transgression, and to make an end of sin, and to forgive iniquity.* By the weight of their afflictions, their transgression would be finished, their sins would be made an end of, and their iniquity would be forgiven. Afterwards, He would bring everlasting righteousness, of which David said, *Truth springs out of the earth and righteousness springs down from heaven* (Ps. 85:12). This refers to Messiah, the son of David, for whom we hope and of whom it is said *to anoint the most holy.* In his days, there would appear everlasting righteousness which would never turn into deceit. How deceitful is the world [as it is, made up] of gentiles (*goyim*), and Ishmaelites, and Jews. At that time, however, there will be fulfilled *For then I will turn to the peoples a pure language . . . to serve Him with one consent* (Zeph. 3:9). Then will there be everlasting righteousness. The meaning of *to seal vision and prophet* is that then every vision and prophet will be completely fulfilled, for the words of the prophets [consist of] nothing [but] chastisement [or] consolation. Thus all of the words of the prophets will be fulfilled as it is said in the psalm of Solomon, *Give the king your judgments, O God, and Your righteousness to the king's son* (Ps. 72:1), which he concluded with *the prayers of David, the son of Jesse, are ended* (*ibid.*, vs. 20), for his prayers will no longer be said. How will they say, "save us," when they are saved; "deliver us," when they are already delivered; "forgive our sins," when He has already said *You will be clean from all your uncleanness and I will cleanse you from your idols* (Ezek. 36:25). Then will they acknowledge and bless the name of our God. Of this he said *to seal vision and prophet and to anoint the most holy.*

22.

KUZARI

Judah Halevi

THE PRE-EMINENCE OF THE COUNTRY

THE KHAZARI: What thou meanest by 'His people' is now intelligible to me, but thy word 'His country' is difficult for me to appreciate.

THE RABBI: But no difficulty is attached to (the assumption) that one country may have higher qualities than others. Obviously there are places in which particular plants, metals, or animals thrive well, or where the inhabitants are distinguished by their form and character— through the mingling of humors resulting in the perfection or imperfection of the soul.

THE KHAZARI: Yet I have not heard that the inhabitants of Palestine are better than other people.

THE RABBI: It is the same case as with your hill on which you say the vines thrive so well. If they had not planted vine branches on it and cultivated them well, it would never have produced grapes. So precedence belongs to those particular people who, as stated before, represent the 'pick' and the 'heart' (of mankind); the land has also its part in this and so have the religious acts connected with it, which I would compare to the cultivation of the vineyard. But no other place could share with this pre-eminent people the influence of the Divine power, whereas other hills are also able to produce good wine.

THE KHAZARI: How can this be? Were there not prophets in other

places, between Adam and Moses, as Abraham in Ur-Kasdim, and
Ezekiel and Daniel in Babylon, and Jeremiah in Egypt?

THE RABBI: Whosoever prophesied, did so either in Palestine or
for its sake, viz. Abraham to reach it, Ezekiel and Daniel on account
of it, to prepare the return. The two latter, moreover, lived during the
time of the first temple and under the influence of the apparition of the
Shekinah, through which any member of the 'picked' people who was
duly prepared became able to prophesy. But Adam had there his native
place, and died there, according to tradition: 'in the cave of Makpelah
were buried the four pairs: Adam and Eve, Abraham and Sarah, Isaac
and Rebeccah, Jacob and Leah' (Gen. Rabba 58:4). This is the land
which bore the name 'before the Lord' and of which it is said 'the eyes
of the Lord thy God are always upon it' (Deut. 11:12). It was also
the first object of jealousy and envy between Cain and Abel: they desired to know which of them would be Adam's successor, his 'picked
one' and his 'heart' to inherit the Land, and to stand in communion
with the Divine power, whilst the other would be merely the 'shell'.
Then Abel was killed by Cain, and the realm was without an heir.
Cain 'went out of the presence of the Lord' (Gen. 4:16), which means
that he left the land; (for) he says: 'Thou hast driven me out this day
from the land, and from thy face shall I be hid (4:14); in the same
way it is said: 'Jonah rose up to flee unto Tarshish from the presence
of the Lord' (Jonah 1:3); he only fled, indeed, from the place of
prophecy; God, however, brought him back there out of the belly of the
fish and there He appointed him prophet. When Seth was born, who
was like Adam—for 'he begat in his own likeness, after his image' (Gen.
5:3)—he took Abel's place; for Adam says 'God has appointed me
another seed, instead of Abel, whom Cain slew' (4:25). He merited
to be called 'son of God', like Adam, and to live in that land, which is
the next step to paradise. The land was then the object of jealousy
between Isaac and Ishmael, till the latter was rejected as the 'shell'; the
words 'I have blessed him and I will multiply him exceedingly' (Gen.
17:20) refer to worldly prosperity; but the following words 'my covenant will I establish with Isaac' refer to the emanation of the Divine
power and happiness in the world to come; with Ishmael and Esau
there was no covenant, in spite of their prosperity. About this land
there arose also the jealousy between Jacob and Esau for the birthright
and the blessing, till Esau was rejected, despite his strength, in favor of
Jacob, despite his weakness. Jeremiah's prophecy in Egypt was inspired

by Palestine and was made for its sake. This was also the case with Moses, Aaron and Miriam. Sinai and Paran are reckoned as belonging to Palestine as they are on this side of the Red Sea, as it is said: 'I will set your bounds from the Red Sea, even unto the sea of the Philistines, and from the desert unto the River' (Ex. 23:31). There were the altars of the Patriarchs, who were answered by fire from heaven and the Divine light. The 'binding' of Isaac took place on a desolate mountain, viz. Moriah; in the days of David, when it was inhabited, the secret was revealed that it was the place specially fit and suitable for the Shekinah; Arauna the Jebusite tilled it at that time. Thus it is said: 'And Abraham called the name of the place the Lord sees—about which will one day be said: 'In the mount the Lord shall be seen' (Gen. 22:14). In the book of Chronicles (2, 3:1) it is stated clearly that the Temple was built on Mount Moriah. There (in Palestine) are, without doubt, the places worthy of being called the gates of heaven. Dost thou not see that Jacob ascribed the vision which he saw, not to the purity of his soul, nor to his belief, nor to his integrity, but to the place, as it is said: 'He was afraid and said: How awful is this place' (Gen. 28:17): prior to this it is said: 'He lighted upon the place' (28:11), viz. the distinguished place. Abraham, the 'heart' of the 'picked' people, when he came to maturity and was ready to accept the influence of the Divine power—was he not removed from his country to a place where his perfection could mature, as the agriculturist who finds the root of a good tree in a desert place transplants it into properly tilled ground, in order that the wild root may be transformed into a cultivated one, producing much in the place of little? Having been found in an accidental moment at an accidental place, it produces a luxuriant crop. It was the same with the gift of prophecy among Abraham's descendants in Palestine: it was an asset of many as long as they remained in the land and observed the necessary conditions, viz. purity, worship, and sacrifices, and, above all, the influence of the Shekinah. For the Divine power, one might say, is attendant on the man who appears worthy of the favor, waiting to be attached to him and to be his God, as in the case of the prophets and the pious man; thus Reason is attendant on those whose natural gifts are perfect and whose soul and character are so harmonious that it can find its perfect dwelling among them, viz. philosophers; thus, likewise, the Soul is attendant on a being whose natural powers are perfected to such a degree that a higher power is able to dwell within it, viz. animals; so also Nature (organic power) is attendant on a harmonious mingling of qualities in order to dwell therein, and to form the plant.

THE KHAZARI: These are the general rules of a complete science which must be specified. Continue thy discourse about the advantages of Eretz Israel.

THE RABBI: The land was appointed for the instruction of mankind and apportioned to the tribes of Israel from the time of the confusion of tongues, as it is said: 'When the Most High divided among the nations their inheritance, when He separated the sons of Man, He set up the frontiers of the nations according to the number of the sons of Israel' (Deut. 32:8). Abraham, also, was not fit to be associated with the Divine power and to enter into a covenant with Him—the covenant 'of the pieces of sacrifice' (Gen. 15)—until he had reached that land. And what is now thy opinion of a 'picked community' which has merited the appellation 'people of God', in a land, called 'the inheritance of God' (I Sam. 26:19; Ps. 79:1), and of seasons fixed by Him, not agreed upon or settled by astronomical calculations, and therefore styled: 'feasts of the Lord', of the observance of rules regarding purity and worship, prayers and performances fixed by God and therefore called 'work of the Lord' and 'services of the Lord'?

THE KHAZARI: In such a way we may expect the glory of God to be manifest.

THE RABBI: Thus the knowledge of the 'sabbath of the Lord' and the 'festivals of the Lord' (Lev. 23:38 and 2) depends upon the country which is called 'the inheritance of the Lord', and, as thou didst read, 'His holy mountain', 'His footstool', 'gate of Heaven' (Gen. 28:7); it is also said 'for the Torah goes out from Zion' (Micah 4:2). How greatly did the Patriarchs strive to live in the country, whilst it was in the hands of pagans, how they yearned for it and ordered their bones to be carried thither as, for example, Jacob and Joseph (Gen. 47:30; 50:25). Moses prayed to see it; he considered it a misfortune when this was denied him, and as an act of grace, when the land was shown to him from the summit of Pisgah. Persians, Indians, Greeks, and other nations begged to have sacrifices offered and prayers to be said for them in that Holy House, and they spent their wealth on it, though they believed in other religions, since the true religion did not admit them. Today, also, the country is honored, although the Shekinah no longer appears in it; all nations make pilgrimages to it, long for it— excepting we ourselves, being oppressed and homeless.

THE KHAZARI: If this be so, thou fallest short of thy religious duty, by not endeavoring to reach that place, and making it thy abode in life and death, although thou sayest: 'Have mercy on Zion, for it is the house of our life', and thou believest that the Shekinah will return thither. And had it no other distinction than that the Shekinah dwelt there nine hundred years, this would be sufficient reason for the souls to trust in it and to purify themselves there, as it has been done near the abodes of the pious and the prophets; moreover, it is the gate of Heaven; all nations agree on this point: Christians believe that the souls are gathered there and then lifted up to heaven; Islam teaches that it is the place of Mahomet's Ascension and that prophets are made to ascend from there to heaven, and further, that it is the place of gathering on the day of Resurrection. Everybody turns to it in prayer and visits it in pilgrimage. Thus, thy bowing and kneeling in the direction of it is either hypocrisy or thoughtless practice. Yet thy earliest forefathers chose it as an abode in preference to their birthplaces, and lived there as strangers rather than as citizens in their own country.

THE RABBI: That is a justified reproach, O King of the Khazars! It was that sin which kept the Divine promise with regard to the second Temple from being fulfilled: 'Sing and rejoice, O daughter of Zion; for I come to dwell in the midst of thee' (Zechariah 2:14). For the Divine power was ready to prevail in Zion as it had in the first place, if they had all willingly consented to return. But only a part of the people were prepared to do so; the majority and the men of rank remained in Babylon, preferring dependence and slavery, because they were unwilling to leave their houses and their easy circumstances. The power of the promises was weakened in accordance with their weakness. For the Divine power inspires human power only in such measure as the latter is prepared to receive it: if the readiness is little, little will be obtained, and much will be obtained, if it be great. Were we prepared to meet the God of our forefathers with a pure mind, we should find the same salvation as our fathers did in Egypt. But when we only say: 'Bow to His holy hill, bow to His footstool' (Ps. 99:9, 5), 'He who restoreth His glory to Zion', and similar words, this is but as the chattering of the starling and the nightingale. We do not realize what we are saying through these and other words, as thou observest, O Prince of the Khazars!

23.

ON THE PROMISED LAND

Jerome

You ask, Dardanus, most noble of Christians and most Christian of nobles, about that Promised Land of which the Jews took possession when they returned from Egypt. [You ask too if] it was not promised but rather returned since their ancestors had possessed it previously. In asking this, you seem to share an opinion which is agreeable to most of us: that one must look for another Promised Land of which David spoke in the psalm: "I believe that I shall see the bounties of the Lord in the land of the living" (Ps. 26:13). The Lord too said in the Gospel: "Blessed are the meek for they shall possess the land" (Mt. 5:4). Certainly, David was in the Promised Land when he sang these inspired words. He not only dwelt within Judea but he had conquered many of the surrounding nations from the Torrent of Egypt, i.e. at Rhinocorura [El Arish], to the Euphrates River. Elsewhere he said: "Upon Edom shall I cast my shoe; the Philistines shall submit to me" (Ps. 59:10). How could he then believe that he was yet to receive what he already possessed by conquest? Then, in order to prevent any possibility that his readers, the Jews, might misunderstand the nature of this land that he desired to see, he said explicitly: "I believe that I shall see the bounties of the Lord in the land of the living." Now, the land of Judea, which was under his rule, is not the land of the living— of Abraham, Isaac, and Jacob, of whom the Lord said when questioned of the resurrection: "He is not the God of the dead but of the living" (Mt. 22:32). It is rather the land and the region of the dead of which Ezekiel speaks: "The soul that sins shall die" (Ezek. 18:4). Further, "the dead praise You not, O Lord, but we who live" (Ps. 113: B:7f.), to go before the Lord and Savior at the resurrection. Of this the Apostle said: "I say to you by the word of the Lord, we who live, who are left until the coming of the Lord, shall not precede those who have fallen asleep" (I Thess. 4:14). Jeremiah too speaks of them: "They that forsake You shall be written in the land" (Jer. 17:13). When David asserts "I believe that I shall see the bounties of the Lord," he clearly leads us to the spiritual sense. What other bounties did he seek? What did this king lack? He had power enough and had amassed riches enough so as to satisfy his son Solomon whom no one in the world surpassed in wealth. But in the land of the living he sought those bounties "which no eye has seen, nor ear heard, nor which have been conceived in the heart of man but which God has prepared for those who love Him" (I Cor. 2:9). The statement in the Gospel, "Blessed are the meek for they shall possess the land," seems to harbor a contradiction if understood literally. The land is not usually possessed by the meek and the timid, who often lose what their kin have left them on account of their meekness, but by strong and violent men who are always ready for battle. In addition, Psalm 44, which refers to Christ, under the name of Solomon, and His Church, states: "Gird Your sword upon Your thigh, O mighty one. In Your beauty and Your glory, move forth; prosper and rule for the cause of meekness and justice and truth, and Your right hand will lead You marvelously" (Ps. 44:4f.). The psalmist said the same elsewhere: "Remember David, O Lord, and all his meekness" (Ps. 131:1). Further: "The Lord supports the meek" (Ps. 146:6). Even more clearly in the Gospel: "Learn from Me for I am humble and meek in heart" (Mt. 11:29). Moses prefigured Him for it is written that he was the most humble man on earth.

As we have said, the land of the living is that in which the bounties of the Lord are prepared for the saints and the meek. Before the advent in the flesh of the Lord and Savior, these were not accessible to Abraham, Isaac, Jacob, or any prophet. Indeed, Abraham was seen with Lazarus in the nether-world even though they were not in precisely the same place. Jacob, who was a righteous man, said: "Weeping and sighing I shall descend to the lower world" (Gen. 37:35). The blood of Christ is the key to Paradise, as He said to the thief: "Today you will be with Me in Paradise" (Luke 23:43). This, as we have said, is the land of the living, the land of the riches and bounties of God, which the first Adam lost and the second [Christ] found or, rather, which the first lost and the second restored. "Death reigned from Adam to Moses (by whom the Law is meant) in resemblance to the prevarication of Adam who prefigures the future" (Rom. 5:14). If we wish to know more clearly what that land is, let us read Malachi: "They will call you all blessed, says the Lord, for you will be a desirable land" (Mal. 3:12). . . . Isaiah agrees with these words when he says: "And he shall be a man who hides his speech. He will appear in the land of Zion like a glorious river in a parched land" (Isa. 32:2). What is the land of Zion in which a glorious river shall appear? It is surely that of which David sings in another psalm: "Glorious things are spoken of you, O city of God;" "The Lord loves the gates of Zion more than all the tents of Jacob" (Ps. 86:3, 2). Does God love these gates which we see turned into ashes and dust? I say that not even fools, let alone wise men, could be persuaded of this. I think that that which we read in Psalm 64 is to be understood in this sense: "You have visited the land and have watered her, greatly enriching her. The river of God is full of water. You have prepared their nourishment for so You prepare her. Water her furrows, multiply her sprouts. Under her showers she will rejoice as she sprouts forth" (Ps. 64:10f.). This land is visited daily by God and is watered; it is full of riches. From it, there goes forth the river of God of which it is written, "The stream of the river makes the city of God rejoice!" (Ps. 45:5). It is this river of which Ezekiel speaks when he describes the Temple in mystical allegorical language. On its banks are trees which abound in new fruit every month (Ezek. 47). The wisest of men [Solomon] has written of this land in Proverbs: "He who tills his land shall have plenty of bread" (Prov. 12:11). Does anyone believe that this is the physical land which we see and which is possessed primarily by sinners, of which it is written: "Cursed is the land for your sake" (Gen. 3:17). Then let him explain the verse, "He who tills his land shall have plenty of bread." How many indeed till the land and cultivate it with the plow, yet are afflicted by poverty and penury because of countless hardships? One must consider then what Scripture says: "He who tills *his* land"—the land which is properly his and from which he cannot be expelled. . . .

We must treat here of another point which we shall learn from the authority of Scripture. It is not the saints of the land, which the Jews hold to be the Promised Land, which are its inhabitants but strangers and sojourners. We read this in the words of a righteous man: "I am a stranger and a sojourner as all my fathers were" (Ps. 38:13). Having been long condemned to live in the darkness of that land, he sighs and cries and says: "Woe is me that my exile is so prolonged; that I dwell with the inhabitants of Kedar; my soul has full long been a sojourner" (Ps. 119:5f.). Wherever the expression "inhabitant of the land" appears, let us study the beginning, the middle, and the end of the passage. It may be clearly shown that sinners are always called "inhabitants of the land." There is an example in the Apocalypse of John: "Woe to the inhabitants of the land" (Rev. 8:13). The promise was first made to Abraham when the Lord said: "I will give this land to you and your posterity" (Gen. 12:7). According to the discourse of Stephen, the first Christian martyr, it is said that Abraham did not even receive a "foot's length" (Acts 7:5). Here indeed is what is written: "Then he departed from the land of the Chaldeans and lived in Haran. After his father died, he migrated to that land in which you are now living. He gave him no inheritance in it, not even a foot's length, but promised to give it to him in possession and to his posterity after him" (Acts 7:4f.). Lest the tacit reflection of the reader lead him to think that what was not given to the fathers might yet revert to the sons, the Chosen Vessel [Christ, Acts 9:15] said to the Hebrews: "By faith Abraham obeyed when he was called to go out to a place which he was to receive as an inheritance; and he went out, not knowing where he was to go. By faith he sojourned in the Promised Land as in a foreign land, living in tents with Isaac and Jacob, heirs with him of the same promise. For he looked forward to the city which has foundations, whose builder and maker is God" (Heb. 11:8ff.). Then, after having spoken of Abel, Enoch, Noah, and Sarah (*ibid.,* vss. 4, 5, 7, 11), He added: "These all died in faith not having received what was promised, but having seen it and greeted it from afar, and having acknowledged that they were strangers and foreigners on the land. Those who speak thus make clear they are seeking a homeland. If they had been thinking of that land from which they had gone out, they would have had opportunity to return. But as it is, they desire a better land, that is, a heavenly one" (Heb. 11:13ff.). Then, after discussing a number of the saints, He added: "And all these, though well attested by their faith did not receive the promise; since God had foreseen something better for us, that apart from us they should not be made perfect" (*ibid.,* vss. 39f.). "But you

have come to Mount Zion and to the city of the living God, the heavenly
Jerusalem, and to innumerable angels in festal gathering, and to the
assembly of the first-born who are enrolled in heaven" (Heb. 12:22f.).
It does not escape me that Jewish unbelief does not accept these evi-
dences, even though they are well supported by the authority of the
Old Testament. . . .

Those who believe that this land (which has now become a Promised Land for us by virtue of the passion and resurrection of Christ)
was possessed by the Jewish people—let them tell me: How much of
it did they possess after they returned from Egypt? The distance from
Dan to Beersheba is scarcely 160 miles. Scripture attests that even the
very powerful kings, David and Solomon, possessed no more than this—
if we exclude that which they received in peace treaties after their
victories. And I have not even mentioned the five cities of the Philistines
—Gaza, Ashkalon, Gath, Ekron, and Ashdod—or the Edomites in the
south who were scarcely seventy-five miles from Jerusalem, or the
Arabs and the Hagarites, which they now call Saracens, in the vicinity
of Jerusalem. I am embarrassed to mention the length of the Promised
Land, lest I be accused of giving pagans an opportunity to blaspheme.
It is forty-six miles from Jaffa to our village of Bethlehem. Beyond,
there is a vast desert, populated by ferocious barbarians of whom it is
said: "You shall dwell over against all your kinsmen" (Gen. 16:12).
. . . This, O Jew, is the length and breadth of your lands. You pride
yourself on them; you boast of them to the ignorant of various provinces:
"The outer trappings for the people; I know you deep under the skin"
(Persius, *Satires* III:30).

You may object that the Promised Land is that which is defined
by the Book of Numbers: From south of the Salt Sea to Sinai and
Kadesh-Barnea as far as the Torrent of Egypt which empties into the
Great Sea near Rhinocorura; to the west, the Sea itself which extends
along Palestine, Phoenicia, Coelesyria, and Cilicia; to the north, Mount
Taurus and Zephyrium as far as Hamath; to the east, passing Antioch,
Lake Chinnereth, now called Tiberias, and the Jordan, which empties
into the Salt Sea which is now called the Dead Sea. On the other side
of the Jordan is the territory of the two tribes of Reuben and Gad and
the half tribe of Manasseh. Now I will admit that these lands were
promised to you—although not handed over to you—on the condition
that you observe God's commandments and that you conduct yourself
according to His precepts; that you not serve Baal-peor and the Baals,

Beelzebub and Chemosh instead of Almighty God. Because you chose them over God, you have lost all that was promised you. The Kingdom of Heaven, which the Old Testament does not mention at all, was also promised to me by the Gospel. But if I were not to do what was commanded, the fault would not lie with Him who promised but with me, for I would not be worthy of having the promise fulfilled. . . . Read the Books of Joshua and Judges and you will see in what a narrow territory you are confined. Why even recall the aliens of various cities which the Jews could not expel from their cities and holdings? Your very capital (first Jebus, then Salem, still later Jerusalem, now Aelia) could not expel the Jebusites. She abode with them (despite the scandalous example of their vices) so that your Temple was built on the threshing-floor of Arauna the Jebusite. Was not your Temple constructed by pagans: 80,000 quarriers and 70,000 porters, that is 150,000, without counting the foremen. Such was the multitude of uncircumcised among you.

I do not say this to deride the land of Judea as some deceiving heretic might; nor do I wish to destroy the historical reality which is the foundation of the spiritual sense. I only wish to cast down the arrogance of the Jews who prefer the narrowness of the synagogue to the breadth of the Church. If they would follow the letter that kills and not the spirit that makes alive, let them show us a Promised Land flowing with milk and honey. But if they were to accept that these expressions are used tropologically [figuratively] for an abundance of all things, then we might prefer the land of divine praise, the land of the living, to the land of thorn-bushes. Of the rejection of Israel and the election of the Gentiles the Lord said to Moses: "Let Me alone that I may destroy this people and make of you a great nation" (Exod. 32:10). Indeed, the Father said to the Son: "Ask of Me, and I will make the nations your heritage, and the ends of the earth your possession" (Ps. 2:8). Isaiah said even more clearly: "It is too light a thing that you should be My servant to raise up the tribes of Jacob and to restore the refuse—or the remnants —of Israel" (Isa. 49:6). It thus follows clearly that everything concerning this people is an adumbration—image, prefiguration, and symbol—of that which has been written for us "upon whom the end of the ages has come" (I Cor. 10:11).

You have committed many crimes, O Jew; you have been the slave of all the surrounding nations. For what reason? Surely because of your idolatry! You were frequently enslaved. Yet God took pity on you and

sent judges and deliverers who redeemed you from enslavement to
Moabites, Ammonites, Philistines and various other nations. At the last,
you offended God under the kings, and the entire province, devastated
by Babylonia, was destroyed. Cyrus, king of the Persians, released the
captives; Ezra and Nehemiah report this in detail. The Temple was
rebuilt under Darius, king of the Persians and Medes, by Zerubbabel
the son of Shealtiel and Joshua the son of Jozadak, the high priest.

I shall not recount what you suffered under the Medes, Egyptians,
and Macedonians. I shall not remind you of Antiochus Epiphanes, the
cruelest of all tyrants. I shall not repeat the names of Pompey, Gabinius,
Scaurus, Varus, Cassius, and Sossius who triumphed over your cities,
especially Jerusalem. Then at last, the city was captured and the Temple
demolished under Vespasian and Titus. The city then lay in ruins for
fifty years until the reign of Hadrian. Now only a little less than four
hundred years after the destruction of the Temple, the city and the
Temple remain in ruins. For what great villainy? You no longer worship
idols; even while enslaved to the Persians and the Romans and subjected to the yoke of captivity, you knew no strange gods. How is it
that the most merciful God, who has never forgotten you, is not moved
by your sufferings after all this time to release you from captivity—or
more precisely, to send you your awaited Antichrist? For what villainy,
I say, and for what vile misdeed has He turned aside your eyes? You
do not know? Remember the cries of your fathers: "His blood be upon
us and our children" (Mt. 27:25); "Come let us kill him and the inheritance will be ours" (Mk. 12:7); "We have no king but Caesar"
(John 19:15). You have what you chose: Until the end of the world
you shall serve Caesar "until the full number of the Gentiles come in,
and so all Israel shall be saved" (Rom. 11:25f.), so that that which
was once at the head shall now be at the tail. . . .

REJECTIONS AND AFFIRMATIONS

Abraham Joshua Heschel was professor of Jewish ethics and mysticism at the Jewish Theological Seminary of America until his death in 1972. His Hasidic background and western philosophical training are reflected in the two aspects of his life's work: the interpretation of the classical sources of the Jewish religion and the exposition of an original philosophy of Judaism. His writings in English and Hebrew are widely read.

One of the major themes of Heschel's theology is that Judaism hallows time over against the spatial categories of modern thought. This conception was most fully developed in his essay, *The Sabbath: Its Meaning for Modern Man* (1951). It was apparently not until the Six Day War that Heschel fully realized that space too has its sacred dimension. *Israel: An Echo of Eternity* is the expression of that realization. It is worthy of note that one Christian reviewer of that volume observed that if even Heschel could not fully come to grips with the religious meaning of the Land of Israel until the occurrence of a near traumatic experience, how much more difficult would it be for a Christian to realize Israel's meaning for the Jew!

In the passage below, Heschel recounts the possible difficulties that Christians might encounter in accepting the fact of the State of Israel. He demonstrates the persistence of the ancient theology in the minds of those who believe themselves to have abandoned such modes of thought. In this way, the old letter and spirit dichotomy (sels. 13, 23) is transferred to the Jewish people and its land. They, the people and the land, are not concrete realities but Christian theological abstractions. (The reader might compare the use of the word "Zion" in the name of a synagogue and in that of a Baptist church.) The reaction of Heschel, a twentieth-century Jewish theologian, is remarkably like that of Joseph Kimhi in the twelfth. Kimhi, stressing the concrete character of Israel's redemption, declares that the Messiah must rebuild a Jerusalem of "wood and stones." Heschel, as it were, reiterates: "Hewing stones, paving roads, planting gardens, building homes, can be carried out as prayer in the form of deeds."

Another major obstacle to Christian acceptance as stated by Heschel is that discussed in selection 24. He relates how the return of political sovereignty to the Jewish people is seen by some Christians as a threat to their faith and how the myth of the wandering Jew lingers. Heschel concludes with an interpretation of a gospel passage, problematic for Christian theologians, which, he maintains, shows that the disciples of Jesus themselves expected the political renewal of the Kingdom of Israel.

Selection 24 has been reprinted from *Israel: An Echo of Eternity,* New York: Farrar, Straus and Giroux, 1967, pp. 139-147, 161-167.

In 1942, the same year in which Karl Barth was drawing theological implications from the Jews' plight in Europe (sel. 6), Reinhold Niebuhr was considering the practical aspects of post-war reconstruction. Niebuhr (1892-1971), who taught at Union Theological Seminary, was concerned throughout his life with the application of Christian ethics to the structures and dynamics of large social groups. Niebuhr sought the relationship between Christian *agape*—a heedless love involving sacrifice of self—and justice, which by its nature demands prudent, discriminate judgments. He was engaged in determining how this love could be related to national policy when a political leader's first responsibility is to national security and national interest. Concerns of this nature caused him to study and comment upon world events constantly. In the words of Gordon Harland: ". . . Niebuhr's thought has been forged in daily encounter with the shattering events of our age. . . . Nothing is more exciting and instructive than to see Reinhold Niebuhr week in and week out, year in and year out, wrestling to speak the prophetic and clarifying word of Christian understanding in the midst of the momentous events and decisions of the past three decades" (*The Thought of Reinhold Niebuhr,* New York: Oxford, 1966, p. x). It is in this context that Niebuhr broached the question of Jewish existence after World War II. Niebuhr had, for theological considerations of his own, rejected the attempt at religious assimilation of the Jew and felt that the mission to Israel should be abandoned. (See bibliographic survey.) In a two-part article in *The Nation* (CLIV [1942], 214-16, 253-55), Niebuhr argued against the ethnic assimilation of the Jew as well. On the one hand, he claimed, the Jew who seeks assimilation to ward off antisemitism is only deluding himself. On the other hand, liberal Gentiles who are willing to accept Jews at the price of their collective extinction are practicing a false liberalism. Yet while he advocates that nations should grant full rights to their Jewish citizens, this is not enough. Nations, as well as individuals, have their own individuality, their collective will to live—and this will is expressed through a national homeland. Niebuhr maintained that "the type of liberalism that fights for and with the Jews [for civil rights and tolerance] but leaves them to fight alone [for a state] is informed by unrealistic universalism."

In reading Niebuhr's words over three decades after they were written, one cannot fail to be impressed by his insight (and his *agape*) into the problems he dealt with. His observation that the world could not face what was happening to the Jews in Europe ("Even the Jews are loath to bring the problem to our attention in all its tragic depth.") shows that the events were evident to those with eyes to see.

Niebuhr's advocacy of a Jewish state in Palestine was coupled with a realistic outlook toward the future. He knew that this objective would not be easily achieved but he placed responsibility on the Anglo-Saxon nations for a comprehensive settlement which would safeguard both Arab rights and Jewish national sovereignty.

No better example of the translation of Christian anti-Jewish categories of thought into secular language can be found than Arnold J. Toynbee's *A Study of History* (10 vols., London: Oxford University Press, 1934-54). In this work, considered by some monumental and by others pretentious, the Jews are transformed from an accursed race rejected by God into "a fossil of the Syriac civilization." As such, their pretensions to statehood are, in Toynbee's eyes, bizarre. With all his lack of appreciation for Pharisaic Judaism, he invokes its "way of gentleness" to show that political Zionists betray their own heritage. In fact, he makes every attempt to associate Zionism with nazism—a most extraordinary equation coming from a noted historian.

In 1961, Toynbee published a supplementary volume (vol. 12), entitled *Reconsiderations,* to *A Study of History.* In it, he observed: "We may say with our lips that, when we are making an historical study of our fellow human beings, we suspend our moral judgments and suppress our feelings; but, if we fancy that we can do that, we are deceiving ourselves" (p. 54). More specifically, on the subject of the Jews he notes:

> It is difficult for anyone brought up in the Christian tradition to shake himself free from the official Christian ideology. He may

have discarded Christian doctrine on every point; yet on this particular point he may find that he is still influenced, subconsciously,
by the traditional Christian view in his outlook on Jewish history.
. . . I am conscious that my own outlook has been affected in this
way (p. 478).

This bit of self-revelation, however, led to no really fundamental altera-
tion of his position.

Toynbee's views on the Jews and Judaism have been examined by
Maurice Samuel in *The Professor and the Fossil*. Samuel has written
widely on Zionism and on the question of the Jew in Gentile society.
He at one time sardonically observed that antisemitism was a Gentile
affliction to which Jews would have to become accustomed. That this
did not mean passive acceptance is attested by his spirited critique of
Toynbee in which he exposes some of the British historian's biases and
misconceptions. Selection 26 is abridged from the chapter "Zionism and
Neo-Zionism," *The Professor and the Fossil*, New York: Alfred A.
Knopf, 1956, pp. 183-216. Of particular interest in this chapter is the
discussion of Toynbee's reservations concerning the Hebrew language,
the like of which are frequently heard among academicians in the
British world.

Toynbee's attitudes toward Zionism have lately been the subject of
a detailed and incisive study by Oskar K. Rabinowicz in *Arnold Toynbee
on Judaism and Zionism: A Critique*, London: W. H. Allen, 1974. Cf.
Harry M. Orlinsky, "On Toynbee's Use of the Term *Syriac* for One of
His Societies" in D. J. Silver, ed., *In the Time of Harvest*, New York:
Macmillan, 1963, pp. 255-269. For some revealing insights into Toynbee's attitudes toward the Jews, the reader is referred to his debate with
Yaacov Herzog, "The Herzog-Toynbee Debate," CBS phonodiscs CP
13-14.

While Toynbee writes in the guise of a secular historian who is
perforce influenced by his Christianity, there are anti-Zionists who voice
their opinions *qua* Christians. Much of this Christian anti-Israel writing
is to be found in such self-styled liberal journals as *Christianity and
Crisis*, the *United Church Observer* (Canada), and, to a lesser extent,
The Christian Century. An example of this is "Christians and the Mideast Crisis" (*Christian Century* LXXXIV [July 26, 1967], pp. 961-65)
by Willard G. Oxtoby, a Presbyterian minister and professor of religious

studies at the University of Toronto. The article is so blatant that it speaks for itself. It may be noted, however, that Professor Oxtoby reconsidered his remarks in a later piece in the same journal ("The Middle East: From Polemic to Accommodation," *Christian Century* LXXXVIII [October 13, 1971], pp. 1192-97). Among these reconsiderations are: "But the demand that gentiles today acknowledge a divine role [*sic!*] for the State of Israel seems like a counterpart to the Inquisition's demand that Jews acknowledge the divinity of Christ." (p. 1193) "So where were we in early 1967? Knowing that there had been a crescendo of threats and counterthreats, many of us concluded that much of what was going on was angry rhetoric. . . . We contend that Israel's existence was in no serious danger and the events proved us right." (p. 1194) "The Israelis are not Nazis. However much the Israeli state may be racist in principle. . . ." (p. 1196) "A subtle contribution to reconciliation between pro-Arabs and pro-Israelis would be a moratorium on *either side's* referring to Nazism and the Holocaust as a description of anything now happening or likely to happen in the eastern Mediterranean." (pp. 1196f.)

One further point should be remarked. Like medieval polemicists, Oxtoby invokes a Jewish source to document his case—here, a declaration of a meeting of American Reform rabbis in 1885 (the "Pittsburgh Platform") which asserts that "we are no longer a nation but a spiritual community and therefore expect no return to Palestine." Since the use of this statement may be somewhat misleading, it requires some historical perspective. One familiar with post-biblical Judaism will know that Jewish literature from 70 C.E. on shows a relentless preoccupation, nay obsession, with the return to Zion; that the abandonment of the Zionist aspiration by assimilationists in the late eighteenth and nineteenth centuries was a temporary aberration from this perennial Jewish longing; that the trauma of the Holocaust, which began in the very heartland of emancipation and assimilation, jolted even the assimilationists themselves into realizing the tragic failure of their attempted solution; that the aforementioned plank of the Pittsburgh Platform, a product of assimilationist thinking, has been long repudiated by American Reform, let alone by the remainder of American Jewry who never espoused it at all.

Professor Oxtoby maintains that "Christians must defy pressure on them to sit by silently, muzzled by the fear of being called anti-

Semitic" for "anti-Semitism has to do with the spirit in which criticism is given." With this last, few could disagree.

A. Roy Eckardt's "The Devil and Yom Kippur" (*Midstream* XX [1974], 67-75) was not written as a direct reply to Oxtoby but may be read as such. The essay, written in response to certain Christian reactions to the 1973 Mideast war, deals with the relationship between antisemitism and anti-Zionism or anti-Israelism.

Eckardt is a United Methodist clergyman and professor of religious studies at Lehigh University. He has written extensively on Jewish-Christian relations and the status of Jews in Christian theology. As have several Protestant theologians, Eckardt has argued that the Old Covenant made with Israel has not been abrogated and superseded by the Christian Covenant but remains in force. This viewpoint has been elaborated in *Elder and Younger Brothers* (See Bibliographic Survey) and more recently and more radically in *Your People, My People: The Meeting of Jews and Christians* (New York: Quadrangle, 1974). Here he maintains that Christians have no right to theologize about Jews but must take them at their own self-evaluation.

Eckardt has been an advocate of the State of Israel in the face of Christian theological opposition to it. In the same issue of the *Christian Century* in which Oxtoby's anti-Israel statement appeared and in the following issue, Eckardt and his wife, Alice Lyons Eckardt, published a two-part article, "Again, Silence in the Churches" (reprinted in *Elder and Younger Brothers,* pp. 163-70). This essay concerned itself with the silence of official Christianity in the critical period prior to the Six Day War. Eckardt's commitment "on Christian grounds to bespeak the integrity of Israel among Jews as among Christians" has been elaborated in further writings. (See Bibliographic Survey.)

"The Devil and Yom Kippur" expresses Eckardt's reaction to Christian responses to the 1973 crisis. In 1967, Eckardt complained of Christian silence. In 1973, he complained of Christian animosity—the attacks made on Israel in speeches and in the perennial letters to the editor; the allegation that the "Jews, the 'victims' of 'aggression' are, in actuality, the aggressors, the ones to be brought to trial and punished." Eckardt explains this phenomenon in terms of the symbolism of the devil—an expression of despair over the Holocaust and of the perpetuation of antisemitism by Christians in the name of Christianity. The devil and antisemitism are, he maintains, "correlative realities: anti-

Semitism is born of the devil, and the devil receives his sustenance from anti-Semitism." Eckardt develops the implications of this premise and denies what is for him the fictitious distinction between antisemitism and anti-Israelism.

In the fall of 1974, American Jews found themselves confronted with a spate of antisemitic remarks emanating from the very highest levels of U.S. civil and military authority. Commenting on this in the *New York Times* of November 29, 1974, the Rev. Edward H. Flannery observed: "The only thing somewhat unusual about these performances is the political level of the persons involved. We are not dealing here with guttersnipes but with presumably educated and sophisticated people. The very level of these personages raises questions. If individuals of some cultivation, or stature, fall prey to the virus of anti-Semitism as readily as anyone else, where are the boundaries of its power? Is anyone beyond its reach? Have we underestimated the dimensions of the phenomenon of anti-Semitism?"

The fact is that in addition to popular antisemitism, there is another kind, learned and academic, which is far more pernicious since it lays claim to intellectual respectability. For many years, the university was a center of this sort of antisemitism. Over and beyond the question of the *numerus clausus,* Jewish Studies as such were not viewed as having a place in the university curriculum. In traditionalist terms, the history of the perfidious Jews ended with the Great Perfidy. In liberal terms, the Christian could only recognize the great universality of mankind. In either case, Jewish history was a non-existent subject and could not therefore be taught.

To be sure, great breakthroughs have been achieved in the fostering of Jewish Studies in the North American university throughout the last two decades. But this has not been without its problems or pockets of resistance. Discussion of Judaism and Jewish Studies in academic circles often has a strange dialectic all its own. One encounters wonder at the fact that Jews born in Anglo-Saxon countries have learned to speak English like Anglo-Saxons. Yet at the same time, it is asked (by a "Hebraist") if the Jews are really serious about trying to "revive" Hebrew since it would be so much more convenient for them to speak English. One meets puzzlement over the possibility that a non-Jew should want to study or teach Jewish Studies. Yet, on the other hand, it is maintained that such courses are not warranted unless a sufficient number of non-Jews are enrolled, since "we're not here to provide a service to the Jewish community." It is maintained too that Jewish Studies must be "internationalized;" that a non-Jew should teach Jewish Studies whether qualified or not. (Of course, at such institutions, it is never suggested that Biblical Studies be internationalized and that a Jew, let alone a Roman Catholic, be allowed to teach Bible, since this is considered to be the peculiar preserve of the post-Protestant.)

Academic antisemitism is nowhere as vocal as when it is transmuted into anti-Israelism. And none are more vehement on this subject than some specialists on the Ancient Near East. This goes back a long way. A North American Orientalist visited Palestine during the "disturbances" in the late 1920's. It is related that when he returned home, he met a Jewish acquaintance and remarked: "You know, your people almost killed me. I was riding on a bus from Jerusalem to Hebron and the Arabs attacked us." "Why then *my* people?," he was asked. "Because if your people weren't there to begin with, the Arabs wouldn't be doing these things." In more recent times, Professor Oxtoby notes that "(in 1967) at least a considerable number of Old Testament scholars did not side with Israel, where one might have supposed their natural affinities would lie. Protestant biblical scholars are probably as well and as sympathetically informed as any group concerning the Jewish tradition—its ideals, *if not its postbiblical history.* . . . And *knowing Judaism well,* they could be critical of Israeli policies without the guilt of an evil hatred." (*Christian Century* LXXXVIII (October 13, 1971), p. 1193. Italics mine—(F.E.T.) Professor Oxtoby relates this fact to their "compassion for their Palestinian acquaintances." There may, however, be other factors at play.

For one thing, until the Jews began to rebuild it, Palestine remained an ideal museum piece for the Orientalist. The land of the patriarchs had changed little in four thousand years. The supermarket, the automobile, and the high-rise—considered indispensable at home— have no place in the Holy Land. It is no accident either that many of those who think this way have had seminary training; indeed, some have had only seminary training. They have learned their lessons well. They have learned that the Jews are doomed to wander forever because of their sins—and the existence of a Jewish state in Palestine does not sit well with this revealed truth.

Selection 29 is based on a reaction to one of several anti-Zionist and anti-Jewish incidents experienced in academic circles during the past few years. First published in *Commentary* (LIX [1975], 57-62), the paper was originally delivered in a slightly different form at a Jewish-Christian colloquium at the University of Pittsburgh in January, 1974. The quotation from Jacques Maritain is from *On the Church of Christ,* Notre Dame: Notre Dame University Press, 1973, pp. 170f. The italics are mine.

24.

ISRAEL: AN ECHO OF ETERNITY

Abraham J. Heschel

THE ALLEGORIZATION OF THE BIBLE

While it is proper and even necessary to seek to derive by a variety of interpretive methods new meaning from ancient sources, it is a fact that the attempt of traditional Christian theology to reduce concrete narratives, hopes, expectations connected with a living people and a geographic land, to paradigms of Church dogma has had detrimental results for Christian theology.

The radical use of the method of allegorization of the Hebrew Bible, the tendency to spiritualize the meaning of its works and to minimize its plain historical sense has made many Christians incapable of understanding or empathy for what the Holy Land means to the Jewish people and to the authors of the Hebrew Bible, or for what the people Israel means in the flesh, not just as a symbol or as a construct of theological speculation. Even many Christian theologians who are no longer committed to the method of allegorization react in a way as if the concrete people Israel, the city of Jerusalem, the hope of the restoration of Zion, were illusory entities.

"The allegorical method essentially means the interpretation of a text in terms of something else, irrespective of what that something else is." Its use in biblical exegesis which goes back to Philo has often been accompanied by the assumption that we must distinguish in Scripture a body and a soul, a literal sense and a spiritual sense. The literal sense is depreciated, the spiritual sense exalted.

The allegorical method developed by Philo has its echoes in the Epistle to the Hebrews. By the middle of the second century, allegory, though not generally used by the New Testament writers, finds acceptance in the Church, for example, in the Epistle of Barnabas, and in Justin Martyr.

Allegoric interpretation is based on the supposition that Scripture intended to express some other meaning than what is literally said. Extreme allegorization, or the exclusive nonliteral method of interpreting Scriptures, particularly when adopting neo-Platonic methods of thinking, tends to contrast the real which is heavenly and eternal with the apparent which is earthly and temporary. By such a method biblical history and laws were construed as being, in reality, mere intimations of the mysteries of faith. Over and above that, it was maintained that in the Bible the spirit is concealed in the letter, that the immediate and apparent meaning of the Bible is but a shadow of the mystery, the "shadow" tending to obscure the mystery.

Since the Hebrew Bible was but a foreshadowing, and the New Testament a reality, it was possible to allegorize the Hebrew Bible while taking the words of the New Testament literally. While Philo used the method of allegorizing to derive from the Hebrew Bible timeless truths of philosophy, the New Testament writers sought to demonstrate that the events of the present are fulfillments of predictions contained therein. Subsequently, Christian typological exegesis saw the events of the Hebrew Bible as the prefiguration of the events in the New Testament. It saw in the facts of the Hebrew Bible something in preparation, something sketching itself out, of which the writers themselves were not aware because it lay quite beyond their purview.

"The proper motive was the firm belief that the Old Testament was a church document. For the church, the allegorical method was its primary means of making the Old Testament a church document." The allegorization of the Bible became the recognized method of dealing with the Hebrew Scriptures within the Church. This method enabled the exegetes to find intimations of the life of Jesus nearly everywhere. The two goats which are brought into the Sanctuary on the Day of Atonement typified the two advents of Jesus. Jacob served Laban for sheep, so Jesus became a servant so that he might purchase his flock.

Moses holding up his hands during the battle with Amalek is a type of Jesus on the cross.

There was also a tradition of more sober exegesis cultivated by Theodore in the Antiochene School. Epiphanius mentioned that "Scripture does not need allegory; it is as it is. What it needs is contemplation and sensitive discernment."

Luther insisted that the Word of God is imparted through Scripture and that Scripture is above the Church. Yet what he meant by the Word was not the Bible itself but the divine offering itself to man. "Take Christ out of the Scripture and what else will you find in them? Understanding the Bible means finding Christ in it."

It was modern critical scholarship that paved the way for the understanding of the literal and historical dimensions of the Bible that we now consider indispensable for theological understanding.

Few men today could accept the view that the mind of man created the universe as it created the principles of logic, that the universe is a form of the mind's activity deriving its being from it, authentic and authoritative only as possessed by the mind and authorized by it. It is rather difficult to comprehend how a contemporary scholar can appreciate the insight expressed in the following statement: Jesus "created the Scripture as He created the Church; both are forms of His activity, valid as they derived their being from Him, authentic and authoritative as possessed of Him and authorized by Him." It is thus mentioned that "this christocentric understanding of the Bible is the right way of approach."

"When the historical sense of a passage is once abandoned, there is wanting any sound regulative principle to govern exegesis. . . . the mystical [allegorical] method of exegesis is an unscientific and arbitrary method, reduces the Bible to obscure enigmas, undermines the authority of all interpretation, and, when taken by itself, fails to meet the apologetic necessities of time."

"This I consider the first principle in prophetic interpretation," writes Davidson, "to assume that the literal meaning is *his* meaning— that he is moving among realities, not symbols, among concrete things like people, not among abstractions like *our* Church, world, etc." Davidson treats with a measure of scorn those interpreters who blithely make Zion or Jerusalem the Church, and the Canaanite the enemy of the Church, and the land the promises to the Church, etc., as if the prophet moved in a world of symbols and abstractions.

That "Israel has a great future is clear from Scripture as a whole. There is a large unfulfilled element in the Old Testament which demands it, unless we spiritualize it away or relinquish it as Oriental hyperbole."

BODY AND SPIRIT

Religious existence is not limited to prayer, dogma, and observance of rituals. Hewing stones, paving roads, planting gardens, building homes, can also be carried out as prayers in the form of deeds. Seeking to conquer helplessness and infirmity, to overcome despair and despondency, are acts that forge reminders that there are deeds in which God is at home in the world.

In Judaism there is no absolute bifurcation of the secular and the religious, of the concrete and the spiritual, of the common and the marvelous. The spiritual is not the antithesis of the material. Both aspects are interrelated. We must seek to endow the material with the radiance of the spirit, to sanctify the common, to sense the marvelous in everydayness.

It was well within the spirit of classical Jewish thinking that the following statement was coined: "Body and soul are like friends and lovers to each other."

Before God sanctified time, He created things of space. What is the meaning of living in the world of space? To master things of space in order to sanctify moments of time. Even before He blessed the Seventh Day and made it holy, God blessed man and said, "Be fertile and increase, fill the earth and master it and rule the fish of the sea, the birds of the sky, and all the living things that creep on earth" (Genesis 1:27).

Just as we are told, "Remember the Sabbath day to keep it holy," we are commanded, "Six days you shall labor" (Exodus 20:8-9). The upbuilding of the land of Israel was inspired by a new awareness of the sanctity of physical labor.

The dichotomy of spirit and letter is alien to Jewish tradition. What man does in his concrete, physical existence is directly relevant to the divine. Man is body and soul and his goal is so to live that both "his heart and his flesh should sing to the living God" (Psalm 84:3). While the soul without the body is a ghost, the body without the soul is a corpse.

The Hebrew Bible is not a book about heaven—it is a book about the earth. The Hebrew word *erets,* meaning earth, land, occurs at least five times as often in the Bible as the word *shamayim,* meaning heaven.

We will never be able to sense the meaning of heaven unless our lives on earth include the cultivation of a foretaste of heaven on earth. This may also explain why the promise of the land is a central motif in biblical history. God has not given the land away—He remains the Lord and ultimate owner: "For Mine is the land" (Leviticus 25:23). Living in the Holy Land is itself a witness to the almost forgotten truth that God is the Lord and owner of all lands.

We must cultivate the earth as well as reflect on heaven. The Hebrew Bible is a book dealing with all of man, and redemption involves spiritual purification as well as moral integrity and political security.

Harmony of heaven and earth rather than their perennial tension is the hope. Everything certifies to the sublime, the unapparent working jointly with the apparent. Security, justice and renewal on earth are prerequisites to such merging. According to Rabbi Yochanan of the third century, who lived in Palestine: "The Holy One Blessed Be He said: I will not enter heavenly Jerusalem until I can enter earthly Jerusalem" (Ta'anit 5a).

The destiny of heavenly Jerusalem depends upon the destiny of Jerusalem on earth.

The agony of our people particularly in this century was dreadfully concrete and redemption of our people and all peoples, we believe, must also be concrete. It is not enough to be concerned for the life to come. Our immediate concern must be with justice and compassion in life here and now, with human dignity, welfare, and security.

The task is not to abandon the natural order of creation but to purify it; to humanize the sacred, to sanctify the secular.

The hope is for universal redemption, for ontological transformation. Yet it seems that fulfillment will come about by degrees.

Judaism insists upon the single deed as the instrument in dealing with evil. At the end of days, evil will be conquered by the One; in historic times evils must be conquered one by one.

"The inner history of Israel is a history of waiting for God, of waiting for His arrival. Just as Israel is certain of the reality of the Promised Land, so she is certain of the coming of 'the promised day.' She lives by a promise of 'the day of the Lord,' a day of judgment followed by redemption, when evil will be consumed and an age of glory will ensue.

"The climax of our hopes is the establishment of the kingship of God, and a passion for its realization must permeate all our thoughts. For the ultimate concern of the Jew is not personal salvation but universal redemption. Redemption is not an event that will take place all at once at 'the end of days' but a process that goes on all the time. Man's good deeds are single acts in the long drama of redemption, and every deed counts. One must live as if the redemption of all men depended upon the devotion of one's own life. Thus life, every life, we regard as an immense opportunity to enhance the good that God has placed in His creation. And the vision of a world free of hatred and war, of world filled with understanding for God as the ocean is filled with water, the certainty of ultimate redemption, must continue to inspire our thought and action."

THE CHRISTIAN APPROACH

There is little doubt that the establishment of the State of Israel came as a shock, even a scandal, to some Christians. They held that in punishment for the crucifixion of Christ the Jews would not return to their ancient homeland unless they came to believe in him. There was the cry of the crowd before Pilate's palace: "His blood be on us and on our children" (Matthew 27:25); there were other biblical texts—all seemed to tell of lasting exile. Thus, the present restoration, partial though it was, seemed a contradiction of the inspired word.

Examples of the belief that Scripture demanded the barring of the Jews from the Holy Land are not lacking in recent times, nor have they been confined to the market place. When in 1869 the Spanish Cortes (the legislature) debated freedom of worship, Professor Emilio Castelar took up the cause of the Jews. He was answered by Vicente de Manterola, a deputy, who advised the Jews not to rebuild the Temple in Jerusalem, not to reorganize as a people under a scepter, a flag, or a president, for the moment they succeeded, "the Catholic Church will have been slain, because the word of God will have been slain." Francisco Mateo Gago went further. In an open letter he insisted that the Jews "walk the earth" because they carry a curse; that till the last judgment they will be without a country of their own, without a fixed abode, without prince, without sacrifice. This seemed to him the clear teaching of the prophet Hosea (see 3:4).

However, there is nothing in the words of Jesus "to lead us to believe that He envisioned a physical desolation that would endure to the end of days. . . . A study of the patristic and scriptural sources makes us conclude that the belief the Jews could never regain their lost nationhood did not have its origin in Scripture or in a dogmatic patristic tradition. Rather it is based on the writings of several of the Fathers of the later fourth century—principally Chrysostom—who, unduly influenced by the dramatic failure of Julian the Apostate to reconstruct the Temple, interpreted certain texts of the Old and New Testaments in the light of this event and read into them temporal specifications which an exacting exegesis cannot discover or support. Hence, the existence of a Jewish state, be it the state of Israel or another, does not contradict sacred Scripture." (Edward H. Flannery, "Theological Aspects of the State of Israel," *The Bridge,* Vol. III, pp. 304, 312 ff.).

There is, moreover, a passage in the New Testament that seems to reflect the belief of the early Christian community in the restoration of the kingdom to the Jewish people. According to the Book of Acts, the disciples to whom Jesus presented himself alive after his passion, asked him: "Lord, is it at this time that thou restorest the kingdom to Israel?" And he said to them: "No one can know times and seasons which the Father fixed by His own authority" (Acts 1:6-7).

What is the meaning of this question and this answer? It was a time when Jerusalem was taken away from the Jewish people, the holy Temple destroyed, Jews sold into slavery. Pagan Rome ruled in the Holy Land.

But there was a hope, a hope of deliverance from the pagans, there was the promise offered by the prophets, of returning Jerusalem to the kingdom of Israel. It was the most urgent question. So when they saw Jesus for the first time in these extraordinary circumstances, it is understandable that this was the first question they asked, their supreme concern: "Is it at this time that thou restorest the kingdom?" In other words, they asked the question about the restoration.

Jesus' answer was that the times of the fulfillment of the divine promise were matters which lay within the Father's sole authority. So, earlier, he had assured them that he himself did not know the day or hour of his parousia. "But of that day or the hour [of the parousia] no one knows, not even the angels in heaven, nor the Son, but only the

Father" (Mark 13:32). A similar awareness is common in Rabbinic literature. "Nobody knows when the house of David will be restored." According to Rabbi Shimeon the Lakish (*ca.* 250), "I have revealed it to my heart, but not to the angels." Jesus' answer is as characteristic of the Rabbinic mind of the age as the question.

However, this passage is generally interpreted in a different way. Reflecting a dichotomy in early Christian thinking, the position of the Galilean disciples was different from that of the Hellenistic Christians. The original hope of the disciples was that the kingdom was at hand in the apocalyptic sense, but the Hellenistic Christians, who in the end conquered the empire, preached the Gospel as having present importance for each individual apart from the eschatological kingdom. True to the tendency of disregarding any secular or political relevance to the early Christian message, the question contained in this message was criticized rather than appreciated.

Thus Augustine explains the meaning of the question to be that Jesus after the resurrection was visible only to his followers, and they asked whether he would now make himself seen to everyone. Calvin maintains that "there are as many errors in this question as words." According to modern commentators, the question reflects the spiritual ignorance and hardness of heart of the disciples, "the darkened utterance of carnal and uninspired minds," and the answer of Jesus as a rebuke.

However, the simple meaning of the entire passage has a perfect *Sitz im Leben* [life context], and both question and answer must be understood in the spirit of their times. The Apostles were Jews and evidently shared the hope of their people of seeing the kingdom of God realized in the restoration of Israel's national independence. So now, hearing their Master speak of the new age, they asked if this was to be the occasion for restoring the kingdom to Israel. We can scarcely fail to realize or to understand the naturalness of their question. The expectation was burned into their very being by the tyranny of the Roman rule. The answer confirms the expectation that the kingdom will be restored to Israel—an expectation expressed again and again in ancient Jewish liturgy. The point in history at which that restoration will take place remains the secret of the Father.

It is very likely that following Daniel and Ezra, calculations were made to predict the time of the coming of the restoration. However, most rabbis disapproved computations that dealt with the "time, two times, and half a time" of Daniel 7:25. Jesus' answer is not a rebuke of the Apostles' hope; it is, rather, a discouragement of Messianic calculations (see Luke 17:20-21).

Jesus' expectation that Jerusalem will be restored to Israel is implied in his prediction that "Jerusalem will be trodden down by the Gentiles, until the times of the Gentiles are fulfilled" (Luke 21:24). This saying announces not only the destruction of Jerusalem, but the end of Israel as a political entity as well. The Gentiles are, commentators agree, the Romans, whose armies set fire to the Temple and laid Jerusalem in ruins under Titus in A.D. 70, and who humbled her again when Hadrian, about the year 135, sought to turn her into a pagan city in the Greek style.

Some commentators, indeed, see in these words a prediction of "the re-establishment of Jerusalem as a capital of the Jewish nation."

25.

JEWS AFTER THE WAR

Reinhold Niebuhr

The position of the Jews in Europe and the Western world is by no means the least of the many problems of postwar reconstruction that must engage our minds even while our energies are being exhausted in achieving the prerequisite of any reconstruction, that is, the defeat of the Axis. It is idle to assume that this defeat will solve the problem of the Jews; indeed, the overthrow of nazism will provide no more than the negative condition for the solution of any of the vexing problems of justice that disturb our consciences.

Millions of Jews have been completely disinherited, and they will not be able to obtain the automatic restoration of their rights. An impoverished Europe will not find it easy to reabsorb a large number of returned Jews, and a spiritually corrupted Europe will not purge itself quickly of the virus of race bigotry with which the Nazis have infected its culture. It must also be remembered that the plight of the Jews was intolerable in those parts of Europe which represented a decadent feudalism—Poland and the Balkans—long before Hitler made their lot impossible in what was once the democratic world. The problem of what is to become of the Jews in the postwar world ought to engage all of us, not only because a suffering people has a claim upon our compassion but because the very quality of our civilization is involved in the solution. It is, in fact, a scandal that the Jews have had so little effective aid from the rest of us in a situation in which they are only the chief victims. The Nazis intend to decimate the Poles and to reduce other peoples to the status of helots; but they are bent upon the extermination of the Jews.

One probable reason for the liberal world's failure to be more instant in its aid to the Jews is that we cannot face the full dimensions of this problem without undermining the characteristic credos of the democratic world. Even the Jews are loath to bring the problem to our attention in all its tragic depth. We will not face it because we should be overwhelmed by a sense of guilt in contemplating those aspects of the problem which Hitler did not create but only aggravated. Some Jews have refused to face it in dread of having to recognize that the solutions provided by the liberal Jewish world have failed to reach the depths of the problem.

The liberal world has sought to dissolve the prejudice between Jews and Gentiles by preaching tolerance and good will. Friends of the Jews have joined the Jews in seeking to persuade their detractors that the charges against them are lies. But this does not meet the real issue. The real question is, Why should these lies be manufactured and why should they be believed? Every cultural or racial group has its own characteristic vices and virtues. When a minority group is hated for its virtues as well as for its vices, and when its vices are hated not so much because they are vices as because they bear the stamp of uniqueness, we are obviously dealing with a collective psychology that is not easily altered by a little more enlightenment. The fact is that the relations of cultural and ethnic groups, intranational or international, have complexities unknown in the relations between individuals, in whom intelligence may dissolve group loyalties and the concomitant evil of group friction.

American theories of tolerance in regard to race are based upon a false universalism that in practice develops into a new form of nationalism. The fact that America has actually been a melting pot in which a new amalgam of races is being achieved has given rise to the illusion that racial and ethnic distinction can be transcended in history to an indeterminate degree. Russian nationalism has the same relation to Marxist universalism as American nationalism has to liberal universalism. There is a curious, partly unconscious, cultural imperialism in theories of tolerance that look forward to a complete destruction of all racial distinctions. The majority group expects to devour the minority group by way of assimilation. This is a painless death, but it is death nevertheless.

The collective will to survive of those ethnic groups in America which have a base in another homeland is engaged and expressed in their homeland, and need not express itself here, where an amalgam of races is taking place. The Finns need not seek to perpetuate themselves in America, for their collective will to live is expressed in Finland. But the Jews are in a different position. Though as an ethnic group they have maintained some degree of integrity for thousands of years, they are a nationality scattered among the nations. Does the liberal-democratic world fully understand that it is implicitly making collective extinction the price of its provisional tolerance?

This question implies several affirmations that are challenged by both Jewish and Gentile liberals; it is therefore important to make these affirmations explicit and to elaborate them. One is that the Jews are really a nationality and not merely a cultural group. Certainly the Jews have maintained a core of racial integrity through the ages. This fact is not disproved by the assertion that their blood is considerably mixed. There are no pure races. History develops new configurations on the bases of nature, but not in such a way as to transcend completely the natural distinctions. Who would deny that the Germans have a collective will to live, or think that this simple statement can be refuted by calling attention to the admixture of Slav blood in people of German nationality?

The integrity of the Jews as a group is, of course, not purely biological; it has also a religious and cultural basis. But in this Jews are not unique, for there are no purely biological facts in history. The cultural and religious content of Jewish life transcends racial particularity, as does the culture of every people, though never so absolutely as to annihilate its own ethnic core. The one aspect of Jewish life that is unique is that the Jews are a nationality scattered among the nations. I use the word "nationality" to indicate something more than "race" and something less than "nation." It is more than race by reason of the admixture of culture and less than nation by reason of the absence of a state. The Jews certainly are a nationality by reason of the ethnic core of their culture. Those Jews who do not feel themselves engaged by a collective will have a perfect right to be so disengaged, just as Americans of French or Greek descent need feel no responsibility for the survival of their respective nationalities. But Jews render no service either to democracy or to their people by seeking to deny this ethnic foundation of their life, or by giving themselves to the illusion that they might dispel all prejudice if only they could prove that they are a purely cultural or religious community.

The fact that millions of Jews are quite prepared to be *spurlos versenkt,* to be annihilated, in a process of assimilation must affect the program of the democratic world for dealing with the Jewish question. The democratic world must accord them this privilege, including, of course, the right to express the ethos of their history in purely cultural and religious terms, in so far as this is possible, without an ethnic base. The democratic world must resist the insinuation that the Jews are not assimilable, particularly when the charge is made in terms of spurious friendship, as it is by Albert Jay Nock. They are not assimilable but they have added to the riches of a democratic world by their ethnic and cultural contributions. Civilization must guard against the tendency of all communities to demand a too simple homogeneity, for if this is allowed complete expression, it results in Nazi tribal primitivism. The preservation of tolerance and cultural pluralism is necessary not only from the standpoint of justice to the Jews but from the standpoint of the quality of a civilization.

The assimilability of the Jews and their right to be assimilated are not in question; this conviction must prompt one half of the program of the democratic world, the half that consists in maintaining and extending the standards of tolerance and cultural pluralism achieved in a liberal era. But there is another aspect of the Jewish problem that is not met by this strategy. That is the simple right of the Jews to survive as a people. There are both Jews and Gentiles who deny that the Jews have such a survival impulse as an ethnic group, but the evidence of contemporary history refutes them, as does the evidence of all history in regard to the collective impulses of survival in life generally. Modern liberalism has been blind to this aspect of human existence because its individualist and universalist presuppositions and illusions have prevented it from seeing some rather obvious facts in man's collective life.

One proof of the Jews' will to survive is, of course, that they have survived the many vicissitudes of their history. They have survived in spite of the fact that they have been a nationality scattered among the nations, without a homeland of their own, since the dawn of Western European history. They are a people of the Diaspora. Modern assimilationists on both sides sometimes suggest that the survival of the Jews through the centuries was determined on the one hand by the hostility of the feudal world and on the other by the toughness of an orthodox religious faith; and they suggest that the liberal era has dissipated both the external and the internal basis of this survival. They assume that the liberal ideals of tolerance are infinitely extensible and that the breaking of the hard shell of a traditional religious unity will destroy the internal will to live.

The violent nationalism of our period proves the error of the first assumption. While we need not believe that nazism or even a milder form of national bigotry will set the social and political standards of the future, it is apparent that collective particularities and vitalities have a more stubborn life than liberal universalism had assumed. The error of the second has been proved by the Jews themselves. For Zionism is the expression of a national will to live that transcends the traditional orthodox religion of the Jews. It is supported by many forces in Jewish life, not the least of which is an impressive proletarian impulse. Poor Jews recognize that privileged members of their Jewish community may have achieved such a secure position in the Western world that they could hardly be expected to sacrifice it for a Zionist venture. But they also see that for the great multitude of Jews there is no escape from the hardships a nationality scattered among the nations must suffer. They could, if they would, be absorbed in the Western world. Or they could, if they desired, maintain their racial integrity among the various nations. But they know that the price that must be paid for such survival is high. They know from their own experience that collective prejudice is not as easily dissolved as some of their more favored brothers assume.

The poorer Jews understand, out of their experience, what is frequently withheld from the more privileged—namely, that the bigotry of majority groups toward minority groups that affront the majority by diverging from the dominant type is a perennial aspect of man's collective life. The force of it may be mitigated, but it cannot be wholly eliminated. These Jews, therefore, long for a place on the earth where they are not "tolerated," where they are neither "understood" nor misunderstood, neither appreciated nor condemned, but where they can be what they are, preserving their own unique identity without asking "by your leave" of anyone else.

It is this understanding of a basic human situation on the part of the less privileged portion of the Jewish community which has given Zionism a particular impetus. There are of course individuals in the more privileged groups who make common cause with the less privileged because they have the imagination to see what their more intellectualist brothers have not seen. But on the whole Zionism represents the wisdom of the common experience as against the wisdom of the mind, which tends to take premature flights into the absolute or the universal from the tragic conflicts and the stubborn particularities of human history.

The second part of any program for the solution of the Jewish problem must rest upon the recognition that a collective survival impulse is as legitimate a "right" as an individual one. Justice, in history, is concerned with collective, as well as with individual, rights. Recognition of the legitimacy of this right must lead, in my opinion, to a more generous acceptance of the Zionist program as correct in principle, however much it may have to be qualified in application.

The Jewish religionists, the Jewish and Gentile secularists, and the Christian missionaries to the Jews have, despite the contradictory character of their various approaches, one thing in common. They would solve the problem of the particularity of a race by a cultural or religious universalism. This is a false answer if the universal character of their culture or religion demands the destruction of the historical—in this case racial—particularism. It is just as false as if the command "thou shalt love thy neighbor as thyself" were interpreted to mean that I must destroy myself so that no friction may arise between my neighbor and myself.

The author, who happens to be a Christian theologian, may be permitted the assertion, as a postscriptum, that he has his own ideas about the relation of the Christian to the Jewish religion. But he regards all religious and cultural answers to the Jewish problem that do not take basic ethnic facts into consideration as the expressions of either a premature universalism or a conscious or unconscious ethnic imperialism.

I offer "a" solution rather than "the" solution to the problem of anti-Semitism precisely because a prerequisite for any solution of a basic social problem is the understanding that there is no perfectly satisfactory formula. A perennial problem of human relations can be dealt with on many levels of social and moral achievements, but not in such a way that new perplexities will not emerge upon each new level. The tendency of modern culture to find pat answers and panaceas for vexing problems —one aspect of its inveterate utopianism—has confused rather than clarified most issues with which it has occupied itself.

I have previously suggested that the problem of the relation of the Jews to our Western democratic world calls for at least two different approaches. We must on the one hand preserve and if possible extend the democratic standards of tolerance and of cultural and racial pluralism that allow the Jews *Lebensraum* as a nation among the nations. We must on the other hand support more generously than in the past the legitimate aspiration of Jews for a "homeland" in which they will not be simply tolerated but which they will possess. The type of liberalism that fights for and with the Jews on the first battle line but leaves them to fight alone on the second is informed by unrealistic universalism. If its presuppositions are fully analyzed, it will be discovered that they rest upon the hope that history is moving forward to a universal culture that will eliminate all particularities and every collective uniqueness, whether rooted in nature or in history. History has perennially refuted this hope.

The late Justice Louis D. Brandeis illustrated in his person and his ideas exactly what we mean by this double strategy. Brandeis was first a great American, whose contributions to our national life prove that justice to the Jew is also a service to democracy in that it allows democracy to profit from the peculiar gifts of the Jew—in the case of Brandeis and many another leader, the Hebraic-prophetic passion for social justice. But Brandeis was also a Zionist; his belief in the movement was regarded by some of his friends, both Gentile and Jewish, as an aberration that one had to condone in an otherwise sane and worthy man. Brandeis' Zionism sprang from his understanding of an aspect of human existence to which most of his fellow liberals were blind. He understood "that whole peoples have an individuality no less marked than that of single persons, that the individuality of a people is irrepressible, and that the misnamed internationalism that seeks the elimination of nationalities or peoples is unattainable. The new nationalism proclaims that each race or people has a right and duty to develop, and that only through such differentiated development will highest civilization be attained." Brandeis understood in 1916 what some of his fellow Jews did not learn until 1933 and what many a Gentile liberal will never learn. "We Jews," he said, "are a distinct nationality of which every Jew is necessarily a member. Let us insist that the struggle for liberty shall not cease until equal opportunity is accorded to nationalities as to individuals."

It must be emphasized that any program that recognizes the rights of Jews as a nationality and that sees in Zionism a legitimate demand for the recognition of these rights must at the same time support the struggle for the rights of Jews as citizens in the nations in which they are now established or may be established. This strategy is demanded, if for no other reason, because there is no possibility that Palestine will ever absorb all the Jews of the world. Even if it were physically able to absorb them, we know very well that migrations never develop as logically as this. I cannot judge whether Zionist estimates of the millions that a fully developed Palestine could absorb are correct. They seem to me to err on the side of optimism. But in any case it would be fantastic to assume that all Jews could or would find their way to Palestine, even in the course of many centuries.

It is more important, however, to consider what democracy owes to its own ideals of justice and to its own quality as a civilization than what it owes to the Jews. Neither democracy nor any other civilization pretending to maturity can afford to capitulate to the tendency in collective life that would bring about unity by establishing a simple homogeneity. We must not underestimate this tendency as a perennial factor in man's social life. Nor must we fail to understand the logic behind it. Otherwise we shall become involved in the futile task of seeking to prove that minority groups are not really as bad as their critics accuse them of being, instead of understanding that minority groups are thought "bad" only because they diverge from the dominant type and affront that type by their divergence. But to yield to this tendency would be to allow civilization to be swallowed in primitivism, for the effort to return to the simple unity of tribal life is a primitive urge of which nazism is the most consistent, absurd, and dangerous contemporary expression. In the case of the Jews, with their peculiar relation to the modern world and the peculiar contributions that they have made to every aspect of modern culture and civilization, any relaxation of democratic standards would also mean robbing our civilization of the special gifts that they have developed as a nation among the nations.

The necessity for a second strategy in dealing with the Jewish problem stems from certain aspects of the collective life of men that the modern situation has brought into tragic relief. The Jews require a homeland, if for no other reason, because even the most generous immigration laws of the Western democracies will not permit all the dispossessed Jews of Europe to find a haven in which they may look forward to a tolerable future. When I say the most "generous" immigration laws, I mean, of course, "generous" only within terms of political exigencies. It must be observed that the liberals of the Western world maintain a conspiracy of silence on this point. They do not dare to work for immigration laws generous enough to cope with the magnitude of the problem that the Jewish race faces. They are afraid of political repercussions, tacitly acknowledging that their theories do not square with the actual facts. Race prejudice, the intolerance of a dominant group toward a minority group, is a more powerful and more easily aroused force than they dare admit.

A much weightier justification of Zionism is that every race finally has a right to a homeland where it will not be "different," where it will neither be patronized by the "good" people nor subjected to calumny by bad people. Of course many Jews have achieved a position in democratic nations in which the disabilities from which they suffer as a minority group are comparatively insignificant in comparison with the prestige that they have won. A democratic world would not disturb them. Their situation would actually be eased to an even further degree if the racial survival impulse were primarily engaged in Palestine. Religious and cultural divergences alone do not present a serious problem, particularly under traditions of cultural pluralism. But there are millions of Jews, not only in the democratic world, but in the remnants of the feudal world, such as Poland and the Balkans, who ought to have a chance to escape from the almost intolerable handicaps to which they are subjected. One reason why Jews suffer more than any other minority is that they bear the brunt of two divergences from type, religious and racial, and it is idle for the Jews or Gentiles to speculate about which is the primary source of prejudice. Either would suffice, but the prejudice is compounded when both divergences are involved.

Zionist aspirations, it seems to me, deserve a more generous support than they have been accorded by liberal and democratic groups in Western countries. Non-Zionist Jews have erred in being apologetic or even hostile to these aspirations on the ground that their open expression might imperil rights painfully won in the democratic world. Non-Jewish liberals have erred equally in regarding Zionism as nothing but the vestigial remnant of an ancient religious dream, the unfortunate aberration of a hard-pressed people.

Whether the Jews will be allowed to develop a genuine homeland under their own sovereignty, within the framework of the British Empire, depends solely upon the amount of support that they secure in the two great democracies, for those democracies will have it in their power if Hitler is defeated to make the necessary political arrangements. The influence of the American Government will be indirect but none the less effective—which is why American public opinion on this issue cannot be a matter of indifference. It is obviously no easy matter for British statecraft to give the proper assurances and to make basic arrangements for the future while it is forced to deal with a vast and complex Arab world still in danger of falling under the sway of the Nazis. Yet it must be observed that the Arabs achieved freedom and great possessions in the last war, and that this war, in the event of victory for the United Nations, will increase the extent and cohesion of their realm. The Anglo-Saxon hegemony that is bound to exist in the event of an Axis defeat will be in a position to see to it that Palestine is set aside for the Jews, that the present restrictions on immigration are abrogated, and that the Arabs are otherwise compensated.

Zionist leaders are unrealistic in insisting that their demands entail no "injustice" to the Arab population since Jewish immigration has brought new economic strength to Palestine. It is absurd to expect any people to regard the restriction of their sovereignty over a traditional possession as "just," no matter how many other benefits accrue from that abridgment. What is demanded in this instance is a policy that offers a just solution of an intricate problem faced by a whole civilization. The solution must, and can, be made acceptable to the Arabs if it is incorporated into a total settlement of the issues of the Mediterranean and Near Eastern world; and it need not be unjust to the Arabs in the long run if the same "imperial" policy that established the Jewish homeland also consolidates and unifies the Arab world. One may hope that this will not be done by making the Jewish homeland a part of an essentially Arab federation.

It must be noted in conclusion that there are both Jews and Gentiles who do not believe that Palestine is a desirable locus for a Jewish homeland, though they do believe that a homeland must be created. They contend that there is as yet no evidence of Palestine's ability to maintain an independent economic existence without subsidies; that the co-operative agricultural ventures of the Jews, impressive in quality but not in size, offer no hope of a solid agricultural basis for the national economy; that the enmity of the Arab world would require the constant interposition of imperial arms; that the resources of Palestine could not support the millions whom the Zionists hope to settle there; and that the tendency to use Arab agricultural labor may once more create a

Jewish urban caste. It is difficult to know to what degree such criticisms are justified. The fact that 25 per cent of the Jewish settlers in Palestine are engaged in agriculture tends to refute the argument that the Palestinian economy has no adequate agricultural base. The criticism that Palestine cannot, under the most favorable circumstances, absorb all the Jews who must find a new home and security after the war is more serious. However, even if fully borne out, it would not affect the thesis that the Jews require a homeland. It would simply raise the question whether a different or an additional region should be chosen. It is barely possible that a location ought to be found in Europe.

The whole matter is so important that it should be explored by an international commission, consisting of both Jews and Gentiles, both Zionists and non-Zionists. The Jews were the first, as they have been the chief, victims of Nazi fury. Their rehabilitation, like the rehabilitation of every Nazi victim, requires something more than the restoration of the *status quo ante*. We must consider this task one of the most important among the many problems of postwar reconstruction. We cannot, in justice either to ourselves or to the Jews, dismiss it from our conscience.

26.

ZIONISM AND NEO-ZIONISM

Maurice Samuel

It is a pity that we cannot dispense with the word Zionism. It is of recent coinage, and gives the phenomenon to which it refers a false appearance of recentness and simplicity. A true definition of Zionism shows the phenomenon to be old and complex.

Zionism is the activation by wordly means of the Jewish longing for the re-creation of the Jewish State in Palestine. Zerubbabel, Nehemiah, Ezra, and the other exiles who returned to Judea to create the Second Jewish State after the destruction of the First by Babylon were Zionists. The False Messiahs of the exile, of whom Sabbatai Zevi is the best-known, were also Zionists. It follows from this definition that from the point of view of the preservation of Judaism, Zionism can manifest itself destructively as well as constructively; and the Zionism of the nineteenth and twentieth centuries, which I shall call neo-Zionism, has to be assessed accordingly. . . .

[Professor Toynbee's] opposition to neo-Zionism is . . . total and consistent; that is to say, he condemns it from all the contradictory points of view which he adopts from time to time. He regards it as a purely secular phenomenon of particular unholiness, a mixture of the worst features of European nationalism and race delusion; above all, it is to him the systematic effort of the Jewish people (or that part of it which is Zionist and pro-Zionist) to achieve assimilation by another name. In this opposition to Zionism Professor Toynbee displays what

210

may be called a standard or permissible partisanship. It is when he comes to the State of Israel and groups its creators with the Nazis that his position becomes morally and intellectually impermissible. I shall deal first with his ideological objections to neo-Zionism. He writes:

> The ultimate aim of the Zionists is to liberate the Jewish people from the peculiar psychological complex induced by the penalization to which they have been subject for centuries in the Gentile World. In this ultimate aim, the Zionists are at one with the Assimilationist School among the 'emancipated' Jews in the enlightened countries of the West. They agree with the Assimilationists in wishing to cure the Jews of being 'a peculiar people' [II, 252].

The Zionist view is, he says, that

> . . . to be a Jew is to be a human being whose social environment is Jewry. It is an essential part of the Jew's individuality that he is a member of the living Jewish community and an heir to the ancient Jewish tradition. . . . Thus, in the Zionist view, the emancipation *and assimilation* of the Jew as an individual is a wrong method of pursuing a right aim. *Genuine assimilation* is indeed the true solution for the Jewish problem and ought therefore to be the ultimate goal of Jewish endeavors. . . . If they are to succeed in becoming 'like all the nations,' they must seek assimilation on a national and not on an individual basis . . . they must try to assimilate Jewry itself to England and France . . . [II, 253].

Then, assessing the results of the Zionist movement till 1933, he adds:

> Though the Zionist Movement as a practical undertaking is only half a century old, its social philosophy has already been justified by results. In the Jewish agricultural settlements that have been founded in Palestine within the last fifty years, the children of the ghetto have been transformed out of all recognition into a pioneering peasantry which displays many of the characteristics of the Gentile European colonial type in the New World. The Zionists have made no miscalculation in their forecast of the effect which the establishment of a Jewish national home in Palestine would

have upon Jewry itself. The tragic misfortune into which they have fallen, in company with the Mandatory Power, is their inability to arrive at an understanding with the existing Arab population of the country . . . [II, 253f.].

The captivation of the Irish by Nationalism, like the captivation of the Jews by Zionism, signifies the final renunciation of a great but tragic past in the hope of securing in exchange a more modest but perhaps less uncomfortable future [II, 425].

. . . the Turkish legatees of the arrested Ottoman Civilization are today content—like the Zionist legatees of a fossilized Syriac Civilization next door and the Irish legatees of an abortive Far Western Christian Civilization across the street—to live henceforth in comfortable nonentity as a welcome escape from the no longer tolerable status of being 'a peculiar people' [III, 49].

A note on the general tenor of these statements is in order before we proceed to an examination of the neo-Zionist movement. We have already seen that Professor Toynbee considers Judaism to be a fossil relic even though it perpetuates itself by the cultivation of a noble ethos. Now we learn that to lose the fossil status means for the Jews "the final renunciation of a great but tragic past." That the preservation of this past conferred some distinction on the Jews is apparent from the "fact" that in Zionism the Jews (like the Turks in their new nationalism) have chosen to live "*henceforth* in comfortable nonentity." They must accordingly decide whether they will remain a worthless and unsightly archaeological curiosity of distinction or become contented nobodies. This is a hard choice, partly because it is quite unintelligible and partly because "comfortable" is not a very accurate description of the Israeli part of Zionism. Professor Toynbee foresees with confidence that nothing of high value will ever come out of the State of Israel (or the new Turkey), just as he is confident that no high values have come out of the Jewish people in the last two thousand years. What can one do in the face of this double omniscience, historical and prophetic? . . .

In the early and middle part of the nineteenth century there began a movement toward Palestine on the part of extreme orthodox Jews, Russian followers of the Gaon of Vilna, and Hungarian Hassidim, followers of the "Hatam Sofer" [Rabbi Moses Sofer]. They were assisted first by German and Dutch Jewish communities, and later by Sir Moses Montefiore, himself an orthodox Jew, and by scattered groups of Jews

in France and America. These were the Jews who began the modern
city of Jerusalem outside the old walls and, later, the first modern agricultural settlement, Petah Tikvah. There was observable at the same
time, outside the Jewish world, a renewed interest in the idea of the
Restoration as a practical, immediate, mundane enterprise. (For details
see Nahum Sokolow's *History of Zionism,* 1919.)

Once more, let it be noted that these pious Jews did not think of
themselves as the vanguard of a Jewish state. But their action was
taking place in a very different setting from that of the medieval settlers
in the Holy Land. They were fleeing from a Europe that was to all
appearances becoming more habitable for Jews; and they were being
assisted by Jews who, however deluded, believed that their emancipation
in Europe would proceed rapidly from the political to the moral. The
impulse behind this movement, the real beginning of neo-Zionism, long
antedating the appearance of Herzl and the first Zionist Congress, was
the folk feeling that the something drastically new which was needed in
Jewish life was a specific Jewish center in the Holy Land, such as had
not existed hitherto since the Destruction, from which Jewish influence,
not denaturized by assimilative infiltration, might radiate to the Diaspora.

In other words, neo-Zionism was an instinctive countermove on
the part of the Jewish people against the threat of assimilation presented
by specifically modern conditions. Later on, toward the end of the nineteenth century, the philosophy of the "radiating center" was made articulate and systematized in a "secular" neo-Zionism, of which Aḥad Ha-Am
was the first exponent and Chaim Weizmann, like most of his colleagues,
a protagonist. The word "secular" must be taken here in a special sense.
The neo-Zionism of the east European Jews has always been largely
religious in intent even when secular in terminology. The ethos of
Judaism was deeply embedded in it. It would be absurd to say of Weizmann, Bialik, Aḥad Ha-Am, Shmarya Levin, Menahem Mendel Ussis-
skin, and the other east-European Zionist leaders (I will not speak of
the rabbinic leaders) that they were irreligious. They did discard some
of the symbols and terms of accepted orthodoxy; but in effect they were
looking for new symbols and terms for the teaching of the original
God-inspired ethos.

Can the pious Jews of the early period of neo-Zionism, the followers of the Gaon of Vilna and the "Hatam Sofer," be called neo-
Zionists? Let us consider. By their practical efforts in Palestine, by their
unconscious recognition of the need for a new technique of survival,

they assisted the Zionist movement. If they later turned violently on the "secular" and the genuinely secular neo-Zionists, it was not because these wanted to settle in Palestine or help Jews settle there, but because they did not follow the ritualistic observances, did not use the old terminology, and did not subscribe to the Messianist formula of the Restoration. As in medieval times, had tens of thousands followed the original neo-Zionists to Palestine, but with the right ritual and terminology, they would have been welcomed instead of opposed.

It is difficult, again, to define in terms of neo-Zionism the assimilating and semi-assimilating Jews who began giving their financial support to the Jewish Homeland when it became a burning, practical issue. They, like the early pietists who settled in Palestine, did not aim at a Jewish state and did not want one; but they have been just as useful in the creation of the State of Israel. They were drawn into the building up of Jewish Palestine by inescapable philanthropic duty, and again, like the orthodox, they have made their peace with the idea of the Jewish State. Another inevitable change has taken place. The steady raising of funds for Palestine and Israel, though accompanied by a minimum of intelligent pedagogic effort (Hadassah, the Women's Zionist Organization, with its significant influence on the Jewish home, is a notable exception), has awakened in numbers of semi-assimilating American Jews an interest in more than their philanthropic duty; the humanitarian appeal had stimulated a longing, still vague and uninformed, but of mounting intensity, for the fundamentals of Judaism. This is the parallel to which I have already referred between the Diaspora's payment of Temple dues in the Second Jewish State and the Diaspora's participation today in the support of Israel. Here too, as I have mentioned, is one of the explanations, perhaps the most important, of the restless groping among third-generation American Jews for the heritage of the Jewish people.

Neo-Zionism became a battleground when non-orthodox Jews, with the Jewish ethos, but without some of its symbols and dogmas, entered the movement toward Palestine. To what degree these were irreligious or secularist I shall discuss shortly. The conflict deepened when a purely European nationalism, such as Professor Toynbee mistakenly ascribes to neo-Zionism as a whole, and a flatly irreligious and anti-religious element (coming much later) also entered the movement.

Some of Professor Toynbee's observations (and one need not agree with his blanket repudiation of modern nationalism, which has been creative as well as destructive) apply to part of the secularist-nationalist elements in neo-Zionism; what he does here, however, is what the New Testament (with Professor Toynbee following suit) has done with the Pharisees: ignore everything that does not fit in with a negative picture. There are large numbers of neo-Zionists who certainly want the Jewish people, or that part of it which will settle in Israel, to become "like all the nations," and who see it becoming just that. They do not, I think, subscribe to the prophecy that the new nation will be a "comfortable nonentity," but they want to be done with "the peculiar people." . . .

I have been careful to point out . . . that we are dealing with "part of the secular-nationalist element in neo-Zionism." I shall be challenged by those who believe that secular nationalism is vicious through and through, and that all secular nationalists are mobsters. Here one can open an endless debate. One can also debate endlessly whether the Jewish ethos can exist outside of orthodox circles. . . . The Jewish ethos still exists most intensely in orthodox circles, but . . . secular-nationalism can be, and in many places is, consistent with purity of moral purpose and action, and my objection to it (as to atheism) among non-Jews as well as Jews lies in its ultimately fatal pedagogic impotence.

Professor Toynbee asks:

> . . . how was a God-fearing Jewry to reconcile itself with a secular Zionist movement that numbered agnostics among its leaders, and whose program had been inspired, not by the messianic visions of post-Exilic Jewish prophets, but by the blue-prints of a Western Gentile Nationalism whose prophets had been a King Louis XI of France, a King Henry VII of England, and the Florentine publicist Niccolò Machiavelli? [VIII, 300].

This brings us to the heart of the present discussion. We have seen that a God-fearing Jewry has in fact reconciled itself to a Jewish state—that is, unless the Mizraḥi never was, and unless the *Agudat Israel* has ceased to be God-fearing—without reconciling itself to the present leadership of Zionism and Israel. [The *Mizraḥi* and the *Agudat Israel* are orthodox Jewish groups active in the political life of the State of Israel.] But what is the nature of the agnosticism of the "agnostic" leaders, and what is the true character of the secularist branch of the movement?

I have already touched on these phenomena in their extreme manifestations of the right and left, pointing out that they constitute, in the sum, a minority of the Israeli people. They are not representatives of the solid body of so-called Secular Zionism.

If I think of recent secular Zionist leaders and teachers who are no longer among the living—of Herzl, Aḥad Ha-Am, Weizmann, Sokolow, Jabotinsky, Shmarya Levin, Haim Nahman Bialik—I am not able to fasten on a single one of them the label of Agnostic or Atheist in the usual sense of either word, as it could be fastened, for instance, on a Voltaire, a Bradlaugh, a Huxley, or an Ingersoll. The men to whom it properly belongs are to be found only in the Communist-Zionist (strange yoking of words!) group. As to the leaders I have just mentioned by name, they no doubt varied in the degrees of their faith in God, and the least believing was still in some sense a believer. Of Herzl and Jabotinsky it may be said that they became the patron saints of the most secular branch of secular Zionism outside of the Communists; but I am not sure that the followers have not outrun their masters. It should be borne in mind that these two men did not receive the traditional Jewish education in their childhood, and that Herzl acquired very little knowledge of Judaism later, and none at all of Hebrew. Jabotinsky as an adult made good the deficiency as far as the language was concerned. The others were steeped in the tradition; their knowledge of Judaism was both folkist and academic, and it was a knowledge of emotional participation. Their ethos was Jewish.

Their nationalism was not that founded by Louis XI of France, Henry VII of England, and Niccolò Machiavelli. It was the nationalism I have described as felt by the simple Jewish masses. It was interwoven with the Bible—all of them had a deep love of it, and read it continually in the original—and with a sense of a non-secular meaning in human history. It was not based, like the nationalisms of the modern Western countries, on the economic developments of territorial units. It had its economic argumentation in relation to the Jewish position, but it had not grown with the internecine European struggle for markets; it had not followed the line from feudalism to mercantilism, from mercantilism to capitalism. It adapted itself to these stages in the European scene; it did not imbibe post-medieval European nationalism any more than it had imbibed the tradition of medieval chivalry. . . .

A note on Professor Toynbee's treatment of the revival of Hebrew as a spoken language. He cites four other instances of what he calls "linguistic Archaism" in the modern Western World: the Norwegian, the Irish, the Ottoman Turk, and the Greek. He writes:

> Our fifth instance . . . is the reconversion of Hebrew into a ver-
> nacular language of everyday life on the lips and in the ears of the
> Zionist Jews from the Diaspora who have settled in Palestine; and
> this is the most remarkable case of all the five . . . [VI, 70].

This statement is preceded by a satirical reference to the little peoples which, in new-found freedom, or in renaissance, are seeking to re-establish cherished languages, their own. He speaks of

> the laborious and ludicrous expedient of fabricating the 'mother-
> tongue' that they are determined to possess, in the temper of a
> *nouveau-riche* who furnishes himself with portraits of appropriate
> ancestors [VI, 63].

Ignorant of the values to be found in the languages the four other peo-ples are attempting to revive, I will confine myself to the meaning of the rebirth of Hebrew, with the preliminary observation that in this general question the Toynbeean statistical, over-all method of classifica-tion is peculiarly inept and impertinent; each case must be examined separately. Laborious the re-establishment of Hebrew certainly was; it certainly had and has its ludicrous moments—there are always comical episodes in the learning of a language; and Professor Toynbee, with ostentatious shyness, pleads with Greek scholars not to make fun of the Greek poem he has written as a preface to *A Study of History.* (What did he want to do that for?) But those who know from the inside the Judaizing effect that the revival of Hebrew has had on some segments of the Jewish people will be puzzled by Professor Toynbee's metaphor of the "*nouveau riche.*"

Myself an indifferent Hebraist, I was led by the Zionist movement to establish living contact with the language of the Prophets, and if I have indeed to some extent recaptured their message in the original, I am again indebted in a great measure to this contact. *Nouveau riche?* Here is a national heritage considerably older than the English of Pro-fessor Toynbee or even the Greek with which he adorns his opus. He calls the revival of Hebrew the most remarkable of the five instances of "linguistic Archaism," but does not tell us why; and I cannot guess whether he knows as little about the other four as he knows about the fifth. But certainly one section of the Zionist movement was drawn to Hebrew by a spiritual impulse akin to that of Isaiah and Amos, and this is not less true because there are Hebrew-speaking atheists and agnostics —as there were, of course, in the days of Isaiah and Amos. Let us note, too, as one of the fantastic features of this complex movement called Zionism, or neo-Zionism, that many Hebrew-speaking agnostics and atheists, even on the extreme left, cannot rid themselves of the Prophetic Books. I have heard them again and again driven for self-expression to the moral intuitions of the Hebrew Prophets, whom they frequently quote at length by heart while contemptuously denying any intellectual community with them. Is this the Devil quoting Scripture or is it a spiritual anchor to windward? Which is more significant, their quotations or their disclaimers? We may be sure of one thing: the apostates of the time of Isaiah did not go about repeating his moral pronouncements with the passion (and the intellectual confusion) of many Israeli unbelievers.

There were purely practical reasons for the revival of Hebrew as the language of the new homeland which was to gather its inhabitants from the four corners of the earth. Yiddish predominated among the newcomers until recently, and yet it was the Yiddish-speaking neo-Zionists who converted themselves, with a painful effort, into Hebrew-speaking Israelis. They felt that no particular language of the exile, whether Yiddish, or Ladino, or any other, had the right to impose itself on other exile languages. It is an astonishing fact that the—at one time —fanatical opponents of Yiddish in Palestine were Yiddish-speaking neo-Zionists who were tormenting themselves into the use of Hebrew. As a unifier of the fragmented Jewish groups who came into Palestine, Hebrew was strategically indispensable. . . .

But the most powerful reasons for the cultivation of Hebrew were of a spiritual practical nature. There was felt to be a profound impropriety in a reunion of the Jewish people and the Holy Land which did not also include a reunion with Hebrew, the language in which the spiritual self-consciousness of the Jewish people had crystallized with this landscape as background. That secularists and even leftists and avowed unbelievers, as against a dwindling group of the super-orthodox, should have shared this feeling with orthodox Jews is another of the fascinating oddities of neo-Zionism; and this is what gives a special coloration to the "secularism" of a great many Zionists. It is a secularism tinged with a corrective nostalgia for the tradition.

Of all this Professor Toynbee glimpses nothing. Nor does it ever occur to him that in re-establishing Hebrew as a living language the neo-Zionists have opened to the world a pathway to the original sources of the faith of the Western World. But I am forgetting. Professor Toynbee is allergic to this "old-fashioned Syriac oracle."

27.

CHRISTIANS AND THE MIDEAST CRISIS

Willard G. Oxtoby

When is attack not aggression? When it is self-defense. And self-defense, it seems, has all along been the position of both Moshe Dayan and Gamal Abdel Nasser, of Israeli and Arab alike. Though the shooting has stopped (at least for the time being), the war of words goes on in the continuing story of the Middle East as it has done for decades. From the United Nations and diplomatic circles, from pulpits and editorial pages issue appeals to the principles of morality, decency and justice. Speaking individually or officially, people agree that self-defense is legitimate but differ as to whether particular acts in the recent Arab-Israeli war were self-defense. They agree that there has been more than enough violence but disagree as to the steps to be taken to forestall further violence.

In the Arab-Israeli clash of 1967, the combatants were primarily Jew and Moslem, and political leaders on both sides appealed to religious sympathy and tradition and skillfully manipulated these in support of the war effort. But this was Christendom's war too; or at least a fair number of people were trying to make it so—morally if not theologically.

Christian leaders have been called on, and no doubt will continue to be called on, to adjudicate the moral issues of the Holy Land. They form a "third party" in the bargaining, though they are far from being as disinterested as one might wish. A typical pro-Israeli appeal to

Christians was the three-quarter-page ad published in the *New York Times* on Sunday, June 4, the day before the Israeli attack. Headed "The Moral Responsibility in the Middle East"—the moral responsibility being "to support Israel's right of passage through the Straits of Tiran"—the ad declared that the threat to peace lay in "the recent Arab military mobilization along Israel's borders." "Let us recall," the ad continued, "that Israel is a new nation whose people are still recovering from the horror and decimation of the European holocaust." As the next six days were to prove, Israel was not so decimated that it had not been able to mobilize an army of men—and women! Presumably the signers of the ad—including such luminaries as John C. Bennett, Martin Luther King, Reinhold Niebuhr and Robert McAfee Brown— did not view Israel's own mobilization as a threat to peace.

That Israel took the offensive in the war only increased the pressure on Christian leaders for moral support. In city after city, representatives of the churches were called on to share the platform at meetings and rallies with rabbis and public officials and to affirm that Israel's cause was just. Clergymen were urged to assert what only a jurist or a Near Eastern specialist could competently assert, that the Israeli attack was not aggression but legitimate self-defense.

This is nothing new. Over the years pro-Israeli interests have systematically cultivated the Christian clergy. Until the mid-'50s, when it was exposed as a Zionist front and so discredited, the so-called American Christian Palestine Committee worked unremittingly to convince church leaders of Israel's moral and biblical claims to the territory she won by force of arms in 1948. Clergymen were offered free trips to the Holy Land, and during the past decade other agencies have continued an Intourist-type treatment for ecclesiastical V.I.P.s visiting Israel. Thus we have a generation of church leaders schooled not to raise questions when Israel's 1948 war is called the "war of liberation." Apparently they are unaware that some crucial and embarrassing facts about that war have been swept under the red carpet.

Of course, there have been appeals from the other side. But these are mainly humanitarian—appeals for the relief, however minimal, of the thousands of refugees and other Palestinian Arabs who lost their livelihood in the war of 1948. (In the past month, incidentally, the number of refugees has increased by perhaps 100,000.) The focus is on the human need for two reasons: first, because it is immediate; second, because it is nonpolitical. Whereas Zionist political and philan-

thropic activities in the United States go hand in hand, American chari-
table and educational organizations working in Arab countries feel the
need to remain scrupulously aloof from politics, lest there be a legal
challenge to their philanthropic endeavors. The net effect is that the
churches have been frightened away from any pro-Arab position. The
refugees are dealt with as a virtually unexplained fact, and it is left to
the individual to ask why they are refugees at all.

Indeed, the churches have been remiss in regard to the refugee
problem. When the first phase of the recent war erupted, the church
agencies and boards apparently were concerned chiefly for the safety of
their personnel stationed in the Arab countries. The evacuation of these
people made it impractical for the churches to commit themselves to
extensive relief operations. Only on the 13th day of the crisis did timid
TV coverage of Christian interests appear. Informed individuals in the
churches campaigned here and there, but as of the last week of June
official church support for the Arabs in their time of suffering remained
seemingly sporadic.

The first public appeal for refugee relief appeared in the *New
York Times* on the 20th day after the war began. Paid by private persons, this appeal called for contributions to three secular organizations
working through United Nations channels. UNRWA, with an international staff already on the scene, was during the early weeks of the
crisis better prepared than the American churches to offer aid; yet it
took three weeks to muster support even for UNRWA. Meanwhile,
appeals for support of Israel had been broadcast throughout the U.S.

The Middle East crisis poses several problems for Christian ethics.
One is how to support the desire of both Israelis and Palestinian Arabs
for an assurance of national and personal peace and security. Even
more difficult is the problem raised by U.S. national interest in the
Middle East. Coming after a couple of winters of theological discontent
with our military involvement in Vietnam, the question of what should
be the nature of our involvement in the Middle East will doubtless
prompt lively discussion when seminaries resume classes in the fall.

Comparisons of U.S. policy in the Middle East and in Vietnam
have swirled on editorial pages across the land. Seldom have newspapers had so much free copy from professionals. Historian Barbara
Tuchman fired one of the first salvos in a letter appearing in the *New
York Times* (and also in the *Washington Post*) on May 30. Claiming
that Israel, as representing the source of the Judeo-Christian tradition,

concerns America more nearly than South Vietnam, Mrs. Tuchman argued that our government's standing by while the Gulf of Aqaba was blockaded was "the ultimate paralysis of power." "Futile fiddling" in the "cynical farce" of the United Nations is useless, she said, for "the family of nations is an illusion with which we comfort ourselves like a teething-ring." The fate of the Western democracies hangs on "independent action in support of our stated policy [which] is not intervention, nor is it something to be afraid of."

Three days later the *New York Times* published a reply by David Lelyveld, who described Mrs. Tuchman's "discussion of the issue as a question of American 'prestige' and a battle between higher civilization and lesser breeds" as

> a return to the rhetoric of the era of high imperialism which she usually writes about. What is saddening is that respected public leaders like Martin Luther King who have courageously opposed American actions in Vietnam should now associate themselves with vague calls for American intervention on behalf of Israel.

Now the fat was in the fire. How could the Vietnam dove be the Israel hawk? Most liberal intellectuals, following Mrs. Tuchman, argued that our interests were more seriously threatened in the Middle East. It is astonishing that for three weeks practically no one engaged in the hawk-dove discussion suggested that our commitment to Israel had been, or ought to be, anything less than unlimited.

The issue was put clearly on June 25 by Yale's David Little in his important letter to the *Times*:

> Neither is our commitment to South Vietnam as "minimal" as is alleged, nor is our commitment to Israel as "maximal" as is implied. . . . Our commitments do not obligate us to support, or even to condone, Israel's patent acts of expansionism, particularly against Jordan. . . . Self-defense in both the case of Vietnam and of Israel seems to be a just cause. In neither case may arbitrary expansionism be so designated. . . . Premier Eshkol's recent declaration which implied that Israel alone is "entitled to determine what are [its] true and vital interests and how they shall be secured" . . . is a cynical doctrine that undermines the notions of justice and law.

Why, during June, did so many of our liberals urge American support of Israel? Mainly because they saw Israel as the bastion of democracy in the Middle East. Israel, they declared, is our only friend, a bulwark against Russian influence in the Middle East—despite the evidence that the spread of Russian influence there is a result of America's long-standing favoritism toward Israel. Or, they said, Israel is a showplace of progressive Western ways—despite the fact that the capital required for technology has been uniquely available to Israel and that comparison of living standards in, say, Gaza Strip or Jordan (which have had so much less U.S. aid per capita) with those in Israel is acutely offensive to Arabs, who would develop a technology if they had the capital. Or again, they said that Israel is the only nation seeking peace in the Middle East—despite Israel's defiance of U.N. peace-keeping efforts for these 19 years, despite the speed with which she seems to have exhausted all alternatives to armed attack when Nasser closed the Straits of Tiran, and despite her delay in matching the Jordanian cease-fire until she had achieved her military objectives.

While Israel was winning the war, Secretary Dean Rusk stated America's position: "neutrality in thought, word, and deed." One wonders whether Washington would have been so calm if the Egyptians had deliberately torpedoed an American ship, if the Syrians had struck deep into Israel, if the Jordanians had systematically demolished an Israeli hospital or looted a museum or executed children at a boys' school. Our "neutrality" was partiality, the effects of which on future American-Arab relations can only be catastrophic.

Language of this sort, indeed even the mildest criticism of Israel, raises still a third cluster of problems for Christians: Christian-Jewish relationships on the American scene. The current crisis has revealed Jewish loyalties whose passionate intensity few Christians had been aware of.

Note first the genuinely gratifying advances that have been made in interfaith relationships among us. In the past two decades especially, we have witnessed a "coming of age" of the American Jewish community. The old barriers of prejudice have been falling away in most neighborhoods and professions. No longer are Jews "strange" people. Ours has become a religiously and culturally pluralistic world in which Jews are intelligent, talented neighbors. In this we rejoice.

But many of us Christians assume that Jews are almost exactly like us religiously, too—a naive and even pernicious assumption which, though it may seem to make for brotherhood, is based largely on ignorance. What separates Jews and Christians, alike heirs of Moses and the Prophets? Apart from the status of Jesus, not much, we have thought. The messiahship of Jesus is central to the Christian understanding of man and of God. Hence Judaism appears to be a rejection of the heart of Christianity, a kind of hereditary Unitarianism. But such a view fails utterly to convey a *Jewish* understanding of man and God. To discover the heart of Judaism we must shift the focus from the messiahship of Jesus to the peoplehood of Israel.

In the rich complex of religious connotations attached to the idea of Jewish peoplehood two main themes are survival and suffering. Over the millenniums the scattered people of the Jews has clung to this religious tradition and this sense of national identity as the fortunes of politics drove it from land to land. In modern times the tradition has been realized in the State of Israel. But to the Jew the triumphs of the people are a sign of divine favor and its tragedies a divine testing. Nobody who watched the Shavuoth observances televised from the Wailing Wall in June could miss the note of tragedy underlying the song of triumph. The trauma inflicted on the Jew in 20th century Europe intensifies his feeling of urgency about a homeland, and as long as this feeling is alive there is slim chance of a reaffirmation of the American Reform rabbis' 1885 Pittsburgh platform: "We are no longer a nation but a spiritual community and therefore expect no return to Palestine."

Thus while in the Christian's view the State of Israel is simply a political fact, for many Jews it is also a profoundly religious fact. That explains why by mid-June fund drives for Israel launched in the United States had brought in more than twice the amount she was reported to have spent on the June 5-10 battle. For example, a synagogue in Connecticut contributed the $10,000 it had salted away for its building fund. A Jewish businessman who led in organizing an Israel rally is reported as saying that he didn't know much about the Bible or about Middle Eastern politics but that for him giving to Israel is a *mitzvah,* a religious obligation.

For many American Jews, Zionism functions as a defense against assimilation to modern secular culture. They have no particular interest in traditional theology and ritual observance, but their community can achieve a sense of meaning and relevance by rallying around a tangible campaign. American Jews who feel guilty for having escaped the suffering of their European fellow Jews can atone by sacrificing financially now. Israel is the answer to European Jewry's need for a haven *for* everyday life, but it also meets American Jewry's need for a haven *from* the secular embrace of everyday life. That is to say, what is secular nationalism in Israel is piety in America. American Christians, so accustomed to doctrinal formulations of religion, have generally failed to grasp the nature of Jewish loyalty. And in the eyes of their brethren those American Jews who steadfastly object to political involvement with Israel are victims of an unduly spiritual (i.e., American) concept of religion.

Thus we can understand why American Jews view as a personal affront any criticism of the State of Israel. In the eyes of many such criticism amounts to a blasphemous attack on their religious identity, almost as we would regard an attack on Christ. To assert that Israel has no historic claim to Palestine is to deny the Jew's interpretation of Scripture. To assert that Israel has no moral claim to Arab land is to deny the Jew compensation for Auschwitz and Buchenwald and thus to question divine justice. To assert that Israel had inadequate provocation for launching its preventive attack in June is to cast doubt on the fact of Jewish suffering and thereby on the "sacramental theology" which undergirds the fund drives. To suggest that Israel deserves no support from religious men because it inflicted suffering through acts of premeditated brutality is to question the concept of Jewish peoplehood. And, finally, to liken Israel's militancy to the Germans', the annexation of Old Jerusalem to Hitler's *Anschluss,* is the unpardonable sin.

All of which is to say that anything short of total commitment to the rightness of Israel's cause is interpreted as anti-Semitism. As a matter of fact, even the grass-roots anti-Semites of the radical right have been silent of late, probably because our "enemy," the Soviet Union, supports the Arabs. All the same, the Anti-Defamation League of B'nai B'rith, a body generally distinguished for liberality and intellectual integrity, has seemed downright paranoid in the current crisis. For example: Arthur Spiegel, Connecticut regional director for the A.D.L., commenting on William Buckley's protest against the league's monitoring of broadcasts, declared that Buckley "never lets a fact get in the way of his obsessive hatred of the A.D.L."—a remark irrelevant to the crisis at best and a piece of defamation at worst. Again, Arnold Forster, B'nai B'rith general counsel, dismissed Arab spokesman Mohammad T. Mehdi as "an Iraqi citizen who refuses American naturalization" and declared that "as a guest in this country Mehdi should refrain from criticizing activities of its citizens"—surely neither an invitation to examine the substance of Mehdi's statements nor a suggestion that American Jewish comments on developments in Iraq were off limits.

Jewish spokesmen have directed their scorn not only at political conservatives and "irresponsible Arab propagandists"; they have blasted the mainline churches whose clergy have been brotherhood-minded for years. For example, on June 22 Rabbi Balfour Brickner, director of Reform Judaism's Commission on Interfaith Activities—a normally cordial quarter—denounced the "Christian establishment" as silent "on support for the integrity of the State of Israel." To counter "these failures on behalf of the Christian church," he said, "let us first talk about Israel and its role in the life of the Jew. . . . Understanding the very existence of the Jew precedes any interfaith conversations we might wish to have about Christian-Jewish understanding of conscience, morality or worship."

This, then, is the church's dilemma. For many Jews this war is a holy war. But is it therefore a holy war for Christians? In interfaith matters it is one thing to understand, quite another to agree. Anti-Semitism has to do with the spirit in which criticism is given; it must not be equated with the fact of disagreement.

Christians, clearly, have moral concerns besides the concern for interfaith harmony. The concern for truth and justice, in my opinion, overrides the concern for harmony. Hence outright disagreement with Israel's carefully planned conquest of June 1967 is required of us. Christians must defy pressure on them to sit by silently, muzzled by the fear of being called anti-Semitic.

Besides caring for the hundreds of thousands of blamelessly suffering Palestinian Arabs and working to end their suffering through resettling them somewhere (even in America), the churches must look toward the preservation of free speech in our nation, in fact as well as in law. The right of dissent—staunchly defended by religious and secular intellectuals in respect to other issues—has been effectively suppressed in respect to the current crisis.

The powerful pressures which have made it possible for subtle pro-Israeli evaluations to pass as fact in the news have also caused even the most restrained mediating position to be assessed as Arab propaganda. For a time, virtually the only place in North America where the Arabs could be heard was the U.N. Official Washington, sensitive to the opinions of the voters, appears unable to penetrate the smokescreen of Israeli self-righteousness through which the Arab picture comes and seems ready to sacrifice American interests in the Arab world. Included in such a sacrifice would be Christian educational, medical and evangelistic work built up over the past hundred years.

But the Christian losses will not only be overseas. Here in America, church leaders have unwittingly played into the hands of a militant foreign nationalism. So far as they have been victims of slanted sources of information they may perhaps be pardoned—Bennett on mobilization, Eugene Carson Blake on control of the Old City, any Christian spokesman who confers his blessing on Israel's nationalistic excesses. But so far as they have been victims, so far they cast doubt on the reliability of the church's official judgments.

28.

THE DEVIL AND YOM KIPPUR

A. Roy Eckardt

Following upon the Six-Day War I was enabled to present in *Midstream* an interpretation of the meaning of Israel for me. I was impelled to lament the persisting anti-Semitism of the Christian world of which I am a part. I shall not duplicate that testimony or that lamentation, although I should like to reaffirm the former and I am forced to stay with the latter. (It may be that between the Six-Day War and the Yom Kippur War the devil's armies within the Christian community were forced to retreat a little; I incline to leave that kind of assessment to the experts and to the public and community relations people.)

It is now several months since the Arabs' warfare, and indeed the world's warfare, was once again visited upon the Jewish people. In the context of the Yom Kippur War the immediate connotation of the title of this essay is the demonic utilizing of holy times for unholy purposes. But that point has been made by others. I should like to move in a quite different direction, introducing certain considerations that are much less evident and much more arguable, but a direction that will fully vindicate the title.

With other interpreters, Jewish and Christian, and in the interests of an intended fairness, I have in the past been careful to distinguish between anti-Semitism (*Judenfeindschaft,* enmity toward Jews) and anti-Zionism/anti-Israelism. I now believe that the distinction is no longer permitted. The major reason is that the distinction has come to be utilized by the enemies of Jews for the sake of their nefarious purposes. The distinction has been captured by ideology. How repeatedly in recent months have we been assailed by the allegation that defenders of Israel are always trying to confuse things by linking criticisms of that country with anti-Semitism! The allegation remains false; it is a ploy that comes straight from the devil. To fall prey to it would be to give a victory to him. For the anti-Semites could then continue to castigate Israel with total impunity, and their opponents would have to keep silent. (The devil has always sought to abolish free speech.)

In its January 21, 1973 number *Time* published three letters responding to its December 31, 1973 account of Father Daniel Berrigan's tirade of last fall against Israel. A Jewish reader understood Berrigan's speech as one more example of the exploiting of hatred through the development of anti-Semitism. The president of the Association of Arab-American University Graduates identified Berrigan's statement about Israel as "added testimony to his courage and sincerity as an advocate of peace and justice." And a gentile reader denied that Berrigan is an anti-Semite "of any kind," and then denounced Rabbi Arthur Hertzberg's rejoinder to Berrigan for its linking of criticism of Israel with anti-Semitism. Of the three, the third letter is, I think, the really significant one. That the gentile reader could so readily falsify the rabbi's rejoinder (Hertzberg did *not* link criticism of Israel with anti-Semitism; he linked Berrigan's lies with anti-Semitism) was made possible by the ploy above described. With respect to Israel, today's anti-Semites seem to "have it made"; their acts of hatred against Jews can be effectively camouflaged by the protest that, after all, the State of Israel is not immune to criticism. Here is another in the infinity of cases where the devil uses moral truth—who could possibly plead the exemption of any nation-state from criticism?—in order to advance his lying purposes against Jews. The simple fact stands that the would-be destruction of Israel involves the would-be destruction of the Jewish people. The two acts are of the one evil piece. So let us call anti-Israelism and anti-Zionism by their correct name: anti-Semitism. (If the responsibilities of discriminating analysis demand a qualifying expression, we need merely refer to anti-Semitism in its anti-Israeli dimension.)

The question of God pursues the Jewish people as it pursues us all. Men suffer. But it is Jews who, in Martin Buber's idiom, uniquely feel the lack of redemption against their skin and taste it on their tongue. What is the Jew to do before the fact of the Holocaust and its intended repetition through the destruction of Israel? Is the Jew to cast God away (cf. Richard L. Rubenstein) or is he to affirm God in spite of all (cf. Emil L. Fackenheim)? Yet it is not primarily the question of God to which I here address myself. I allude to the question of God more than once, but I do so in the context of its powerful analogy to the question of the devil: Are we to deny the fact of the devil, or are we condemned (or at least required) to assent to the devil's reality? The abiding persecution of the Jews of the Middle East, as elsewhere, surely burdens us with the question of God. But to me at this time, early in 1974, the much more terrible and vital question is that of the devil.

"God" is our imperative symbol for the absolutely unique power of righteousness and creativity; "devil" is the symbol of the absolutely unique power of evil and destructiveness, a symbol possessed, therefore, of comparable necessity with "God." The devil is not the reality of "evil" in any abstract or generalized sense; he is other than the power of evil as such (just as God is anything but generalized goodness or divineness). The devil is the totally unique power that concentrates upon totally unique evil. But is there an evil in this world that is totally unique? Yes. That evil is called anti-Semitism (as explained below). The point is, the "devil" and "anti-Semitism" are correlative realities: anti-Semitism is born of the devil, and the devil receives his sustenance from anti-Semitism. The elucidation or disclosure of the devil is required etiologically and existentially because the hatred of Jews is not, in essence, a matter of evil as such, but is *this* evil, an evil absolutely incomparable and absolutely incredible (just as the choice of the Jews by God is absolutely incredible, the one totally unique act of salvation in this world). Incredibility is normally or linguistically the opposite of credibility, but it is not necessarily the opponent of truth. To speak of the unbelievable destiny of the Jews is somehow to testify to God, for he is the unbelievably unique One. Were the divine election of the Jews comparable to other elections, we should have to settle for "the factor of the gods" or some other mundane explanation. In the same way, were the ongoing persecution of Jews comparable to other persecutions, we should have to settle for "the element of evil forces" or some equally mundane explanation. But there is nothing like anti-Semitism. Accordingly, we have no choice but to speak of the devil.

From the above it follows that within one frame of reference, and one frame of reference alone, the devil is to be denominated "god": he is the god of anti-Semitism.

I have referred to the "reality" of the devil, but this is a manner of speaking. Strictly, and on the basis of the ontological gulf between God and the devil, it is more accurate to speak of the devil's "unreality." But I cannot here offer an exhaustive clarification or "defense" of the devil. The doubter would probably remain unconvinced—as men tend to be unaffected by "proofs" for God. I may be permitted, however, to add one literary and substantive gloss: the devil does not deserve a capital "D." In point of truth, he deserves nothing.

There are no parallels to anti-Semitism. It is not a question of "human prejudice" in a general sense. For whether we speak of time or space, of temporal enduringness or geopolitical pervasiveness, no "prejudice" comes anywhere near to anti-Semitism. Various forms of prejudice remain, by contrast, fleeting and localized; they are instances of historical transience and spatial contingency. The kingdom of God extends to mankind, yet God sustains his chosen people. So too the devil covets a universal kingdom, and so too he retains his elected ones, his "faithful remnant," his special witnesses. These are the anti-Semites. Through the millennia and across all boundaries the devil's faithful persist. Men and nations who are normally foes always have the opportunity to join hands, in the devil's peace, against the one foe, the Jew. Membership in the religion of anti-Semitism is ever open to all. It is the only universal faith. The language of anti-Semitism is the devil's native tongue; it quickly becomes the second language of the devil's disciples, and soon it takes command of their original language.

Thus, the one substantive or operative bond that unites or can unite the disparate Arab peoples is the surety that Israel is the world enemy. In this, the Muslim-Arab entity has become, fantastically, the heir of centuries of Christendom, with its persuasion that the Jews, and only the Jews, are engaged in a conspiracy against humanity. An even more fantastic (though not unrelated) heir—and because of its larger scope and great power an infinitely more threatening heir—is the United Nations, which has become the operative center of world anti-Semitism. Just before his premature death Robert Alden described in *The New York Times* the anti-Israeli tone in that body. Alden saw the expressed anti-Jewishness as reflective of a seething hostility brewing for many years. Before the packed chamber of the Security Council, Yakov Malik of the Soviet Union spoke recently of the Israelis as "murderers and international gangsters"—whereupon the room exploded into prolonged applause (an act normally frowned upon in the chamber). One delegate said of the atmosphere in the Council, "At times I felt that I was in the middle of a lynch mob." But the incredible thing was the date of the meeting: four days after the Arabs initiated the Yom Kippur War.

When in the history of humanity has there been a counterpart to such spectacles? These are the "highest councils" of the nations! The international wrath reserved for Israel is unparalleled in time and place.

Part of the devil's work is the confusing of identities, including his very own identity. Were the State of Israel to die, many parties would be thrown into disarray and metaphysical despair. This would surely happen to the Arab nations for whom Israel is identified as the devil. These real disciples of the devil would face the dreadful trauma that the devil had died. How could they then endure their continuing distresses as human beings? Members of the United Nations would be confronted by a similar crisis. What would the delegation from the Soviet Union do without Israel? Massive disorientation would occur. A typical sermon of Yakov Malik reads: "Like savage, barbaric tribes, in their mad destruction they [the Jews] have annihilated, destroyed and tried to remove from the surface of the earth cities, villages, the cultural heritage of mankind. They have ravaged entire civilizations." (One need not be a psychoanalyst to discern in the above sermon a quite accurate description of the history of the Soviet Union through the simple substitution of "Russians" for "Jews.") With a non-existent Israel, Comrade Malik would be forced to change his entire theme. For his is an international pulpit, where the behavior of states is the only proper universe of discourse. Apart from Israel, the Jews are not of much utility to Malik. But perhaps he would recover, and offer a variation upon his favorite theme: the abolition of a visible Israel has been a clever Jewish plot to confound, and ultimately to ravage, humanity.

We are beset by the incomparably horrible proposition that the devil acts to deceive the world into seeing in the Jew his own incarnation. This is the only masquerade that is possible for him. For who, then, could ever accuse him of being the real father of anti-Semitism? His masquerade is an absolute necessity. But the knife cuts two ways and the truth comes out: that the Jewish people are uniquely and unremittingly accused of being the devil proves that anti-Semitism is the absolutely unique work of the devil. Only the devil could stoop to the demonic depth of claiming the Jew as his singular confrere.

One familiar and viable way of living with the shattering truth that God is relentlessly our judge yet infinitely our font of mercy is through the assurance that he afflicts the comfortable and comforts the afflicted. The devil, by contrast, afflicts the afflicted and comforts the comfortable. He is the wellspring of every false prophet (i.e., lying spirit; cf. I Kings 22:21-23). The main difference between the behavior of God and the behavior of the devil is that God grieves over his people's suffering while the devil delights in that suffering. The building-blocks of the reestablished State of Israel are the dried tears that God shed during the Holocaust. Between 1933 and 1945 the devil spent his days and nights convulsed in laughter. Those who strike men when they are down are agents of evil; those who strike Jews when they are down are agents of the devil.

The enigma of true versus false prophecy is resolved in the triad of God, devil, and *kairos* ("right time"). In the community of Pennsylvania in which I work there lives a man who writes to local newspapers expressing deep hostility to Israel. But he does so only under one exacting condition. By actual count, the letters appear immediately after the Jewish people have experienced tragedy and suffering at the hands of their enemies. The man has been doing this for seven years. His real name is Satan.

Why is Father Daniel Berrigan also to be numbered among the devil's elect? Because he afflicts the afflicted Jews. His diatribe against the Jewish people—Israel is essentially a criminal community, a racist state like Nazi Germany, a manufactory of human waste that seeks "a biblical justification for crimes against humanity"—was not even delivered in a (mythical) time of Israeli well-being. Berrigan chose a moment of intense suffering shared by Jews around the world. Moreover, the unvalidated lies were delivered in the company of Israel's avowed enemies. Had Berrigan expressed a given criticism of Israel (as many Israelis and Jews themselves do)—let us say the criticism that she does not do enough for her Oriental Jews or for her Arab citizens —and had he done so amidst a (theoretical) time of prosperity and peace for her, Berrigan might have qualified as a true prophet. But to condemn Israel in the very hour of her aloneness and peril—Berrigan's speech was delivered on October 19, 1973—is to be taught by the devil. "Do not attack the attacker; attack the Jewish victim; do it while the Jew is 'down' "—here are cardinal entries in the devil's manual of instructions. The anti-Semites sometimes stay in the woodwork—as long as little attention is being paid to Israel. The correct time to come forth is when Israel's physical existence has just been subjected to possible abolishment.

In alluding to Father Berrigan, I should not wish to give the impression that such manifestations among Christians are limited only to the Roman Catholic Church. I still remember with revulsion and horror the declaration in July, 1967 by a former (Presbyterian) teacher of mine, Henry P. Van Dusen, that the Israeli response to Arab action in the Six-Day War was like unto the *Blitzkrieg* and behavior of the Nazi hordes. And in 1973 another (United Methodist) teacher of mine, a theologian named Robert E. Cushman, now at the Duke Divinity School, also waited for the devil's *kairos*. Professor Cushman's *kairos* was identical with Berrigan's: the period immediately after the occasion of the Yom Kippur War. Cushman's thesis is that Israel is not worth all the trouble she causes us. The price of Israel's existence is simply too high. In "the order of international justice" American support for the State of Israel is without wisdom and without right. It contravenes the Jeffersonian dictum of "decent respect to the opinion of mankind." Cushman is in effect seeking here to guide gentiles back beyond their Christianity into paganism. The pagan enticement of Cushman has done two things for him: it has blinded him to the truth that "the opinion of mankind" often stands in direct contradiction to what is right; and it has enabled him to replace the Christian norm of self-sacrifice with the pagan readiness to sacrifice the lives of other human beings, and more especially Jews.

God judges his people in their sins; the devil judges the Jews whenever others sin against them. Were God to afflict the comfortless, he would turn into the devil (many Jews in the "kingdom of night" and at other times have seriously asked whether God had become the Evil One). Were the devil to afflict the comfortable, he would become as God. The primary working distinction between God and the devil is not so much that God does what is right and the devil does what is wrong. The decisive thing is that God does what is right at the right time, whereas the devil supplants required mercy with ruthless judgment.

We are provided with a most decisive criterion for adjudging when criticisms of Jews and Israel comprise or do not comprise anti-Semitism. Everything depends upon the timing.

In carrying forward his work, the devil pays tribute to virtue and justice, although only in characteristically diabolic ways. We are assured that the Jew is not the victim after all! There must be something about the Jew as "victim" that justifies the attack upon him. One of the devil's time-dishonored insights is the finding that, secretly, the Jew always remains the victor, the conqueror. The Jew only *seems* to be "down," to be weak; for this is how he conceals his power. His reputed suffering is an insidious weapon for obscuring the Jewish world-conspiracy. (As Berrigan points out, it is *millionaires* and *generals* and *entrepreneurs* who sustain powerful Israel, that supposedly weak little nation.) Here is the reason why the right time to subject the "victim" to deserved condemnation is precisely when the Jewish nation comes under military or "terrorist" attack. Justice must be done! Traditionally, he who starts wars is the culpable party. But in the case of the Jews, and only the Jews, the "victims" of "aggression" are, in actuality, the aggressors, the ones to be brought to trial and punished. Alone among all nations, Israel is to return territory captured from an invading antagonist. This is because Israel is the real invader.

It is clear, then, why the occasion of "suffering" (it is only the *appearance* of suffering; Jews never really suffer; they are too powerful for that) becomes the time to inflict rightful suffering ("rightful" as defined by, and the peculiar obligation of, the devil). Hence, the policy of waiting to attack Israel until she has been attacked and is on the edge of seeming destruction is the one sane course and the one just course. The policy follows logically from the insight that the Jew's threat to mankind is greatest when, to surface appearances, he is at his weakest. It is the victim who is the real menace.

The devil requires total commitment, purity of action and belief. But are Messrs. Berrigan, Cushman, Van Dusen et al. entirely faithful to the devil's program in all its carefulness? We have been concentrating upon their one qualification: the readiness instantly to afflict Jews whenever Jews are afflicted. But in one fateful respect these protagonists are not good soldiers of the devil: their denunciations of the Jews are totally open and public. This must be upsetting to their master. Does it not constitute a threat to the secrecy of his operation? The devil does his best not to expose himself openly in struggles between right and wrong.

His higher method is evenhandedness, neutrality. His ultimate strategy is to deny that he ever takes sides—indeed, to insist that sides not be taken. This accords with his essential aim to convince the world of his non-existence. The method also enables him to claim purity of motive: Who would ever dare to gainsay fairmindedness?

Consequently, in our search for truly faithful disciples of the devil we must turn to such an establishment as the World Council of Churches and such a publication as *The Christian Century*. With the Yom Kippur War both the Council and the *Century* fully observed the devil's *kairos* all right but they did so after the devil's peculiar fashion. Through Philip Potter, its general secretary, the World Council of Churches' response to the heinous Arab attack on October 6 was to offer a plea for peace. Underneath the "evenhandedness" lay a message of approval of Arab holy wars. For in its statement of October 17, 1973, the Council totally avoided the issue of Israel's survival and made no mention whatsoever of the Arab attack. (Reading the statement, a chance visitor from another planet would be left wondering how the war could possibly have started.) Johan M. Snoek, executive secretary of the World Council of Churches' Consultation on the Church and the Jewish People advised his fellow-members that on the basis of discussions, "also with friends from Israel" (*sic!*), it was decided not to issue a public statement; instead attention was drawn to a letter in *The Times* (London) by a British churchman counseling the avoidance of any laying of blame in the Israeli-Arab conflict. Representatives of the devil are strictly forbidden to condemn morally any attack upon Jewish lives.

The procedure followed by *The Christian Century,* Protestantism's most influential weekly in this country, was to issue an editorial polemic against onesidedness. Readers were advised that the Christian's instinctive and "natural affinity" for Israel (*sic!*) can never justify "an automatic assumption that the Israeli government's position is correct." There simply cannot be any "emotional taking of sides" in the Middle East conflict. "Our Jewish friends" must stop demanding "absolute commitment" to their side, absolute commitment to Israel in a religious sense. The editor-in-chief, James M. Wall, subsequently wrote that the way to provide support for Israel is by retaining an "equally powerful commitment to the Palestinian Arabs—Christian and Muslim—who seek freedom and self-determination." Wall perpetuated and reenforced established *Century* "evenhandedness": "there are no 'sides' to be taken" in the Middle East.

238 A. ROY ECKARDT

However, while the devil is clever, he is not all that clever. Or at least his cleverness is not able to abrogate the divine insistence that men are responsible beings who are required to make responsible moral judgments. As the true prophet Reinhold Niebuhr declared, "the essence of immorality is the evasion or denial of moral responsibility." The context of this particular declaration was Dr. Niebuhr's call for the repeal of this country's Neutrality Act of 1939 on the ground of its immorality, an immorality accentuated, as he put it, "by the misguided idealism which was evoked" to support the act.

Further, the devil is not clever enough finally to succeed in sowing complete confusion respecting what it means to "take sides." Over a number of years *The Christian Century* editors have charged that Jewish criticisms of the Christian world "erroneously assume that Christian commitment to Judaism and Israel requires hostility to Arabs. This charge together with the related allegation cited above that Jews demand absolute commitment to Israel in a religious sense comprise fairly pedestrian representations of a traditional technique of the devil: utilization of the Big Lie. But the morally crucial truth is that all that Israel's advocates are asking is the right for her to live in peace in ways no different from any other people. To be pledged to equal rights for two antagonists is the diametrical opposite of an "absolute religious commitment." The pledge comprises an entirely *relative* human commitment: each antagonist is possessed of a full right to exist relative to the other party's presence. Simply put, *The Christian Century* and allied spokesmen utilize the universally acknowledged norm of fairmindedness as a trick to hide the ongoing Arab effort to annihilate Israel. There is no such thing as a partial right to exist. The moral truth is that anyone who is committed equally to Arab rights and Jewish rights is thereby obligated to "take sides" with Israel—*not* against Arab rights (Arab integrity is in no way questioned) but against the dismemberment of the Jewish state and the destruction of Jews.

If the delicate and painful task of making relative moral judgments constitutes a divine-human rebuttal of devilish evenhandedness, it is yet foolhardy to expect that the devil's defeat is imminent or that it is even possible. "The devices of the devil" have stood the tests of time and place; they are fully sanctioned by "the authorities and potentates of this dark world" and by "superhuman forces of evil" (Ephesians 6:11-12). The one divine opportunity of our period is Jewish sovereignty, the perpetuation and prosperity of which begs therefore for our highest resolve. Jewish national sovereignty is not the death of the devil but it is one effective way of laughing at him.

I hope that my closing observation won't sound pollyannish. What I wish to say is that the devil is a dreadful bore. I limit myself to two random examples from among thousands within the Christian world. It was just after the destruction of the Six Million that G. L. B. Sloan of the Near East Christian Council wrote, with appropriately devilish timing, that the Palestinian Jewish leadership is "spreading a spirit of intolerance and narrow jingoism" scarcely distinguishable from "the Nazi race doctrine." And in 1948 Henry Sloan Coffin, former president of the Union Theological Seminary in New York, followed Sloan by assailing the "resurgence of fanatical Jewish nationalism," Israel's "parasitic economic basis," and "the aggressiveness of this new state" with its "covetous eyes" on Arab lands.

The devil's vituperations forever overwhelm the devil's tact. These Christians could just as well be speaking in 1974, and of course they are, through other equally infected mouths. The more Christendom changes, the more it remains quite the same. We have heard it all before. The devil's nemesis is his banality. Year upon year, century upon century, epoch upon epoch he repeats himself ad nauseam. In him is prescribed a universal emetic.

The voices of the anti-Semites have grown hoarse and old. Their accusations form a cosmic broken record. There is no way for them to come up with anything fresh; all the satanic concepts have long been exhausted. The devil has run out of ideas.

I find a little comfort in this state of affairs. The devil simply has no talent for creativity, for newness. Thus does his Adversary act to shame him:

> Here and now I will do a new thing; this moment it will break
> from the bud.
> Can you not perceive it? (Isaiah 43:19)
> The Lord's mercies are new every morning (Lamentations 3:23).

29.

CHRISTIANITY AND THE JEWISH PEOPLE

Frank Ephraim Talmage

Rome. The 13th century. In his disputational work, *The Testimony of the Lord Is Faithful,* Solomon ben Moses cautions his readers:

> I have advised my friends . . . not to argue or debate with Christians. They should avoid disputing with them on matters of religion. . . . If the Jew be victorious he will provoke wrath upon himself for belittling and refuting their faith. But if he is defeated and shamed and if on his account and through ignorance truth is silenced, his punishment is twofold. Yet if the Jew be forced to debate, let him not do so with ignoramuses for that is forbidden by the authorities. . . . Neither should he dispute with his enemies and those who are of ill will toward him, for they will inform on him and on us. . . .

Master Solomon was clearly not an advocate of dialogue. Nor were most medieval Jews. Joseph Kimhi, the 12th-century author of the first European Hebrew polemical work, tells us he is writing to refute "the children of the impudent of our people," apostates from Judaism. His son, David, whose polemics became famous and widely quoted, seems also to have been more concerned with renegades than with born Christians. It was also a common phenomenon for apostates to write polemical works against their former co-religionists, trying to convince them to join the new faith. Thus, Petrus Alphonsi in the 11th century writes a dialogue in which he persuades his old self, Moyses, of the justice of his conversion.

For most medieval Jews, however, no matter what crises they may have had to endure, the identity crisis was not one of them. Religio-cultural, linguistic, and social bonds allowed them to find their place within the texture of Jewish history. Confrontations with representatives of other faiths were *ad hoc* or *ad hominem*. And being secure in their own faith, Jews had no compelling need to denigrate others. Most major medieval thinkers appraise Christianity in a rather positive light —to the extent that they give it attention at all. Not surprisingly, this remained true throughout later centuries in the case of those Jews who stayed rooted in the Jewish sources (while not necessarily cut off from Western thought). The views of Christianity of Jacob Emden (1698-1776), Nahman Krochmal (1784-1840), and Abraham Isaac Kook (1865-1935) are couched in the same sympathetic spirit as those of Moses Maimonides (1135-1204) and Menahem ha-Meiri of Perpignan in the 13th century.

The point is made in a strangely charming way, not by any of these exalted figures but by the acerbic Russian bibliophile and bibli-ographer, Ephraim Deinard, who settled in the United States before the turn of the century. Deinard reprinted in 1904 the *Refutation of the Principles of the Christians* by the 14th-century philosopher, Hasdai Crescas. In his introduction, Deinard observes:

> I know very well that even if we print thousands of books like this, we will not convert the Christians. Rather, I have another aim. My principal object in the publication of such books is my own breth-ren and people: to give the sons of Judah the weapons with which to defend their faith against their Hebrew assailants, the rabbis who preach Reform who harm us more than the Christians. If only the pious Christians would abolish the missionaries and place Reform rabbis in their place, they could expect the speedy demise of the Jewish religion.

But our concern today is not with people such as these, who— whether they lived in Denmark, Galicia, Jerusalem, or New Orleans— read, wrote, and lived in Hebrew, those whom the late Simon Rawido-wicz called Jews-in-the-original. Our concern nowadays is, rather, with Jews-in-translation.

The gradual admission of Jews into European society at the beginning of the 19th century brought with it the disorientation that
accompanies a change of address. The newly emancipated Europeanized
Jew had less and less access to the primary sources of his tradition.
He had been sprinkled with a knowledge of European culture but was
not quite ready for total immersion. He thus began to look at his
Christian neighbor with new interest. By determining who the latter
was, at least, he could know who he was not. Thus, with these Jews-in-
translation, we find, from Moses Mendelssohn on, a continuing dialectic
between Judaism and Christianity in which the one is defined in terms of
the other. The format is usually that of a theological chess game. As is
common in a chess game, one side is black and the other white. Generally, the white knight is Judaism, the religion of reason, and paganism,
the religion of nature, the black. Christianity is the gray area, a syncretism of the two, becoming more and more alienated from its Jewish
origins and inclining toward paganism.

A look at several representative Jewish thinkers of the period shows
the prevalence of this typological approach. Saul Ascher (1767-1822),
Samuel Hirsch (1815-1899), and Solomon Formstecher (1808-1889)
see Judaism as the religion which teaches man's freedom and his consequent ability to liberate himself from sin. The Frenchmen, Joseph
Salvador (1796-1873) and Elie Benamosegh (1823-1900), oppose the
otherworldliness of Christianity with the faith of Israel that unites both
this world and the next. Abraham Geiger (1810-1874), a leader of the
Wissenschaft des Judentums movement and an exponent of German
Reform, sees in the Jewish-Christian relationship a reenactment of the
Pharisee-Sadducee conflict.

The failure of most of these analyses is that in them Judaism is
stripped of any specific content. For Salvador it is identical with the
Social Contract or the ideals of the French Revolution; for some of the
Germans, the principles of German idealism were revealed at Sinai.
Specific Jewish practice is shunted to the side. Saul Ascher, for example,
finds the content of Jewish tradition a defense against Egyptian paganism, while Samuel Hirsch wishes Jewish practice preserved for historical
but not theological reasons. Finally, Formstecher, as a representative of
Reform, sees in Jewish ritual observances impediments to the ultimate
unification of mankind.

This trend of thought continues into the 20th century, with the
types becoming more sophisticated but the methodology the same. Thus

Leo Baeck, the Reform distiller of the essence of Judaism, defines the religion of Israel as classical, seeking the future and in a constant ferment. Christianity, on the other hand, is romantic: passive, with sights set toward the past. It was thinking such as this that made Franz Rosenzweig quip that in Baeck, author of *The Essence of Judaism,* he found more essence than Judaism.

This was more than a quip—Rosenzweig himself had been through one of the best known disputations of the 20th century with his Christian kinsman, Eugen Rosenstock-Huessy. The debate is based on a correspondence conducted in the foxholes of the German lines in 1916. In the eyes of Rosenzweig, this was not dialogue but "a bombardment between two learned cannons with a lyrical urge." Indeed, the correspondence can only be fully appreciated by one born in Germany at the turn of the century and possessed of a classical education. Yet through the rich and polished repartee, we find, on Rosenstock-Huessy's part, an interesting meld of classical and modern anti-Jewish motifs. He, too, speaks in typological terms. In talking of Judaism as the "law," he finds a religion archaic, self-righteous, and passive—a characterization not entirely removed from Baeck's view of Christianity. To such a Judaism, Christianity is contrasted, spiritual, dynamic, liberating the individual from his national limitations. Rosenstock-Huessy throws the paradox of German Jewish life in Rosenzweig's face. What is the point, he asks, of being a Jew who "plays the organ and thinks in a non-Jewish way," who has no Temple and no Law, who does not marry at the age of eighteen, and, when he does, takes a non-Jewish girl and converts her?

Reflecting on Israel's pride, Rosenstock-Huessy asserts:

I know that Judea will outlive all the "Nations," but you have no capacity for theology, for inquiry after truth or for beauty. Thou shalt not make any image. At this price the Eternal Jew may live because he hangs on tenaciously to the life granted to him. But he is cursed to live by the sweat of his brow, taking loans everywhere, and making loans everywhere. The Jew dies for no fatherland and for no mission. He lives because his life does not approach the margin of life. He lives in a chimerical reflection of a real life that cannot be envisaged without the sacrifice of death and the nearness of the abyss. . . . You do not know that the world is movement and change; the Christian says there is day and there is night, but you are so moonstruck that you think that the night view is the only

view that exists and you consider as the ideal conception the minimum of light, the night. You consider that this encompasses day
and night.

Rosenzweig answers that the way of life of Eastern Europe is not
the only legitimate approach to Jewish living. Judaism can adapt itself
to many environments. "However much these phenomena may hold of
the alien," he observes, "Judaism cannot but help assimilate them to
itself." But more to the point, Rosenzweig asserts:

> The serious acceptance in reality in which the theological principle
> about Jewish stubbornness is being worked out is Jew-hatred. You
> know as well as I that all the realistic explanations of this hatred
> are only so many fashionable dressings to hide the only true meta-
> physical reason, which is, metaphysically formulated, that we re-
> fuse to take part in the fiction of the Christian dogma that has
> gained world acceptance because (although reality) it is fiction
> (and *fiat veritas, pereat realitas,* for "Thou God art truth"), and,
> formulated in the manner of enlightenment (by Goethe in *Wilhelm
> Meister*): that we deny the basis of present culture (and *"fiat
> regnum Dei, pereat mundus,"* for "a kingdom of priests shall ye be
> unto me, and a holy people"); to formulate it in an unenlightened
> way: that we have crucified Christ and, believe me, we shall do it
> again any time, we alone in all the world (and *fiat nomen Dei
> Unius, pereat homo,* for "whom shall you make equal to me that
> I will be equal").

Rosenzweig thus finds himself participating in a classical Jewish-
Christian disputation. Rosenstock-Huessy reveals his structure of dogma,
which rests on the all-important foundation of Jewish obduracy; Rosenzweig, probably without knowing it, answers in practically the same way
as had 12th-century Franco-German polemicists. But this is not the 12th
century; and Rosenzweig's vexation is clear. He is ready to put the chess
board away. He may not have been an Eastern European Jew but he
could still immerse himself in the Hebrew sources of his religion. Like
his medieval forebears, he knew who he was and had no need to fall
back upon a negative anthropology. Like them, he wished to leave, and
be left, alone.
Rosenzweig, then, attempted to turn his back on the old typological

approach. In his *magnum opus,* the *Star of Redemption,* which appeared in 1921, Rosenzweig proposes the thesis that both religions, Judaism and Christianity, be held to possess equal validity and to be mutually complementary. Neither is the arbiter of the truth, which will only be fully known at the end of days. Judaism is the Life—the faith that was with the Father at the beginning—while Christianity is the way toward the Father of those who are not yet with Him. Judaism is the fire; Christianity the rays. Judaism is the Star of Redemption turned in upon itself; Christianity the Cross with its arms branched outward.

Yet despite this attempt, Rosenzweig could not completely rid himself of the old dichotomies. For one, his interpretation of Christianity as the rays emanating from the center did not preclude the possibility of those rays turning back upon the center. To ward off such a reflection, Rosenzweig was forced to have recourse to defensive apologetics. He writes in his famous letter to Pastor Ehrenburg: "Christianity acknowledged the God of Judaism, not, however, as God, but as the 'Father of Jesus Christ.' Christianity cleaves to Jesus because it knows that the Father can be reached only through him. Precisely the good Christian forgets God Himself in the face of the Lord Jesus." If neither is the true religion, Christianity is less true than Judaism; the new thesis of equal validity is destroyed, and with it the new desire for dialogue on equal terms.

On January 14, 1933, on the eve of catastrophe, the failure of dialogue could be seen again in a debate between Martin Buber and Karl Ludwig Schmidt. In the bizarre setting of Nazi Germany, Jews were invited at a public meeting to brotherhood with Christians, German style, with the understanding that the Church is the spiritual Israel. Schmidt invokes the ancient arguments: ". . . The Christian message says in this context: God has willed all this; Jesus, the Messiah rejected by his people, prophesied the destruction of Jerusalem. Jerusalem has been destroyed, so that it will never again come under Jewish rule. Until the present day the Jewish diaspora has no center."

Buber, however, refuses to be alarmed. Calmly and confidently, he responds to Schmidt's ancient argument as David Kimhi had refuted it centuries before. Israel's condition is not a proof of Christianity. Rather, it is a proof that despite all, the covenant still exists. In a moving statement which reflects the depths of his own experience, Buber asserts his counter-claim:

I live not far from the city of Worms, to which I am bound by the tradition of my forefathers; and, from time to time, I go there. When I go, I first go to the cathedral. It is a visible harmony of members, a totality in which no part deviates from perfection. I walk about the cathedral with consummate joy, gazing at it. Then I go over to the Jewish cemetery consisting of crooked, cracked, shapeless, random stones. I station myself there, gaze upward from the jumble of a cemetery to that glorious harmony, and seem to be looking up from Israel to the Church. Below, there is no jot of form; there are only the stones and the dust lying beneath the stones. The dust is there, no matter how thinly scattered. There lies the corporeality of man, which has turned to this. There it is. There it is for me. There it is for me, not as corporeality within the space of this planet, but as corporeality within my own memory, far into the depths of history, as far back as Sinai.

I have stood there, have been united with the dust, and through it with the Patriarchs. That is a memory of the transaction with God which is given to all Jews. From this the perfection of the Christian house of God cannot separate me, nothing can separate me from the sacred history of Israel.

I have stood there and have experienced everything myself; with all this death has confronted me, all the dust, all the ruin, all the wordless misery is mine; but the covenant has not been withdrawn from me. I lie on the ground, fallen like these stones. But it has not been withdrawn from me.

The cathedral is as it is. The cemetery is as it is. But nothing has been withdrawn from us.

Nothing has been withdrawn from us. In the formulation of Professor H. H. Ben-Sasson, "To the harsh and uncompromising postulate that the Jews can live in Europe only on acceptance of Christian conditions and conceptions, Buber presents his thesis of open dialogue between Israel as a nation and religion, and Christianity as a religion for other nations."

What happened to Buber's readiness for dialogue at this point is well known. And so back to Rome. In the year of infamy, 1942, a German Jesuit was expressing his views concerning the place of the Jews in the divine economy. Peter Browe ends his work, *The Papacy and the Medieval Mission to the Jews,* with a section explaining the slender success of the medieval Christian mission to the Jews. The book concludes:

> The entire fate of the Jewish people, its life and wandering throughout the centuries, the preservation of its race and its peoplehood in the midst of countless conflicts and persecutions cannot be satisfactorily explained on the basis of purely political and sociological considerations; the rejection and ultimate reelection of the Jewish people completely elude these. Only through faith can we somehow understand the resolution when we with St. Paul must recognize that God's election is mysterious and unfathomable, "that His judgments are unsearchable and His ways past finding out" (Romans 11:33).

In the same year in Protestant Switzerland, no less a theologian than Karl Barth makes the following observations:

> . . . Israel's unbelief cannot in any way alter the fact that objectively, and effectively, even in this senseless attitude beside and outwith the Church, it is the people of its arrived and crucified Messiah, and therefore the people of the secret (concealed from it as yet) Lord of the Church. . . . Over against the witness of the Church it can set forth only the sheer, stark judgment of God, only the obduracy and consequent misery of man, only the sentence and punishment that God in His mercy has chosen to undergo Himself to prevent them from falling on us. . . . This is how Israel punishes itself for its sectarian self-assertion. But it cannot alter the fact that even in this way it discharges exactly the service for which it is elected. Even in this way it really gives to the world the very witness that is required of it . . . even in the spectral form of the Synagogue. The existence of the Jews, as is generally recognized, is an adequate proof of the existence of God. It is an adequate demonstration of the depths of human guilt and need and therefore of the inconceivable greatness of God's love in the event in which God was in Christ reconciling the world to Himself. The Jews of the ghetto give this demonstration involuntarily, joylessly, and ingloriously, but they do give it. They have nothing to attest to the world but the shadow of the cross of Jesus Christ that falls upon them. But they, too, do actually and necessarily attest Jesus Christ Himself.

Rosenstock-Huessy. Schmidt. Browe. Barth. Twentieth century or 2nd? Do these statements differ in essence from what Tertullian had preached to the Jews eighteen-hundred years before?

> Since, therefore, the Jews were predicted as destined to suffer these calamities *on Christ's account,* and we find that they *have* suffered them, and see them sent into dispersion and abiding in it, manifest it is that on Christ's account these things *have* befallen the Jews, the sense of the Scriptures harmonizing with the issue of the events and of the order of the times. Or else, if Christ is not yet come, on whose account they were predicted as destined thus to suffer, when He *shall have come* it follows that they *will* thus suffer. And where will then be a daughter of Sion to be derelict, who *now* has no existence? Where the cities to be burnt which are already burnt and in heaps? Where the dispersion of a race which is now in exile? Restore to Judea the condition which Christ is to find, and [then, if you will,] contend that some other [Christ] is coming.

In terms of content, the 20th century formed a micro-aeon which encapsulated with little essential change the rhetoric and invective of nineteen-hundred years. Yet as in all periods of radical upheaval in Jewish history—the destruction of the Temple, the Crusades, the expulsion from Spain—the rise of Nazism and the Holocaust altered the syntax of the polemical idiom, if not the morphology. Considerations of doctrine and dogma, Scripture and social critique, changed the nature of disputation from a sporting event and theological chess game to a confrontation in which the disputants found their national identity and indeed their very lives at stake. Statements that in earlier times were merely vexing to the Jew, in 1942 were blasphemy.

Yet Jews were learning to "blaspheme" as well. Shortly after the war they fulfilled Tertullian's condition, restoring to Judea the condition which Christ was to find. In 1948, in a moment of weakness, Jewish "arrogance" was given free reign and the State of Israel was allowed to happen. The birth of the Jewish state was greeted in Christian circles with mixed reactions. Millar Burrows, representative of a whole class of theologian-Orientalists, responded in the *Christian Century*:

> The central issue between Judaism and Christianity lies in their answer to the question: What do you think of Christ? . . . There

are some points, however, on which all Christians are united. While orthodox Judaism believes that the Messiah is to come and liberal Judaism holds that there is no Messiah except the Jewish people itself, all Christians believe that the messianic prophecies of the Old Testament have their true and only fulfillment in Jesus. The present resurgence of Jewish nationalism is a repetition of the same fatal error that caused Israel's rejection of Jesus. It is the focal point at which Christian opinion, in all brotherly love, should make clear and emphatic its disagreement with the dominant trend in contemporary Judaism. For the enthusiastic, dominating, just now apparently all-conquering devotees of political Zionism we would feel the sorrow that Jesus felt when he wept over Jerusalem. We must not relinquish or forget our conviction that the Messiah is Jesus, and that the fulfillment of the promises of the Old Testament is to be found in the universal Kingdom of God which He came to establish. The Christians' final attitude must be that of Paul: "Brethren, my heart's desire for Israel is that they may be saved."

So it was that where the Jews were a proof of Christianity, the Jewish state was a stumbling block. And so it was that for the next two decades Zionist apologists attempted to convince the Christian world of the compatibility of the Jewish state with Christian ideals, and of the justice of Christian recognition of the right of the Jews to political independence in their historic homeland. Scribes and Pharisees, these apologists compassed the sea and land to earn one proselyte, but the proselytes—distinguished as they may have been—were few indeed. Nevertheless, in Jewish ranks, only an occasional voice of dissent was heard. One such dissident, Eliezer Berkovits, called his co-religionists to task for fighting a futile battle. In an article entitled "Judaism in the Post-Christian Era," published in 1966, Berkovits turned the table on its head: Christianity is on the way out. The Jewish people, the old Israel, are the New Israel as well. To the former New Israel—the Christians—there is nothing to say.

Such "bigotry" was unpalatable to most Jews. Jacob Neusner, in a letter to the editor of *Judaism,* where the essay had appeared, decried its narrowness of mind: we must keep the doors open. Then came June 1967. Americans fear a second Vietnam; Jews dread a second Auschwitz. As A. Roy Eckardt put it: "Again Silence in the Churches." Jacob

Neusner writes a second letter to *Judaism*: he was wrong. Berkovits was right. Overnight the Jewish people turned into a nation of Berkovitses. Writing in a *Christian Century* series, "How My Mind Has Changed," Emil L. Fackenheim gave eloquent testimony to this development in 1970:

> Thirty years ago I had become convinced that what had once divided Jews and Christians was now dwarfed by the demonic forces threatening both. In the years that followed I became involved in Jewish-Christian dialogues on that basis and formed lasting personal and theological friendships. Today I am confronted by another, less comforting aspect of Jewish-Christian relations. In regard to it I find myself misunderstood or even abandoned by most, though not all, Christian theologians. Nazi anti-Semitism, anti-Christian, would have been impossible without centuries of Christian anti-Semitism. Why drag up this dead past? Because, alas, I can view it as past no longer, and because I owe the victims of Auschwitz (and . . . Christianity itself) a relentless truthfulness.
>
> Once I held the mild view that Christian anti-Semitism was vanishing in the wake of Jewish-Christian dialogues which confined attention to what the two faiths have in common. I have now been forced into a more radical view: anti-Semitism exists wherever it is held (or implied) that "the Jewish people" is an anachronism which may survive, if at all, only on sufferance. Anti-Semitism of this kind survives in such post-Christian phenomena as a liberalism which maintains that of all peoples Jews alone are obliged to be men-in-general, and in a Communism which affirms that of all nationalisms Jewish nationalism alone is "petty-bourgeois." Its ultimate root, however, lies in the Christian view—perpetuated through the centuries, lingering on even where Christianity itself is undermined by atheism or agnosticism—that the birth of the new Israel entails the death of the old.

Thus the impasse at which Jewish-Christian dialogue finds itself. Is this then to be the last word? Perhaps we should look elsewhere and go beyond the sphere of learned theological debates. Perhaps we should examine the situation as it is on an "everyday" plane. One runs the risk in doing so, of course, of slipping over the unguarded border between scholarship and journalism—the one consists of relating anecdotes about others, the other of relating anecdotes about oneself—but perhaps the risk is minimal after all.

On October 19, 1973, a letter favoring support for the State of Israel and signed by a group of distinguished Christian theologians and laymen was published in the Toronto *Globe and Mail*. Since "Jewish nationalism is the stepchild of Christian prejudice," the letter claimed, "Christians must affirm Israel as the visible and tangible manifestation of both Jewish survival and Jewish security." A Jewish friend of mine at the University of Toronto, where I teach, while finding the letter well-intentioned, objected that it sounded as if it were advocating the establishment of a game-preserve for an endangered species. Could not even our friends take the Jewish right to a state at face value?

The real answer, however, appeared in the *Globe and Mail* of October 23, in a letter submitted by, among others, some members of my own department. This letter took serious issue with the first and found it "rife with prejudice, and an often subtle, but nonetheless virulent anti-Semitic prejudice against the Arabs (for they too are Semites and cousins of the Jews)." Several days later, I was confronted by a signatory of this letter. As Burrows would have put it, in all brotherly love, he made clear and emphatic his disagreement with the dominant trend in contemporary Judaism. Still under the unspeakable strain of those days, I listened—as had my forefathers on many occasions in past centuries—to a sermon of Christian love and charity. The keynote was of course philo-Semitism: We Christians should treat you so well that you won't want to run off somewhere else! You are too valuable to lose! You can function perfectly well in the Diaspora! Look at the Golden Age of Spain! Why do you want to set up a Levantine state, another Lebanon? What a pity that all the Oriental Jewish communities have now been lost!

I was not left speechless, but I knew—and was later assured— that my response fell on deaf ears. Then the conversation shifted to a discussion of the general atmosphere of the department and I remarked that I did not enjoy the strain of its constant tension. My interlocutor looked at me and replied: "But isn't that what being a Jew is all about?

Isn't that what being a Jew is all about? So we have been told. So was Trypho the Jew told many hundreds of years ago:

Indeed the custom of circumcising the flesh . . . was given to you as a distinguishing mark, to set you off from other nations and from us Christians. The purpose of this was that you and only you might suffer the afflictions that are now justly yours; that only your land be desolate, and your cities ruined by fire; that the fruits of your land be eaten by strangers before your very eyes; that not one of you be permitted to enter your city of Jerusalem. Your circumcision of the flesh is the only mark by which you can certainly be distinguished from other men. Therefore, the above-mentioned tribulations were justly imposed upon you for you have murdered the Just One, and His prophets before Him; now you spurn those who hope in Him, and in Him who sent Him, namely, Almighty God, the Creator of all things. . . .

Yes, so we have been told. But now—for afflictions, read tension. For distinguishing marks, read: "You don't look Jewish." For desolation, read: "You have no history." And for exile, read exile. To be sure, the 20th-century Jew has an advantage which his forefathers did not: he knows how to exploit technology to the fullest. He can use plastic surgery to remove his horns and Right Guard to mask his *foetor judaicus.* He can go to Berlitz and learn to speak like an Anglo-Saxon. And Alka-Seltzer, labeled in Hebrew script, is sold all over the State of Israel to relieve his divinely ordained tension.

Rome. January 26, 1904. Theodor Herzl writes in his diary:

I saw the Pope yesterday.
I presented my request briefly, but he answered: "We cannot look with favor upon this movement. We cannot prevent the Jews from going to Jerusalem—but we can never favor it." "But, Holy Father, the Jews are having a terrible time. I do not know whether your Holiness is acquainted with the whole scope of this melancholy situation. We need a country for these persecuted people."
"Must it be Gerusalemme?"
"We are not asking for Jerusalem, but for Palestine, only the profane part of the country."

Herzl's desacralization of the sacred was not as some Christians might envision the Jewish state: further evidence of Jewish obstinacy, doomed—for as long as it might last—to a mediocre levantinism. Rather, it was a notice that after having been forced to participate in a two-thousand-year-old drama, the Jew was ready for his stage directions to say "Exit." His role-playing in someone else's passion play is over. Yet for some Jews, new-found independence has not been enough. They want the state to be accepted, recognized, acknowledged—not only politically but theologically; and when it is not, they feel frustration, disappointment, and despair. This pattern repeated itself only recently in response to the Vatican's failure to come to grips with the state of Israel in its latest guidelines on relations with the Jews. Significantly, Israeli Jews—and especially native-born Israelis—are least concerned. What matters to them is what the U.S. State Department thinks and not what U.S. churches think. But the Diaspora Jew, far less secure, is far more sensitive. For him, perhaps, the restoration is no less a mystery than for the Christian; and perhaps in explaining it to the Christian, he is really trying to explain it to himself. He does not yet realize that the posture of a supplicant is no longer appropriate to a sovereign nation.

To such Jews, and to their Christian partners in dialogue, one may address the words of the distinguished Catholic philosopher, Jacques Maritain:

> It is a strange paradox to see disputed with the Israelis the sole territory to which, considering the entire spectacle of human history, it is absolutely, *divinely* certain that a people has incontestably a right. . . .
>
> In speaking thus I [am] not making of the State of Israel a state by divine right. The State of Israel is only a state like the others. But the return of a portion of the Jewish people and its regroupment in the Holy Land (of which the existence of this state is a sign and the guarantee)—this is the reaccomplishment, under our eyes, of the divine promise which is without repentance. . . . And I do not doubt that the event, however enigmatic it may be for the Jews as for the Christians, carries in it the mark of the faithful love and of the pity of God toward the people which is ever His. It appears to me, consequently, that once the Jewish people has put its feet again upon the land which God gave to it, no one will be able anymore to wrest it from it; and that to wish the disappearance of the State of Israel is to wish to reject into nothingness this return which finally was accorded to the Jewish people, and which permits it to have a shelter of its own in the world; in other words, it is—in another manner, but as grave, than that of ordinary anti-Semitism—to wish that misfortune hound again this people, and that once more it be the victim of iniquitous aggression. *"Anti-Israelism" is no better than anti-Semitism.*

PART V

IMPASSE, COEXISTENCE, DIALOGUE

Although it had many positive aspects, the Jewish-Christian relationship in the Middle Ages was characterized, above all, by the *vikkuah* or *disputatio*. As one can see from the examples of Joseph and David Kimhi, debates with Christians seem to have been a frequent if not a favored pastime. One such as Nahmanides would be coerced into debating an opponent as repugnant to him as Pablo Cristiá. Over and beyond the debates, both public and private, there was that other ever present phenomenon of the medieval mission to the Jews: the compulsory sermon. Jews were regularly herded or assembled in churches or synagogues to have the gospel preached to them. Later, in the period of the Inquisition, they would listen to lengthy and venomous harangues about their obstinacy and perfidy while waiting to be penanced or burnt at the stake. Such preachings of the gospel of love are generally labeled "medieval." There is, however, no special need to insult the Middle Ages. The crusade against the Jews was not limited to any one time period. One generally begins the modern era in Jewish history with the

255

emancipation of the Jews in the eighteenth century. There we find that although they begin to gain civil and political rights, they are still considered by the Church or the churches as objects of the Mission to Israel which will solve the Jewish problem by eliminating the Jews. Indeed, the modern period bestowed on the struggle *adversus Judaeos* new dimensions of subtlety and callousness never conceived of in the Middle Ages. Thus, at the very moment when Jewry in Germany appeared to be on the ascendant, we find J. C. Lavater attempting to undo all in his public challenge to Moses Mendelssohn. Nor did the nineteenth and twentieth centuries bring many advances. Missions to the Jews proliferated in Europe and America. In Germany, in a great hour of peril, Martin Buber was called upon to respond to such Missions and to make peace with demands made upon the Jews by nazi Christianity. The history of these events would surely require several volumes in the telling. However, even these few remarks are sufficient to provide some notion of the associations and connotations that religious discussions with Christianity convey to the Jewish mind.

To be sure, this reluctance to engage in theological discussions has not precluded Jewish interest and participation in a common world of thought. Jewish theologians—and among them the most vocal opponents of dialogue—have long made use of Christian theology and philosophy in their own thought, employing and adopting that which was meaningful in a Jewish context.

Yet in the post-war period, it appeared as if new developments were in the offing. In partial response to the Holocaust, the churches became more sensitive to the phenomenon of antisemitism—especially the antisemitism within Christianity. Indeed, in the view of Franklin H. Littell, the Holocaust is the central theological event for *Christianity* in the twentieth century. Consequently, Vatican II and the expectations that a new relationship between Judaism and Christian churches might develop led to a modification of the traditional Jewish reluctance to engage in dialogue. In certain circles, principally Reform and Conservative, both popular and learned scholarly dialogues with Christians took place following the example of the ecumenical movement in Christianity itself. All this was short-lived however. The crisis of June 1967 and the failure of most of official North American Christianity to respond to it disillusioned many Jewish participants in dialogue. In all fairness, however, it should be noted that before 1967 Jews seldom, if ever, raised Israel as an issue in these discussions. Nevertheless, it appeared as if the churches had reacted to the possibility of a second Holocaust as if the first had never happened.

Today, new voices are being heard which call for a radical change in the Jewish-Christian relationship. Once and for all, they say, the missionary stance of Christianity must be abandoned—Jews and Christians are to address each other without preconditions and preconceptions. This is not the literal reading of Vatican II. Yet some North American Roman Catholic theologians choose to interpret Vatican II in this fashion. Their efforts to reconcile this new approach to Judaism with Christian tradition or to modify tradition where necessary have done much to foster interfaith understanding. Among them are Gregory Baum and Rosemary Ruether. Among Protestants, of course, similar attitudes had been expressed before the start of the ecumenical movement. Reinhold Niebuhr is one notable example; more recently, A. Roy Eckardt has become a leading exponent of this point of view. Here we present the remarks of Dean Krister Stendahl of Harvard Divinity School after a Jewish-Christian colloquium in which he reflects on possibilities for the future. And finally, a suggestive approach to interfaith relations by Abraham Joshua Heschel.

FOUR PHASES OF JEWISH RELUCTANCE

In the mid-eighteenth century, western European Jewry was slowly groping its way towards civil emancipation. Individual Jews gradually began to achieve prominence of one sort or another in German society. Foremost among these was Moses Mendelssohn (1729-1786), who was, at one and the same time, a philosopher of the Enlightenment and an exponent of traditional Judaism. This dual role created a certain ambivalence towards him on the part of some of his contemporaries. Their admiration for Mendelssohn as a philosopher and intellectual was clouded by their frustration at his failure to convert to Christianity. In 1763, Mendelssohn met Johann Caspar Lavater, a young theologian from Zurich. In a private meeting, Lavater and some friends prodded Mendelssohn into stating his attitude toward Christianity. After considerable hesitation, Mendelssohn remarked that he saw Jesus as an important moral figure. Yet, he asserted, he would have to withdraw that opinion if it were indeed demonstrated to him that Jesus thought himself divine. Lavater took careful account of these words and drew unwarranted encouragement from them. Lavater was a millenarian; he believed that if Mendelssohn were converted, the other Jews would follow and the Millennium would arrive. For several years then, he was preoccupied with the task of Mendelssohn's conversion. Lavater had read the *Palingenesis* of the Genevan philosopher, Charles Bonnet. This work contained a section devoted to proofs of Christianity which Lavater thought would be the perfect instrument by which to win Mendelssohn to Christianity. He thereupon translated Bonnet's work into German in 1769 and sent it to Mendelssohn with a covering letter. This letter bluntly challenged Mendelssohn "to do what wisdom, love of truth, and honor require, and what a Socrates would have done had he read the treatise and found it irrefutable." As we have seen in the Buber-Kittel encounter (sel. 7), it was the fact that Lavater made it a *public* challenge that made the situation so critical: ". . . When a Lavater calls upon me, I have no choice but to express my convictions in public, lest my silence be misconstrued as contemptuous disregard or acquiescence." Again after considerable hesitation, Mendelssohn drafted

259

a sharp reply with a detailed critique of Bonnet. He then reconsidered, however, and adopted a different position. He would not accept Lavater's challenge. He makes it clear, of course, that he has hardly been convinced by Bonnet. His adherence to Judaism is a result of many years of examination and reflection. In the face of the unenviable civic status of the Jew and Israel's general degradation, he would not have stubbornly held on to his faith if he did not believe in it. (Here one may hear an echo of David Kimhi's claim that the continued although degraded existence of Israel is proof of the covenant. How could they have survived at all if God had not been protecting them?) He maintains, however, that to engage in polemics would run counter to the spirit of tolerance inherent in Judaism. The Jewish religion rejects any thought of attempting to convert the Gentile. "Convert a Confucius or a Solon? What for? . . . It seems to me that anyone who leads men to virtue in this life cannot be damned in the next. . . ." Here, Mendelssohn's argument would draw support from certain Enlightenment circles which supported this notion of tolerance.

On another level, however, Mendelssohn candidly states another major objection to criticizing Christianity publicly: the precarious situation of the Jews in European society. For "a member of an oppressed people which must appeal to the benevolence of the government for protection and shelter," restraint was the far more prudent course. Thus in one stroke, Mendelssohn succeeded in avoiding an open critique of Christianity while portraying its conversionist posture as benighted, arrogant, and unworthy.

Mendelssohn's letter has been reprinted from A. Jospe, ed., *Jerusalem and Other Jewish Writings,* New York: Schocken, 1969, pp. 113-122. An analysis of the controversy may be found in Alexander Altmann's excellent biography, *Moses Mendelssohn: A Biographical Study,* University, Ala.: University of Alabama Press, 1973, pp. 194-263.

The tensions between Judaism and Christianity were the same at the demise of German Jewry as they were in the period of its emancipation and growth. Martin Buber, as one of the spiritual leaders of this community before World War II, was frequently called upon to serve as an apologist for Judaism in the face of Christian provocations. The increasing nazification of certain wings of German Christianity created ever more difficult challenges for Buber. His encounter with Gerhard

Kittel has been discussed above (sel. 7). His essay "The Question to the Single One" was written in this period as a reply to Friedrich Gogarten, who attempted a justification of the authoritarian state on theological grounds. Again in the crucial year of 1933, Buber faced Karl Ludwig Schmidt in a debate in which Schmidt too expressed the concept of divine rejection in terms of racial inferiority (See sel. 29; Buber's response to Schmidt is now available in the English translation of William Hallo in D. W. McKain, ed., *Christianity; Some Non-Christian Appraisals,* New York: the McGraw-Hill, 1974, pp. 175-88.) Even before these disputations, in March, 1930, Buber was invited to address the four German-language missions to the Jews at Stuttgart. The subject was the nature of the Jewish soul. Buber at first displayed the usual reluctance (note the beginning of his address), but finally "fell in with their request." Buber's address, "The Two Foci of the Jewish Soul," does not limit itself to a strategy of defense. Placing the burden of proof upon Christianity, he demands evidence that the Christian claim is true—that the world has indeed been redeemed. In a widely quoted passage, he observed that "the Jew, as part of the world, experiences, perhaps more intensely than any other part, the world's lack of redemption. He feels this lack of redemption against his skin, he tastes it on his tongue, the burden of the unredeemed world lies on him."

Buber's appeal is strongly reminiscent of the words of the Spanish poet and philosopher, Judah Halevi, written eight centuries earlier. In the *Kuzari,* a philosophical defense of Judaism (see above, sel. 22), Halevi describes the Jewish people as the heart of the world—the most sick and the most healthy of the organs at the same time. It is the most sick because the heart is exposed to all sorts of ills stemming from external causes. It is the most healthy because it has the capacity to reject these harmful influences; it can afford no defect lest it cease to function. So it is with Israel:

> Our relation to the Divine Influence is the same as that of the soul to the heart. For this reason it is said: "You only have I known of all the families of the earth, therefore I will punish you for all your iniquities" (Amos 3:2). These are the illnesses. As regards its health, it is alluded to in the words of the sages: He forgives the sins of his people, causing the first of them to vanish first. He does not allow our sins to become overwhelming, or they would destroy us completely by their multitude. Thus he

says: "the iniquity of the Amorites is not yet full" (Gen. 15:16).
He left them alone till the ailment of their sins had become fatal
Just as the heart is pure in substance and matter, and of even temperament, in order to be accessible to the intellectual soul, so
also is Israel in its component parts. In the same way as the heart
may be affected by disease of the other organs, . . . Israel is exposed to ills originating in its inclinings towards the Gentiles.

In these words Judah Halevi would concur in Buber's assertion
that Christian doctrine cannot disprove that which Israel knows from
its very being.

"The Two Foci of the Jewish Soul" first appeared in *Israel and
the World: Essays in a Time of Crisis,* New York: Schocken, 1948,
pp. 28-40.

The early 1960's saw the highpoint of interfaith dialogue in North
America. The Second Vatican Council (1962-65), raised expectations
of new breakthroughs in religious understanding—not only within Christianity but between Christianity and other religions. For Jews, there was
the possibility that the Council would declare that Judaism had in fact
not been superseded by Christianity; that the Church would abandon
its missionary stance toward the Jews. Representatives of Jewish bodies
—officially observers—lobbied at the Council in the hope that they
could influence a positive outcome of the deliberations. In America,
church and synagogue groups met together in both organized and in-
formal sessions to discuss the differences and similarities of their respective faiths. Many Jews savored this new experience. Judaism had
completely suppressed any missionary instincts since Hellenistic times.
Now for the first time in almost two millennia, Judaism had an opportunity, if not to proselytize, to display its wares. Yet not all Jews were
equally enthusiastic. Most efforts at dialogue were conducted among
Reform and Conservative Jews; Orthodox Jews generally eschewed
such activity. What, they asked, did Jews have to gain from such conversations? They had nothing to gain; they felt no need to judaize
Christianity. They could only lose. At bottom, they were concerned
that the old dialogue was nothing but a masking of the new mission.

When the Vatican schema on non-Christian religions was finally
promulgated in 1965, most Jews found it less encouraging than they
had expected it to be. It appeared that at most Judaism was considered

to bear a ray of divine light; that the Jews had been "absolved" of their sins against the founder of Christianity. This made some Jews feel an even more intense need for dialogue. Others became more adamant in their opposition. Among these was Eliezer Berkovits, who teaches Jewish philosophy at the Hebrew Theological College in Skokie, Illinois. In an article in *Judaism* (XV [1966], 74-84), Berkovits voiced traditional skepticism toward Christian overtures to Jews and observed that Christianity was reaching out only because it itself was in need; because it no longer dominated the world; because the post-Christian era had come. If the Church sought tolerance, it was tolerance for itself in the non-Christian and Communist anti-Christian world.

Berkovits considered dialogue unacceptable on several grounds. Emotionally, Jews are not yet ready to deal with a religion which bears so much responsibility for Jewish suffering. Theologically, Judaism is self-sufficient; the Judeo-Christian tradition is a myth. There is no need for a philosophical dialogue; the realm of thought is universal. (Some may find it paradoxical that some of those Jewish thinkers who reject dialogue most vehemently are most deeply influenced by Christian thought.) Finally, there is the implication that Jews and Christians share responsibility for a mutual misunderstanding when in fact there was only unilateral oppression.

It has already been noted that many Jews were profoundly shocked and disillusioned at Christian indifference or enmity to the State of Israel in the spring of 1967. Those who had actively been engaged in Jewish-Christian dialogue now wondered at the purpose of their efforts. Those who might have thought Berkovits's words shortsighted or narrow at the time they were written now came to feel themselves in agreement with them. Throughout North America, formal dialogue programs were interrupted as Jews began to rethink their attitudes. The conclusion reached through such rethinking was not necessarily that Jews no longer had anything to say to Christians. It did, however, influence what would be said.

Emil L. Fackenheim, professor of philosophy at the University of Toronto, is one of North America's leading Jewish theologians and authorities on modern philosophical thought. His *Quest for Past and Future, The Religious Dimension in Hegel's Thought* (both Bloomington: Indiana U., 1968), *God's Presence in History* (New York: N.Y.U., 1970), and *Encounters Between Judaism and Modern Philosophy* (New

York: Basic Books, 1973) have had wide-ranging influence. In an article in *The Christian Century* series, "How My Mind Has Changed" (LXXXVII [May 6, 1970], 563-68), Fackenheim relates how he had moved to a neo-orthodox theology from a "liberal ideology which had confused the messianic days with achievements and promises of the modern world." This liberal ideology had entailed an anti-Zionist distinction between Jewish "religion" and "nationalism" which he rejected as well. The decisive fact in his theological development, however, was the Holocaust which, with Elie Wiesel, he "dares to compare . . . with Sinai in its revelatory significance." The lesson learned is a commitment to Jewish survival through which "after Auschwitz every Jew represents all humanity."

In dialogues with Christians, Fackenheim had held the conviction that "what had once divided Jews and Christians was now dwarfed by the demonic forces threatening both." Yet, in June 1967, he realized that Jewish-Christian dialogues were doing little to erode Christian anti-semitism; that "antisemitism exists wherever it is held (or implied) that 'the Jewish people' is an anachronism which may survive, if at all, only on sufferance." Fackenheim's doubt as to whether Jewish-Christian dialogue is possible is not unqualified: Christians could come to understand Israel (people and state) if they came to terms with Auschwitz and its implications for Christianity as well as for Judaism. In this, they might indeed find their own renewal.

30.

LETTER TO JOHANN CASPAR LAVATER

Moses Mendelssohn

Dear Friend,

You have found it advisable to dedicate your translation from the French of Bonnet's *Examination of the Proofs for Christianity* to me and to request me publicly and solemnly to refute this treatise if I felt that its arguments in support of the claims of Christianity were erroneous. Should I, however, find the arguments convincing, you ask me "to do what wisdom, love of truth, and honor require, and what a Socrates would have done had he read the treatise and found it irrefutable," namely, to abandon the religion of my fathers and to embrace the faith advocated by M. Bonnet. For even if I were ever tempted to stoop so low as to place expediency above my sense of truth and probity, my course of action would in this particular case obviously be dictated by all three elements.

I am convinced your motives are pure and reflect nothing but your loving concern for your fellowmen. Indeed, I should not be worthy of anyone's respect if I did not gratefully reciprocate the affection and friendship for me that are evident in your dedicatory inscription. Yet I must confess that your action has shocked me deeply. I should have expected anything but a public challenge from a Lavater.

Since you recall the confidential conversations I had with you and your friends in my home, you cannot have forgotten how often I attempted to shift the discussion from religious issues to more neutral and conventional topics and how strongly you and your friends had to prod me before I would venture to express my views on these matters [i.e., Mendelssohn's views on Jesus and Christianity], which touch upon man's deepest convictions. Unless memory betrays me, I was assured on these occasions that our conversations would be kept confidential. I would, of course, rather be mistaken in my recollection than accuse you of a breach of promise.

Nevertheless, you could easily have foreseen how repugnant it would be to me to issue a public statement about these matters after I had carefully tried to avoid discussing them even in the privacy of my own home and among just a few trusted men, of whose good will I was certain. The fact that the voice that now challenges me cannot easily be disregarded or dismissed only adds to my embarrassment. What could therefore possibly have motivated you to single me out against my will in order to drag me into the arena of public controversy, which I had hoped never to enter? Even if you had ascribed my reticence merely to timidity and shyness, should a loving friend not have shown some tolerance and leniency for such personal shortcomings?

My disinclination to enter into religious controversy has, however, never been the result of fear of folly. My study of the foundations of my religious faith does not date from yesterday. Very early in my life I had already become aware of the need to examine my views and actions. And the principal reason for which I have spent my leisure time since then in the study of philosophy and the humanities was precisely that I wanted to prepare myself for this task. I had no other motives. I knew that my studies could not possibly bring the slightest material advantage to someone in my situation. I realized there was no promising career for me in this field. And as for inner rewards? O, my dear friend! The civic status and position of my coreligionists are not conducive to the free development of our intellectual capacities. To ponder the true state of our affairs can hardly increase our happiness. Let me refrain from elaborating this point. Any person who knows our plight and who has a human heart will understand more than I can possibly say here.

If my decision, after all these years of study, had not been entirely in favor of my religion, I would certainly have found it necessary to make my convictions known publicly. I fail to see what could have kept me tied to a religion that is so severe and generally despised had I not, in my heart, been convinced of its truth. Whatever the result of my studies, I would have felt compelled to leave the religion of my fathers had I ever begun to feel that it was not true. And had my heart been captured by another faith, it would have been depravity not to admit to the truth. What could possibly cause me to debase myself [by not admitting it]? There is only one course, as I have already pointed out, that wisdom, love of truth, and honesty can choose.

If I were indifferent to both religions or mocked and scorned all revelations, I might indeed follow the counsel which expediency dictates while conscience remains silent. What could deter me? Fear of my fellow Jews? They lack the power to intimidate me. Stubbornness? Inertia? Blind adherence to familiar customs and conventions? Since I have devoted a large part of my life to the examination of my tradition, I hope no one will expect me to sacrifice the fruits of my studies to such personal failings.

You can, therefore, see that I would have been impelled to make a public statement about the results of my studies had they left me without the sincere conviction of the validity of my faith. However, inasmuch as my investigations strengthened me in the faith of my fathers, I was able to continue in it quietly, without feeling that I had to render an account to the world of my convictions.

I do not deny that I see certain human excesses and abuses that tarnish the beauty of my religion. But is there any friend of truth who can claim that his religion is completely free of man-made accretions and corruptions? All of us know that the search for truth can be impeded by the poisonous breath of hypocrisy and superstition. We wish we could dispel both without damaging the beauty and truth of the essentials of our religion. Nevertheless, of the validity of the essentials of my faith I am as firmly and irrefutably convinced as you or M. Bonnet is of his, and I declare before God, who has created and sustained both you and me—the God in whose name you have challenged me—that I shall adhere to my principles as long as my soul remains unchanged.

My inner remoteness from your religion has remained unchanged since I disclosed my views to you and your friends [in our earlier conversations]. And I would even now be prepared to concede that my respect for the moral stature of its founder has not diminished since then, were it not that you have clearly disregarded the reservation which I had attached to my views at that time. But there comes a moment in a man's life when he has to make up his mind about certain issues in order to be able to go on from there. This happened to me several years ago with regard to religion. I have read; I have compared; I have reflected; and I have made up my mind [about my religion].

Still, I admit that I would never have entered into a dispute about Judaism, even if it had been polemically attacked or triumphantly held up to scorn in academic textbooks. There would have been no counterargument from me even against the most ridiculous notion which anyone, whether trained or merely semi-literate in the field of rabbinics, might have discovered in some literary trash that no serious-minded Jew bothers to read. I wanted to refute the world's derogatory opinion of the Jew by righteous living, not by pamphleteering. However, it is not only my station in life but also my religion and my philosophy that furnish me with the most cogent reasons why I wanted to avoid religious controversy and discuss, in my publications, only those religious verities which are of equal importance to all religions.

According to the principles of my religion, I am not expected to try to convert anyone not born into my faith. Even though many people think that the zeal for proselytizing originated in Judaism, it is, in fact, completely alien to it. Our rabbis hold unanimously that the written as well as the oral laws that constitute our revealed religion are binding only for our own people. "*Moses* had given *us* the law; it is the inheritance of the House of *Jacob*" [Deut. 33:4]. All other nations were enjoined by God to observe the law of nature and the religion of the patriarchs. All who live in accordance with this religion of nature and of reason are called "the righteous among other nations"; they too are entitled to eternal bliss. Far from being obsessed by any desire to proselytize, our rabbis require us to discourage as forcefully as we can anyone who asks to be converted. We are to ask him to consider the heavy burden he would have to shoulder needlessly by taking this step. We are to point out that, in his present state, he is obligated to fulfill only the Noachide laws in order to be saved but that upon his conversion he will have to observe strictly all the laws of his new faith or expect the punishment which God metes out to the lawbreaker. Finally, we are to paint a faithful picture of the misery and destitution of our people and of the contempt in which they are held, in order to keep him from a hasty decision he may later regret.

As you see, the religion of my fathers does not ask to be propagated. We are not to send missionaries to the two Indies or to Greenland in order to preach our faith to distant nations. . . . Anyone not born into our community need not observe its laws. The fact that we consider their observance incumbent upon us alone cannot possibly offend our neighbors. Do they think our views are absurd? No need to quarrel about it. We act in accordance with our convictions and do not mind if others question the validity of our laws, which, as we ourselves emphasize, are not binding on them. Whether they are acting fairly, peaceably, and charitably when they mock our laws and traditions is, of course, something else that must be left to their own consciences. As long as we do not want to convince or convert others, we have no quarrel with them.

If a Confucius or a Solon were to live among our contemporaries, I could, according to my religion, love and admire the great man without succumbing to the ridiculous desire to convert him. Convert a Confucius or a Solon? What for? Since he is not a member of the household of Jacob, our religious laws do not apply to him. And as far as the general principles of religion are concerned, we should have little trouble agreeing on them. Do I think he can be saved? It seems to me that anyone who leads men to virtue in this life cannot be damned in the next. . . .

It is my good fortune to count among my friends many an excellent man who is not of my faith. We love each other sincerely, although both of us suspect or assume that we differ in matters of faith. I enjoy the pleasure of his company and feel enriched by it. But at no time has my heart whispered to me, "What a pity that this beautiful soul should be lost. . . ." Only that man will be troubled by such regrets who believes that there is no salvation outside his church.

Every man, admittedly, has a duty to teach his fellowmen understanding and virtue and to seek to eradicate prejudice and error in every possible way. Consequently, one could assume that a man has the responsibility of taking a public stand against religious notions that he considers erroneous. Nevertheless, not every prejudice or weakness we seem to detect in our fellowmen is equally harmful. Nor should we react to all of them in the same manner. Some prejudices strike directly at the happiness of mankind. Their influence on morality is pernicious; we cannot expect even an incidental benefit from them. These prejudices must be attacked immediately and unhesitatingly by anyone who has the interests of mankind at heart. Any delay or detour would be irresponsible. Fanaticism, hatred of one's fellowmen and the wish to persecute them, levity, self-indulgence, amoral atheism—these are among the failings that disturb man's inner peace and happiness and destroy his latent capacity for truth and goodness before it can unfold.

But some of my fellowmen hold views and convictions which, although I may consider them wrong, do belong to a higher order of theoretical principles. They are not harmful, because they have little or no relationship to the practical concerns of daily life. Yet they frequently constitute the foundation on which people have erected their systems of morality and social order and are therefore of great importance to them. To question such notions publicly merely because we consider them biased or erroneous would be like removing the foundation stones of a building in order to examine the soundness of its structure. Any person who is interested more in man's welfare than in his own fame will refrain from public statements in such matters. He will proceed with the utmost care in order not to destroy someone else's ethical principles, even though he may suspect they are faulty, until the other person is prepared to accept the truth in their stead.

Therefore, I find it possible to remain silent despite the fact that I may encounter racial prejudices and religious errors among my fellow citizens, as long as their views do not subvert natural religion or undermine natural law. In fact, these views may incidentally even produce some good. I admit that our actions do not deserve to be called moral if they are grounded in error and that the cause of the good will be advanced more effectively and lastingly by truth, where truth is known, than by prejudice and error. Nevertheless, as long as truth is not yet known or not yet sufficiently accepted to have the same impact upon the masses that their old prejudices did, their preconceived notions must be considered inviolate by any friend of true virtue.

We must show this kind of discretion especially where a people, though harboring seemingly erroneous beliefs, has otherwise distinguished itself intellectually and morally and has produced a number of great personalities who rank high among the benefactors of mankind. We should, with respectful silence, overlook the errors of so noble a member of the human family even if we think it is all too human on occasion. Is there really anyone among us who is entitled to ignore the excellent qualities of such a people and to criticize it for a single weakness he may have discovered?

These are the reasons, rooted in my religious and philosophical convictions, for which I carefully avoid religious controversy. If you add to them the circumstances of my life among my fellowmen, I am sure you will find my position justified. I am a member of an oppressed people which must appeal to the benevolence of the government for protection and shelter—which are not always granted, and never without limitations. Content to be tolerated and protected, my fellow Jews willingly forego liberties granted to every other human being. Barred even from temporary residence in many countries, they consider it no small favor when a nation admits them under tolerable conditions. As you know, your circumcised friend may not even visit you in Zurich, because of the laws of your own home town. Thus, my coreligionists owe much grateful appreciation to any government that shows them humanitarian consideration and permits them, without interference, to worship the Almighty in the ways of their fathers. They enjoy a fair amount of freedom in the country in which I live. Should they therefore attack their protectors on an issue to which men of virtue are particularly sensitive? Or would it not be more fitting if they abstained from religious disputes with the dominant creed?

These considerations governed my actions and motivated my decision to stay away from religious controversies unless exceptional circumstances were to force me to change my mind. To the private challenges of some men whom I respect highly I was bold enough to react with silence, while for the little minds that think they can bait me publicly because of my religion, I have nothing but contempt. But when a Lavater solemnly calls upon me, I have no choice but to express my convictions in public, lest my silence be misconstrued as contemptuous disregard or acquiescence.

I have read your translation of Bonnet's essay with close attention. After everything I have already said, I hope there can no longer be any doubt as to whether I found his arguments convincing. In addition, however, I must confess that I do not consider his reasoning even adequate as a defense of the Christian religion, as you seem to do.

Judging him by his other works, I consider M. Bonnet an excellent author. But I have read many vindications of Christianity by our fellow Germans, if not by Englishmen, that are far more thorough and philosophically more acceptable than M. Bonnet's essay, which you have recommended for my conversion. Unless I am mistaken, most of the writer's philosophical hypotheses are of German origin, and even the author of the *Essai de psychologie* [an anonymous work written by Bonnet himself], whose arguments M. Bonnet follows so faithfully, owes nearly all his views to German scholars. Where philosophical principles are concerned, a German rarely has need to borrow from his neighbor.

Nor are the general reflections with which M. Bonnet prefaces his work very profound. In fact, I could hardly recognize Bonnet from the illegitimate and arbitrary manner in which he uses this section of his work as an apologia for his religion. I regret that my opinion is so much at variance with yours in this respect; but I have the impression that M. Bonnet's personal convictions and laudable religious zeal led him to ascribe to his truths a cogency that no one else can see in them. Most of his conclusions do not follow from his premises; moreover, I would venture to defend any religion whatever with the identical arguments. This may not even be the author's fault. He evidently wrote only for people who already share his convictions and who read such treatises simply in order to be confirmed in their beliefs. When an author and his reading public hold identical preconceived notions about an issue under discussion, they will readily agree upon its truth.

What amazes me, however, is that you, Sir, consider this study of sufficient caliber to convert a man whose principles must be diametrically opposed to it. It was probably impossible for you to project yourself into the mind of someone for whom these views are not foregone conclusions, but who must first be persuaded of their validity. If you attempted to do this, yet still believe, as you say you do, that Socrates himself should have found M. Bonnet's proofs irrefutable, it can only mean that one of us must be a remarkable example of the influence which prejudice and upbringing exert even upon those who search for the truth with all their heart.

I have given you the reasons for which I fervently wish to have nothing to do with religious disputes. But I have also intimated to you that I could easily present strong arguments in refutation of M. Bonnet's thesis. If you insist, I shall have to overcome my reservations and publish my arguments against M. Bonnet's apologia in the form of a "Counterinquiry." I hope you will spare me this disagreeable task and permit me to return to the peaceful stance which is so much more natural to me. I am sure you will respect my preference if you put yourself in my place and look at the situation from my point of view, not yours. I should not like to be tempted to go beyond the limits that I have set for myself after mature consideration.

I am, with sincerest respect,

your obedient servant,
M. M.
Berlin, December 12, 1769.

31.

THE TWO FOCI OF THE JEWISH SOUL

Martin Buber

You have asked me to speak to you about the soul of Judaism. I have complied with this request, although I am against the cause for which you hold your conference, and I am against it not "just as a Jew," but also truly as a Jew, that is, as one who waits for the Kingdom of God, the Kingdom of Unification, and who regards all such "missions" as yours as springing from a misunderstanding of the nature of that kingdom, and as a hindrance to its coming. If in spite of this I have accepted your invitation, it is because I believe that when one is invited to share one's knowledge, one should not ask, "Why have you invited me?" but should share what one knows as well as one can—and that is my intention.

There is however one essential branch of Judaism about which I do not feel myself called upon to speak before you, and that is "the Law." My point of view with regard to this subject diverges from the traditional one; it is not a-nomistic, but neither is it entirely nomistic. For that reason I ought attempt neither to represent tradition, nor to substitute my own personal standpoint for the information you have desired of me. Besides, the problem of the Law does not seem to me to belong at all to the subject with which I have to deal. It would be a different matter were it my duty to present the teaching of Judaism. For the teaching of Judaism comes from Sinai; it is Moses' teaching. But the *soul* of Judaism is pre-Sinaitic; it is the soul which approached Sinai, and there received what it did receive; it is older than Moses; it is patriarchal, Abraham's soul, or more truly, since it concerns the *product* of a primordial age, it is Jacob's soul. The Law put on the soul and the soul can never again be understood outside of the Law; yet the soul itself is not of the Law. If one wishes to speak of the soul of Judaism, one must consider all the transformation it underwent through the ages till this very day; but one must never forget that in every one of its stages the soul has remained the same, and gone on in the same way.

This qualification, however, only makes the task more difficult. "I should wish to show you Judaism from the inside," wrote Franz Rosenzweig in 1916 to a Christian friend of Jewish descent, "in the same 'hymnal' way as you can show Christianity to me, the outsider; but the very reasons which make it possible for you to do so make it impossible for me. The soul of Christianity may be found in its outward expressions; Judaism wears a hard protective outer shell and one can speak about its soul only if one is within Judaism." If, therefore, I still venture here to speak about the soul of Judaism from the outside, it is only because I do not intend to give an account of that soul, but only some indication of its fundamental attitude.

It is not necessary for me to labor the point that this fundamental attitude is nothing else than the attitude of faith, viewed from its human side. "Faith," however, should not be taken in the sense given to it in the Epistle to the Hebrews, as faith that God exists. That has never been doubted by Jacob's soul. In proclaiming its faith, its *emunah,* the soul only proclaimed that it put its trust in the everlasting God, *that he would be present* to the soul, as had been the experience of the patriarchs, and that it was entrusting itself to him, who was present. The German romantic philosopher Franz Baader did justice to the depth of Israel's faith relationship when he defined faith as "a pledge of faith, that is, as a tying of oneself, a betrothing of oneself, an entering into a covenant."

The fealty of the Jew is the substance of his soul. The living God to whom he has pledged himself appears in infinite manifestations in the infinite variety of things and events; and this acts both as an incentive and as a steadying influence upon those who owe him allegiance. In the abundance of his manifestations they can ever and again recognize the One to whom they have entrusted themselves and pledged their faith. The crucial word which God himself spoke of this rediscovery of his presence was spoken to Moses from the midst of the burning bush:

"I shall be there as I there shall be" (Exod. 3:14). He is ever present to his creature, but always in the form peculiar to that moment, so that the spirit of man cannot foretell in the garment of what existence and what situation God will manifest himself. It is for man to recognize him in each of his garments. I cannot straightaway call any man a pagan; I know only of the pagan in man. But insofar as there is any paganism, it does not consist in not discerning God, but in not recognizing him as ever the same; the Jewish in man, on the contrary, seems to me to be the ever renewed rediscernment of God.

I shall therefore speak to you about the Jewish soul by making a few references to its fundamental attitude; I shall regard it as being the concretion of this human element in a national form, and consider it as the nation-shaped instrument of such a fealty and rediscernment.

I see the soul of Judaism as elliptically turning round two centers.

One center of the Jewish soul is the primeval experience that God is wholly raised above man, that he is beyond the grasp of man, and yet that he is present in an immediate relationship with these human beings who are absolutely incommensurable with him, and that he faces them. To know both these things at the same time, so that they cannot be separated, constitutes the living core of every believing Jewish soul; to know both, "God in heaven," that is, in complete hiddenness, and man "on earth," that is, in the fragmentation of the world of his senses and his understanding; God in the perfection and incomprehensibility of his being, and man in the abysmal contradiction of this strange existence from birth to death—and between both, immediacy!

The pious Jews of pre-Christian times called their God "Father"; and when the naively pious Jew in Eastern Europe uses that name today, he does not repeat something which he has learned, but he expresses a realization which he has come upon himself of the fatherhood of God and the sonship of man. It is not as though these men did not know that God is also utterly distant; it is rather that they know at the same time that however far away God is, he is never unrelated to them, and that even the man who is farthest away from God cannot cut himself off from the mutual relationship. In spite of the complete distance between God and man, they know that when God created man he set the mark of his image upon man's brow, and embedded it in man's nature, and that however faint God's mark may become, it can never be entirely wiped out.

According to hasidic legend, when the Baal Shem conjured up the demon Sammael, he showed him this mark on the forehead of his disciples, and when the master bade the conquered demon begone, the latter prayed, "Sons of the living God, permit me to remain a little while to look at the mark of the image of God on your faces." God's real commandment to men is to realize this image.

"Fear of God," accordingly, never means to the Jews that they ought to be afraid of God, but that, trembling, they ought to be aware of his incomprehensibility. The fear of God is the creaturely knowledge of the darkness to which none of our spiritual powers can reach, and out of which God reveals himself. Therefore, "the fear of God" is rightly called "the beginning of knowledge" (Ps. 111:10). It is the dark gate through which man must pass if he is to enter into the love of God. He who wishes to avoid passing through this gate, he who begins to provide himself with a comprehensible God, constructed thus and not otherwise, runs the risk of having to despair of God in view of the actualities of history and life, or of falling into inner falsehood. Only through the fear of God does man enter so deep into the love of God that he cannot again be cast out of it.

But fear of God is just a gate; it is not a house in which one can comfortably settle down—he who should want to live in it in adoration would neglect the performance of the essential commandment. God is incomprehensible, but he can be known through a bond of mutual relationship. God cannot be fathomed by knowledge, but he can be imitated. The life of man who is unlike God can yet be an *imitatio Dei.* "The likeness" is not closed to the "unlike." This is exactly what is meant when the Scripture instructs man to walk in God's way and in his footsteps. Man cannot by his own strength complete any way or any piece of the way, but he can enter on the path, he can take that first step, and again and again that first step. Man cannot "be like unto God," but with all the inadequacy of each of his days, he can follow God at all times, using the capacity he has on that particular day—and if he has used the capacity of that day to the full, he has done enough. This is not a mere act of faith; it is an entering into the life that has to be lived on that day with all the active fullness of a created person. This activity is within man's capacity: uncurtailed and not to be curtailed, the capacity is present through all the generations. God concedes the might to abridge this central property of decision to no primordial "Fall," however far-reaching in its effects, for the intention of God the Creator is mightier than the sin of man. The Jew knows from his knowledge of creation and of creatureliness that there may be burdens inherited from prehistoric and historic times, but that there is no overpowering original sin which could prevent the late-comer from deciding as freely as did Adam; as freely as Adam let God's hand go the latecomer can clasp it. We are dependent on grace; but we do not do God's will when we take it upon ourselves to begin with grace instead of beginning with ourselves. Only our beginning, our having begun, poor as it is, leads us to grace. God made no tools for himself, he needs none; he created for himself a partner in the dialogue of time and one who is capable of holding converse.

In this dialogue God speaks to every man through the life which he gives him again and again. Therefore man can only answer God with the whole of life—with the way in which he lives this given life. The Jewish teaching of the wholeness of life is the other side of the Jewish teaching of the unity of God. Because God bestows not only spirit on man, but the whole of his existence, from its "lowest" to its "highest" levels as well, man can fulfil the obligations of his partnership with God by no spiritual attitude, by no worship, on no sacred upper story; the whole of life is required, every one of its areas and every one of its circumstances. There is no true human share of holiness without the hallowing of the everyday. Whilst Judaism unfolds itself through the history of its faith, and so long as it does unfold itself through that history, it holds out against that "religion" which is an attempt to assign a circumscribed part to God, in order to satisfy him who bespeaks and lays claim to the whole. But this unfolding of Judaism is really an unfolding, and not a metamorphosis.

To clarify our meaning we take the sacrificial cultus as an example. One of the two fundamental elements in biblical animal sacrifice is the sacralization of the natural life: he who slaughters an animal consecrates a part of it to God, and so doing hallows his eating of it. The second fundamental element is the sacramentalization of the complete surrender of life; to this element belong those types of sacrifice in which the person who offers the sacrifice puts his hands on the head of the animal in order to identify himself with it; in doing so he gives physical expression to the thought that he is bringing himself to be sacrificed in the person of the animal. He who performs these sacrifices without having this intention in his soul makes the cult meaningless, yes, absurd; it was against him that the prophets directed their fight against the sacrificial service which had been emptied of its core. In the Judaism of the Diaspora prayer takes the place of sacrifice; but prayer is also offered for the reinstatement of the cult, that is for the return of the holy unity of body and spirit. And in that consummation of Diaspora Judaism which we call hasidic piety, both fundamental elements unite into a new conception which fulfils the original meaning of the cult. When the purified and sanctified man in purity and holiness takes food into himself, eating becomes a sacrifice, the table an altar, and man consecrates himself to the Deity. At that point there is no longer a gulf between the natural and the sacral; at that point there is no longer the need for a substitute; at that point the natural event itself becomes a sacrament.

The Holy strives to include within itself the whole of life. The Law differentiates between the holy and the profane, but the Law desires to lead the way toward the messianic removal of the differentiation, to the all-sanctification. Hasidic piety no longer recognizes anything as simply and irreparably profane: "the profane" is for hasidism only a designation for the not yet sanctified, for that which is to be sanctified. Everything physical, all drives and urges and desires, everything creaturely, is material for sanctification. From the very same passionate powers which, undirected, give rise to evil, when they are turned toward God, the good arises. One does not serve God with the spirit only, but with the whole of his nature, without any subtractions. There is not one realm of the spirit and another of nature; there is only the growing realm of God. God is not spirit, but what we call spirit and what we call nature hail equally from the God who is beyond and equally conditioned by both, and whose kingdom reaches its fulness in the complete unity of spirit and nature.

The second focus of the Jewish soul is the basic consciousness that God's redeeming power is at work everywhere and at all times, but that a state of redemption exists nowhere and never. The Jew experiences as a person what every openhearted human being experiences as a person: the experience, in the hour when he is most utterly forsaken, of a breath from above, the nearness, the touch, the mysterious intimacy of light out of darkness; and the Jew, as part of the world, experiences, perhaps more intensely than any other part, the world's lack of redemption. He feels this lack of redemption against his skin, he tastes it on his tongue, the burden of the unredeemed world lies on him. Because of this almost physical knowledge of his, he *cannot* concede that the redemption has taken place; he knows that it has not. It is true that he can discover prefigurations of redemption in past history, but he always discovers only that mysterious intimacy of light out of darkness which is at work everywhere and at all times; no redemption which is different in kind, none which by its nature would be unique, which would be conclusive for future ages, and which had but to be consummated. Most of all, only through a denial of his own meaning and his own mission would it be possible for him to acknowledge that in a world which still remains unredeemed an anticipation of the redemption had been effected by which the human soul—or rather merely the souls of men who in a specific sense are believers—had been redeemed.

With a strength which original grace has given him, and which none of his historic trials has ever wrested from him, the Jew resists the radical division of soul and world which forms the basis of this conception; he resists the conception of a divine splitting of existence; he resists most passionately the awful notion of a *massa perditionis*. The God in whom he believes has not created the totality in order to let it split apart into one blessed and one damned half. God's eternity is not to be conceived by man; but—and this we Jews know until the moment of our death—there can be no eternity in which *everything* will not be accepted into God's atonement, when God has drawn time back into eternity. Should there however be a stage in the redemption of the world in which redemption is first fulfilled in one *part* of the world, we would derive no claim to redemption from our faith, much less from any other source. "If You do not yet wish to redeem Israel, at any rate redeem the goyim," the rabbi of Koznitz used to pray.

It is possible to argue against me, that there has been after all another eschatology in Judaism than that which I have indicated, that the apocalyptic stands beside the prophetic eschatology. It is actually important to make clear to oneself where the difference between the two lies. The prophetic belief about the end of time is in all essentials autochthonous; the apocalyptic belief is in all essentials built up of elements from Iranian dualism. Accordingly, the prophetic promises a consummation of creation, the apocalyptic its abrogation and super-session by another world, completely different in nature; the prophetic allows "the evil" to find the direction that leads toward God, and to enter into the good; the apocalyptic sees good and evil severed forever at the end of days, the good redeemed, the evil unredeemable for all eternity; the prophetic believes that the earth shall be hallowed, the apocalyptic despairs of an earth which it considers to be hopelessly doomed; the prophetic allows God's creative original will to be fulfilled completely; the apocalyptic allows the unfaithful creature power over the Creator, in that the creatures' actions force God to abandon nature. There was a time when it must have seemed uncertain whether the current apocalyptic teaching might not be victorious over the traditional prophetic messianism; if that had happened, it is to be assumed that Judaism would not have outlived its central faith—explicitly or imperceptibly it would have merged with Christianity, which is so strongly influenced by that dualism. During an epoch in which the prophetic was lacking, the Tannaites, early talmudic masters, helped prophetic messianism to triumph over the apocalyptic conception, and in doing so saved Judaism.

Still another important difference separates the two forms of Jewish belief about the end of days. The apocalyptists wished to predict an unalterable immovable future event; they were following Iranian conceptions in this point as well. For, according to the Iranians, history is divided into equal cycles of thousands of years, and the end of the world, the final victory of good over evil, can be predetermined with mathematical accuracy.

Not so the prophets of Israel: They prophesy "for the sake of those who turn." That is, they do not warn against something which will happen in any case, but against that which will happen if those who are called upon to turn do not.

The Book of Jonah is a clear example of what is meant by prophecy. After Jonah has tried in vain to flee from the task God has given him, he is sent to Nineveh to prophesy its downfall. But Nineveh turns —and God changes its destiny. Jonah is vexed that the word for whose sake the Lord had broken his resistance had been rendered void; if one is forced to prophesy, one's prophecy must stand. But God is of a different opinion; he will employ no soothsayers, but messengers to the souls of men—the souls that are able to decide which way to go, and whose decision is allowed to contribute to the forging of the world's fate. Those who turn co-operate in the redemption of the world.

Man's partnership in the great dialogue finds its highest form of reality at this point. It is not as though any definite act of man could draw grace down from heaven; yet grace answers deed in unpredictable ways, grace unattainable, yet not self-withholding. It is not as though man has to do this or that "to hasten" the redemption of the world— "he that believes shall not make haste" (Isa. 28:16); yet those who turn co-operate in the redemption of the world. The extent and nature of the participation assigned to the creature remains secret. "Does that mean that God cannot redeem his world without the help of his creatures?" "It means that God does not will to be able to do it." "Has God need of man for his work?" "He wills to have need of man."

He who speaks of activism in this connection misunderstands the mystery. The act is no outward gesture. "The ram's horn," runs an haggadic saying, "which God will blow on that day will have been made from the right horn of the ram which once took Isaac's place as a sacrifice." The "servant" whom God made "a polished shaft" to hide apparently unused in his quiver (Isa. 49:2), the man who is condemned to live in hiding—or rather, not one man, but the type of men to whom this happens generation after generation—the man who is hidden in the shadow of God's hand, who does not "cause his voice to be heard in the street" (Isa. 42:2), he who in darkness suffers for God's sake (*ibid.*)—he it is who has been given as a light for the tribes of the world, that God's "salvation may be unto the end of the earth" (Isa. 49:6).

The mystery of the act, of the human part in preparing the redemption, passes through the darkness of the ages as a mystery of concealment, as a concealment within the person's relation to himself as well, until one day it will come into the open. To the question why according to tradition the Messiah was born on the anniversary of the day of the destruction of Jerusalem, a hasidic rabbi answered: "The power cannot rise, unless it has dwelt in the great concealment. . . . In the shell of oblivion grows the power of remembrance. That is the power of redemption. On the day of the Destruction the power will be lying at the bottom of the depths and growing. That is why on this day we sit on the ground; that is why on this day we visit the graves; that is why on this day was born the Messiah."

Though robbed of their real names, these two foci of the Jewish soul continue to exist for the "secularized" Jew too, insofar as he has not lost his soul. They are, first, the immediate relationship to the Existent One, and second, the power of atonement at work in an unatoned world. In other words, first, the *non-incarnation* of God who reveals himself to the "flesh" and is present to it in a mutual relationship, and second, the unbroken continuity of human history, which turns toward fulfilment and decision. These two centers constitute the ultimate division between Judaism and Christianity.

We "unify" God, when living and dying we profess his unity; we do not unite ourselves with him. The God in whom we believe, to whom we are pledged, does not unite with human substance on earth. But the very fact that we do not imagine that we can unite with him enables us the more ardently to demand "that the world shall be perfected under the kingship of the Mighty One."

We feel salvation happening; and we feel the unsaved world. No savior with whom a new redeemed history began has appeared to us at any definite point in history. Because we have not been stilled by anything which has happened, we are wholly directed toward the coming of that which is to come.

Thus, though divided from you, we have been attached to you. As Franz Rosenzweig wrote in the letter which I have already quoted: "You who live in an *ecclesia triumphans* need a silent servant to cry to you whenever you believe you *have partaken* of God in bread and wine, 'Lord, remember the last things.' "

What have you and we in common? If we take the question literally, a book and an expectation.

To you the book is a forecourt; to us it is the sanctuary. But in this place we can dwell together, and together listen to the voice that speaks here. That means that we can work together to evoke the buried speech of that voice; together we can redeem the imprisoned living word.

Your expectation is directed toward a second coming, ours to a coming which has not been anticipated by a first. To you the phrasing of world history is determined by one absolute midpoint, the year nought; to us it is an unbroken flow of tones following each other without a pause from their origin to their consummation. But we can wait for the advent of the One together, and there are moments when we may prepare the way before him together.

Pre-messianically our destinies are divided. Now to the Christian the Jew is the incomprehensibly obdurate man, who declines to see what has happened; and to the Jew the Christian is the incomprehensibly daring man, who affirms in an unredeemed world that its redemption has been accomplished. This is a gulf which no human power can bridge. But it does not prevent the common watch for a unity to come to us from God, which, soaring above all of your imagination and all of ours, affirms and denies, denies and affirms what you hold and what we hold, and which replaces all the creedal truths of earth by the ontological truth of heaven which is one.

It behooves both you and us to hold inviolably fast to our own true faith, that is to our own deepest relationship to truth. It behooves both of us to show a religious respect for the true faith of the other. This is not what is called "tolerance," our task is not to tolerate each other's waywardness but to acknowledge the real relationship in which both stand to the truth. Whenever we both, Christian and Jew, care more for God himself than for our images of God, we are united in the feeling that our Father's house is differently constructed than our human models take it to be.

32.

JUDAISM IN THE POST-CHRISTIAN ERA

Eliezer Berkovits

There was a phase in world history that may be called the Christian era. It designates that period in which Christianity, including Christian civilization and culture—all that goes under the name of the West—was the dominant and dominating force. We suggest that this phase is now at an end. We propose that Judaism ought to take adequate cognizance of this important change in the world situation and develop its attitude and its religious policies accordingly.

The Christian era did not start with the birth of Jesus. It dates from the first half of the fourth century, commencing when Constantine the Great established Christianity as the state religion of the Roman Empire. The characteristic mark of the era was militancy. This was inherent in its beginnings: Christianity did not capture the Roman Empire by the power of a religious idea but by the sword of the emperor. As soon as Christianity was established, Judaism was declared an odious heretic sect, and its propagation was forbidden under the penalty of death. All other religions were completely oppressed and actually exterminated. Christianity's conquering march all over Europe began. It was a conquest in the true sense of the word: Europe was Christianized by the power of the imperial sword. The Saxons, the Franks, many of the aboriginal tribes, were placed before the choice: baptism or death. Uncounted numbers chose death. *Cuius regio cuius religio* [the religion of a country is that of its ruler], the principle by which faith was determined in the religious wars that tore Europe apart after the Reformation, was also the principle by which, from the earliest days of the established church, Christianity was spread across the face of the earth. Even the vast missionary activities in Asia and Africa were possible only because the Western colonizing powers which opened up these new lands were Christian. The preachers of the gospel marched in the wake of the swift and terrible sword of Constantine.

This era has come to an end in our days, before our own eyes. It has reached its conclusion because the sword of Constantine has been passed on to numerous other hands. The Soviets are holding it mightily in their grip; Red China has taken possession of it; the dark millions of Africa are acquiring it; hundreds of millions of Moslems, Buddhists and Hindus have learned to wield it. Christianity is no longer the decisive power or influence. From now on, world history will be determined by the interplay of many forces, many cultures and civilizations, most of them non-Christian, some of them anti-Christian.

This change in the world situation carries with it weighty consequences for Christianity, which the Church, especially the Roman Church, has not been slow to appreciate. *Nolens volens* the age of Christian militancy is over; "baptism or death" is gone forever. The reason, as we noted, is that now so many non-Christians, too, have acquired the sword of Constantine. They can wield it no less effectively than the Christian powers did in the past; they are in the majority, and now they, in turn, have the power to be intolerant, to oppress and persecute no less crushingly than did Christianity through the long and dark centuries of the Christian era.

The new revolutionary distribution of the balance of power in the *ecumene* is ultimately responsible for the new Christian ecumenism. An interesting illustration of this was provided by the discussion on human freedom which took place at the Vatican Council. It would seem that, notwithstanding the arguments in the Council about the theological niceties of the final formula, the Church now affirms the principle of freedom of religious worship and human conscience. Following the discussion, we could not help thinking of the old adage about the mills of God which, though they grind slowly, grind exceedingly fine. We recalled that the freedoms of religion and conscience existed in the Roman Empire at the beginning of the rule of Constantine the Great. In fact, they were affirmed anew in Constantine's own Edict of Tolerance. But that was before he converted to Christianity. When Christianity became the state religion of the empire tolerance was abolished, freedom of religion proscribed, and freedom of conscience eradicated. This state of affairs continued through the dark centuries that followed in the form of oppression, persecution, auto-da-fés, religious wars and massacres. But now things are changing. After sixteen centuries of Christianity regnant in the world, the Church is ready to champion ideals which were realized by mankind in the heathen Roman Empire, not to speak of Judaism or the secularisms of the last four centuries. What has brought about this *volte-face* of the Church? Nothing but the fact that Christianity is no longer supreme in the world. When the Church leaders speak of freedom of religion, they mean first of all freedom for Christians to adhere to their faith in Communist lands. When they affirm freedom of conscience, they mean primarily freedom for the Church to propagate Christianity in Asia and Africa among Moslems, Buddhists, Hindus, and among the followers of all kinds of tribal cults. Christianity is now on the side of tolerance because this is the post-Christian age of world history, because in this post-Christian era the old policies of intolerance are no longer viable. Any policy of Christian intolerance would be self-defeating, for it would justify intolerance on the part of the non-Christian powers, civilizations and religions. It would ultimately boomerang onto the heads of hundreds of millions of Christians the world over. Ecumenism or no ecumenism, tolerance and a measure of official friendliness toward other religions and philosophies of life have today become matters of practical politics for the Church and for Christianity.

What should be the Jewish attitude, facing Christianity in the post-Christian era of world history?

We must, above all, understand history—that this is, in fact, the post-Christian era. We must understand the significance and the implications of this revolutionary change. From now on Christianity will have to rely for its propagation, as any decent religion should, on the methods of persuasion. All the friendlier statements about Jews and Judaism made in this new age by the Church and Christianity must be comprehended in the light of the change imposed by external historic developments upon Christianity. This certainly applies to the Vatican Council's schema on the Jews. It was forced on the Church by the new historic constellation. There are, of course, many Christians who feel ashamed of the abominable crimes committed by Christendom against Judaism and the Jewish people. However, the uncharitable haggling in the Council about the final version of the schema in itself proved that the sense of shame in some Christian consciences alone would never have sufficed to produce even that extremely guarded and political declaration.

An understanding of the implications of the new situation itself ought to help those Jews who are in contact with Church authorities and Christian leaders. Often they represent Judaism and the Jewish people without a mandate. At least let them speak with courage, self-assurance and with all the dignity to which sixteen centuries of Jewish martyrdom in Christian lands obligates them. For the first time since the early days of the fourth century there may be a confrontation between Judaism and Christianity in freedom. Let it, indeed, take place in freedom!

Confrontation in freedom means that the scope of the confrontation must not be reduced to the provincial dimensions of Jewish-Christian understanding in the United States. Its significance must not be falsified for cheap considerations of public relations. Jewish-Christian confrontation in freedom is confrontation in the world-historic context of Israel's own Messianic history. In this new type of encounter with Christianity our generation must stand for all the generations that ever lived and suffered in Christian lands. It must stand for all the innumerable generations that never beheld the light of day because those who were destined to be their progenitors perished before their time under the bloody yoke of Christian oppression. We must face Christianity as the children of the *am olam,* the eternal people, viewing historic developments *sub specie aeternitatis.* I have never sensed so acutely that we are indeed the *am olam* as in these days when we are able to survey the Christian performance from the beginning of the Christian era to its end. We have been there all the time, we alone know what it has meant.

It is our responsibility to sum up the meaning of that era, unimpressed by Christian claims, guided exclusively by our own experience. In terms of the Jewish experience in the lands of Christendom, the final result of that age is bankruptcy—the moral bankruptcy of Christian civilization and the spiritual bankruptcy of Christian religion. After nineteen centuries of Christianity, the extermination of six million Jews, among them one-and-a-half million children, carried out in cold blood in the very heart of Christian Europe, encouraged by the criminal silence of virtually all Christendom, including that of an infallible Holy Father in Rome, was the natural culmination of this bankruptcy. A straight line leads from the first act of oppression against the Jews and Judaism in the fourth century to the holocaust in the twentieth. In order to pacify the Christian conscience it is said that the Nazis were not Christians. But they were all the children of Christians. They were the fruit of nineteen centuries of Christianity—the logical fruit of violence and militancy, oppression and intolerance, hatred and persecution, which dominated European history for the sixteen centuries since Constantine the Great. Without the contempt and the hatred for the Jew planted by Christianity in the hearts of the multitude of its followers, Nazism's crime against the Jewish people could never have even been conceived, much less executed. What was started at the Council of Nicea was duly completed in the concentration camps and the crematoria. This has been a moral and spiritual collapse the like of which the world has never witnessed before for contemptibility and inhumanity. Judged in the light of our own experience and under the aspects of the Messianic history of the *am olam,* we are confronting a morally and spiritually bankrupt civilization and religion. This knowledge should determine our attitude. In its light ought we define our position in relationship to the various issues which have arisen in the wake of this new Jewish-Christian encounter in freedom.

The schema on the Jews has now been officially promulgated by the Vatican Council. It has thought fit to declare solemnly before all the world that the Jews are not to be considered a people accursed by God; the Jews are not collectively guilty for the death of Jesus. We cannot help wondering whether in the opinion of the leaders of the Church these are still the Middle Ages or almost the Middle Ages. For many centuries it was they who have been doing the persecuting, they who perpetuated abominable acts of inhumanity against the Jewish people, but now they condescend to tell the world that we are perhaps not guilty nor to be considered accursed by God.

Underneath such lack of sensitivity to historic truth still lingers the barbarous concept that the fact that someone is persecuted and made to suffer by others is proof that something is wrong with him. For many centuries Christian clerics, theologians and historians have maintained that the fact that Jews had lost their homeland, were scattered over the face of the earth, everywhere persecuted and held in contempt, was in itself proof that they were an accursed people, punished for the crime of having killed Jesus. In 1947 this thesis could still be found in history books written for the enlightenment of Christian youth (see *The Foot of Pride,* Malcolm Hay, p. 22).

If it ever occurred to an isolated Christian that the "proof" was perhaps not altogether convincing, since it was man and not God who imposed all this suffering on the Jew, he could easily calm his conscience with the Christian logic of the Church Father, St. John Chrysostom, who showed that it was really God after all who was punishing the Jews. For, he argued, could man do all this to the Jews "unless it had been God's will?" By the same logic, not so long ago in Christian lands they would light the faggots under the poor creatures accused of witchcraft or cast them into deep water. If they burned or drowned, they were guilty of the crime of which they were accused. The Vatican Council's declaration about the Jews reveals how deeply rooted the logic of Chrysostom still is in the Christian psyche. Given the premises of Chrysostom's logic, it might seem Christian charity to declare that these Jews, though they suffered and were persecuted, are nevertheless not to be considered a people accursed by God.

This is, indeed, progress. A non-Christian, however, is not impressed. To such noble Christian sentiments he might prefer the teaching of the heathen Socrates who maintained that it was better to suffer than to inflict suffering, nobler to be martyred than to inflict martyrdom. Followers of Socrates will be inclined to say that those who make others suffer are more likely to be a people accursed by God than those who are made to suffer by them. In this respect Jews are much closer to the heathen Socratic tradition than to the Christian. Many centuries ago their Pharisaic teachers interpreted for them the words of *Ecclesiastes,* "God seeketh that which is pursued," to mean: "The wicked pursues the righteous—God seeketh the pursued; the righteous pursues the righteous—God seeketh the pursued; the righteous pursues the righteous —God seeketh the pursued; the wicked pursues the wicked—God seeketh the pursued; and even when the righteous pursues the wicked, God seeketh the pursued" (*Vayikra Raba,* 27:5, and *Tanhuma, Emor,* 9). Always God seeks the pursued. To be told after sixteen centuries of oppression and persecution in Christian lands by those responsible for these acts of inhumanity that the Jews are not a people accursed by God is an offense not so much to Jews as to God.

At one point, when it seemed that the Vatican Council was about to exonerate the Jewish people completely of the guilt of deicide, there were some precipitate Reform rabbis who felt that the Jews ought to reciprocate such a noble gesture by acknowledging Jesus as a prophet. It would seem to us that if there were to be any reciprocating Jewish acknowledgment, it should be commensurate with the Christian pronouncement. It might be said, for example, that the appropriate reciprocating gesture on the part of Jewry could be a solemn declaration that the man who endured the crucifixion is not to be regarded as accursed by God. Of course, Jews will never issue such a declaration, because they have never believed in Chrysostom's type of reasoning. Nor do they suffer from the illusion that they personally and humanly represent God on earth. They are, therefore, in no position to dispense God's curse or His blessing. They deem it more respectful toward God to leave such dispensations to Him.

Many Christians and Jews are these days advocating the idea of a Jewish-Christian dialogue. The schema on the Jews recommends such "fraternal dialogues," in order to foster "a mutual knowledge and respect." We ought to analyze this from several approaches—emotional, philosophical, theological, and practical.

We feel that, emotionally, we are not as yet ready to enter into a fraternal dialogue with a church, a religion, that has been responsible for so much suffering, and which is ultimately responsible for the murder of our fathers and mothers, brothers and sisters in the present generation. There are, of course, Jews who are only too eager to undertake such a dialogue. They are either Jews without memories or Jews for whom Judaism is exclusively a matter of public relations, or confused or spineless Jews unable to appreciate the meaning of confrontation in full freedom. For Jewry as a whole an honest fraternal dialogue with Christianity is at this state emotionally impossible. The majority of the Jewish people still mourn in a very personal sense. In a hundred years, perhaps, depending on Christian deeds toward Jews, we may be emotionally ready for the dialogue.

On the level of philosophical thought, contact and interchange of ideas are certainly to be desired. Jews are familiar with Barth and Tillich, Maritain and Marcel, no less than with Sartre or Radhakrishnan. This, however, is not a specific Jewish-Christian dialogue. It is the dialogue in the intellectual realm which Judaism has carried on with all cultures and religions at all times. There is no more reason or need for a Jewish-Christian dialogue than for a Jewish-Moslem, Jewish-Hindu, Jewish-existentialist, or Jewish-atheist dialogue. The realm of thought is universal.

As to a dialogue in the purely theological sense, nothing could be more fruitless and pointless. Judaism is Judaism because it rejects Christianity, and Christianity is Christianity because it rejects Judaism. What is usually referred to as the Judeo-Christian tradition exists only in Christian or secularist fantasy. As far as Jews are concerned, Judaism is fully sufficient. There is nothing in Christianity for them. Whatever in Christian teaching is acceptable to them is borrowed from Judaism. Jews do not have to turn to the New Testament for the "two laws"; Jesus was quoting them from the Hebrew Bible. And whatever is not Jewish in Christianity is not acceptable to the Jew.

There are many who believe that Jews and Christians have at least the "Old Testament" in common. This is a serious misunderstanding. The Jews have no "Old Testament." The very fact that for the Christians it is the "Old Testament" indicates that it is not identical with the Hebrew Bible. This is not a matter of mere semantics. The "Old Testament" asks for a New Testament; the Hebrew Bible is complete within itself. The Christian interpretation of Biblical Judaism is not the Judaism of the Hebrew Bible. The Christian, reading his "Old Testament," discerns history and teaching which are essentially different from what is contained in the Jewish Bible: from the Christian point of view Biblical Judaism, as found in the "Old Testament," is altogether *preparatio evangelica*—a preparation for the divine epiphany as the Christian finds it in the New Testament. From the Jewish point of view, the very essence of Biblical Judaism and the very core of Biblical teaching about God rule out such divine self-revelation. From the Jewish point of view, the "Old Testament" is the Gentile's misinterpretation of the very gist of the message of the Hebrew Bible. When Christians use the term "Judeo-Christian," "Judeo" means something fundamentally different from what is Jewish for the Jew. Nor does Judaism have a common spiritual patrimony with Christianity in the Patriarchs and the Prophets: in Jewish understanding, the God of Abraham is not the triune deity of Christianity.

There is a noteworthy contradiction as regards this matter of the "fraternal dialogue" in the pronouncements of the Vatican Council. On the one hand, the Council encourages dialogues with other religions; on the other, it also affirms that the Roman Catholic Church is the only repository of all true religion. What then is the purpose of the dialogue for the Church? There is nothing that Christianity may gain by it. The schema on non-Christians concedes that other religions may contain some rays of divine light in their beliefs and teaching. Yet, it is to be understood that all these rays of light are comprehended in greater purity and perfection in the Church. How then is dialogue possible? One does not enter into a dialogue in honesty when one is convinced from the beginning that one is in possession of all the truth and one's partner in the dialogue is in error. This is not dialogical encounter. It can have only one purpose—to spread the good tiding to the unfortunate ones who have not yet seen one's own light.

This, we have seen, is the post-Christian era. In former times Jews were commanded to appear before popes, bishops, and kings in order to defend their beliefs in religious disputations. These popes, bishops, and most Christian kings were also the judges. In these disputations the Jews could never be sure whether to win or lose was better for them. It also used to be customary to impose on Jewish communities the indignity of compelling them to admit missionary preachers into the synagogues to listen to their sermons and boorish insults. These channels of "communication" with the Jewish people are no longer open. They are now to be replaced by "fraternal dialogue."

But there is no reason why Jews should be interested. Judaism does not have the ambition to save mankind, because it never maintained that mankind was lost without it. Judaism is the only possible way of life for Jews. Only Jews are lost without it. As to non-Jews, Judaism maintains that "the righteous of all the peoples have a share in the world-to-come." Judaism is free from missionary zeal. In turn, there is no reason on earth why it should make itself accessible to "fraternal dialogue" with a religion which, by its very premises, declares others to be in error and thus, from the outset, destroys the basis of a true dialogical situation.

But might not a Jewish-Christian dialogue have some beneficial, practical effects? Would it not further inter-religious understanding? The strange reality, however, is that whereas among Christians it is the clerics, theologians, and the more committed and knowledgeable Christians who propagate the idea of inter-religious understanding, the Jewish enthusiasts include the less committed Jews, the public-relations experts, the secularists. From such a dialogue, that in its very premises lacks intellectual honesty and emotional sincerity, it would be most unwise to expect any genuine deepening of inter-religious understanding. The greater the hopes one places in such a "dialogue," the greater the disappointments which must follow.

However, independently of all considerations of inter-religious politics, we reject the idea of inter-religious understanding on ethical grounds.

First of all, it represents a distortion of historic truth; it is a falsification of the true nature of the Judeo-Christian tragedy. It suggests a measure of mutuality in the responsibility for that tragedy; as if there had been friction and conflict because we did not know each other well enough; as if there had been struggle between Jews and Christians because they were not familiar with each other's noble religious traditions and beliefs. This is not the case. There were no conflicts or wars. There was only unilateral oppression and persecution. We reject the idea of inter-religious understanding as immoral because it is an attempt to whitewash a criminal past.

Further, the idea of inter-religious understanding is ethically objectionable because it makes respect for the other man dependent on whether I am able to appreciate his religion or his theology. In the official summary of the Vatican Council's schema on non-Christians we read that "the Council wants to foster and recommend a mutual knowledge and respect which is the fruit, above all, of Biblical and theological studies as well as of fraternal dialogues." We find the suggestion that mutual knowledge and respect among people should be the fruit of Biblical and theological studies, as well as of inter-religious dialogue, repugnant. It implies that if I am able to appreciate another man's religious belief I ought to respect and love him; if not, my contempt for him is understandable and justifiable. This is still conceived in the old questionable tradition of religious persecution. It is not a matter of whether Christianity acknowledges fragmentary truths in Judaism. All we want of Christians is that they keep their hands off us and our children! Human beings ought to treat each other with respect and hold each other dear independently of theological dialogues, Biblical studies, and independently of what they believe about each other's religion. I am free to reject any religion as humbug if that is what I think of it; but I am duty-bound to respect the dignity of every human being no matter what I may think of his religion. It is not inter-religious understanding that mankind needs but inter-*human* understanding— an understanding based on our common humanity and wholly independent of any need for common religious beliefs and theological principles.

There are some who believe that, in an age such as ours, when religion is being assailed on all sides by secularism, materialism, and atheism, Judaism and Christianity ought to form a common religious front in defense of religious values and ideals.

It will be found that the policy of a common front may be laid down as a general principle only in areas of inter-human endeavor and not in the specifically inter-religious realm. A common front is useful and necessary in the struggle for freedom of conscience and worship, for peace and social justice; our interests are identical in these fields of human striving. In the post-Christian era, however, these goals of freedom, peace, and social justice have universal validity. It would be extremely foolish to seek their realization by means of a narrowly Jewish-Christian religious front. On the other hand, in the specifically religious realm, a common interest cannot be predicated as a general principle. There, Jewish and Christian interest may occasionally coincide in certain specific situations; in others, it may not. Under a condition of freedom, each group ought to decide on its course of action in accordance with its own insight and understanding.

The confrontation between religion and secularism occurs first in the intellectual realm, in the heart and mind of the believer himself. Here Judaism must maintain its complete independence. In the intellectual confrontation with secularism Judaism must not become a mere adjunct to Protestant or Roman Catholic theology. Any close association with Christian thought is ultimately bound to cause confusion within Jewish thinking. It may cripple our ability to articulate the relevance of the specific Jewish position in our times. It would also be detrimental to Judaism's effectiveness: because of its fewer dogmas, Judaism is intellectually in a far better position to develop a philosophy or theology which can meet the intellectual onslaught of secularism. This is not easy, but it will be easier without the burden of a common religious front.

Even in the field of ethics and of the application of ethical principles to actual social or international conditions, one must be cautious about any joint Jewish-Christian endeavor. In many parts of Asia and Africa, Christianity has been compromised because of the close connection between colonial conquest and missionary activities. Closer to home, in the light of the Christian performance in the past and because of the practical requirements of Christian politics in the post-Christian era, it is not always easy to determine what is humanitarian-ethical deed and what is Christian propaganda. An example to ponder is Pope Paul VI's peace mission to the United Nations. The speech on behalf of world peace was a fine oration. It came, of course, rather late in history. In earlier periods, a pope's stand on universal peace and brotherhood could have stopped wars, expulsions, and massacres. Unfortunately, when it could have been most effective—in the Christian era—the papacy was unaware of its universal mission for peace. Today, peace is a popular slogan. What was once placed by Isaiah before the conscience of mankind as an ideal has now become an inescapable demand of practical world politics. Today the bomb itself is the most convincing argument for peace. "Make peace or perish" is its unmistakable message. In the final reckoning, when in a situation of world crisis the issue of war or peace in this atomic age will be decided, the pontifical plea will count for very little.

It would seem then that, on the whole, we have to go our own way. We have to work hard to make Judaism a significant philosophy of life in the intellectual climate of our age. We have to prove it to be a significant form of living which takes due cognizance of the moral predicaments of our days. We must equip it with the ability to articulate the truth of God in relationship to the vital issues of present-day human existence. If, as we develop our own position in the intellectual, ethical, theological, and religious realms of twentieth-century human endeavor, we find other religions working beside us, all the better. If not, we shall not be concerned. An awe-inspiring task lies ahead of us. Hard work, challenging and exacting, is to be done on the interpretation of Judaism and its implementation in this new era. We have every reason to continue with faith and confidence in our path. This is one of those rare turning points in history when we feel the breath of eternity about us. Having survived miraculously, the world historic mystery of Israel has been deepened ever more by Israel's return to the land of its origins, in accordance with the faith of the dark centuries of homelessness.

No one can foretell what this new era holds in store for mankind. But we are here at the threshold of the new age. We who were there when the Christian era began; we in whose martyrdom Christianity suffered its worst moral debacle; we in whose blood the Christian era found its end—we are here as this new era opens. And we shall be here when this new era reaches its close—we, the *edim,* God's own witnesses, the *am olam,* the eternal witness of history.

33.

THE PEOPLE ISRAEL LIVES

Emil L. Fackenheim

As I reread my theological writings of ten—or of 15 or 20—years ago I am filled with religious and theological guilt and repentance. In this report, however, I can deal only with the theological. More than 30 years ago, largely under the influence of Martin Buber and Franz Rosenzweig, I had responded to the demonic fact of nazism by turning my back on my 19th century liberal Jewish heritage and embracing what may broadly be called a neo-orthodox faith and theology. I had rejected the dissipation of the distinction between the Word of God and the word of man, between the divine covenant with Israel and the random events of history—above all, an ideology which had confused the messianic days with the achievements and promises of the modern world.

To this day I remain largely within this neo-orthodox stance. I remain, too, in the bond with Christians made possible by that stance, a bond which first became fully actual for me when in a nazi concentration camp before the war two of my closest fellow-sufferers and -witnesses were Christians. There was, however, one omission in my position of that time, and that omission remained in my writings for more than two decades. Having recognized "the demonic" in principle, I abused that recognition to ignore the scandalous uniqueness of Auschwitz. Having taken hold of what, after Hitler, unites Jews with Christians, I overlooked the utter abandonment of the children of Treblinka by the world, Christians included. And even as my Jewish brethren in Europe suffered an agony without precedent inside or outside Jewish history, I was at work on a theology which sought to show that nothing unprecedented could call into question the Jewish faith—that it is essentially immune to all "secular" events between Sinai and the Messianic days.

For the past half-dozen years or so I have recognized my guilt and sought to do repentance. And I can only plead that other Jews—religiously and nonreligiously minded—are likewise only now able to begin to face the Holocaust.

My mind and spirit are still numbed. I have, however, acquired one religious certainty as great as any in this religiously uncertain age. Søren Kierkegaard once perceived his "knight of faith" as forever obliged to retrace Abraham's road to Mount Moriah, the place where he was to sacrifice Isaac. The Jewish believer and theological thinker today—as well as a century or a millennium hence—is obliged to retrace, again and again, the *via dolorosa* which led one-third of his people to the human sacrifice in the nazi gas chambers. He is forbidden the cheap and often sacrilegious evasions which tempt him on every side: the "progressive" ideology which asserts that memory is unnecessary, that Auschwitz was an accidental "relapse into tribalism" (an insult to any tribe ever in existence); the "psychiatric" ideology which holds that memory is masochism even as Auschwitz itself was sadism, thus safely belittling both; the "liberal-universalist" ideology which asserts that memory is actually immoral, that because Jews must care about Vietnam, the black ghetto and Arab refugees, they are obliged to forget the greatest catastrophe suffered by their own people.

That last-named ideology is especially insidious, for good Jews are tempted by it. When I first called Auschwitz unique my assertion was at once taken to mean that a dead Jewish child at Auschwitz is a greater tragedy than a dead German child at Dresden. That was a misunderstanding possible only because of an anti-Semitism (conscious or unconscious) which distinguishes "universalistic" Jews concerned with others to the point of consenting to group suicide, and "particularistic" Jews who deserve this nasty epithet if they show any concern whatever for the fate of their own people. This ideology, I say, tempts many: witness the countless Jews today who risk much in behalf of Vietnam or the black ghetto but will not utter a word against Polish or Soviet anti-Semitism. Hate of Jews on the part of others has always produced self-hating Jews—never more so than when disguised as a moral ideology.

I call Auschwitz unique because it *is* unique. As my wife, Rose, put it in a letter to a minister, Auschwitz was

> overwhelming in its scope, shattering in its fury, inexplicable in its demonism. Unlike Hiroshima, it was no miscalculation of a government at war. It was minutely planned and executed over a 12-year period, with the compliance of thousands of citizens, to the deafening silence of the world. Unlike slaughtered Russian villagers, these were no chance victims of the fury of war. They were carefully chosen, named, listed, tabulated, and stamped. The Nazis went to incredible lengths to find even a single missing Jew. It did not help but hindered the war effort. For while anti-Semitism was in the beginning politically advantageous to the Nazis the actual crime of genocide had often to be carefully hidden from their own people. Troop trains were delivered from the Russian front in order to transport Jews to Auschwitz. Unique in all human history, the Holocaust was evil for evil's sake.

The woman who wrote those words is a Christian. I doubt whether I or any other Jew could have been so relentless as she was in her evaluation.

No wonder the mind seeks refuge in comparisons—some shallow, some obscene, all false—between Auschwitz and Hiroshima, or Vietnam, or the black ghetto, or even the American campus. Indeed, the very words "Holocaust" and "6 million" are evasive abstractions, empty universal substitutes for the countless particulars each of which is an inexhaustible mystery of sin and suffering. And when Jewish theologian Richard Rubenstein writes (in his essay in *The Religious Situation* [Beacon, 1968]) that "the facts are in" and that since "the theological options . . . will not magically increase with the passing of time" we may as well make our choice now, we must conclude that he does not know whereof he speaks.

Let me take just one of those particulars. In issuing "work permits" which were designed to separate "useless" Jews to be murdered at once from "useful" ones to be kept useful by diabolically contrived false hopes and murdered later, the nazis customarily issued two such permits to an able-bodied Jewish man. One was untransferable, to be kept for himself; the other was to be given at his own discretion to his able-bodied mother, father, wife or one child. The nazis would not make the choice, even though to do so would have produced a more efficient labor force. Jewish sons, husbands or fathers themselves were forced to decide who among their loved ones was—for the time being—to live, who to die at once.

I search the whole history of human depravity for comparisons. In vain. I would reject the comparisons cited above even if they compared the comparable: let each human evil be understood in its own terms. What makes the comparisons utterly odious is that in effect if not intention they abuse Auschwitz, deny that it ever happened, rob its victims even of memory. There is a qualitative distinction between evils—even gigantic ones—perpetrated for such "rational" ends as gain, victory, real or imagined self-interest, and evils perpetrated for evil's sake.

Moreover, there can be a difference even among evils for evil's sake. Theologians call these "the demonic," and I myself once found escape in this theological abstraction. I find it no more. In the history of demonic evil (which, incidentally, in this age of uncritical theological celebrations, someone should write) conceivably there are examples comparable to the nazi custom of issuing the two work permits. But until such examples are found my religious life and theological thought must lack the comfort of comparisons as I retrace the *via dolorosa* which leads to Auschwitz, trying at the desperate utmost to match the solitude, the despair, the utter abandonment of every one of my brethren who walked that road. And I shall always fail.

If the crime of Auschwitz is unique, so is the threat to the faith of its victims. I search the history of religious suffering for comparisons. Once again, in vain. Other believers (Jewish and Christian) have been tortured and murdered for their faith, secure in the belief that God needs martyrs. Black Christians have been tortured and murdered for their race, finding strength in a faith not at issue. The children of Auschwitz were tortured and murdered, not because of their faith nor despite their faith nor for reasons unrelated to the Jewish faith. The nazis, though racists, did not murder Jews for their "race" but for the Jewish faith of their great-grandparents. Had those great-grandparents failed to show the minimum commitment to the ancient covenant on the raising of Jewish children, their 20th century offspring might have been among the nazi murderers; they would not have been among the Jewish victims. At some time in the mid-19th century European Jews, like Abraham of old, brought a child sacrifice; but unlike Abraham they did not know what they were doing—and there was no reprieve. It is as if Satan himself had plotted for 4,000 years to destroy the covenant between God and Israel, and had at last found the way.

For the desperate question for us after Auschwitz is this: 19th century European Jews did not know—what if they *had* known? And what of us who *do* know? Dare we *morally* raise Jewish children, exposing our offspring to a possible second Auschwitz decades or centuries hence? And dare we *religiously not* raise Jewish children, completing Satan's work on his behalf?

My soul is aghast at this impossible choice, unprecedented in the annals of faith anywhere. And I am filled with shame of mind as well as of soul when I consider that my earlier theology had ruled it out on neat a priori grounds, when it implied that nothing radically new could happen in Jewish religious history between Sinai and the Messianic days. My intentions, I still think, were good, for I had sought to make the Jewish faith immune to "merely empirical" and "secular" history, irrefutable as well as unprovable. The result, however, was a betrayal, however unwitting, of the victims of Auschwitz—a betrayal committed even as they were suffering their unique martyrdom.

Moreover, I now think that my earlier theological aim lacked Jewish authenticity. To be sure, when the Romans destroyed the second Temple the Talmudic rabbis refused to despair of God's covenant with Israel, but at the same time they let the catastrophe call it into question. Whether picturing God as in exile with Israel or as lamenting his own decision or even as engaged in bitter self-recrimination, they showed the courage to make their faith vulnerable to actual—i.e., empirical and "secular"—history. How shall we live with God after Auschwitz? How without him? Contend with God we must, as did Abraham, Jacob, Job. And we cannot let him go.

Rather than venturing to enter in this brief essay into this still-unknown territory, I quote here two texts, both of which have been used in prayers in Jewish services:

THE RESURRECTION

One day they will assemble in the valley of bones—
Ashes sifted out of furnaces, vapors from Luneburg,

Parchments from some fiend's books, cakes of soap,
Half-formed embryos, screams still heard in nightmares.
God will breathe upon them. He will say: Be men.

> *But they will defy Him: We do not hear you. Did you hear us?*
> *There is no resurrection for us. In life it was a wondrous thing*
> *For each of us to be himself, to guide his limbs to do his will.*
> *But the many are now one. Our blood has flowed together,*
> *Our ashes are inseparable, our marrow commingled,*
> *Our voices poured together like water of the sea.*
> *We shall not surrender this greater self.*
> *We the Abrahams, Isaacs, Jacobs, Sarahs, Leahs, Rachels*
> *Are now forever Israel.*

Almighty God, raise up a man who will go peddling through the
    world.
Let him gather us up and go through the world selling us as
    trinkets.
Let the peddler sell us cheaply. Let him hawk his wares and say:
Who will buy my souvenirs? Little children done in soap,
A rare Germanic parchment of the greatest Jew in Lodz.
Men will buy us and display us and point to us with pride:
A thousand Jews went into this and here is a rare piece
That came all the way from Crakow in a box car.
A great statesman will place a candle at his bedside.
It will burn but never be consumed.
The tallow will drip with the tears we shed
And it will glow with the souls of our children.
They will put us in the bathrooms of the United Nations
Where diplomats will wash and wash their hands
With Polish Jews and German Jews and Russian Jews.
Let the peddler sell the box of soap that once was buried
With Kaddish and Psalms by our brothers.

> *Some night the statesman will blow upon the candle*
> *And it will not go out.*
> *The souls of little children will flicker and flicker*
> *But not expire.*
> *Some day the diplomats will wash their hands and find them*
> *   stained with blood.*

Some day the citizens of the German town
Will awake to find their houses reeking
With all the vapors from all the concentration camps,
From Hell itself, and the stench will come from the
Soap box.

Then they will all rise up, statesmen, diplomats, citizens
And go hunting for the peddler: You who disturb our rest
And our ablutions, you who haunt us with your souvenirs,
You who prick our conscience, death upon you!

But the peddlers shall never cease from the earth
Until the candles die out and the soap melts away.

YOSSEL RAKOVER'S APPEAL TO GOD

. . . I believe in You, God of Israel, even though You have done everything to stop me from believing in You. I believe in Your laws even if I cannot excuse Your actions. My relationship to You is not the relationship of a slave to his master but rather that of a pupil to his teacher. I bow my head before Your greatness, but will not kiss the lash with which You strike me.

You say, I know, that we have sinned, O Lord. It must surely be true! And therefore we are punished? I can understand that too! But I should like You to tell me whether *there is any sin in the world deserving such a punishment as the punishment we have received!*

You assert that You will repay our enemies? I am convinced of it! Repay them without mercy? I have no doubt of that either! I should like You to tell me, however—*is there any punishment in the world compensating for the crimes that have been committed against us?*

You say, I know, that it is no longer a question of sin and punishment, but rather a situation in which Your countenance is veiled, in which humanity is abandoned to its evil instincts. But I should like to ask You, O Lord—and this question burns in me like a consuming fire—*what more, O what more, must transpire before You unveil Your countenance again to the world?*

I want to say to You that now, more than in any previous period of our eternal path of agony, we, we the tortured, the humiliated, the buried alive and burned alive, we the insulted, the mocked, the lonely, the forsaken by God and man—we have the right to know *what are the limits of Your forbearance?*

I should like to say something more: Do not put the rope under too much strain lest, alas, it snap! The test to which You have put us is so severe, so unbearably severe, that You should— You must—forgive those members of Your people who, in their misery, have turned from You.

. . . I tell You this because I do believe in You, because I believe in You more strongly than ever, because now I know that You are my Lord, because after all You are not. You cannot possibly be after all the God of those whose deeds are the most horrible expression of ungodliness!

. . . I die peacefully, but not complacently; persecuted but not enslaved; embittered but not cynical; a believer but not a supplicant; a lover of God but no blind amen-sayer of His.

I have followed Him even when He rejected me. I have followed His commandments even when He has castigated me for it; I have loved Him and I love Him even when He hurls me to the earth, tortures me to death, makes me the object of shame and ridicule.

. . . God of Israel, . . . You have done everything to make me stop believing in You. Now lest it seem to You that You will succeed by these tribulations to drive me from the right path, I notify You, my God and God of my father, *that it will not avail You in the least!* You may insult me, You may castigate me, You may take from me all that I cherish and hold dear in the world, You may torture me to death—I shall believe in *You,* I shall love You no matter what You do to test me!

And these are my last words to You, my wrathful God: nothing will avail You in the least. You have done everything to make me renounce You, to make me lose faith in You, but I die exactly as I have lived, a believer!

Eternally praised be the God of the dead, the God of vengeance, of truth and of law, Who will soon show His face to the world again and shake its foundations with His almighty voice.

Hear, O Israel, the Lord our God, the Lord is One.
Into your hands, O Lord, I consign my soul.

Authentic Jewish theology cannot possess the immunity I once gave it, *for its price is an essential indifference to all history between Sinai and the Messianic days.* The distinction between "sacred" and "secular" history is in any case Christian in origin, and whether Christianity (for which the decisive divine incursion into history has already occurred) can pay the price of indifference to "secular" history I must let Christian theologians decide. Jewish theology, at any rate, cannot pay that price, for *its* God of history (whose work is as yet incomplete) must be capable of continued presence *in* history, not merely at its messianic end.

I must strain my mind and heart to enter into the soul of the father or son or husband subjected to the nazi "two work permits" custom. As my thought enters into this terrible solitude it is itself solitary, for it finds no help from any source. Camus's reflections on suicide and Sartre's philosophy of the absurd seem childish games in comparison. Moreover (if orthodox Jews will forgive me), I find no help in pious rabbis slaughtered by the crusaders; nor (if refugees from the iron curtain will forgive me) in the victims of Stalin's massacres; nor (if Christians will forgive me) in the solitary self-sacrifice of the Christ. Indeed, I am attempting the impossible. The father and son and husband I speak of must be multiplied many times. And the soul of each is a many-sided mystery which can never be fathomed, but only revered.

Yet my impossible attempt is necessary. Moreover, it has uncovered for me a revelation which, as I again and again behold it, fills me with an ever-new radiating light and power. I ask: Why did not each and every father, husband and son subjected to the nazi two work permits go mad? Or not going mad and surviving, why did he not commit suicide? Or choosing life rather than death, why did he stay a Jew, remarry and raise Jewish children? Why did even a single Jew who stayed sane and chose life and remained a Jew and raised Jewish children remain faithful to his ancient God?

Elie Wiesel has dared to compare Auschwitz with Sinai in its revelatory significance—and he has added that we are not listening. As, still shrinking from such a listening, I attempt to listen at least to those who survived, I hear in the very existence of each and every one a totally astonishing, albeit totally fragmentary, faithfulness and testimony: in him who stayed sane, to the sacredness of sanity; in him who chose life, to the sacredness of life; in him who raised Jewish children, to the sacredness of the survival of the Jewish people; in him who stayed with his God, to a sacred bond between God and Israel which even Satan himself did not break.

I cannot resort to a glib theologizing which holds fast to but one of these testimonies, implicitly presuming to judge among them. (Where was I at the time of Auschwitz? Who would I be today if I were a survivor?) If nevertheless I focus attention on the last two testimonies, it is because, taken together, they reveal a fact revolutionary for Jewish theology.

Once there was a sharp, perhaps ultimate, dichotomy between "religious" and "secular" Jews. It exists no longer. After Auschwitz the religious Jew still witnesses to God in history, albeit in ways which may be revolutionary. And the "secular" Jew has become a witness as well—against Satan if not to God. His mere commitment to Jewish survival without further grounds is a testimony; indeed, Jewish survival after Auschwitz is neither "mere" nor without grounds. At Auschwitz *every* Jew represented all humanity when for reasons of birth alone he was denied life; after Auschwitz every Jew represents all humanity when he commits himself to Jewish survival. For this commitment is *ipso facto* testimony that there can be, must be, shall be, no second Auschwitz anywhere; on this testimony and this faith the secular no less than the religious Jew stakes his own life, the lives of his children and the lives of his children's children. A secular holiness, side by side with the religious, is becoming manifest in contemporary Jewish existence.

Nowhere is this more obvious than in the state of Israel. When I set out on my first visit to Israel two years ago I expected religious Jews to be religious and secular Jews to be secularists. Brought up in an anti-Zionist tradition, I had been taught a neat distinction between Jewish "religion" and Jewish "nationalism." And though I had long rejected these inapplicable pseudo-Protestant distinctions (and along with them, anti-Zionism) I was still altogether unprepared for one totally astonishing discovery: *the religious quality of the "secularist" Israeli Jew*. Perhaps I would not have seen it had I still been in head-long flight from the Holocaust. Of the truth of what I saw, however, I have no doubt. Jerusalem, while no "answer" to the Holocaust, is a response; and every Israeli lives that response. Israel is collectively what every survivor is individually: a No to the demons of Auschwitz, a Yes to Jewish survival and security—and thus a testimony to life against death *on behalf of all mankind*. The juxtaposition of Auschwitz and Jerusalem recalls nothing so vividly as Ezekiel's vision of the dead bones and the resurrection of the household of Israel. Every Israeli—man, woman or child—stakes his life on the truth of that vision.

This vision came alive for all with eyes to see when in June 1967 Jews at Jerusalem had no choice but to fight for life, whereas 25 years earlier Jews at Auschwitz had had no choice but death. Why did this vision come less alive for the Christian press, which might have remembered Ezekiel, than for the secular press, which presumably did not remember him?

This brings me to a most painful aspect of my recent religious and theological development. Thirty years ago I had become convinced that what had once divided Jews and Christians was now dwarfed by the demonic forces threatening both. In the years that followed I became involved in Jewish-Christian dialogues on that basis and formed lasting personal and theological friendships. Today I am confronted by another, less comforting aspect of Jewish-Christian relations. In regard to it I find myself misunderstood or even abandoned by most, though not all, Christian theologians. Nazi anti-Semitism, while anti-Christian, would have been impossible without centuries of Christian anti-Semitism. Why drag up this dead past? Because, alas, I can view it as past no longer, and because I owe the victims of Auschwitz (and, as I shall endeavor to show, Christianity itself) a relentless truthfulness.

Once I held the mild view that Christian anti-Semitism was vanishing in the wake of Jewish-Christian dialogues which confined attention to what the two faiths have in common. I have now been forced into a more radical view: Anti-Semitism exists wherever it is held (or implied) that "the Jewish people" is an anachronism which may survive, if at all, only on sufferance. Anti-Semitism of this kind survives in such post-Christian phenomena as a liberalism which maintains that of all peoples Jews alone are obliged to be men-in-general, and in a communism which affirms that of all nationalisms Jewish nationalism alone is "petty-bourgeois." Its ultimate root, however, lies in the Christian view—perpetuated through the centuries, lingering on even where Christianity itself is undermined by atheism or agnosticism—that the birth of the new Israel entails the death of the old. Deliberately using hyperbole in order to shock Christian conscience, the Christian theologian J. Coert Rylaarsdam has said that Christians have generally thought that the only good Jew is a dead Jew or a Christian.

Such a formulation is enough to show that after Auschwitz any kind of anti-Semitism is intolerable. Yet anti-Semitism survives in Christian attitudes—in none so obviously as those vis-à-vis the state of Israel. Why did the Christian press remain undisturbed by 19 years of Jordanian control of the Christian holy places (and desecration of Jewish cemeteries and synagogues), but become greatly agitated by Israeli control? Why does it fill its pages with accounts of the plight of Arab refugees but rarely even mentions the nearly as numerous Jewish refugees from Arab countries? Why are there moral equations between Israel's claims to the right to exist and Arab claims to the right to destroy her? I have no answer to these questions except a theology of a new Israel to which, consciously or unconsciously, the resurrected old Israel remains an affront.

Few Jews are indifferent to the plight of the Arab refugees. For my part, I cannot deny the Palestinian Arabs the right to a state of their own which I claim for my own people. What fills me with a frustration bordering on despair—and indeed with doubt whether, after all, such a thing as Jewish-Christian dialogue is possible—is any Christian view that the survival of the Jewish state is a "merely political" matter to which I must be "religiously" indifferent if I am to be a worthy partner in Jewish-Christian dialogue. Do Christians think that Judaism could survive a second Holocaust—or that Israel could survive without her army? Are they to have dialogue with dead Jews?

I speak bluntly for the sake of Christianity as well as for the sake of Judaism. Dostoevsky once wrote a legend about the Grand Inquisitor and the returning Christ. No Christian has yet been able to write the infinitely more traumatic legend of the Christ returning to nazi-occupied Europe. Hitler gave a perverse reality to the ancient fact that one is born into the Jewish covenant but that one chooses the Christian covenant. He murdered Jews if they had one Jewish grandparent, Christians only if they chose to be saints. And, alas, there are few saints among Jews or Christians. (Had I been born a gentile, would I have been a saint? Or a bystander? Or a nazi murderer?)

Christians cannot yet face the fact that the returning Christ would have gone to Auschwitz voluntarily, for few of them did so. Still less can they face the fact that he would have gone involuntarily if not voluntarily. For not only is the view that his people are dead in spirit— a view without which physical death at Auschwitz would have been impossible—an evil, centuries-old heritage within Christendom itself; it survives, consciously or unconsciously, in the Christian mind to this day.

Like all evil, centuries-old heritages, that view will continue to

survive until Christians themselves turn consciously and uncompromis-
ingly against it. To do so will be an act of spiritual self-liberation. I
have no doubt that if masses of Christians in Hitler's Europe had voluntarily put on the yellow star there would today be no doubt or confusion in the Christian churches, no talk of the death of God. I also
have an uncanny feeling that Christians might find the renewal they
presently seek if they were to close the tragic, centuries-old gulf between
themselves and the "old" Israel; if their souls were to enter into the
despair and the hope-despite-despair of Auschwitz.

May one hope that a Christian will one day be able—nay, compelled—to write the legend of the Christ returning to nazi-occupied
Europe? While Christians even now are turning against one great sin
of their past, sharing in the chant of their erstwhile black slaves: "Freedom now!" Will the time come when all Christians will turn against
their other, far older sin—when, dancing in Jerusalem with the people
of their Lord, they will chant in astonishment, gratitude and joy: "*Am
Yisrael Chai*—The people Israel lives"?

PRELUDE TO DIALOGUE

In 1966, the Harvard Divinity School held a Jewish-Christian Colloquium on the model of the Roman Catholic-Protestant Colloquium which took place in 1963. The impressive results of the latter, however, were hardly equaled by the former. Even with participants well disposed to discussion, there was little feeling of progress. As one of the organizers of the colloquium, Krister Stendahl, Dean of the Harvard Divinity School and a distinguished New Testament scholar, analyzes some of the reasons for this. Stendahl is aware, of course, of the Jewish aversion to the Christian mission. Yet the problem goes deeper. One difficulty is the anti-Jewish tradition in Christian literature itself. Here Stendahl speaks with utter frankness about the problems inherent in the New Testament before it was yet fashionable to do so. Another difficulty—more pronounced in Lutheranism than in Roman Catholicism—is the Law-Gospel dichotomy.

In the face of these obstacles, Stendahl calls not so much for a dialogue as for a careful Christian listening to Jewish views in which "we are not primarily anxious to impart our views as [we are that] they impart theirs." It is hoped that from this there will come a new beginning based on the conviction that the tragic history of Jewish-Christian relations was not according to divine plan; that Church and Synagogue may develop a positive relationship without sacrificing their integrity and peculiar character. Stendahl's very sensitive appreciation of the religious significance of Zion is surely a measure of the possibility of such a relationship.

The essay reprinted here appeared originally under the title "Judaism and Christianity II: After a Colloquium and a War" in *Harvard Divinity Bulletin*, N.S. I (1967), 2-8 (reprinted in *Cross Currents* XVII (1967), 445-58). It is a continuation of "Judaism and Christianity: Then and Now" in *Harvard Divinity Bulletin* XXVIII (1963), 1-9 reprinted in M. E. Marty, ed. *New Theology No. 2,* New York: Macmillan, 1965, pp. 153-64.

Gregory Baum, a respected Roman Catholic theologian and professor of religious studies at St. Michael's College of the University of

Toronto, has long been concerned with the problematics of fostering a new relationship between Judaism and Christianity. Baum's original approach was apologetic. He relates: ". . . In the late fifties . . . in a book entitled *The Jews and the Gospel* [New York: Newman Press, 1961; revised under the title *Is the New Testament Anti-Semitic?*, New York: Paulist, 1965], I readily acknowledged the anti-Jewish trends present in Christian preaching, but I then thought that it was my religious duty as a Christian theologian to defend the New Testament itself from the accusation of prejudice and falsification." Since that time he has changed his point of view. Reading Vatican II as a call for Christian reexamination, he affirms that the Church must "examine the very center of its proclamation and reinterpret the meaning of the gospel for our times." (From the introduction to R. Ruether, *Faith and Fratricide*, pp. 2, 7). Baum, along with other liberal Roman Catholic theologians, is thus concerned with the roots of Christian anti-Jewish ideology and the ways in which they are perpetuated. In a short piece which appeared in *The Christian Century* (LXXXIX [July 19, 1972], 775-77), Baum examines the mechanics of ideology. A majority group develops a rhetoric of exclusion, comparing "us" to "them" so that "they" always manage to appear inferior. Because this process is often unconscious, it is all the more dangerous. The majority tends to create myths about the minority: in the United States, whites about blacks; in Ontario, the English about the French; Protestants about Catholics. Baum claims that the "objectivity" (here too, the current word would be "evenhandedness") which majority groups invoke with respect to minorities is an abdication of their responsibilities. Neither the blacks nor the Jews are simply another minority group. The white and the Christian must examine his own ideological past in order to determine the integrity of his attitudes towards them.

It is precisely this that Rosemary Radford Ruether does in *Faith and Fratricide*. In this work, Ruether, a prolific author who teaches theology at Howard University School of Religion and Yale Divinity School, traces the development of the anti-Jewish theme in Christianity through the New Testament, the fathers, and post-Christian secular phenomena. While historical studies of this sort have been undertaken previously, Dr. Ruether's approach is strikingly different. It is her contention that the affirmation of Jesus as Christ entailed and became de-

pendent upon a denigration of Judaism. It is this "left hand of Christology" which is the source of Christian anti-Semitism. She maintains:

> . . . The anti-Judaic myth is neither a superficial nor a sec-
> ondary element in Christian thought. The foundations of anti-
> Judaic thought were laid in the New Testament. They were de-
> veloped in the classical age of Christian theology in a way that
> laid the basis for attitudes and practices that continually produced
> terrible results. Most Christians today seem more than willing to
> prune back the cruder expressions of these attitudes and practices.
> But to get at the roots from which these grew is a much more
> profound problem. The wheat and the tares have grown together
> from the beginning, and so it may seem impossible to pull up the
> weed without uprooting the seed of Christian faith as well. Yet as
> long as Christology and anti-Judaism intertwine, one cannot be
> safe from a repetition of this history in new form. The end of
> Christendom may seem to have brought an end to the possibility
> of legislating theological anti-Judaism as social policy. But we
> witnessed in Nazism the ability of this virus to appear in even worse
> form in secular dress. Yet I believe that this is actually a critical
> moment when a deep encounter with the structures of anti-Judaism
> is not only necessary to atone for this history, but may be essential
> to revitalizing the original Christian vision itself. (p. 226)

Dr. Ruether's provocative proposals for achieving this are presented
here in a selection from *Faith and Fratricide,* New York: Seabury Press,
1974, pp. 251-61.

"No Religion Is an Island," Abraham Joshua Heschel's exposition
of his views on interfaith relations, was delivered as an address at Union
Theological Seminary in 1965 where Professor Heschel spent a year as
Harry Emerson Fosdick Visiting Professor. The essay is a learned and
sensitive examination of the possibilities, from a Jewish point of view,
for a meeting between Judaism and Christianity.

Once again, in traditional fashion, there is the appeal for an end
to the Christian mission to Israel. As always, this is a precondition for
dialogue. His argument is Mendelssohnian and draws from rabbinic and
medieval statements concerning relations between different faith communities. As reinforcement, he cites the supporting views of Protestant

and Roman Catholic theologians. To be sure, there might be those who would see no value in talking to Jews if there was no hope of converting them. Then too, if Christian creedal statements are foreign to the Jew, why should he talk to the Christian? On either side, this represents shortsightedness. Disagreement? Yes! Disparagement? No! One cannot afford to live without the other. Just as nations with varying points of view and commitments must learn to function together (as in the United Nations), so must it be with religions. To deny this is arrogance; yet men do not incline easily to humility. Heschel therefore jars us into it: "Religion is a means, not the end. . . . To equate religion and God is idolatry." He points out the positive things that the two faiths have done for each other and draws from a number of medieval Jewish authorities who held Christianity (and Islam) in esteem. In this, it seems as if his appeal is addressed more to Jews than to Christians.

Heschel's remarks raise certain questions for us. For one, they were written before 1967 and before 1973. Do they have the same force today? Does not the use of the United Nations as a model harm the argument rather than benefit it? Finally, how did Heschel himself envision this enterprise? Interfaith, he observes, "is not an enterprise for those who are half learned or spiritually immature. If it is not to lead to the confusion of the many, it must remain a prerogative of the few." If so, what is the role of the many? To such questions, perhaps dialogue can—in all humility—find the answers.

"No Religion Is An Island" originally appeared in *Union Seminary Quarterly Review* XXI (1966), 117-33.

34.

SALVATION IS FROM THE JEWS:
A STORY OF PREJUDICE

Gregory Baum

Although the Christian faith is derived from the experience and history of Israel, a strong anti-Jewish bias was built into Christian preaching almost from the beginning. While we proclaimed the doctrine of love, we also—unconsciously, most of the time—spread the seed of contempt of an entire people.

Initially there was the tendency to glorify the New Testament by belittling the Old. Christian preachers presented the religion of the old covenant as legalistic, as based on justice instead of love, as therefore inferior and unspiritual—forgetting that this religion was grounded on the covenant of mercy which God made with the people he saved from Egyptian oppression. More than that, we slandered Jewish religion as it was practiced at the time of Jesus by presenting it as corrupt, materialistic and self-centered. We tended to project the qualities of Jesus' opponents onto all Jews of the time and, later, onto Judaism as a whole. Often we disguised the fact that Jesus himself was Jewish, that his mother and his disciples were Jewish, that the entire early church in Jerusalem was Jewish. We even blamed the Jews for the crucifixion of Christ, and eventually put the burden on the whole Jewish people. We interpreted the prophetic condemnations uttered over the people of Jerusalem as literal predictions of the future of the Jews. Ultimately

313

we preached that their presence in the world was the visible sign of God's wrath and judgment.

Especially after the fourth century, when Christianity became the established religion of the Roman Empire, the Jews were represented in Christian preaching as the symbol of unredeemed humanity—of the earthly man estranged from God and his own destiny, man who had lost his way—and was slightly less than human. This symbolism nourished the church's imagination for centuries and pervaded the deep recesses of the Western mind.

At first the tension between church and synagogue arose from rivalry. All wanted to be the sons of Abraham. When the church permitted gentiles to become sons of Abraham, the younger sons sought to supplant the older. As the church became mainly a gentile community, it viewed Judaism as the parent religion which it wanted to replace. Christians began to call themselves the true Israel, implying that the Jews were the false Israel. The Jews were the people whose mission had been voided. They no longer made sense in the Christian understanding of history; indeed their very existence was a nuisance to the church. The story of Christian anti-Jewish preaching is a complex fabric woven of political, religious and pathological elements.

That story remained hidden from the Christian world for centuries —until the anti-Semitism of the Nazis, based not on Christian but on pagan, biological ideals, took on monstrous forms and led to the murder of millions of Jews in the heart of Christian Europe. It was then that the church began to study its own history and to discern in its past the ever-present anti-Jewish bias. The churches were not, of course, responsible for Nazism or for Nazi anti-Semitism—to claim that would be nonsense: but they generated a symbolism, a typology regarding the Jew and his "inferiority" that was exploited by evil, power-hungry men for their own political and imperialistic ends.

"Ideology" is a technical word employed to account for the anti-Jewish trend in Christian preaching. It refers to the unconscious process by which a society or group generates a set of ideals that legitimize and reinforce the power of that society or group over others. First we speak in terms of "we" and "they." "We" are the exponents of true humanity, the enlightened ones; "we" have good sense, the true values, the right understanding. "They," on the other hand, are inept, unenlightened, blind, inferior. We create what is called a rhetoric of exclusion. Our way of speaking (and joking) about the others nourishes our sense of our own superiority and their inferiority. A rhetoric of exclusion will eventually generate social attitudes of contempt, give rise to social institutions that legitimize exploitation of others, and at the same time preserve a good conscience in the dominant group. Having learned to think and speak of others as slightly less than human, we ultimately feel justified in treating them as less than human. This is ideology, a disguised, unconscious power game from which none of us—no society, no group—is ever totally free. A classical case of ideology is the anti-Jewish bias in the Christian community through the ages.

Since I wish to clarify the meaning and power of ideology, let me give a few more examples of it. The dominant group judges "the others" by its own values, finds them inferior, despises them, and creates social institutions that perpetuate its own superiority. Prior to the ecumenical movement, Protestants and Catholics developed ideologies which became part of their religion. At the same time the preaching of the gospel became a way of triumphing over others, of confirming our own superiority and fostering contempt for others. This took place unconsciously. We thought we were friendly to Catholics, or to Protestants, just because we smiled at them across the street, but we did not examine the hidden social attitudes that excluded Catholics, or Protestants, from participating in society. The greater harm is always done by the dominant, ruling group. Since the rise of the ecumenical movement, however, we have become conscious of this inherited ideology and have wrestled against it.

We can study ideology in connection with all of today's major conflicts. We are well aware of the white man's power over the black in the U.S. and of the deep emotional roots of these attitudes in the nation. Closer to home, we Canadians have begun to realize that our English-speaking people have created an ideology in regard to the conquered French. The dominant group measured them by its own standards and values, found them wanting, and, despite the assurances given them in Canadian law, felt deep down that their privileges of language and culture were unfortunate concessions. We felt that Canada would be better off if we all spoke English. It is this hidden ideology that keeps the people of Ontario from paying sufficient attention to the French fact and makes Torontonians read accounts of French-Canadian problems as if these existed in some distant country; and it is this ideology that may eventually strike us with a blindness endangering the nation's survival. So successful have English-speaking people been in the Western world that they have created the myth that it is difficult to learn other languages. This, again, is ideology. The dominant group finds it difficult to learn other languages because this is a way of assuring their hegemony. In fact, people who must learn languages for survival and success do so quite easily.

Another good example of ideology is the myth invented by men to preserve their dominance over women. It is useful for the male to think of the female as a weak, dependent, unreliable creature in need of protection. This view pervades our culture and religion. In the ordinary marriage ceremony, for instance, the power game is symbolized and acted out. The dependent girl, the minor, who cannot give herself away (as the bridegroom can), is led in, given away by the father, and placed under the protection of the bridegroom. Ideology is so deeply disguised that it is often absorbed even by the victim.

Today the churches have discovered this hidden power game operative in their symbols, and are trying to purify themselves of it. The Second Vatican Council and many Protestant and Anglican church councils and boards have taken significant steps to remove the ideological deformation from the Christian gospel. But these trends have so deeply penetrated the Christian imagination that it is impossible to root them out all at once. Overcoming the heritage of the centuries is a slow process.

Let me give an example of how profoundly the anti-Jewish ideology is rooted in Christian thinking. A. C. Forrest, editor of the *United Church Observer,* has been deeply moved by the plight of the Arab refugees, by the unwillingness of their host nations to integrate them into social life, and by the reluctance of Israel to leave itself unprotected against those who call for its total destruction. Surely everyone honors Mr. Forrest's solicitude for the refugees. But at the same time Forrest presents a one-sided, extremely unfavorable picture of Israel. A Christian may, of course, be critical of the policies adopted by the state of Israel; there are divergent views on those policies in Israel itself. But seeing that the survival of Israel is gravely threatened today and conscious of the ancient Christian death-wish toward "the blind, stiff-necked people of Israel," the Christian will add to his criticism an affirmation of Israel's right to live. If a Christian approaches the political situation of Israel without wrestling with his own ideological past, he will remain caught in the inherited symbols and adopt an anti-Jewish attitude with regard to Israel as well as other social manifestations of Judaism.

Ideology, as I said, is largely unconscious. It may go together with a cheerfully good conscience. But because it is largely unconscious, it will express itself unexpectedly. The man who insists that he is "only" anti-Zionist and not anti-Jewish will eventually reveal the ideological origin of his attitude.

The March issue of Mr. Forrest's *United Church Observer* included an article titled "How Zionists Manipulate Your News," by John Nichols Booth. In this plainly anti-Semitic article we read, for instance: "The French Jewish philosopher Jean-Paul Sartre regards some threat of anti-Semitism as essential to hold Jews together. If there is no actual anti-Semitism, then it must be created." Now, Sartre is not a Jewish philosopher. He has written powerful refutations of anti-Semitism, and while he may have spoken, in a certain context, of the defensiveness or over-defensiveness of Jews induced by their tragic history, it is shocking to see this honorable man used to support the idea that Jews must invent anti-Semitism as a myth necessary for their survival. Such an idea is scandalous in a century that has seen the extermination of millions of Jews, and scandalous in a Christian paper that ought to be conscious of the age-old anti-Jewish trends in Christian preaching.

Since our ideologies are largely unconscious, to discover them takes struggle and willingness to change. This is always painful. The refusal to look at inherited ideological trends, and the denial that they are operative in one's views, is "false consciousness." False consciousness, we note, is always allied to a cheerfully good conscience. I wish to analyze false consciousness in greater detail because there is a blatant example of it in the letters columns of the same March issue of the *United Church Observer*.

The man whose consciousness is false in regard to a class or group of people assumes a stance of objectivity toward them. He refuses to acknowledge that his own history is interwoven with that of this class or group, that he has derived benefits from the power of his own group over these others, and so on. If white U.S. Americans look objectively at the black people in their nation, compare them with other minorities in their own and other countries, try to arrive at a scientific assessment of where blacks stand in regard to this or that quality or talent—then they are victims of false consciousness. For they refuse to acknowledge that the blacks are not merely one among many minorities. Since blacks were brought to the U.S. as slaves and were victims over the centuries of exploitation and dehumanizing institutions, their present situation can be understood by whites only if these latter take into account how their own world and their own wealth and power are in part a legacy from the master/slave relationship. Objectivity is here a device for not looking at the whole historical truth. False consciousness disguises the actual power relations; it obscures the past. False consciousness cannot be overcome by science, but only by willingness to change, to abandon a situation of superiority, and to review to a considerable degree one's idea of the world.

For Christians, it would be false consciousness to adopt an objectivist stance in regard to Israel and to other social manifestations of Judaism. This false consciousness is evident in a letter written to the *United Church Observer* by E. M. Howse and defending the magazine's editor against the charge of hostility toward the Jews. Overly sensitive people, Mr. Howse remarks, have discovered "a secret hostility to Jews" in *Observer* editorials, "which sometimes criticized some of the policies and deeds of the State of Israel." But, he says, Mr. Forrest is merely trying to be objective. And he suggests a comparison:

> A sensitivity as pathological elsewhere would discover that editors now criticizing Pakistan are secretly motivated by unconscious hostility to Moslems. Those who criticize India have a similar antipathy to Hindus. And the long Western alienation from China is at last revealed to have its roots in a latent animosity to Confucians. The nonsense is not more blatant in one case than in the other.

In these and in other equally explicit passages, the letter writer refuses to wrestle with the inherited ideology of the Christian Church. The stance of objectivity allows him to look away from the actual historical link between his group and the various peoples and religions he mentions. To classify Israel, or any social manifestation of Judaism, simply as one among several societies is to deny the entire ideological past. For accompanying Christian preaching almost from the beginning were hostile and prejudiced views, not against Moslems, Hindus or Confucians, but against Jews. Those views have entered our ecclesiastical tradition and our language of worship; they have nourished a popular symbolism and generated hostile feelings. To attempt to negate all this by recourse to objectivity is false consciousness. Such a tactic is also unrealistic in regard to the Asian nations mentioned by the letter writer.

For we are linked to these countries not by religious ties but by political and economic interests, and unless we face these in each instance we cannot come to a sound judgment. The man who refuses to wrestle with his ideological past will inevitably become enmeshed in prejudices and false judgments.

Since the Christian community has been totally insensitive to moral issues regarding the Jews for almost two millennia, a sociology of knowledge makes it highly unlikely that Christians will all of a sudden produce sensitive moralists on matters pertaining to Jews. It is sociologically unlikely that people who for centuries overlooked obvious injustices in regard to a particular group, slandered them and denigrated their religion, will quickly become sensitive moral guides as to how this group ought to behave. If, therefore, the Christian wants to express his own critical views of Israeli policies, he can do so with honor only if he reveals that he is also wrestling with his own ideological past.

35.

TOWARD A NEW COVENANTAL THEOLOGY

Rosemary Radford Ruether

The question of a new covenantal theology cannot be solved or even adequately discussed from one side alone. It would be the area where Christians and Jews would have to enter into discussion of their contrary traditions about the nature of covenantal peoplehood. Each of the traditional positions proves inadequate before the facticity of the other people. It is also the area, I believe, where there might be interesting and fruitful dialogue.

Traditional Judaism knew what Israel was intended by God to do. Beyond the horizon of its own identity and revealed Way, it spoke of the others only as "Noachides." As indicated earlier, this term does not define the identity of the others; it simply refers to that minimal commonality that assures the possibility of universal salvation. What the specific identity of others is, what is comparable to Torah for them, Israel does not discuss.

When faced with the phenomenon of a "second people from among the Gentiles," a people who had learned and adopted this Jewish identity, claiming to be the true Israel that supersedes Israel, traditional Jewish categories were at a loss. At first this group was seen as Jewish heretics. When the Church became predominantly gentile, the way was open for looking at the Church simply as "goy." Yet, what does one do with

Gentiles who claim to be the "true Israel"? One can think of them alternatively as Jewish heretics or pagan idolators, a people who mix idolatry (the divinity of Jesus) and polytheism (the Trinity) with Jewish heresy (false messianism, antinomianism). This is traditional Judaism's basic view of Christians. But through association with Christians it became clear that this view was inadequate, as Jacob Katz has shown in his study *Exclusiveness and Tolerance*. The roots of Christian identity —its view of God—was too biblical to be simply regarded as pagan. Christians fall in some indeterminate status between Jewish messianic heretics and incompletely converted gentile proselytes. Seen as gentile semiproselytes, Christians can even be viewed more benignly as one way in which Judaism carries out its mission to spread the true concept of God to "the nations." These options more or less exhaust the traditional Jewish categories for understanding Christianity. One thing it cannot be and that is the "true Israel."

Christians, on the other hand, are hardly content to be regarded as "good Noachides," much less as pagans. They have regarded themselves as the true heirs to the covenant of God with Israel. They are, in fact, the final universal destiny of this covenant, surpassing its "Jewish stage." They are the people of the final messianic covenant which now achieves, through Christ, that inner righteousness which Judaism sought in vain through the outward commandments. This Christian New Covenant supersedes the covenant of God with Israel in the Jews in a way that can leave no room for a continuing covenant of Israel in Judaism. The Christian New Covenant must deny the legitimacy of ongoing Jewish covenantal existence. It can grant them only that negative space in which the Jews are to be preserved until the end of time, when they finally have to admit their error and join the true covenant of Israel, now passed on to its destined heirs, the Christians.

Should we try to replace the Christian concept of the New Covenant and the Jewish concept of the second, Noachian covenant with a plural concept of "separate but equal" covenants of God with each people? Should we say that God has made a covenant with each people in their own context and history and given them each a way to salvation? This would seem to be implied by what we have said earlier about contextualism and relativism. But it is also tinged with an assumption that we can transcend our own context and see everyone as God sees them. A student of mine tried to solve this dilemma by suggesting that there are two covenants: a particularist covenant to the Jews and the universal covenant of the Church for the other peoples. The two are parallel, not supersessionary. This view relativizes the patristic doctrine of the "two peoples." But this translation distorts Jewish and Christian historical reality. It assumes that everyone is supposed to be Christian, except the Jews! It fails to see that Jews in the Diaspora have long since ceased to be identifiable as descendants of a local Semitic tribe. Even the Nazis were never able to describe the Jews genetically as a "race." In fact, Jews today are gathered from as many different peoples as are Christians. The multiregional and multiracial character of the Jews in Israel should demonstrate this fact. The Jews, as much as the Christians, have become a people gathered out of many peoples. They are a people only because they have all adopted the Jewish covenantal identity.

On the other hand, the Christian concept of the New Covenant did not originally signify simply a second covenant which, in a relative and historical way, can be paralleled with a still valid covenant to the Jews. Rather, the New Covenant is the one covenant of God with Israel in its final and ultimate form. This New Covenant is the messianic destiny of the covenant with Israel of Jeremiah 31:31, which overcomes the ambiguities of historical existence and human self-alienation. Christians saw themselves as the people of the New Covenant, in the sense of being the beginning of the final messianic covenant that unites mankind and Israel. Must we not say today that this messianic covenant lies as much ahead of the historical reality of Christianity as it does that of Judaism? Before God, must we not see the Christians as being in the same historical situation as the Jews? Christians are not yet encamping in the Promised Land. Still less does their hope give them the right to usurp access to it altogether. The Christian, as much as the Jew, is still on the way through the desert between the Exodus and the Promised Land, with many a golden idol and broken tablet along the way.

The idea of election is not really original with Israel, although Christians know this idea primarily through Jewish identity. Most ancient peoples tended to see their own identity as being the umbilicus of the universe. A certain concept of election, in this sense, is found among any people who have a sense of identity that links them with heaven. Most ancient peoples also confused their own particular identity with the ultimate and made it the standard for judging humanness in general. Judaism took a step beyond this parochial ideology with the concept of the distinction between the covenant to Israel and the covenant to Noah, recognizing, on the one hand, their own particularism, but also its limitation by the humanity of others. Christianity obliterated this limitation by its fusion of messianic universalism and imperial ideology, making its own identity the one true way for all men. It identified the fulfillment of the covenant to Israel with an already realized covenant to all men, so destroying the delicate balance which Israel had created between the two.

Christianity today might learn a version of the Jewish concept of particularism, which accepts the general humanity and possibility for salvation of others, without trying to define their identity for them. This works for peoples whom Christianity has not known from the inside, such as Hindus or Buddhists or even Moslems (whom Jews must regard as a second offspring of biblical faith). But Christians cannot look at Jews simply as people of another "world religion." Each has known the other from within the same household of faith. Christianity, however gentilized, remains rooted in the Jewish identity of Jesus and the apostles. It is through them that it inherits its claim to identify with the Jewish past as its own past. Judaism may come to speak more benignly of Christians as semiproselytes. In this form, it was able to tolerate Christians in the synagogues. But this view conceals the earlier, more intimate, and angrier knowledge of Christians, not as gentile semiproselytes, but as Jewish heretics, trying to proselytize the synagogue. As such, Christians could not be tolerated in the synagogues. As the gentile adopted descendants of these Jewish heretics, Christians inherit from them their claim to be the true heirs of the Jewish past and identity, appropriating it through the medium of fulfilled messianism. Both remain in unresolved relation to each other, each claiming to carry on the one covenant of God with Israel. The elder brother carries it on through an exegesis still based on the original "cornerstone" of Abraham and Moses. The younger claims it through a foreshortening of history on one side, and a foundation upon the Jew Jesus, who is the aperture through which it inherits Jesus' Jewish identity.

The crisis of the first century produced, then, two ways of carrying on the biblical inheritance. Using Jesus' parable, we might see the Jews as the faithful elder brother who remains tending the father's flocks in the ancestral house. The younger son goes off chasing his vision. Today he can neither renounce that vision that drove him out of the father's house, nor can he renounce his claim to be a son and heir of the same household of faith. Should we declare that the nonappearance of his

fortune—i.e., Jesus' *parousia*—must finally force him to admit that inheritance of the covenant rests solely on its original cornerstone, i.e.,
Abraham and Moses? There is nothing to prevent any Christian from
accepting this option and using Christianity as a way to full conversion
to Judaism. But, for most, the story cannot become simply a circular
one. The younger son refuses to see his adventure simply under the
rubric of a "prodigality," calling for repentance and return. This is
because a development took place which Jesus did not anticipate when
he told the story. Jesus' faith rested on the original cornerstone, the
Mosaic covenant. He did not become for himself a "new cornerstone."
But the Christian cannot return to Jesus' Jewish identity before the Easter
experience. The vision which drove Christians into separation from the
parental faith, however unrealized, still determines our religious consciousness and the way we appropriate the older stories. However much
we may repent of having pursued this vision falsely, we cannot forget
our own story. The messianic encounter which originally inspired us
continues to be our foundational paradigm, through which we appropriate the earlier stories and out of which our history flows. Jesus, as the
new cornerstone, continues to divide the two brothers, giving Christians
a different day of appropriating the biblical past and relating to its future
hope.

   We have seen that this Christian paradigm tends to double back
on itself constantly, oscillating between new messianic sectarianisms
and the absolutizing of what has been actualized out of it. Yet, in the
very dialectic between these two errors, Christianity again and again
proves its ability to mediate new breakthrough experiences. By bringing
history into constant collision with eschatology, it makes history itself
dynamic. The Christian paradigm has been the foundation of the Western revolutionary tradition, which constantly rediscovers the imminent
eschatological horizon from out of its past immanences. This is the
paradigm through which Christianity mediates encounter with God and
constantly reawakens messianic hope, projecting again upon the future
what has been absolutized in its past moment of experience. When we
are able to see those past places of experience, beginning with Jesus,
as proleptic, rather than final and fulfilled, then we may be able to
validate messianic hope in Jesus in a way that is no longer anti-Judaic.
This also means that we can use this paradigm to mediate new breakthrough experiences in a way that need not demonize the past of the
"others" who are the antagonists of the experience.

Before it was anything else, the Christian messianic experience in Jesus was a Jewish experience, created out of Jewish hope. As an experience of messianic ecstasy, born of the dream of biblical faith, it becomes paradigmatic and foundational for reaffirming this hope in the final coming of God's Kingdom that is definitive for the heirs of that community which experienced it. But others remember this history quite differently, as a time when no Messiah came, although many frantically hoped for his coming. This people survived by continuing to base their hope on the original stories of Abraham and Moses. For them, the Exodus continues to be the breakthrough experience that founds their hope for ultimate salvation. The messianic experience, which happened to a small group of companions of Jesus, failed to become paradigmatic for most Jews. Those who loved Jesus could not mediate this gap between their own vibrant encounter with the messianic horizon through Jesus and the nonexperience of other Jews. Each then comes to invalidate the experience of the other by his own experience or nonexperience. The two rapidly become incapable of living in the same house.

When we find a way of accepting the situational validity of these differing experiences, which give different communities different foundations for their faith, then the Christian story can cease to be an assault on the right of Jews to continue to exist. Christians must be able to accept the thesis that it is not necessary for Jews to have the story about Jesus in order to have a foundation for faith and a hope for salvation. The story of Jesus parallels, it does not negate, the Exodus. It is another story, born from Abraham's promise, which becomes the paradigm of salvation for Christians. In each case, the experience of salvation in the past is recounted as the paradigm for continued hope experienced in the present and pointing to that final hope which is still ahead of both Jews and Christians. When Easter is seen, not as superseding and fulfilling the Exodus, but as reduplicating it, then the Christian can affirm his faith through Jesus in a way that no longer threatens to rob the Jew of his past, eliminate his future and surround his present existence with rivalrous animosity.

EDUCATION FOR A NEW RELATIONSHIP

In order to give this acceptance of ongoing Jewish covenantal existence flesh and blood, Christians must learn the story of the Jews after the time of Jesus. Christians must accept the oral Torah as an authentic alternative route by which the biblical past was appropriated and carried on. This requires the learning of a suppressed history. Learning history is never really an act of "detached" scholarship, as academicians like to think. Learning history is, first of all, a rite of collective identity. Christians learn who they are by learning the story of the Jews from Abraham to the time of Jesus and, through Jesus, carrying down a history created by the Christian Church and society. The history of the Jews disappears at the time of Jesus. This testifies to the Christian claim that it is the true Israel which alone carries on the biblical legacy. This Christian way of learning history negates ongoing Jewish existence. If we learned not only New Testament, but rabbinic midrash; if we viewed the period of the Second Temple, not merely through the eyes of early Christianity, but through the eyes of the disciples of Rabban Yohanan ben Zakkai; if we read Talmud side by side with the Church Fathers; if we read the Jewish experience of Christendom side by side with the Christian self-interpretation, this Christian view of history would fall into jeopardy. For this reason, Jewish history "after Christ" is not merely unknown, but repressed. Its repression is essential for the maintenance of Christian identity.

For Christians to incorporate the Jewish tradition after Jesus into their theological and historical education would involve ultimately the dismantling of the Christian concept of history and the demythologizing of the myth of the Christian Era. It would mean the opening of the mind to the other side that must provide the decisive critique at each stage of development of this myth. If, when the Christian student, especially the seminarian, studied the Hebrew Bible through Christian exegesis, both ancient and modern, he also had to know something about rabbinic midrash and modern Jewish biblical studies, the myth of Jewish Scripture as "Old Testament" would have to be taken apart. The seminarian would have to deal seriously with a second line, other than "New Testament," through which this legacy was appropriated. If, in studying New Testament, the Christian student also studied rabbinic thought in Jesus' time, he would have to see Jesus in his Jewish setting in a new way. The myth of Pharisees as hypocrites and Judaism as "dead legalism" would be exploded. He would also have to see the crucifixion in the context of Roman imperialism and Jewish messianism and resistance. These things are sometimes mentioned in biblical courses in liberal seminaries. But real entry into the perspective of those who salvaged Judaism after the fall of the temple is not undertaken. So this criticism remains abstract and without flesh and blood. The old anti-Judaic myths live on in attenuated forms.

Because the anti-Judaic myth and its social workings in Christendom is almost never taught in Church history or "Western civilization," the questionableness of Christendom and the roots of anti-Semitism remain buried. The vital key for understanding an aspect of Western history is thus lost. Avoidance of this knowledge also allows the Christian theologian to continue to turn out Christologies which are implicitly, if not explicitly, imperialist and anti-Judaic. The dilemma of messianic ideology and its career in Western history also remains mostly untouched or is not connected with Christian theology. This selective ignorance is then passed on in the teaching and preaching of Christianity in the churches in a way that continues to inculcate the myth of the carnal, legalistic, and obsolete "Jew." This very suppression of Jewish history and experience from Christian consciousness is tacitly genocidal. What it says, in effect, is that the Jews have no further right to exist after Jesus. We repress the memory of their continued existence and our dealings with them so that it appears that "after Christ" Jews disappear, and only Christians remain as the heirs of Jewish history and the people with a future.

The Christian anti-Judaic myth can never be held in check, much less overcome, until Christianity submits itself to that therapy of Jewish consciousness that allows the "return of the repressed." This means establishing a new education for a new consciousness, the sort of new consciousness that would make us grapple with the need for a new way of formulating Christian identity that allows space for the Jewish brother to live—live not on our terms, but on his. To a committee of the American Association of Theological Schools, I recently proposed the following reforms of current theological curricula:

1. Christian biblical scholarship must learn and teach the Jewish line of commentary and interpretation of Hebrew Scripture in midrash, questioning thereby the treatment of Judaism as something fulfilled and made obsolete by Christianity, to which the Hebrew Scriptures are assigned the status of "Old Testament."

2. New Testament scholarship must import into its teachings the rabbinic context of the thought of Jesus and Paul and correct the stereotypes of the Pharisees and the Torah which occur in the New Testament. Christians must grapple especially with the myth of Jewish "blood guilt"

and seek ways of overcoming the anti-Judaic implications of Christian
Scriptures for preaching.

3. Church historians should teach the history of the legal and social
persecution of Jews in Christendom by ecclesiastical and political rulers,
inspired by the myth of Jewish reprobation, and make Christians aware
of the responsibility of Christianity for the translation of theological
anti-Judaism into social anti-Semitism.

4. Christian theology must question the anti-Judaic side of its re-
demptive language and ask itself how these formulations can be eliminated from its interpretation of the gospel.

5. Christian seminaries should cultivate face-to-face conversation
between faculty and students and the living Jewish religious consciousness, so that Christians can become aware of the conflict between the
way in which Christians perceive the "Judaeo-Christian tradition" and
the way this history has been experienced and appropriated by Jews.
Field education courses should establish contact with rabbinic leadership
and Jewish community agencies and work out internships where insight
into Jewish concerns may be gained first-hand.

6. Above all, courses on preaching and Christian education must
work conscientiously to overcome anti-Judaic language in its hermeneu-
tics and in the educational and liturgical materials which teach Christianity to the people.

Such material is in no way intended to substitute for courses in
the history of Jewish thought and society which should go on in depart-
ments of Jewish studies and which Christians also should study. It is
the repressed side of a history which Christians, especially seminarians,
presently study as their own tradition.

These concrete steps toward a new consciousness do not mean that
Christians can now claim this Jewish history and tradition as their own.
The very content of this tradition precludes such easy appropriation,
for it makes it necessary for the Christian to understand the Jew, not as
the Christian has seen him, but as the Jew sees himself. This would
strike the anti-Judaic myth as its root, establishing Jewish consciousness
in its autonomy and its rejection of the Christian appropriation. But
since the Christian anti-Judaic myth has been not only a means of hating
Jews, but a means establishing Christian identity as the "true Israel,"
this Jewish consciousness means also a rethinking of Christian identity
in such a way as to accept Judaism as still the "true Israel." What this
will mean for Christian identity, we do not yet know. It means at least

a certain relativization of Christian absolutism which can accept the independent salvific validity of the Jewish tradition, the authenticity of this alternate way of approaching the biblical heritage. Perhaps, for some, it may become a real mutuality, an imaginative appreciation of each other's revelatory stories, an interpenetration of each other's identities. It is doubtful that these two streams will soon merge. It is, more importantly, not necessary to anyone's salvation that they should. Today, the tyranny of unity needs to be replaced by a valuing of the enrichment of dialogue that happens when various traditions cultivate their distinct perspectives. Perhaps Christianity needs a separate Judaism to keep it honest! God, who creates the many peoples, also can allow for many ways to the Father, which only become one at that end of history which is truly "final." The fratricidal side of Christian faith can be overcome only through genuine encounter with Jewish identity. Only then might a "Judaeo-Christian tradition," which has heretofore existed only as a Christian imperialist myth, which usurps rather than converses with the Jewish tradition, begin to happen for the first time.

36.

JUDAISM ON CHRISTIANITY: CHRISTIANITY ON JUDAISM

Krister Stendahl

In 1963 the Harvard Divinity School arranged for a Roman Catholic-Protestant Colloquium. Many factors converged into that decision and invitation. Some of our faculty had served as Observers at the sessions of the Second Vatican Council and were following closely its further developments. In 1958, the Charles Chauncey Stillman chair for Roman Catholic Studies had been established at Harvard University, and it had been decided that this chair should be in the Divinity School rather than in the Faculty of Arts and Sciences. For the academic year 1962-63, we were granted permission to use the funds for this Colloquium in lieu of the visiting professorship envisaged. And, above all, it was the right moment to highlight and scrutinize the new spirit of ecumenism by placing it in the crucible of academic inquiry. For all of us who participated in the seminars, the Colloquium was a stimulating and reassuring experience. Our scholarly deliberations indicated that the image of an ecumenical breakthrough—as pictured by the press-coverage of the Vatican Council—was, indeed, a well-founded one, and we could push beyond what was already achieved. In addition, there were the symbolic effect of Cardinal Bea's lectures and the demonstration that Roman Catholics were not guests but co-workers in the theological enterprise of the Divinity School.

In some ways things turned out differently with the Jewish-Christian Colloquium to which the Divinity School invited an equal number of scholars in the fall of 1966. And these differences are symptomatic of the present state of Jewish-Christian relations. The outward arrangements were similar. A wide range of such consultations had taken place, the press-coverage of which usually highlighted a new "ecumenical" spirit. It was deemed timely to choose this topic for the major scholarly celebration of our 150th anniversary year as a Divinity School. Names like those of George Foot Moore and Harry A. Wolfson indicated Harvard's substantial part in the serious academic study of the topic. The present faculty had played its part in these areas, both in the States and in the Middle East. The generous interest of the American Jewish Committee allowed us to plan on strong international participation. The aim was the same as three years earlier. We wanted to test, in the sober and sharp light of academic inquiry, where the cutting edge was in studies significant to the wide-spread dialogues of Judaism and Christianity. We wanted to test how well-founded the publicized spirit of brotherhood was, and, hopefully, to suggest lines for further progress. I think it is fair to say that we did not come very far. We did not do so well. But that is also important, since it indicates how mandatory it is to work harder. Thus it may be useful to have me, as one of the participants, reflect in writing on some of the reasons for such a state of affairs.

Here we must consider a basic incompatibility between Judaism and Christianity. We are used to treating them as two "religions" or two "traditions" contributing to Western culture. But in doing so we may well overlook elements which are constitutive. Both as religions and as traditions, Judaism and Christianity are related to each other in ways which make it difficult for them to be merely parallel phenomena. On the one hand, Christianity grew out of Judaism with a claim to be the fulfillment thereof, and, on the other, in the history of ideas they are intertwined beyond disentanglement. It could be argued, for example, that the beneficial contribution of Christianity to Western culture was exactly its function as the vehicle for the Jewish component in Christianity, while some of the less attractive elements of Christian ideology are the properly "Christian" ones. Or—as is often done in Christian circles—such an argument could be put forward in its absolutely opposite form. So complex is the matter when considered in the history of ideas.

When we think of Christianity and Judaism as communities of

faith, as church and synagogue, the incompatibility is perhaps most obvious in the fact that the church is by definition set on mission and conversion, and that this missionary thrust includes the hope that Jews accept Jesus as their long-awaited Messiah. Judaism, on the other hand, has no *equivalent* urge toward evangelization among the Gentiles. While this difference in the theological structure of the two has led to gruesome things where the Jews constituted a minority placed in a so-called Christian society, the problem itself is not dependent on a minority/ majority situation. While it can be alleviated in a secular and pluralistic situation, it remains a problem at any direct confrontation between Church and Synagogue. It is a problem which works both ways. The "pressure" from the Christian side heightens the fear on the Jewish side, and leads to frequent pleas that the Christians declare a non-mission stance, in conformity with that of Judaism. If *we* don't, why do *you?* The incompatibility is a basic one, and is one of the most serious factors in the Jewish dispersion with its concern about assimilation.

This leads us to another factor which troubles a dialogue between Judaism and Christianity: the whole web of guilt and fear which the 2000 years of our common history has made us inherit. It could perhaps be said that one issue in our Colloquium as an academic enterprise was whether the scholarly approach should attempt to stand above this factor, and achieve a non-emotional detachment therefrom. Were Auschwitz and Belsen to be considered admissible evidence in our court of discussion, or not? The problem reminds me of the discussion whether nuclear warfare is just another quantitative development of weaponry, or whether it changes the ethical problems of the world in a qualitative fashion so as to make many earlier forms of argumentation obsolete.

Such discussions can often turn cynical. It seems that the attempted genocide of the 40's, even if considered "only" a quantitative intensification of the pogroms, is a valid reason to ask new and more drastic questions about Christian responsibility, and exactly in that academic fashion. Christian theologians, preachers, and laymen all tend to make a most convenient distinction between Christianity as an ideal phenomenon—a priori beyond suspicion of any guilt in these matters—and bad "Christians" who in their lack of true Christianity have committed heinous crimes. But after 2000 years, such a facile distinction becomes rather suspect. It is a striking example of the most primitive mistake in the comparative study of religions. One compares one's own religion in its ideal form with the actual form and manifestations of other faiths.

We must rather ask openly and with trembling whether there are elements in the Christian tradition—at its very center—which lead Christians to an attitude toward Judaism which we now must judge and overcome. It is an odd form of anti-intellectualism to believe that the theology is all right but the practice and sentiments of individuals are to blame. It may well be that we should be more responsible for our thoughts and our theology than for our actions. To trust in "men of good will" and to leave the theological structures unattended is bad strategy.

The Harvard Colloquium had its challenge exactly at this point. We could take for granted that we were all for brotherhood and against bias and discrimination. We had all done our part at community activities to the betterment of social and personal relations between Christians and Jews. But now we were to test the theoretical bases for such desirable attitudes. And here we found that little had been done which could constitute a consensus. And even less had been done so as to intimate a new starting point.

It could perhaps be argued that this was partly due to a more accidental incompatibility at our Colloquium. We were fortunate in having a wider spread of theological and philosophical opinion among the Jewish participants than was perhaps the case with those who spoke out of a Christian tradition. In the future, this should be corrected by widening the Christian spectrum. The main threat to ecumenical work is that more and more significant voices are frozen out, while those who remain in conversation pride themselves on their increasing agreements. Nevertheless, the radical nature of our problem can perhaps be well exemplified by two publications which have appeared since the Colloquium.

On my desk is an edition of the Gospel of John, the title page and dust-jacket of which state—partly in re-assuring Gothic print—that here is "The Gospel according to Saint John, in the words of the King James Version of the year 1611. Edited in conformity with the true ecumenical spirit of His Holiness, Pope John XXIII, by Dagobert D. Runes. The message of Jesus is offered here without adulteration by hate and revulsion against the people of the Savior." In this edition, some twenty shorter or longer passages of the Fourth Gospel are deleted, and at other points references to the Jews are exchanged for general terms like "the people," "the crowd(s)," etc. In 7:13, 19:38, and 20:19 we read that those friendly to Jesus acted out of fear of the Romans—not of the

Jews, as the text says. Such an edition is based on a laudable sentiment. And many of us would prefer a New Testament without the marks of bitter feelings between Church and Synagogue. But it is hard to believe that the production of a fraudulent text can help anyone. There is no manuscript basis whatsoever for these deletions and changes.

I have not brought up this type of pious fraud in order to ridicule what is intended as a positive attempt toward bettering Jewish-Christian relations. Rather, it points toward the serious fact that the Christian Bible itself contains material about the Jews which must strike the contemporary reader as offensive and hateful.

That such and similar New Testament sayings have functioned as "divine" sanction for hatred against the Jews is well-known and a commonly accepted fact. The more crucial question is whether they should not be defined as having in themselves, and in their very biblical context, that element of bitterness and hateful zeal.

This issue is well and tragically demonstrated in a recent book by Cardinal Bea. It had been his eager expectations to have the Second Vatican Council make a strong statement which in effect would condemn all anti-Jewish sentiment, social and theological, as sin against God and his Christ. Much attention has been given to the ways in which this statement was finally toned down to a far more guarded and general one and placed in the context of the Council's "Declaration on the Relation of the Church to Non-Christian Religions." By his book and by its very title, Bea tries to salvage his original intention and to give as positive an interpretation as possible to what finally was decreed. In that sense the book is a moving personal document. We should, however, not blame the outcome at the Council only on political pressure from the Arab world—Christian and Muslim—nor on an ill intentioned conservatism among the bishops. Bea's own presentation makes it perfectly clear that the theological structure of the New Testament material cannot so easily be brought into harmony with a spirit of love and humility on the side of Christians. 1 Thess. 2:14ff. stands out and bothers Bea continuously (e.g., pp. 74, 87, 158, 165) and he can only counterbalance it with the Pauline sentiment in Rom. 9:1ff. Much attention is given to the fact that the gospels often confine the responsibility for the death of Jesus to the Sanhedrin or to the inhabitants of Jerusalem; hence it is not tied to all "the Jews" of that time, let alone of later generations. This is not the place to argue whether such an interpretation can be defended. If it is, it is a fine point, immensely difficult to retain, in the future development. Nor does it quite suffice to stress the love of Christ as an antidote to the bitter language about the Jews to which the Christian bible-reader is exposed. At least history shows, that so far, that has not been enough. In short, one reason for the defeat of Bea's intentions at the Council was that too many texts from the New Testament were against him. This is the really serious level of Christian anti-semitism: can the church admit to the tinge of anti-Jewish elements in its very Scriptures?

Much of recent discussion, especially the one related to the Vatican Council, has centered around the question of the "guilt" of the Jews for the crucifixion of Jesus and the so-called deicide. It may be that this specific issue is the natural one to focus upon within the Roman Catholic tradition, and within that context the Council's declaration achieves a certain corrective when it declares that "what happened in his (Jesus') passion cannot be charged against all Jews, without distinction, nor against the Jews of today."

But there is a more subtle and, I think, more powerful form of the anti-Jewish element in Christian theology to consider, especially in Protestantism and then most prominently in Lutheranism. I refer to the theological model "Law and Gospel." According to this model, this habit-forming structure of theological thinking, Jewish attitudes and Jewish piety are by definition the example of the wrong attitude toward God. The Christian proposition in the teachings of Jesus, Paul, John and all the rest, is always described in its contrast to Jewish "legalism," "casuistry," "particularism," ideas of "merit" etc. This whole system of thinking, with its image of the Pharisees and of the political Messianism of the Jews, treats Jewish piety as the black background which makes Christian piety the more shining. In such a state of affairs, it is hard to engender respect for Judaism and the Jews. And the theological system requires the retention of such an understanding of Judaism, whether true or not. Even when the seriousness of Jewish piety is commended, it is done with faint praise: it may be admirable in its sincerity but just for that reason, it is more off the mark.

All this adds up to a deep-rooted tension between Judaism and Christianity. In a historical perspective there is little surprise that that should be so. The early Christian movement was a distinct and vigorous sect within Judaism, fierce in its critique of other segments of Jewish religious life. Just as was the Qumran sect at the Dead Sea, the writings of which are filled with scathing and even hateful comments about the

Jewish establishment in Jerusalem. The prophetic tradition within Judaism reaches equally fierce expressions, "for the Lord reproves him whom he loves, as a father the son in whom he delights" (Prov. 3:12, cf. Hebr. 12:5ff.) and the prophet did his part of that reproving. In a prophetic tradition, this is the natural discourse.

What makes for the problem for Christianity versus Judaism is that this prophetic language fell, so to say, into the hands of the Gentiles. It should not be forgotten that perhaps all of our literary remains from the earliest period of the Christian movement are not only in the Greek language (which was used at that time also by many Jews—even by the majority of the Jews), but was shaped in its present form by churches which were predominantly Gentile in their constituency. In seeking its identity, this primarily Gentile church found its rationale partly in the "no of the Jews" to Jesus Christ. To Paul, the Jew, this "no" was a mystery which he treated with awe, and which, according to him, should create even greater awe and reverence in Gentile minds (Rom. 11:20). Nor does he suggest a Gentile mission to the Jews. As a good Pharisee, he leaves the solution in the hands of God (11:25-36).

But once this Jewish context and identification was lost, the words of Jesus and the earliest witnesses of the apostolic period received a new setting. They were not any longer operating within the framework of the Jewish self-criticism. They hardened into accusations against "the Jews," the synagogue across the street, and against the people who claimed the same Scriptures, but denied its fulfillment in Jesus Christ.

The drastic consequence of such form-critical observations could perhaps be stated somewhat like this: The Christian Church has no "right" to the use of these prophetic statements, once it has lost its identification with Judaism. Even if we repeated the actual words of Jesus, preserved by tape-recordings, these very words would mean something else, something contrary to his intention, once they were uttered from without instead of from within the Jewish communities.

The compassionate sorrow of Jesus as he placed himself in the succession of the prophets and wept over Jerusalem (Mt. 23:37-39) hardened into a self-righteous reassurance in the church; and the way in which Jews chose to remain aloof to Christian claims angered the frustrated missionaries and theologians so as to make the Jews the primary example of the enemies of Christ. Such sentiments color practically all expressions of Christian theology, from New Testament times (including the gospels) to the present. There is little reason to wonder about the fear and tensions in this area. The question must be asked—as it was at our Colloquium—if the present attempts to purge Christian liturgies, catechisms and hymnals from overt antisemitic elements are not only coming too late, but are primarily too timid and totally insufficient. The church is not only responsible for its intentions, which may be honorable, but also for what *actually* happens in the minds of its *actual* members and half-members as they have been and are exposed to its Scriptures and message.

What should and could then be done? It is clear to me that Christian theology needs a new departure. And it is equally clear that we cannot find it on our own, but only by the help of our Jewish colleagues. We must plead with them to help us. And as far as we are concerned, it is not a dialogue we need; we are not primarily anxious to impart our views as [we are that] they impart theirs. We need to ask, in spite of it all, whether they are willing to let us become again part of their family, a peculiar part to be true, but, even so, relatives who believe themselves to be a peculiar kind of Jews. Something went wrong in the beginning. I say "went wrong," for I am not convinced that what happened in the severing of the relations between Judaism and Christianity was the good and positive will of God. Is it not possible for us to recognize that we parted ways not according to but against the will of God?

I know that this is a strange way to speak. I know that it may be branded as historical romanticism, an attempt to turn the clock back. But why call it "to turn the clock back"? Why not say instead that the time has come for us to find the alternatives which were lost at that ancient time, alternatives which are the theological expressions of our repentance and of our understanding as they force themselves upon us today?

In this respect the parallel to the ecumenical movement is highly instructive. After a period of improved relations between the churches, Christians came to a point where the parting of ways in the past appeared to have grown out of diverse concerns within the one church. Many of these differences—some of them prefigured already in the rich variations within the New Testament itself—are serious, but none serious enough for the divisions which hardened into distinct "churches" and "sects." And, to be sure, no excuse could or should be found for the way in which this "hardening" developed into walls of suspicion and wars of suppression. So began a new attempt to find ways of growing together again. Not a syncretistic compromising of conflicting views, but a strategy developed by which actual churches begin to express the once lost unity. This is not a romantic way to play the fourth, or eleventh, or sixteenth century. It is a way to respond to one's own faith and understanding in the twentieth.

There are good theological reasons for a similar movement in the relation between Judaism and Christianity. Needless to say, there are differences, too. But if it be true that "something went wrong" in their parting of the ways, we should not elevate the past to an irrevocable will of God, but search for the lost alternatives.

What they are is too early to say. There may be many. The important thing is to accept the possibility that there are such. My own thinking is naturally influenced by my studies of the first century of the Common Era. In the Colloquium, strong arguments were given by Jewish and Christian scholars of that period to the effect that *both* "Judaism" as we know it and "Christianity" have their respective beginnings in the first century. Out of the varied and rich religious life of post-biblical Judaism prior to the year 70, there emerged two main traditions. One was rabbinic Judaism as codified in Mishna and Talmud, the other was Christianity. *Both* claimed their continuity and authenticity from the Scriptures and the ongoing post-biblical tradition. Each came to brand the other as unfaithful and heretical in their respective teaching and practice. Such an admittedly oversimplified model has much to commend it as far as historical scholarship is concerned, and it serves to question many of our traditional views.

It is obvious that a Christian plea for a new relation between Judaism and Christianity of the kind we have wished for here must raise serious questions in the minds of the Jewish community. Even if it were granted that our intentions were serious when we describe our plea as one borne out of repentance and humility—for we are the ones to ask that we be recognized as a peculiar kind of Jews, and it is up to "Judaism" to see if that is possible—it must be recognized that such a question is a new one, and utterly unexpected from our divided and common history. We Christians must be prepared to face "conditions," and that will be the time when the seriousness of our repentance will be tested. Such "conditions" may be interpreted by some as a compromising of our faith. At that point, it will be of utmost importance for Christian theology to see clearly what "our faith" is, and what must be judged to be expressions of that faith which were conditioned by our division, rather than by the revelation in Jesus Christ and by the will of God.

Obviously Judaism, on its side, will have to face similar searching questions. But rabbinic *halakha* [law] knows how the time can be ripe for something new, and this, if any situation, is one "when it is a time to do something for the Lord" (Gittin 60a, cf. M. Ber. 9:5).

It should be noted that our thinking here is openly informed by a theology of history. That is, we do not think about religious matters in terms of timeless truths, revealed in a form unrelated to the situations in which they are given. Both their original form and their continuous interpretation depend on the situations to which they speak. And the religious communities which listen and interpret are organic bodies which must find out what God wants now, as he governs his people and his world. Without attention to that *now,* our interpretations can never be true, although they may sound orthodox in a literal sense.

In such a context, a comment which was made repeatedly at the Colloquium deserves attention. When Christians take for granted that their faith and theology is superior to Judaism, they often do so for the very simple reason that Christianity followed upon Judaism as a new and hence superior "philosophy." Or an argument of Heilsgeschichte [salvation history] makes it easy to see the later stage as superior to an earlier one. If that be so, we should take the emergence of Islam far more seriously than we usually do, for here is a tradition which makes the reasonable claim of having superseded both Judaism and Christianity, and doing so according to the will and plan of God. We should at least not close our minds to the suggestion that future theological reflection, Christian and Jewish, will cut through the immense historical barriers against bringing Islam into our serious consideration.

It may seem almost ironical to bring up such a matter at the present time. Just as centuries of Western history were marked by hatred between Christians and Muslims—while the Jews were treated far better by the latter than by the former, first in Spain and then under the Turks—so today the tension between Muslims and Jews is one of the concerns of the world at large. It should not be forgotten, however, that the Arabs most involved in the present crisis are not to be identified with the Muslims since a sizable number of them are Christians. Also for that reason I find it important to close my reflections about Judaism and Christianity with some observations on the situation after the military victory of the Israelis in the summer of 1967.

It is clear enough from what we have said already that current events and theological work are not unrelated. Theology—be it academic or unconsciously embedded in piety and spontaneous reactions—does inform man's actions, for better or for worse.

The relation between Judaism and the State of Israel is naturally quite complex. It would be wrong to identify the two, both in terms of Israel itself, and in terms of the vast majority of Jewry living in other parts of the world. But it would be equally wrong to consider Israel a purely secular state. To be sure, its constitution guarantees freedom of religion, and retains the religious courts for Christians and Muslims in matters of marriage etc., according to the ancient system inherited from the Turks and the British. But Israel is a Jewish state and its religion is Judaism. Without getting involved in the difficulties of defining "Jew," "Judaism" and "Israel," it is important for Christians and Westerners to realize that a certain kind of "clean thinking" does not work here, although it would be convenient. I refer to the view—expressed also by some Jews—that Israel is a political and secular phenomenon, while Judaism is to be defined in spiritual terms as a religion or a tradition. At this juncture in history, at least, that is not so. The driving forces which made Palestine—rather than Uganda—the goal for Zionism are reason enough for the intertwining of Jewish faith and the State of Israel. That force was rooted in the Scriptures and the tradition. Our evaluation of the present situation must take that into account. Whether we like it or not, when we speak and think about the State of Israel, we are speaking about a very substantial element of Judaism. Not only in terms of so many Jews, but also in terms of Jews who see the State of Israel as the fulfillment of God's promises.

We began our reflections by pointing to the incompatibility of Judaism and Christianity. This is not only a "difficulty" in dialogue. It is also necessary to grant to Judaism its right to work out its own problems according to its own understanding of its Scripture and tradition. It is not for us to impose on Judaism our understanding of what are the "true insights of the best of the prophets." It is not for us to prescribe for Judaism that its religious aspirations should not be tied to a land or a city, "to a piece of real estate" as one Christian writer chose to express it. It is true indeed that Judaism has lived and flourished in the Dispersion for 2000 years, but it did so because somewhere in its soul was the hope for the return. That hope became spiritualized at times, but never really so. Judaism as we know it today is related to the

Land, the *Eretz*. Its rabbis and its believers may differ widely in their interpretations of this fact and its foundations, but it is hardly our task as Christians to lecture the Jews on how they as Jews should read their Scriptures.

For this reason, I am inclined to think that some of the present discussion about the possibilities of an international Jerusalem overlooks one important point. The discussion often centers on the access to the sacred sites. For Christians and Muslims that term is an adequate expression of what matters. Here are sacred places, hallowed by the most holy events, here are the places for pilgrimage, the very focus of highest devotion. It would be cruel indeed if such places were not available to all the faithful.

But Judaism is different—although the Wailing Wall came to take on much of that same character, partly under the influence of the Christian example. The sites sacred to Judaism on the Israeli side have no shrines. Its religion is not tied to "sites," but to the Land, not to what happened in Jerusalem, but to Jerusalem itself.

I would not argue that this settles the matter in favor of Israeli rule in Jerusalem. But I would argue that we as Christians concerned about the right relation to Judaism must recognize the difference between the access to Christian and Muslim sites, and the Jewish attachment to the city. To overlook that is another form of a patronizing *interpretatio christiana* [Christian interpretation]. To Christians, Jerusalem is a holy city by virtue of its shrines. For us it would be more than natural to worship at them in a Jewish city; one could even say that such a situation would be preferable, since that is how it was when it all happened.

In the months and years to come, difficult political problems in the Middle East call for solutions. Christians both in the West and in the East will weigh the proposals differently. But all of us should watch out for the ways in which the ancient venom of Christian antisemitism might enter in. A militarily victorious and politically strong Israel cannot count on half as much good will as a threatened Jewish people in danger of its second holocaust. The situation bears watching. That does not mean that Israel is always right or that its political behavior and demands should always be supported by all who as Christians would like to be considered honorary Jews for Jesus Christ's sake.

Our stance, rather, presupposes our trust in Judaism's capacity to find its own way as it seeks viable structures for the relation between its faith and the political realities of the State of Israel, and of the global community of nations and men. The Christian West has learned far too slowly and reluctantly that a close interplay between religion and politics has dangers so insurmountable that our best choice must be an acceptance of pluralism and the secularization of political decisions. The progress in that direction has also paved the way for many of the improvements in Jewish-Christian relations in the West. For that reason, it is only natural that we hope for similar developments within the Jewish state. To most of us, such a development is the only one in which we can put our realistic hopes for peace and co-existence. When we as Christian theologians want to defend the freedom of Judaism to find its own answers, we cannot help hoping that such answers can be aided by the negative experience we—and they as a minority in Christian societies—have had, experiences which have taught us to fear rather than rejoice in religion as a political factor. In politics the theologian, Christian and Jewish, must recognize that he is an amateur, and his professional concern for the ways of God should not cover over that simple fact.

I have no doubt that Judaism has the spiritual capacity to find its own solutions to the problems at hand. The present political situation may well unleash a type of Christian attitude which identifies Judaism and Israel with materialism and lack of compassion, devoid of the Christian spirit of love. Even a superficial knowledge of Judaism in its own terms makes it abundantly clear that such is not its nature. And an even more superficial acquaintance with church history suffices to silence such a patronizing attitude. Our hope for Israel should rather be for political wisdom in accordance with the riches of the long and varied tradition of the Jewish faith, a faith rich in compassion, as it always remembers the words ". . . for you were strangers in the land of Egypt." (Ex. 22:21).

As we look and work toward a new structure for our common trust in the God of Abraham, Isaac, and Jacob—and of Jesus of Nazareth, that trust includes our personal confidence in Judaism as a force for peace and justice.

37.

NO RELIGION IS AN ISLAND

Abraham Joshua Heschel

I speak as a member of a congregation whose founder was Abraham, and the name of my rabbi is Moses.

I speak as a person who was able to leave Warsaw, the city in which I was born, just six weeks before the disaster began. My destination was New York, it would have been Auschwitz or Treblinka. I am a brand plucked from the fire, in which my people was burned to death. I am a brand plucked from the fire of an altar of Satan on which millions of human lives were exterminated to evil's greater glory, and on which so much else was consumed: the divine image of so many human beings, many people's faith in the God of justice and compassion, and much of the secret and power of attachment to the Bible bred and cherished in the hearts of men for nearly two thousand years.

I speak as a person who is often afraid and terribly alarmed lest God has turned away from us in disgust and even deprived us of the power to understand His word. In the words Isaiah perceived in his vision (6:9-10):

> Then I said, "Here I am! Send me." And he said, "Go, and say to this people: Hear and hear, but do not understand; see and see, but do not perceive. Make the heart of this people fat, and their ears heavy, and shut their eyes; lest they see with their eyes, and hear with their ears, and understand with their hearts, and turn and be healed."

Some of us are like patients in the state of final agony—who scream in delirium: the doctor is dead, the doctor is dead.

I speak as a person who is convinced that the fate of the Jewish people and the fate of Hebrew Bible are intertwined. The recognition of our status as Jews, the legitimacy of our survival, is only possible in a world in which the God of Abraham is revered.

Nazism in its very roots was a rebellion against the Bible, against the God of Abraham. Realizing that it was Christianity that implanted attachment to the God of Abraham and involvement with the Hebrew Bible in the hearts of Western man, Nazism resolved that it must both exterminate the Jews and eliminate Christianity, and bring about instead a revival of Teutonic paganism.

Nazism has suffered a defeat, but the process of eliminating the Bible from the consciousness of the western world goes on. It is on the issue of saving the radiance of the Hebrew Bible in the minds of man that Jews and Christians are called upon to work together. *None of us can do it alone.* Both of us must realize that in our age anti-Semitism is anti-Christianity and that anti-Christianity is anti-Semitism.

Man is never as open to fellowship as he is in moments of misery and distress. The people of New York City have never experienced such fellowship, such awareness of being one, as they did last night in the midst of darkness.

Indeed, there is a light in the midst of the darkness of this hour. But, alas, most of us have no eyes.

Is Judaism, is Christianity, ready to face the challenge? When I speak about the radiance of the Bible in the minds of man, I do not mean its being a theme for "Information, please" but rather an openness to *God's presence in the Bible,* the continuous ongoing effort for a breakthrough in the soul of man, the guarding of the precarious position of being human, even a little higher than human, despite defiance and in face of despair.

The supreme issue is today not the *halakha* for the Jew or the Church for the Christian—but the premise underlying both religions, namely, whether there is a *pathos,* a divine reality concerned with the destiny of man which mysteriously impinges upon history; the supreme issue is whether we are alive or dead to the challenge and the expectation of the living God. The crisis engulfs all of us. The misery and fear of alienation from God make Jew and Christian cry together.

Jews must realize that the spokesmen of the Enlightment who attacked Christianity were no less negative in their attitude toward Judaism. They often blamed Judaism for the misdeeds of the daughter religion. The casualties of the devastation caused by the continuous onslaughts on biblical religion in modern times are to be found among Jews as well as among Christians.

On the other hand, the Community of Israel must always be mindful of the mystery of aloneness and uniqueness of its own being. "There is a people that dwells apart, not reckoned among the nations" (Numbers 23:19), says the Gentile prophet Balaam. Is it not safer for us to remain in isolation and to refrain from sharing perplexities and certainties with Christians?

Our era marks the end of complacency, the end of evasion, the end of self-reliance. Jews and Christians share the perils and the fears; we stand on the brink of the abyss together. Interdependence of political and economic conditions all over the world is a basic fact of our situation. Disorder in a small obscure country in any part of the world evokes anxiety in people all over the world.

Parochialism has become untenable. There was a time when you could not pry out of a Boston man that the Boston state-house is not the hub of the solar system or that one's own denomination has not the monopoly of the holy spirit. Today we know that even the solar system is not the hub of the universe.

The religions of the world are no more self-sufficient, no more independent, no more isolated than individuals or nations. Energies, experiences and ideas that come to life outside the boundaries of a particular religion or all religions continue to challenge and to affect every religion.

Horizons are wider, dangers are greater . . . *No religion is an island.* We are all involved with one another. Spiritual betrayal on the part of one of us affects the faith of all of us. Views adopted in one community have an impact on other communities. Today religious isolationism is a myth. For all the profound differences in perspective and substance, Judaism is sooner or later affected by the intellectual, moral and spiritual events within the Christian society, and vice versa.

We fail to realize that while different exponents of faith in the world of religion continue to be wary of the ecumenical movement, there is another ecumenical movement, world-wide in extent and influence: nihilism. We must choose between interfaith and inter-nihilism. Cynicism is not parochial. Should religions insist upon the illusion of complete isolation? Should we refuse to be on speaking terms with one another and hope for each other's failure? Or should we pray for each other's health, and help one another in preserving one's respective legacy, in preserving a common legacy?

The Jewish diaspora today, almost completely to be found in the Western world, is certainly not immune to the spiritual climate and the state of religious faith in the general society. We do not live in isolation, and the way in which non-Jews either relate or bid defiance to God has a profound impact on the minds and souls of the Jews. Even in the Middle Ages, when most Jews lived in relative isolation, such impact was acknowledged. To quote, "The usage of the Jews is in accordance with that of the non-Jews. If the non-Jews of a certain town are moral, the Jews born there will be so as well." Rabbi Joseph Yaabez, a victim of the Spanish Inquisition, in the midst of the Inquisition was able to say that "the Christians believe in Creation, the excellence of the Patriachs, revelation, retribution and resurrection. Blessed is the Lord, God of Israel, who left this remnant after the destruction of the second Temple. But for these Christian nations we might ourselves become infirm in our faith."

We are heirs to a long history of mutual contempt among religions and religious denominations, of religious coercion, strife and persecutions. Even in periods of peace, the relationship that obtains between representatives of different religions is not just reciprocity of ignorance; it is an abyss, a source of detraction and distrust, casting suspicion and undoing efforts of many an honest and noble expression of good will.

The Psalmist's great joy is in proclaiming: "Truth and mercy have met together" (Psalm 85:11). Yet so frequently faith and the lack of mercy enter a union, out of which bigotry is born, the presumption that my faith, my motivation, is pure and holy, while the faith of those who differ in creed—even those in my own community—is impure and unholy. How can we be cured of bigotry, presumption, and the foolishness of believing that we have been triumphant while we have all been defeated?

Is it not clear that in spite of fundamental disagreements there is a convergence of some of our commitments, of some of our views, tasks we have in common, evils we must fight together, goals we share, a predicament afflicting us all?

On what basis do we people of different religious commitments meet one another?

First and foremost we meet as human beings who have so much in common: a heart, a face, a voice, the presence of a soul, fears, hope, the ability to trust, a capacity for compassion and understanding, the kinship of being human. My first task in every encounter is to comprehend the personhood of the human being I face, to sense the kinship of being human, solidarity of being.

To meet a human being is a major challenge to mind and heart. I must recall what I normally forget. A person is not just a specimen of the species called *homo sapiens.* He is all of humanity in one, and whenever one man is hurt we are all injured. The human is a disclosure of the divine, and all men are one in God's care for man. Many things on earth are precious, some are holy, humanity is holy of holies.

To meet a human being is an opportunity to sense the image of God, *the presence* of God. According to a rabbinical interpretation, the Lord said to Moses: "Wherever you see the trace of man there I stand before you . . ."

When engaged in a conversation with a person of different religious commitment I discover that we disagree in matters sacred to us, does the image of God I face disappear? Does God cease to stand before me? Does the difference in commitment destroy the kinship of being human? Does the fact that we differ in our conceptions of God cancel what we have in common: the image of God?

> For this reason was man created single (whereas of every other species many were created) . . . that there should be peace among human beings: one cannot say to his neighbor, my ancestor was nobler than thine (Sanhedrin 37a).

The primary aim of these reflections is to inquire how a Jew out of his commitment and a Christian out of his commitment can find a religious basis for communication and cooperation on matters relevant to their moral and spiritual concern in spite of disagreement.

There are four dimensions of religious existence, four necessary components of man's relationships to God: a) the teaching, the essentials of which are summarized in the form of a creed, which serve as guiding principles in our thinking about matters temporal or eternal, the dimension of the doctrine; b) faith, inwardness, the direction of one's heart, the intimacy of religion, the dimension of privacy; c) the law, or the sacred act to be carried out in the sanctuary in society or at home, the dimension of the deed; d) the context in which creed, faith and ritual come to pass, such as the community or the covenant, history, tradition, the dimension of transcendence.

In the dimension of the deed there are obviously vast areas for cooperation among men of different commitments in terms of intellectual communication, of sharing concern and knowledge in applied religion, particularly as they relate to social action.

In the dimension of faith, the encounter proceeds in terms of personal witness and example, sharing insights, confessing inadequacy. On the level of doctrine we seek to convey the content of what we believe in, on the level of faith we experience in one another the presence of a person radiant with reflections of a greater presence.

I suggest that the most significant basis for meeting of men of different religious traditions is the level of fear and trembling, of humility and contrition, where our individual moments of faith are mere waves in the endless ocean of mankind's reaching out for God, where all formulations and articulations appear as understatements, where our souls are swept away by the awareness of the urgency of answering God's commandment, while stripped of pretension and conceit we sense the tragic insufficiency of human faith.

What divides us? What unites us? We disagree in law and creed, in commitments which lie at the very heart of our religious existence. We say "No" to one another in some doctrines essential and sacred to us. What unites us? Our being accountable to God, our being objects of God's concern, precious in His eyes. Our conceptions of what ails us may be different; but the anxiety is the same. The language, the imagination, the concretization of our hopes are different, but the embarrassment is the same, and so is the sigh, the sorrow, and the necessity to obey.

We may disagree about the ways of achieving fear and trembling, but the fear and trembling are the same. The demands are different, but the conscience is the same, and so is arrogance, iniquity. The proclamations are different, the callousness is the same, and so is the challenge we face in many moments of spiritual agony.

Above all, while dogmas and forms of worship are divergent, God is the same. What unites us? A commitment to the Hebrew Bible as Holy Scripture. Faith in the Creator, the God of Abraham, commitment to many of His commandments, to justice and mercy, a sense of contrition, sensitivity to the sanctity of life and to the involvement of God in history, the conviction that without the holy the good will be defeated, prayer that history may not end before the end of days, and so much more.

There are moments when we all stand together and see our faces in the mirror: the anguish of humanity and its helplessness; the perplexity of the individual and the need of divine guidance; being called to praise and to do what is required.

In conversations with Protestant and Catholic theologians I have more than once come upon an attitude of condescension to Judaism, a sort of pity for those who have not yet seen the light; tolerance instead of reverence. On the other hand, I cannot forget that when Paul Tillich, Gustave Weigel, and myself were invited by the Ford Foundation to speak from the same platform on the religious situation in America, we not only found ourselves in deep accord in disclosing what ails us, but above all without prior consultation, the three of us confessed that our guides in this critical age are the prophets of Israel, not Aristotle, not Karl Marx, but Amos and Isaiah.

The theme of these reflections is not a doctrine or an institution called Christianity, but human beings all over the world, both present and past, who worship God as followers of Jesus, and my problem is how I should relate myself to them spiritually. The issue I am called upon to respond to is not the truth of dogma but the faith and the spiritual power of the commitment of Christians. In facing the claim and the dogma of the Church, Jews and Christians are strangers and stand in disagreement with one another. Yet there are levels of existence where Jews and Christians meet as sons and brothers. "Alas, in heaven's name, are we not your brothers, are we not the sons of one father and are we not the sons of one mother? . . ."

To be sure all men are sons of one father, but they have also the power to forfeit their birthright, to turn rebels, voluntary bastards, "children with no faithfulness in them" (Deuteronomy 32:20). It is not flesh and blood but honor and obedience that save the right of sonship. We claim brotherhood by being subject to His commandments. We are sons when we hearken to the Father, when we praise and honor Him.

The recognition that we are sons in obeying God and praising Him is the starting-point of my reflection. "I am a companion of all who fear Thee, of those who keep Thy precepts" (Psalms 119:63). I rejoice wherever His name is praised, His presence sensed, His commandment done.

The first and most important *prerequisite of interfaith is faith.* It is only out of the depth of involvement in the unending drama that began with Abraham that we can help one another toward an understanding of our situation. Interfaith must come out of depth, not out of a void absence of faith. It is not an enterprise for those who are half learned or spiritually immature. If it is not to lead to the confusion of the many, it must remain a prerogative of the few.

Faith and the power of insight and devotion can only grow in privacy. Exposing one's inner life may engender the danger of desecration, distortion and confusion. Syncretism is a perpetual possibility. Moreover, at a time of paucity of faith, interfaith may become a substitute for faith, suppressing authenticity for the sake of compromise. In a world of conformity, religions can easily be levelled down to the lowest common denominator.

Both communication and separation are necessary. We must preserve our individuality as well as foster care for one another, reverence, understanding, cooperation. In the world of economics, science and technology, cooperation exists and continues to grow. Even political states, though different in culture and competing with one another, maintain diplomatic relations and strive for coexistence. Only religions are not on speaking terms. Over a hundred countries are willing to be part of the United Nations; yet no religion is ready to be part of a movement for United Religions. Or should I say, not yet ready? Ignorance, distrust, and disdain often characterize their relations to one another. Is disdain for the opposition indigenous to the religious position? Granted that Judaism and Christianity are committed to contradictory claims, is it impossible to carry on a controversy without acrimony, criticism without loss of respect, disagreement without disrespect? The problem to be faced is: how to combine loyalty to one's own tradition with reverence for different traditions? How is mutual esteem between Christian and Jew possible?

A Christian ought to ponder seriously the tremendous implications of a process begun in early Christian history. I mean the conscious or unconscious dejudaization of Christianity, affecting the Church's way of thinking, its inner life as well as its relationshp to the past and present reality of Israel—the father and mother of the very being of Christianity. The children did not arise to call the mother blessed; instead, they called the mother blind. Some theologians continue to act as if they did not know the meaning of "honor your father and mother"; others, anxious to prove the superiority of the church, speak as if they suffered from a spiritual Oedipus complex.

A Christian ought to realize that a world without Israel will be a world without the God of Israel. A Jew, on the other hand, ought to acknowledge the eminent role and part of Christianity in God's design for the redemption of all men.

Modern Jews who have come out of the state of political seclusion and are involved in the historic process of Western mankind cannot afford to be indifferent to the religious situation of our fellow-men. Opposition to Christianity must be challenged by the question: What religious alternative do we envisage for the Christian world? Did we not refrain for almost two thousand years from preaching Judaism to the Nations?

A Jew ought to ponder seriously the responsibility involved in Jewish history for having been the mother of two world religions. Does not the failure of children reflect upon their mother? Do not the sharp deviations from Jewish tradition on the part of the early Christians who were Jews indicate some failure of communication within the spiritual climate of first century Palestine?

Judaism is the mother of the Christian faith. It has a stake in the destiny of Christianity. Should a mother ignore her child, even a wayward, rebellious one? On the other hand, the Church should acknowledge that we Jews in loyalty to our tradition have a stake in its faith, recognize our vocation to preserve and to teach the legacy of the Hebrew Scripture, accept our aid in fighting anti-Marcionite trends as an act of love.

Is it not our duty to help one another in trying to overcome hardness of heart, in cultivating a sense of wonder and mystery, in unlocking doors to holiness in time, in opening minds to the challenge of the Hebrew Bible, in seeking to respond to the voice of the prophets?

No honest religious person can fail to admire the outpouring of the love of man and the love of God, the marvels of worship, the magnificence of spiritual insight, the piety, charity and sanctity in the lives of countless men and women, manifested in the history of Christianity. Have not Pascal, Kierkegaard, Immanuel Kant or Reinhold Niebuhr been a source of inspiration to many Jews?

Over and above mutual respect we must acknowledge indebtedness to one another. It is our duty to remember that it was the Church that brought the knowledge of the God of Abraham to the Gentiles. It was the Church that made Hebrew Scripture available to mankind. This we Jews must acknowledge with a grateful heart.

The Septuagint, the works of Philo, Josephus, as well as the Apocrypha and Pseudepigrapha, and the *Fons vitae* by Ibn Gabirol would have been lost had they not been preserved in monasteries. Credit for major achievements in modern scholarship in the field of Bible, in biblical as well as hellenistic Jewish history, goes primarily to Protestant scholars.

The purpose of religious communication among human beings of different commitments is mutual enrichment and enhancement of respect and appreciation rather than the hope that the person spoken to will prove to be wrong in what he regards as sacred.

Dialogue must not degenerate into a dispute, into an effort on the part of each to get the upper hand. There is an unfortunate history of Christian-Jewish disputations, motivated by the desire to prove how blind the Jews are and carried on in a spirit of opposition, which eventually degenerated into enmity. Thus any conversation between Christian and Jew in which abandonment of the other partner's faith is a silent hope must be regarded as offensive to one's religious and human dignity.

Let there be an end to disputation and polemic, an end to disparagement. We honestly and profoundly disagree in matters of creed and dogma. Indeed, there is a deep chasm between Christians and Jews concerning, e.g., the divinity and Messiahship of Jesus. But across the chasm we can extend our hands to one another.

Religion is a means, not the end. It becomes idolatrous when regarded as an end in itself. Over and above all being stands the Creator and Lord of history, He who transcends all. To equate religion and God is idolatry.

Does not the all-inclusiveness of God contradict the exclusiveness of any particular religion? The prospect of all men embracing one form of religion remains an eschatological hope. What about here and now? Is it not blasphemous to say: I alone have all the truth and the grace, and all those who differ live in darkness, and are abandoned by the grace of God?

Is it really our desire to build a monolithic society: one party, one view, one leader, and no opposition? Is religious uniformity desirable or even possible? Has it really proved to be a blessing for a country when all its citizens belonged to one denomination? Or has any denomination attained a spiritual climax when it had the adherence of the entire population? Does not the task of preparing the kingdom of God require a diversity of talents, a variety of rituals, soul-searching as well as opposition?

Perhaps it is the will of God that in this aeon there should be diversity in our forms of devotion and commitment to Him. In this aeon diversity of religions is the will of God.

In the story of the building of the Tower of Babel we read: "The Lord said: They are one people, and they have all one language, and this is what they begin to do" (Genesis 11:6). These words are interpreted by an ancient Rabbi to mean: What has caused them to rebel against me? The fact that they are one people and they have all one language . . .

> For from the rising of the sun to its setting My name is great among the nations, and in every place incense is offered to My name, and a pure offering; for My name is great among the nations, says the Lord of hosts (Malachi 1:11).

This statement refers undoubtedly to the contemporaries of the prophet. But who were these worshippers of One God? At the time of Malachi there was hardly a large number of proselytes. Yet the statement declares: All those who worship their gods do not know it, but they are really worshipping Me.

It seems that the prophet proclaims that men all over the world, though they confess different conceptions of God, are really worshipping One God, the Father of all men, though they may not be aware of it.

Religions, I repeat, true to their own convictions, disagree profoundly and are in opposition to one another on matters of doctrine. However, if we accept the prophet's thesis that they all worship one God, even without knowing it, if we accept the principle that the majesty of God transcends the dignity of religion, should we not regard a divergent religion as His Majesty's loyal opposition? However, does not every religion maintain the claim to be true, and is not truth exclusive?

The ultimate truth is not capable of being fully and adequately expressed in concepts and words. The ultimate truth is about the situation that pertains between God and man. "The Torah speaks in the language of man." Revelation is always an accommodation to the capacity of man. No two minds are alike, just as no two faces are alike. The voice of God reaches the spirit of man in a variety of ways, in a multiplicity of languages. One truth comes to expression in many ways of understanding.

A major factor in our religious predicament is due to self-righteousness and to the assumption that faith is found only in him who has arrived, while absent in him who is on the way. Religion is often inherently guilty of the sin of pride and presumption. To paraphrase the prophet's words, the exultant religion dwelt secure and said in her heart: "I am, and there is no one besides me."

Humility and contrition seem to be absent where most required—in theology. But humility is the beginning and end of religious thinking, the secret test of faith. There is no truth without humility, no certainty without contrition.

Ezra the Scribe, the great renovator of Judaism, of whom the rabbis said that he was worthy of receiving the Torah had it not been already given through Moses, confessed his lack of perfect faith. He tells us that after he had received a royal *firman* from King Artaxerxes granting him permission to lead a group of exiles from Babylonia: "I proclaimed a fast there at the river Ahava, that we might afflict ourselves before our God, to seek of Him a right way for us, and for our little ones, and for all substance. For I was ashamed to require of the king a band of soldiers and horsemen to help us against the enemy in the way: because we had spoken unto the king, saying, the hand of God is upon all them for good that seek Him" (Ezra 8:21-22).

Human faith is never final, never an arrival, but rather an endless pilgrimage, a being on the way. We have no answers to all problems. Even some of our sacred answers are both emphatic and qualified, final and tentative; final within our own position in history, tentative—because we can only speak in the tentative language of man.

Heresy is often a roundabout expression of faith, and sojourning in the wilderness is a preparation for entering the promised land.

Is the failure, the impotence of all religions, due exclusively to human transgression? Or perhaps to the mystery of God's withholding His grace, of His concealing even while revealing? Disclosing the fullness of His glory would be an impact that would surpass the power of human endurance.

His thoughts are not our thoughts. Whatever is revealed is abundance compared with our soul and a pittance compared with His treasures. No word is God's last word, no word is God's ultimate word.

Following the revelation at Sinai, the people said to Moses: "You speak to us, and we will hear; let not God speak to us, lest we die" (Exodus 20:19).

The Torah as given to Moses, an ancient rabbi maintains, is but an unripened fruit of the heavenly tree of wisdom. At the end of days, much that is concealed will be revealed.

The mission to the Jews is a call to the individual Jews to betray the fellowship, the dignity, the sacred history of their people. Very few Christians seem to comprehend what is morally and spiritually involved in supporting such activities. We are Jews as we are men. The alternative to our existence as Jews is spiritual suicide, extinction. It is not a change into something else. Judaism has allies but no substitutes.

The wonder of Israel, the marvel of Jewish existence, the survival of holiness in the history of the Jews, is a continuous verification of the marvel of the Bible. Revelation to Israel continues as a revelation through Israel.

The Protestant pastor, Christian Furchtegott Gellert, was asked by Frederick the Great, "Herr Professor, give me proof of the Bible, but briefly, for I have little time." Gellert answered, "Your Majesty, the Jews."

Indeed, is not the existence of the Jews a witness to the God of Abraham? Is not our loyalty to the law of Moses a light that continues to illumine the lives of those who observe it as well as the lives of those who are aware of it?

Gustave Weigel spent the last evening of his life in my study at the Jewish Theological Seminary. We opened our hearts to one another in prayer and contrition and spoke of our own deficiencies, failures, hopes. At one moment I posed the question: Is it really the will of God that there be no more Judaism in the world? Would it really be the triumph of God if the scrolls of the Torah would no more be taken out of the Ark and the Torah no more read in the Synagogue, our ancient Hebrew prayers in which Jesus himself worshipped no more recited, the Passover Seder no more celebrated in our lives, the law of Moses no more observed in our homes? Would it really be *ad majorem Dei gloriam* to have a world without Jews?

My life is shaped by many loyalties—to my family, to my friends, to my people, to the U.S. constitution, etc. Each of my loyalties has its ultimate root in one ultimate relationship: loyalty to God, the loyalty of all my loyalties. That relationship is the covenant of Sinai. All we are we owe to Him. He has enriched us with gifts of insight, with the joy of moments full of blessing. He has also suffered with us in years of agony and distress.

None of us pretends to be God's accountant, and His design for history and redemption remains a mystery before which we must stand in awe. It is arrogant to maintain that the Jews' refusal to accept Jesus as the Messiah is due to their stubbornness or blindness as it would be presumptuous for the Jews not to acknowledge the glory and holiness in the lives of countless Christians. "The Lord is near to all who call upon Him, to all who call upon Him in truth" (Psalm 145:18).

Fortunately there are some important Christian voices who expressed themselves to the effect that the missionary activities to the Jews be given up. Reinhold Niebuhr may have been the first Christian theologian who at a joint meeting of the faculties of the Union Theological Seminary and the Jewish Theological Seminary declared that the missionary "activities are wrong not only because they are futile and have little fruit to boast for their exertions. They are wrong because the two faiths despite differences are sufficiently alike for the Jew to find God more easily in terms of his own religious heritage than by subjecting himself to the hazards of guilt feelings involved in conversion to a faith which, whatever its excellencies, must appear to him as a symbol of an oppressive majority culture . . . Practically nothing can purify the symbol of Christ as the image of God in the imagination of the Jew from the taint with which ages of Christian oppression in the name of Christ have tainted it." Tillich has said,

> Many Christians feel that it is a questionable thing, for instance, to try to convert Jews. They have lived and spoken with their Jewish friends for decades. They have not converted them, but they have created a community of conversation which has changed both sides of the dialogue.

And a statement on "relations with the Roman Catholic Church" adopted by the Central Committee of the World Council of Churches in its meeting in Rochester, New York in August, 1963, mentions proselytism as a "cause of offence," an issue "which must be frankly faced if true dialogue is to be possible."

The ancient Rabbis proclaim: "Pious men of all nations have a share in the life to come."

"I call heaven and earth to witness that the Holy Spirit rests upon each person, Jew or Gentile, man or woman, master or slave, in consonance with his deeds."

Holiness is not the monopoly of any particular religion or tradition. Wherever a deed is done in accord with the will of God, wherever a thought of man is directed toward Him, there is the holy.

The Jews do not maintain that the way of the Torah is the only way of serving God. "Let all the peoples walk each one in the name of its god, but we will walk in the name of the Lord our God for ever and ever" (Micah 4:5).

"God loves the Saint" (Psalms 146:8)—"They love Me, and I love them . . . If a person wishes to be a Levite or a priest, he cannot become one. If he wishes to become a saint, even if he is a gentile, he may become one. For saints do not derive their saintliness from their ancestry; they become saints because they dedicate themselves to God and love Him." Conversion to Judaism is no prerequisite for sanctity. In his Code Maimonides asserts: "Not only is the tribe of Levi (God's portion) sanctified in the highest degree, but any man among all the dwellers on earth whose heart prompts him and whose mind instructs him to dedicate himself to the services of God and to walk uprightly as God intended him to, and who disencumbers himself of the load of the many pursuits which men invent for themselves." "God asks for the heart, everything depends upon the intention of the heart . . . all men have a share in eternal life if they attain according to their ability knowledge of the Creator and have ennobled themselves by noble qualities. There is no doubt that he who has thus trained himself morally and intellectually to acquire faith in the Creator will certainly have a share in the life to come. This is why our Rabbis taught: a gentile who studies the Torah of Moses is (spiritually) equal to the High Priest at the Temple in Jerusalem."

Leading Jewish authorities, such as Jehuda Halevi and Maimonides, acknowledge Christianity to be *preparatio messianica* [preparation for the Messiah], while the Church regarded ancient Judaism to have been a *preparatio evangelica* [preparation for the gospel]. Thus, whereas the Christian doctrine has often regarded Judaism as having outlived its usefulness and the Jews as candidates for conversion, the Jewish attitude enables us to acknowledge the presence of a divine plan in the role of

Christianity within the history of redemption. Jehuda Halevi, though criticizing Christianity and Islam for retaining relics of ancient idolatry and feast days, "they also revere places sacred to idols," compares Christians and Mohammedans to proselytes who adopted the roots, but not all the branches (or the logical conclusions of the divine commandments). "The wise providence of God towards Israel may be compared to the planting of a seed of corn. It is placed in the earth, where it seems to be changed into soil, and water, and rottenness, and the seed can no longer be recognized. But in very truth it is the seed that has changed the earth and water into its own nature, and then the seed raises itself from one stage to another, transforms the elements, and throws out shoots and leaves . . . Thus it is with Christians and Moslems. The Law of Moses has changed them that come into contact with it, even though they seem to have cast the Law aside. These religions are the preparation and the preface to the Messiah we expect, who is the fruit himself of the seed originally sown, and all men, too, will be fruit of God's seed when they acknowledge Him, and all become one mighty tree."

A similar view is set forth by Maimonides in his authoritative Code: "It is beyond the human mind to fathom the designs of the Creator; for our ways are not His ways, neither are our thoughts His thoughts. All these matters relating to Jesus of Nazareth and the Ishmaelite (Mohammed) who came after him, served to clear the way for King Messiah, to prepare the whole world to worship God with one accord, as it is written, *For then will I turn to the peoples a pure language, that they may all call upon the name of the Lord to serve Him with one consent* (Zeph. 3:9). Thus the messianic hope, the Torah, and the commandments have become familiar topics—topics of conversation (among the inhabitants) of the far isles and many peoples . . ."

Christianity and Islam, far from being accidents of history or purely human phenomena, are regarded as part of God's design for the redemption of all men. Christianity is accorded ultimate significance by acknowledging that "all these matters relative to Jesus of Nazareth and Mohammed . . . served to clear the way for King Messiah." In addition to the role of these religions in the plan of redemption, their achievements within history are explicitly affirmed: Through them "the messianic hope, the Torah, and the commandments have become familiar topics . . . [among the inhabitants] of the far isles and many peoples." Elsewhere Maimonides acknowledges that "the Christians believe and profess that the Torah is God's revelation (*torah min ha-shamayim*) and given to Moses in the form in which it has been preserved; they have it completely written down, though they frequently interpret it differently."

Rabbi Johanan Ha-Sandelar, a disciple of Rabbi Akiba, says: "Every community which is established for the sake of heaven will in the end endure; but one which is not for the sake of heaven will not endure in the end."

Rabbi Jacob Emden maintains that heretical Jewish sects such as the Karaites and the Sabbatians belong to the second category whereas Christianity and Islam are in the category of "a community which is for the sake of heaven" and which will "in the end endure." They have emerged out of Judaism and accepted "the fundamentals of our divine religion . . . to make known God among the nations . . . , to proclaim that there is a Master in heaven and earth, divine providence, reward and punishment . . . , Who bestows the gift of prophecy . . . and communicates through the prophets laws and statutes to live by. . . . This is why their community endures. . . . Since their intention is for the sake of heaven, reward will not be withheld from them." He also praises many Christian scholars who have come to the rescue of Jews and their literature.

Rabbi Israel Lifschutz of Danzig (1782-1860) speaks of the Christians, "our brethren, the gentiles, who acknowledge the one God and revere His Torah which they deem divine and observe, as is required of them, the seven commandments of Noah . . ."

What, then, is the purpose of interreligious cooperation?

It is neither to flatter nor to refute one another, but to help one another; to share insight and learning, to cooperate in academic ventures on the highest scholarly level, and what is even more important to search in the wilderness for well-springs of devotion, for treasures of stillness, for the power of love and care for man. What is urgently needed are ways of helping one another in the terrible predicament of here and now by the courage to believe that the word of the Lord endures for ever as well as here and now; to cooperate in trying to bring about a resurrection of sensitivity, a revival of conscience; to keep alive the divine sparks in our souls, to nurture openness to the spirit of the Psalms, reverence for the words of the prophets, and faithfulness to the Living God.

* Reprinted from The Study of Judaism: Bibliographical Essays, New York, ADL, 1972, not updated.

BIBLIOGRAPHICAL ESSAY:
JUDAISM ON CHRISTIANITY:
CHRISTIANITY ON JUDAISM *

Frank Ephraim Talmage

The following list, comprised of source collections, historical and theological works, polemical writings, etc., represents the two-thousand-year development of the image of Christianity in the eyes of Judaism and that of Judaism and the Jews in the view of Christianity. The material is organized wherever possible by period (late antiquity, Middle Ages, modern times) although a number of works overlap and may be mentioned more than once. Works are cited in the text by author and title only, with full bibliographic information provided in the numbered list at the end. A supplementary list of titles not discussed in the text is appended.

A. VIEWS OF JESUS

1. *Rabbinic and Medieval Periods*

References or alleged references to Jesus, New Testament figures, or Christians in Talmud and Midrash have been the object of prolonged speculation and controversy among both Jewish and Christian scholars. The problem was rendered more complex by the fact that much of this material, sufficiently obscure in itself, was censored out of the printed editions by Church authorities. The best known and classic attempt to sift through and organize this material is Travers Herford's *Christianity in Talmud and Midrash* (32) in which all the relevant passages are collected in the original Hebrew and Aramaic, translated, and carefully annotated. Herford set himself a twofold task. He first attempted to identify those passages actually referring to Jesus on the basis of philological analysis, from which he proceeded to an examination of the ma-

361

terial concerning the minim, whom he generally identifies with
early Jewish Christians. A correction of certain technical failings
in Herford such as mistranslations and inadequate use of manu-
scripts was essayed by Morris Goldstein in *Jesus in the Jewish
Tradition* (28). This volume has the advantage of having the
passages sorted by period and classified into the three categories
of authentic references to Jesus, references incorrectly identified
with Jesus (e.g. others by the name of Yeshu, Ben Stada, etc.),
and indirect allusions. Possible references to Christianity and
Christian doctrine are examined with the constant awareness that
"with regard to . . . [our positive identifications], too, we deal
with probabilities." In addition to the rabbinic material, the author
adds an English rendition of one of the medieval Hebrew "bio-
graphies" (*Toledot Yeshu*) of Jesus and a review of the medieval
polemical literature. The fairly thorough bibliographic treatment
is helpful.

Although not as conveniently arranged as Goldstein, the most
technically competent and thorough treatment of the subject is
Jacob Zallel Lauterbach's essay "Jesus in the Talmud" in his
Rabbinic Essays (40). In his effort to show that the rabbinic
material has no historical value whatsoever for a study of Jesus
and Christian origins, Lauterbach is even more conservative than
his predecessors in admitting rabbinic references to Jesus of Nazareth. Especially important is his reexamination of the historical
background of the passages in which a number of long-accepted
interpretations are dismissed, though in some instances they are
replaced by others equally conjectural.

2. The Modern Period

Modern Jewish interest in Jesus may be traced from the early
nineteenth-century writers, who, out of apologetic motives, frequently sought to couple a "reclamation" or "re-judaization" of
Jesus with a negative evaluation of Christianity, through more
recent scholarship which interests itself in Jesus as a historical
and religious figure within the framework of the history of Judaism.
A most exhaustive and erudite literary history of this problem is
Gösta Lindeskog's *Die Jesusfrage im neuzeitlichen Judenthum*

(41) which covers the period from the Emancipation to the out-break of World War I. The author first surveys the literature from the period of the *Wissenchaft des Judentums* through the writings, historical, theological, and belletristic, of the thirties. Then topic-ally, he treats, in addition to the major questions of Jewish atti-tudes towards the religion of Jesus and its relation to Judaism, the problems of historiography of the intertestamental period, the person and role of Jesus, the trial and crucifixion, and the found-ing of Christianity. Each chapter is well endowed with full biblio-graphic annotation including references to works written in Hebrew.

A much smaller volume in English, Thomas Walker's *Jewish Views of Jesus* (68) ably summarizes the views of selected Jewish thinkers still significant at the time of writing (1931), allowing them insofar as possible to speak for themselves. These include two orthodox writers (Paul Goodman, Gerald Friedlander), two lib-eral thinkers (Claude G. Montefiore, Israel Abrahams), and two "portraits" (Joseph Jacobs, Joseph Klausner).

An actual example of the kind of writing done by the liberal-apologetic school of the late nineteenth and early twentieth cen-turies is Ernest R. Trattner's *As a Jew Sees Jesus* (67). Without real scholarly merit, the work is of some interest in its reflection of prevailing attitudes. Of some value is the extensive bibliography (pp. 200–208) of books, tracts, and articles in English by Jewish writers on the subject of Jesus.

Joseph Klausner's *Jesus of Nazareth* (38) remains the classic work from the Jewish nationalist point of view. Highly dependent upon liberal Protestant scholarship (it was roundly condemned in Roman Catholic circles), the chief significance of the work lies less in its advancement over previous scholarship than in the fact that it clearly marked the transition from the liberal-apologetic approach to that of historical criticism. Indicative of this, in part, is the fact that the author wrote the volume in Hebrew intending it for members of the *Yishuv* (Palestinian Jewish community). Klausner's view of Jesus is one that perceives him as a nationalist whose goal was the redemption of his people, but who rendered a disservice to Judaism instead by sapping it of its peculiarly

Jewish content and abstracting it into an ethico-religious system. Seeing himself as the awaited redeemer, Jesus was frustrated in his approach to the people who refused to recognize him because of his failure to provide a concrete plan of redemption. A similar approach is found in the chapter on Christianity in another Hebrew work, Yehezkel Kaufmann's *Golah ve-nekhar* (36). Kaufmann brings a heavily documented account of Jesus' unswerving faithfulness to the *halakhah* on the one hand and his deviation from Judaism, on the other, in his role as apocalyptic Messiah.

Less a study of Jesus than of first-century Palestinian Judaism is Robert Aron's *Jesus of Nazareth: The Hidden Years* (1), an exploration of the kind of life Jesus probably led in the years between his early youth and ministry, concerning which the Gospels are silent. In setting Jesus against his Jewish background, Aron presents Jewish life and institutions (despite certain anachronisms) in a way which should prove enlightening for the Christian reader. Of special interest is the chapter on language in which the author points out the influence of Semitic linguistic structure and modes of thinking on Jesus' thought and preaching.

The most recent critical study of Jesus by a Jewish scholar is David Flusser's *Jesus* (27). Succinct, but highly eloquent, Flusser brings to bear on the work his considerable erudition in both New Testament scholarship and Christian origins on the one hand, and in Rabbinic Judaism on the other. According to the author, "the main purpose of this book is to show that it is possible to write the story of Jesus' life." In doing so, he employs the method of isolating the old Markan account and the logia from the later revisions in the Synoptics. This plus his recoveries of Hebrew idiom behind the Greek lead him to his attempted restoration of Jesus' role and mission as he himself understood it.

Among popular or semi-popular writings, most deserving of mention is *Jésus et Israël* (33) by the Franco-Jewish writer Jules Isaac. Isaac presents a Jesus who loves and is loyal to his people and with consummate irony contrasts his own words as found in the Gospels with the attitudes towards the Jews expressed by the Church Fathers and Christian theologians up to the twentieth century. The material so presented attains a particular poignancy when it is recalled that he is writing in the aftermath and as a result of the Nazi holocaust. "This interesting book," writes David Flusser, "which is not written by a professional scholar and which is the product of apologetic enthusiasm deserves to be read by specialists because of the author's acumen and the penetrating analyses of his sources."

Two other semi-popular studies are worthy of mention. Samuel Sandmel's *We Jews and Jesus* (58) contains useful reviews of nineteenth- and twentieth-century New Testament scholarship and an analysis of the Jewish background of the Gospels. Written for Jews as a sort of *praeparatio dialogica,* the author firmly rejects any attempt to reclaim Jesus. Schalom Ben-Chorin's *Bruder Jesus* (9) is, as the title indicates, inspired by Martin Buber's picture of Jesus. The author sets himself the task of portraying Jesus as his Jewish brother in order to demonstrate to Christians how "the belief of Jesus unites us . . . but the belief in Jesus separates us."

3. *The Crucifixion*

The most sensitive topic in the discussion of Jesus' life and ministry is undoubtedly that of the trial and crucifixion. The charge, a major factor in the development of anti-Semitism, has been sounded by Christian theologians and historians from antiquity through to the twentieth century. With the perhaps naive hope that a demonstration of the lack of Jewish, or at least of popular Jewish, complicity in Jesus' death would lead to an amelioration of Christian attitudes, a number of writers in the nineteenth and twentieth centuries began the work of compiling apologies on the subject. While few of these works are of especial interest in themselves any longer, the account of their development is. This has been charted by Lindeskog in his *Jesusfrage* (41). Lindeskog distinguishes between this first apologetic stage and a second phase, the historical, which was still no doubt prompted by apologetic motives, but is characterized by critical evaluation of the sources. Representative of the prevalent point of view is Joseph Klausner, in *Jesus of Nazareth* (38), who advances the basic theory of a Sadducee-controlled Sanhedrin, concerned over Jesus as a possible political revolutionary, and who hand him over to the Romans to prevent the situation from getting out of control. A refinement of this position came with the development of the two-Sanhedrin theory, which originated with Adolph Büchler but was most ably articulated by Solomon Zeitlin, in *Who Crucified Jesus?* (71). As in other writings, Zeitlin notes that two different types of organizations appear to be spoken of in contemporary Hebrew literature, on the one hand, and in Greek literature, on the other. On the basis of this and other observations, he posits the existence of two bodies, a religious Sanhedrin, the *Bet Din,* composed of scholars and authorized to deal with "religious" matters, and a separate organization of a political nature. It was the latter body composed of the Sadducee minority which tried Jesus in league with the Roman authority. Although the subject of Jesus' death is dealt with only tangentially, the treatment in Hugo Mantel's *Studies in the History of the Sanhedrin* (42) is well worth the reader's attention because of the new light shed on it by his detailed and careful review of previous scholarship and his own critical reexamination of the problem.

The most recent major study in this area written by a Jew is a work of considerable scholarly sophistication, Paul Winter's *On the Trial of Jesus* (70). Winter follows the fruitful method of combining literary with historical analysis. Allowing the Gospel materials less credibility than is customary, he attempts to isolate the historical event from the primary report as found in the Gospels and the secondary tradition of the editors. This leads him to distinguish between reasonably certain facts, probable facts, and issues which must remain unanswered. To the first group belong Jesus' arrest by the Romans, his trial by a Jewish administrative authority during the night, his sentencing by the procurator, and his execution according to Roman procedure. Of high probability are the interrogation by the high priest's representatives and the derision of the Roman soldiers. Points which cannot be determined are the immediate cause of Jesus' arrest, the identification of those who initiated this action, and the deeds that Jesus performed to provoke action against himself.

This most sober treatment of the subject may finally be contrasted with the rather novel approach taken by Haim Cohn of the Israel Supreme Court in his *Reflections on the Trial and Death of Jesus* (16). Attacking the problem from the point of view of the legal historian, the author rejects the two-Sanhedrin theory and sees the night meeting of the Sanhedrin, an investigative body conducted under Sadduceean Law, as an eleventh-hour attempt to save Jesus by acquitting him before Pilate. According to Cohn, the attempt proved abortive because of Jesus' refusal to cooperate.

B. VIEWS OF CHRISTIANITY

1. *The Middle Ages*

The Middle Ages saw a continuous output of anti-Christian polemical literature, both in the form of protocols of compulsory disputations, such as those of Barcelona and Tortosa, and of textbooks for combating Christian missionaries or for the dissuasion of potential apostates. Several of these texts have been made available in English translation. Oliver S. Rankin's *Jewish Religious Polemics* (54) presents a selection of polemical texts of several literary genres including the midrashic *Chronicle of Moses* (narrative), *The Book of Contention* of Rabbi Yom Tov Lippman Muelhausen (poetry), the "Letters" of Rittangel and the Jew of Amsterdam (epistolary), and the disputation of Nahmanides with Pablo Christiani (debate). Each of these texts is put into context with a thorough historical and literary introduction and extensive annotation. In addition to these, the three classic medieval disputations of Paris, Barcelona, and Tortosa are presented in Morris Braude's *Conscience on Trial* (13).

A comprehensive study of medieval Jewish polemic remains a *desideratum*.[1] In addition to the older studies of Isidore Loeb (41a, 41b), Salo Baron's treatment in his *Social and Religious History* (4) will serve as the best introduction to the subject. Two chapters, one devoted to the mechanics of the public disputations and the other to literary polemics, take into account the socioreligious factors and consequences of these controversies. Of special value are the bibliographic annotations which, in themselves, read as a literary history of the material. A briefer thematic study of the material is to be found in Hans Joachim Schoeps'

[1] A comprehensive bibliography of this literature has been prepared by J. Rosenthal in *Areshet* II, pp. 130–179; III, pp. 433–437.

lucid *Jewish-Christian Argument* (59). In his chapter on the medieval polemic, he indicates the place of such central issues as the election of Israel, Law and faith, the destruction of the Temple, and the messiahship of Jesus.

The Bible was no doubt the major battleground of the Jewish-Christian argument, and biblical commentaries frequently contained polemical excursuses. An indication of the exegetical procedures and of such motifs as the status of Israel and the nations in the divine economy, christological interpretations, etc., may be found in my "R. David Kimḥi as Polemicist" (65), a study of the thirteenth-century Provençal exegete.

The Christian assertions of the degenerate character of Judaism and the negation of its right to exist, certainly brought forth responses in kind on the part of the Jews. Nevertheless, certain major theoreticians of the Jewish faith accorded to Christianity and its founder a rather high status in their view of the religious development of mankind. The interesting views of the most distinguished of medieval Jewish thinkers, Moses Maimonides, are expanded in Gershon Tchernowitz's brief Hebrew work *The Relation between Israel and the Gentiles According to Maimonides* (66), which also reviews his attitudes towards Islam. Rabbi Menaḥem ha-Meiri declared unequivocally that Christianity was in no sense to be classed as an idolatrous religion and was to be esteemed for its "practical" ethical norms. Ha-Meiri's ideas are very competently discussed in Jacob Katz's Hebrew study, "Religious Tolerance in the Halakhic and Philosophical System of Rabbi Menahem ha-Me'iri" (35) which appeared with an English summary in *Zion*.

2. *The Modern Period*

Treatments of Christianity by European Jewish writers in the nineteenth and twentieth centuries have generally followed the pattern set by Christian interpreters of Judaism which may be characterized as a typological approach. According to this, Judaism would be seen as the embodiment of the finest ideas of Western culture, with Christianity viewed as a poor imitation falling somewhat short of the mark. This trend, which may be said to have begun with Moses Mendelssohn and to have reached a turning point of sorts in the writings of Franz Rosenzweig, is surveyed in two works which commend themselves to the reader. The first is the above mentioned *Jewish-Christian Argument* (59) by Schoeps which gives a brief history of these discussions. The second is the far more exhaustive and highly competent treatment of Jacob Fleischmann, *The Problem of Christianity in Modern Jewish Thought* (Hebrew: [26]). The work analyzes the thought of ten representative Jewish thinkers of the modern period—Mendelssohn, Ascher, Salvador, Formstecher, Hirsch, Steinheim, Geiger, Benamozegh, Cohen, and Rosenzweig. The attempt on the part of all of these to define Judaism in terms of, or at least vis-à-vis, Christianity may be followed throughout the work to its conclusion in the important discussion of Rosenzweig. In his view of Judaism as the Life and of Christianity as the Way, Rosenzweig tried to abandon the apologetic approach and establish a corelationship with Christianity which would affirm the necessity of each. Much of Rosenzweig's approach to Christianity, if not his fully developed doctrine, has recently been made available in *Judaism Despite Christianity* (55), the English translation of his correspondence with Eugen Rosenstock-Heussy, the editor of the volume. Of great interest is the tone of immediacy in which the correspondence is couched, revealing one of those very rare instances of genuine preparedness for dialogue. The volume is enhanced by the illuminating introductions of the editor, of Dorothy Emmett, and of Professor Alexander Altmann.

Two twentieth-century theologians not mentioned by Fleischmann who are concerned with the relative characterization of Judaism and Christianity are Leo Baeck and Martin Buber. Baeck's effort to distill the "essence" of Judaism in response to Harnack's definition of the essence of Christianity led to the famous formulation of Judaism as the classical religion and Christianity as the romantic religion which came to expression in his *Judaism and Christianity* (2). For an analytical approach to Baeck's writings concerning Christianity, the reader may consult Reinhold Mayer's detailed *Christentum und Judentum in der Schau Leo Baecks* (44). Christianity is considered in many places throughout Martin Buber's work, but the central discussion is to be found in his *Two Types of Faith* (14), where faith as trust (Judaism) and faith as *pistis,* the belief *that* something is true (Christianity), are contrasted. An analysis of Buber's views on the subject together with his evaluations of Jesus and Paul are found in an essay, "The Jewish Jesus and the Christ of Faith," in Malcolm Diamond's *Martin Buber: Jewish Existentialist* (18). Of some interest is the reply to Buber from a Roman Catholic point of view in Hans Urs von Balthasar's *Martin Buber and Christianity* (3).

Once again from the "nationalist"-historical point of view, Joseph Klausner continued his examination of Christian origins in his sequel to *Jesus of Nazareth, From Jesus to Paul* (37). The work was able to arouse the enthusiasm of no less a critic than Arthur Darby Nock who was moved to comment that "Klausner has written with a scholar's depth and prophet's passion of issues which for him are never bloodless abstractions. The result is a piece of religious history as well as a study of it." Klausner surveys the history of the first and second centuries to provide the background for his analysis of the role and thinking of the apostle Paul. As in *Jesus of Nazareth,* Klausner's concerns are Jewish-oriented and the object of his effort is to answer the question why Pauline Christianity could never have been accepted by the Jews. Yehezkel Kaufmann in *Golah ve-nekhar* (36) procedes from his evaluation of Jesus to a critique of Christianity. While his interpretation may not be altogether original, it is forcefully and boldly stated. Kaufmann sees in the Christian emphasis on ethics and love a "great deception" in that, unlike Judaism, Christianity created an illusion of spirituality and other-wordliness by "secularizing" its law and ritual. The success of Christianity lies not in its innovations but in its continuing the task of Judaism, viz., the combating of paganism.

Christian interest in "dialogue" with the Jewish people in the wake of the Christian ecumenical movement has evoked a re-evaluation of the temper of the Jewish stance towards Christianity on the part of a number of Jewish thinkers. Still operative, of course, is the traditional apprehensiveness that any overtures on the part of Christians towards Jews are a cover for missionary ambitions. Such concerns are the subject of an essay by Leo Baeck—"Some Questions to the Christian Church from the Jewish Point of View" — in Göte Hedenquist's *The Church and the Jewish People* (31) in which the very premises of Christian evangelism are questioned. Martin Buber's essay "The Two Foci of the Jewish Soul" which appeared in *Israel and the World* (15), is to be commended to any Christian interested in undertaking a program of dialogue. Written shortly after World War II, it is one of the most eloquent responses to the concept of the mission to the Jews.

In addition to this traditional concern, other fundamental questions have been raised with respect to the possibility and desirability of the dialogical enterprise. At issue here are not only attitudes but actions, with the consensus being that the bi-millenial history of Christian complicity in or, at best, indifference to Jewish suffering provides a poor background for conversation at this time. In an essay included as a "Jewish contribution to a Christian-secularist dialogue" in *Quest for Past and Future* (24), Emil Fackenheim raises and examines the charge that "throughout the long struggle for Jewish human rights the secularist liberal has usually fought alongside the Jew, while the established Christian forces were—on the whole, but with very notable exceptions—ranged against him." That this is so, and that no fundamental change in this situation has been brought about, has been noted too by Eliezer Berkovits. In an article entitled "Judaism in the Post-Christian Era" in *Judaism* XV (10) Berkovits ascribes any apparent softening in Christian attitudes to the fact that Christianity realizes itself to be only one world force among many and, of these, not the most powerful. Because of the events of recent history which represent the culmination of Christian traditions of persecution, the Jew could not at this time emotionally face the prospect of Jewish-Christian dialogue. Rather, he suggests, stress should be placed on an "inter-human," non-theological type of dialogue. Stevens S. Schwarzschild, in "Judaism, Scriptures, and Ecumenism" in *Judaism XIII* (61) couples similar reservations with the traditional mistrust of Christian motivations as discussed above. Schwarzschild, in rejecting contemporary ecumenism speaks instead of an eschatological ecumenism implying a loyalty to Scriptures at the end of time. The event which created the heaviest impact on Jewish attitudes towards the question of dialogue was, of course, the 1967 Israel-Arab war. The general silence of the churches in the face of what appeared to be the imminent destruction of the Jewish state, coming as it did only twenty-five years after a similar silence concerning the Jews of Europe, caused many to feel a loss of optimism "in the hope that the long age of Christian triumphalism over Judaism is truly being superseded by an age of Jewish-Christian dialogue." Emil L. Fackenheim, writing in *Commentary* XLVI ("Jewish Faith and the Holocaust") (23) states that the Christian "failed to recognize the danger of a second Holocaust because he has yet to recognize the fact of the first." This he cannot do because "he knows that as a Christian he should voluntarily have gone to Auschwitz where his own Master would have been dragged . . . and he is racked by a sense of guilt the deeper the less he has cause to feel it." The shift in mood created by the Six Day War is poignantly expressed, too, in the two letters of Jacob Neusner in *Judaism* XV (47), one written before and the other after the war, in reaction to the Berkovits article cited above (10).

In conjunction with these statements, it is of profit to examine a closely aligned Christian point of view, A. Roy Eckardt's "Can There Be a Jewish-Christian Relationship?" in the *Journal of Bible and Religion* XXXIII (19). For such reasons as the lack of contrition on the part of the church, the failure of the church to root out anti-Semitic ideology, and the refusal to see anti-Semitic elements in the Gospels, there cannot yet be a relationship "of human equality and justice" between Jews and Christians.

More positive points of view are to be found of course. Representative of these is Abraham Joshua Heschel's "No Religion is an Island" (32a) which calls for the ordering of an association of religions on the model of the United Nations. While the autonomy of each religion would be respected (again an answer to missionary claims), one would "regard a divergent religion as His Majesty's loyal opposition," conceding that "one truth comes to expression in many ways of understanding." Interreligious cooperation is needed for, among other things, finding "ways of helping one another in the terrible predicament of here and now." A similar optimistic—yet nonconciliatory—attitude towards the future of Jewish-Christian dialogue may be seen in the address of Arthur Gilbert (27a) to the Consultation on the Church and the Jewish People sponsored by the World Lutheran Federation at Logumkloster, Denmark in 1964. Rabbi Gilbert's views are expressed with a full consciousness of and perhaps despite the strong currents of opposition to interfaith confrontation at the time.

THE CHRISTIAN VIEW OF JUDAISM

The principal document which was to shape and mold Christian attitudes towards the Jews is, of course, the New Testament and any statements made by Christians forever after on this topic are in the nature of a commentary upon it. However, in this survey our main concern is not what the New Testament itself says concerning the Jews, a subject which would form the basis of a bibliography of New Testament exegesis, but rather what Christians from antiquity to the present believed it or declared it to say. This section will therefore begin with the period of the Fathers and the Middle Ages.

A. THE PATRISTIC AND MEDIEVAL PERIODS

The missionary overtones behind A. Lukyn Williams' *Adversus Judaeos* (69) do not vitiate its usefulness as a compendium of the anti-Jewish polemic of the patristic period and the high Middle Ages. No systematic arrangement of the material is presented. Rather the anti-Jewish works of each author, listed under one of the rubrics, Latin, Greek, Syriac, or Spanish, are outlined and summarized. Both subject and scriptural indices make the work a particularly valuable tool in researching the literature. An excellent collection of texts is Solomon Grayzel's *The Church and the Jews in the XIIIth Century* (29). This source book presents statements of attitude and policy on the part of the ecclesiastical hierarchy of the period in both the original Latin and in English translation. *Aphrahat and Judaism: The Christian-Jewish Argument in Fourth Century Iran* (47a) by Jacob Neusner includes a translation of this early Christian monk's "Demonstrations" plus studies of pertinent issues.

For a good introductory survey to the literature of the period, one would do well to consult George Foot Moore's very competent essay "Christian Writers on Judaism" (45) in the *Harvard Theological Review*. Approaching the subject from the point of view of literary history, the author traces the anti-Jewish polemic as it develops into the Middle Ages.

In terms of more detailed analysis of the material of this period, three major works may be cited. James Parkes' well-documented *Conflict of the Church and the Synagogue* (50) is devoted to an examination of the relationship between the stance and teachings of Christianity with respect to the Jews and anti-Semitism. The work begins with a discussion of the rise of Christianity and Jewish resistance towards it and then moves into the topic of the relationship of the Church to the Jews in Rome and Byzantium. Marcel Simon's *Verus Israel* (62) is a somewhat more systematic treatment of Jewish-Christian relations in the Roman Empire. The patristic polemic against the Jews is discussed both methodologically and topically. The author evaluates the chief uses of the polemic, viz., the status of Israel under the new dispensation, the law, etc. Of particular importance, especially for an understanding of later phenomena, is his analysis of the implications of Christian theology for Christian anti-Semitism. Bernhard Blumenkranz's excellent *Juifs et Chrétiens dans le monde occidental. 430–1096* (11) does the same for the medieval period through the eleventh century. Blumenkranz deals with the theological issues—the mission to the Jews, polemics, use of the Bible, the questions of the crucifixion, election of the gentiles, etc.—against the background of the legal and political status of the Jews, their social position, and their religious life.

A particular aspect of the status of Judaism in the eyes of the early and medieval church is the relationship of Christianity to rabbinic literature. Louis Ginzberg's investigation of *Die Haggada bei den Kirchenvätern* (27b) and Ch. Merchavia's recent comprehensive study of the treatment of Talmud and Midrash by patristic and medieval Christianity from 500–1248 (44a) are additional volumes in which the rather ambivalent stance of the church towards this literature may be traced. On the one hand, it was condemned for being blasphemous and anti-Christian while on the other, it was carefully combed for any possible "proofs" of Christianity which it might contain.

Three highly significant volumes, two by Roman Catholics and one by a Jew, deal with the materials discussed in the above works from the point of view of their influence upon the development of modern anti-Semitism. Malcolm Hay, a Scottish historian, had interested himself early in his career in correcting popular misconceptions and "chains of error" in British history. Following his experience in World War II which made him acquainted with the

Jewish problem, he saw fit to study yet another "chain of error," the anti-Semitic tradition in Christian theology. Hay's *Foot of Pride* or *Europe and the Jews* (30), the result of his research, is a spirited and provocative work which makes its points by juxtaposing medieval and modern texts and accounts and demonstrating thereby how all the stereotypes of both modern Christian and non-Christian anti-Semitism are direct metamorphoses of earlier attitudes. Edward H. Flannery's *Anguish of the Jews* (25) complements Hay's work in that it follows a chronological rather than a thematic arrangement, starting with pre-Christian anti-Semitism and proceeding century by century until modern times. The evolution of modern anti-Semitic attitudes from Christian teachings, finally, is the subject of Jules Isaac's *Teaching of Contempt* (34). As does Hay, Isaac arranges his material topically and follows the method used in *Jésus et Israël* (*Jesus and Israel*) of allowing the sources to speak for themselves. A wide range of materials, especially from the French scene, is used.

One may conclude this section with a reference to an article surveying the subject of "Luther and the Jews" (62a) which appeared in *Lutheran World*. Aarne Siirala presents this well-known saga from both the non-Lutheran and Lutheran perspectives. The former sees the negative turn in Luther's thinking as a result of frustration in his failure to convert the Jews; the latter, as being rooted in his exegesis of Scripture. Siirala raises questions concerning both the assumptions of the latter approach and some of the larger implications of this approach for Lutheranism in general. Of considerable interest in this connection is Haim Hillel Ben Sasson's study of Jewish awareness of and reaction to Lutheran initiatives in *Harvard Theological Review* LIX (9a).

B. THE MODERN PERIOD

The writings of Hay, Flannery, and Isaac trace the continuity of thought patterns and prejudicial attitudes from the patristic and medieval periods into modern anti-Semitism in both its Christian and non-Christian varieties. A number of studies have been done, attempting to evaluate the effect of Christian preaching and teaching on the attitudes of parishioners towards the Jews, which generally measure the relationship of prejudicial attitudes to degrees of orthodoxy. *Christian Beliefs and Anti-Semitism* (27b), a study by two sociologists, Charles Y. Glock and Rodney Stark, records the results of their survey of the "religious roots of anti-Semitism" and establishes "religious particularism" as a direct cause of anti-Jewish prejudice. Bernhard Olson's excellent study, *Faith and Prejudice* (49) remains one of the best of all these studies, however, in that it does not rely on analyses of responses to black-and-white form questions but rather examines the catechetical literature of four basic theological viewpoints: fundamentalist, conservative, neo-orthodox, and liberal. Its analysis demonstrates that an attempt to establish a direct correlation between orthodoxy and anti-Semitic belief must be branded as simplistic. An important deficiency, however, in the Olson work, which has been corrected in the Glock-Stark study, is the failure to assess properly the role of Christian teachings to reinforce and foster anti-Semitic attitudes. This is particularly significant at a time when an increasing number of Christian theologians are becoming aware that anti-Semitism cannot be seriously combated without coming to grips with this problem. The reader is referred too to A. Roy Eckardt's penetrating study "The Theology of Anti-Semitism" (22) in *Religion in Life* XXXI. The author concludes that doctrinal modifications in themselves, except where such doctrines be overtly anti-Semitic, is not the solution to anti-Semitism. Rather the emphasis should be on the correction of distortions of doctrine stemming from subconscious mechanisms. (See below, "Zionism and the State of Israel.") Finally, Alfred de Quervain's *Das Judentum in der Lehre und Verkundigung der Kirche Heute* (53) in the series *Theologische Existenz Heute* discusses the current situation in this area on the European scene, and the Lutheran perspective is presented in Rudolph Pfisterer's "Judaism in the Preaching and Teaching of the Church," in *Lutheran World* (52a).

The legacy of the patristic and medieval periods had its influence, of course, not only on the pulpit and on popular attitudes, but in the academy as well. Recasting the old attitudes into a new mold, nineteenth-century scholarship waged a new polemic against Judaism in its efforts to stress the advance of Christianity over the parent religion. George Foot Moore's essay, "Christian Writers on Judaism" (45) which has been mentioned above, traces the techniques and themes of this polemic which centered around the contrast between Christian piety and Jewish legalism on the one hand, and the theme of the impassable transcendental Jewish view of the Diety on the other.[2] Moore singled out for criticism one work which had and has been most influential in shaping Christian ideas of Judaism, viz., Emil Schürer's *A History of the Jewish People in the Time of Jesus* (60). While the history of the second commonwealth could not be gainsaid, Moore rejected what he felt were Schürer's attempts to prove "that the strictures on Judaism in the Gospels and the Pauline epistles are fully justified." There were, to be sure, correctives to the work of Schürer and similar investigators, written by Christians, notably, Travers Herford, James Parkes, and Moore himself. Worthy of special mention in this regard is the latter's *Judaism in the First Centuries of the Christian Era: The Age of the Tannaim* (46), a work which gave Christian readers a view of rabbinic theology disembarrassed of prejudicial distortions.

An outstanding study of the fruits of the medieval and patristic legacies is Uriel Tal's *Christians and Jews in the "Second Reich" (1870–1914): A Study in the Rise of German Totalitarianism* (Hebrew; 64a). With a preference for middle-brow writers such as students, the "man in the street," and the average intellectual, Tal presents a careful analysis of the dilemma in which the Jews (especially the liberals) found themselves in their double striving after integration into German society and preservation of their identity as Jews. On the one hand, one encounters the opposition of Christian conservatives who did not trust the Jews to be good Germans since, by rejecting their own nationhood, they had not been good Jews. On the other hand, the very similarity and proximity of liberal Judaism to liberal Christianity provoked the Christion liberals to reject the logic of a separate existence for the Jew. The author treats in detail the development from Christian anti-Semitism to racial anti-Semitism which, in itself, becomes anti-

---

[2] This survey has been brought up to date in the first chapter of E. E. Urbach's *ḤaZaL Pirke Emunot ve-De'ot* (Jerusalem: Magnes Press, 1969), pp. 1–14. See also L. H. Silberman, "Judaism and the Christian Theologian," *Journal of Religion* XXXVII (1957), 246–53 in which the author shows "the dangers involved in assuming the 'possibilities of man's present understanding of existence' have a point-to-point correspondence with the 'phenomena of past history' and in then dealing with the past as though it were the prèsent."

Christian. One sees the latter's theoreticians employ traditional Christian critiques of Judaism as a weapon against Christianity itself in their effort to show that the latter was right in trying to extirpate Judaism but wrong in not going far enough. Christianity had to be purged of its Jewish elements—its universalism; its soppish ethics; its squelching of the *joie de vivre* and spontaneity of natural man; its failure to carry the equation "God equals man" to the conclusion that Jesus become the Aryan and the Kingdom of Heaven the German State. In this analysis, the line from the invective of the Second Reich to the slaughter of the Third is clearly traced.

The one event in our time which had the greatest potential for causing a rethinking of Christian attitudes towards the Jews was of course the European Holocaust. In 1948, three years after the end of World War II, the World Council of Churches, meeting in Amsterdam, promulgated a statement concerning the Jews which, while decrying anti-Semitism and expressing similar appropriate sentiments, showed little evidence of a modification of attitudes on basic questions. The report is available in the anthology edited by Göte Hedenquist, *The Church and the Jewish People* (31), a collection of essays by Jews and Christians on contemporary Judaism and the stance of the Church toward it. Most of the essays explore the theological status of the Jewish people as primarily a subject for evangelization, and the discussions center around the proper approach to take to achieve this end, especially in the new State of Israel.

Of roughly the same vintage and the same line is Karl Barth's best known essay on the Jewish question, "The Jewish Problem and the Christian Answer" (5). He too laments the events of the recent past, denounces anti-Semitism, and even gives lip service to Jewish nationalism although rejecting the meaning of Jewish nationhood unless it fits Christian categories of thought. Remarkable is his hypothesis that anti-Semitism stems from the Gentile's resentment of Israel's election when viewed in the light of his failure to mention at all the influence of Christian anti-Jewish teachings. While evangelism is not advocated, the unredeemed character of the Jewish people is made evident as Barth celebrates the mystery of Israel's blindness. One still hears the echo of Frederick the Great's pastor who, on being asked for a proof of Christianity, replied, "Your Majesty, the Jews." Barth's other writings and statements concerning the Jews have been analyzed in detail in *Die Entdeckung des Judentums für die christliche Theologie* (43) by Friedrich Wilhelm Marquardt.

A formal Roman Catholic statement on the Jews took much longer in coming than the report of the World Council of Churches. When it did come in the form of the Vatican II "Declaration on Non-Christian Religions," many among the Jewish people anticipated that it would herald a dramatic change in Jewish-Christian relations while others regarded it with apathy or even indignation. The central issue was, of course, the "deicide" question and the appropriateness of an "exoneration" of the Jews by the Church, again without the slightest hint of contrition for the injustices of two millennia, was held in question. As it turned out, even this "exoneration" was attenuated, and the declaration, in other areas, also, fell short of its anticipated aims. The text of the document with an extensive commentary is found in *The Church and the Jewish People* (8) by Augustine Cardinal Bea, one of the chief and most liberal architects of the schema. The reader is here advised not to read between the lines but beneath them for the footnotes frequently contain revealing *apologiae* for discrepancies between the original and final drafts.

The Church and the Jewish People as a blueprint for action points in the direction of dialogue. Yet the direction and tone which Vatican II-inspired dialogue might take may vary widely as two recent publications would indicate. The one is that of the New Testament scholar Father Jean Daniélou entitled *Dialogue with Israel* (17), a collection of brief essays dealing with a variety of themes, e.g., early Judaism and Christianity, some Jewish views of Jesus, anti-Semitism, and so forth. Although it is, as the title indicates, intended as a contribution to dialogue, the book is a clear example of the kind of impasse reached in an understanding of Judaism when approached by a rigid traditionalist. Of interest is the appended response of Rabbi Jacob B. Agus to several excesses of the work. Dialogue would seem to take on a very different meaning in Father Gregory Baum's "The Doctrinal Basis for Jewish-Christian Dialogue" (7) which appeared in the journal *Dialog*.

The author probes the possibilities of a reevaluation of Judaism in Roman Catholic theology and concludes that the "destiny" of Judaism is not to disappear and give way to Christianity. Judaism continues to exercise a positive role in God's "plan of salvation."

This concession, which radically alters the notion of the Church's mission with respect to the Jews has been as rarely heard in Protestant circles as in Roman Catholic. To be sure, there are important Protestant theologians who have decried attempts at evangelization such as Reinhold Niebhur ("Christians and Jews in Western Civilization" in *Pious and Secular America* [48] and Markus Barth *(The Broken Wall: A Study of the Epistle to the Ephesians* [611]*)*. Yet their point of view may be far from that of Baum's. Niebuhr, for example, claims that the two faiths, despite differences, are sufficiently alike for the Jew to find God more easily in terms of his own religious heritage than by subjecting himself to the hazards of guilt feelings involved in "conversion to a faith which, whatever its excellencies, must appear to him as a symbol of an oppressive majority culture. . . ." This, coupled with his praise in *Christianity and Crisis* (48a) for "Vatican II's ignoring Pauline authority and thereby satisfying the demand of a Jewish minority for a recognition of its authentic autonomy" indicates that he has little sensitivity to what the "autonomy" demand by the Jews really means. (See the strictures of Steven S. Schwarzschild in "Judaism, Scriptures, and Ecumenism" cited above [61]; also G. Harder, "Christian/Jewish Conversation" in *Lutheran World* XI (1964), 326–336. Harder's remarks are put into perspective through a comparison with K. H. Rengstorf's "The Place of the Jew in the Theology of the Christian Mission," in the same issue (pp. 279–295).

The finest expression of a Protestant Christian recognition of the legitimacy of Judaism and of Israel's existence is A. Roy Eckardt's *Elder and Younger Brothers* (20). Eckardt reviews the theological implications of the role of Jews as the consenting people in the "unbroken Covenant God has made with Israel." He shows that "the messiahship of Jesus is both grounded in and yet discontinuous with the salvation-history of Israel. The existence of the Christian Church in no way annuls Israel's abiding meaning and independent destiny" (from the dust jacket). In a different

formulation, James Parkes ("A Reappraisal of the Christian Attitude Toward Judaism" in *Journal of Bible and Religion* XXIX
[52]), affirms Judaism's existence in his thesis that both Judaism
and Christianity are needed as complements in that Christianity
stresses man as a person while Judaism sees man as a member of
a natural community. Finally, Krister Stendahl ("Judaism and
Christianity: Then and Now" in *New Theology No. 2* [63]) calls
for a reexamination of the relationship between Judaism and
Christianity seen as "peoples" rather than "religions," and on the
basis of a new scholarly understanding of both Testaments, the
contribution of Paul, etc.

C. CHRISTIANITY AND THE STATE OF ISRAEL

A subject worthy of special treatment is the attitude of Christianity towards Zionism and the establishment and existence of
the Jewish state. The loss of Jewish national independence early
in the Christian era and the stateless condition of the Jewish people
became for the Church a cardinal proof of the truth of Christianity.
The Jew, who never lost hope in the eventual return, wrote often
of the folly of Muslims and Christians who believed that Eretz
Israel had become their possession, although he was to wait many
centuries before his own hopes could be realized. Although there
were notable exceptions, Christianity as such showed little sympathy and considerable scorn for Zionist aspirations. Judah Rosenthal has traced the history of this relationship in two essays, "The
State of Israel and the Christian Church" (56) and "The State
of Israel in the Light of Christian Theology" (57) which have
appeared most recently in his Hebrew *Texts and Studies*. The
essays chart the development and significance of the idea of Israel's
eternal exile and wandering in Christian theology and document
the attitudes and pronouncements of ecclesiastical leaders, both
Catholic and Protestant, from the inception of modern Zionism
through the establishment of the State. The material in these
studies sheds a great deal of light on the indifference or even
hostility displayed towards the State of Israel on the part of certain
North American churches, especially at the time of the 1967 war.
No full study of this problem is available in English, but much
of the material is fortunately to be found in Hay's *Foot of Pride*

(30) which analyzes the posture of Europe and America towards the emergence of the State of Israel against this theological background. Of interest too is the material in Pinchas Lapide's *Three Popes and the Jews* (39) which outlines the historical hostility of the papacy (with the exception of Benedict XV) toward the Zionist movement.

Perhaps ironically, Christian fundamentalism, which is often most vocal about the unredeemed character of the Jewish people tends to be most enthusiastic about the State of Israel, seeing in it a fulfilment of biblical prophecy and a sign of the imminent return of Christ. It comes as less of a surprise, then, to discover that at the opposite end of the theological spectrum the situation may find itself reversed.

In *The Crime of Christendom: The Theological Sources of Christian Anti-Semitism* (12), Fred Gladstone Bratton presents a Unitarian-Universalist version of the writings of Hay and Flannery. The work seems less an attempt to heal the wounds of the Jews than to scourge orthodox Christology. The author sees in the latter the principal cause of anti-Semitism which, he claims, will persist until the churches radically revise (or abandon) creed. What follows may suitably be described by what Niebuhr has termed "provisional tolerance." The author stipulates that in order to benefit from an amelioration of Christian attitudes, the Jews will have to abandon their own form of particularism, viz., Zionism, and in effect subscribe to a Jewish counterpart of Unitarian-Universalism. In this context, the following remarks of A. Roy Eckardt are especially relevant: "Is it not conceivable that traditional forms of faith may possess greater insight into the perversity of men, into the bond between inhuman behavior and inhuman idolatry, and into the mysteries of God's work than do less traditional and more rationalistic views? Is it really the case that religious liberals know more or do more about social maladies as discrimination against Jews than traditionalists know or do?" (The Theology of Antisemitism," *Religion in Life* XXXI [1962], p. 566.)

Thus do we find on the part of certain representatives of more conservative churches greater sympathy in this regard. Long known is James Parkes' *History of Palestine from 135 A.D. to Modern Times* (51) in which he sets as his task the tracing of the unsevered connection of the Jewish people with the Holy Land throughout the centuries of the dispersion. A. Roy Eckardt closes his *Elder and Younger Brothers* (20) with a supplement, originally published in *Christian Century,* entitled "Again, Silence in the Churches." The essay reproves the churches for their silence during the Six Day War and advances the case for the State of Israel from a Christian point of view. In this regard, see his *Midstream* article, "Eretz Israel: A Christian Affirmation" (21), in which the author explains his commitment on "Christian grounds to bespeak the integrity of Israel among Jews as among Christians," and his latest volume, *Encounter With Israel: A Challenge to Conscience,* (22a) written in collaboration with his wife. Krister Stendahl's "Judaism and Christianity II; After a Colloquium and a War" (64) in the *Harvard Divinity Bulletin* is a continuation of his discussion of the article in *New Theology No. 2* (63) in the light of the Harvard Jewish-Christian Colloquium of 1966 and the 1967 Israel-Arab war. Of particular interest is the author's position concerning the desirability of a united Jerusalem from a Christian standpoint.

PUBLICATIONS CITED IN TEXT

(1) Aron, Robert, *Jesus of Nazareth: The Hidden Years,* trans. F. Frenaye (London: H. Hamilton, 1962).

(2) Baeck, Leo, *Judaism and Christianity,* trans. W. Kaufmann (Philadelphia: Jewish Publication Society of America, 1961).

(3) Balthasar, Hans Urs von, *Martin Buber and Christianity,* trans. A. Bru (London: Harvill Press, 1961).

(4) Baron, Salo W., *A Social and Religious History of the Jews* (New York: Columbia University Press, 1965), Vol. IX, chapters XXXIX, XL.

(5) Barth, Karl, "The Jewish Problem and the Christian Answer," in *Against the Stream,* trans. E. M. Delacour (London: SCM Press, 1954, 193–202).

(6) Barth, Markus, *The Broken Wall: A Study of the Epistle to the Ephesians* (Chicago: Judson Press, 1959).

(7) Baum, Gregory, "The Doctrinal Basis for Jewish-Christian Dialogue," *Dialog* VI (1967), 200–209.

(8) Bea, Augustine, S. J. *The Church and the Jewish People,* trans. P. Loretz, S. J. (New York: Harper & Row, 1966).

(9) Ben-Chorin, Schalom, *Bruder Jesus: Der Nazarener in Jüdischer Sicht* (Munich: Paul List Verlag, 1967).

(9a) Ben Sasson, Haim Hillel, "Jewish-Christian Disputation in the Setting of Humanism and Reformation in the German Empire," *Harvard Theological Review* LIX (1966), 369–390.

(10) Berkovits, Eliezer, "Judaism in the post-Christian Era," *Judaism* XV (1966), 74–84.

(11) Blumenkranz, Bernhard, *Juifs et Chrétiens dans le monde occidental, 430–1096* (Paris: Mouton, 1960).

(12) Bratton, Fred Gladstone, *The Crime of Christendom: The Theological Sources of Christian Anti-Semitism* (Boston: Beacon Press, 1969).

(13) Braude, Morris, *Conscience on Trial* (New York: Exposition Press, 1962).

(14) Buber, Martin, *Two Types of Faith,* trans. N. P. Goldhawk (London: Routledge and Paul, 1951).

(15) ———, "The Two Foci of the Jewish Soul," in *Israel and the World* (New York: Schocken Books, 1948).

(16) Cohn, Haim H., *Reflections on the Trial and Death of Jesus* (Jerusalem: Israel Law Review Association, 1967; reprint from *Israel Law Review* II [1967], 279–332).

(17) Daniélou, Jean, *Dialogue with Israel,* trans. J. M. Roth (Baltimore: Helicon, 1968).

(18) Diamond, Malcolm, *Martin Buber: Jewish Existentialist* (New York: Oxford University Press, 1960); chapter 7: "The Jewish Jesus and the Christ of Faith."

(19) Eckardt, A. Roy, "Can There Be a Jewish-Christian Relationship?" *Journal of Bible and Religion,"* XXXIII (1905), 122–130.

(20) ———, *Elder and Younger Brothers: The Encounter of Jews and Christians* (New York: Charles Scribner's Sons, 1967).

(21) ———, "Eretz Israel: A Christian Affirmation," *Midstream* XIV (1968), 9–12.

(22) ———, "The Theology of Anti-Semitism," *Religion in Life* XXXI (1962), 552–62.

(22a) ——— and Alice L., *Encounter with Israel: A Challenge to Conscience* (New York: Association Press, 1970).

(23) Fackenheim, Emil L., "Jewish Faith and the Holocaust," *Commentary* XLVI (1968), 30–36.

(24) ———, *Quest for Past and Future* (Bloomington: Indiana University Press, 1968); chapter 16.

(25) Flannery, Edward H., *The Anguish of the Jews: Twenty-three Centuries of Anti-Semitism* (New York: The Macmillan Company, 1965).

(26) Fleischmann, Jacob, *The Problem of Christianity in Modern Jewish Thought,* in Hebrew (Jerusalem: Magnes Press, 1964).

(27) Flusser, David, *Jesus,* trans. R. Walls (New York: Herder and Herder, 1969).

(27a) Gilbert, Arthur, "The Mission of the Jewish People in History and in the Modern World," *Lutheran World* XI (1964), 296–310.

(27b) Ginzberg, Louis, *Die Haggada bei den Kirchenvätern* (Berlin: A. Calvary, 1900).

(27c) Glock, Charles Y. and Rodney Stark, *Christian Beliefs and Anti-Semitism* (New York: Harper & Row, 1966).

(28) Goldstein, Morris, *Jesus in the Jewish Tradition* (New York: The Macmillan Company, 1950).

(29) Grayzel, Solomon, *The Church and the Jews in the XIIIth Century* (New York: Hermon Press, 1966).

(30) Hay, Malcolm, *The Foot of Pride: The Pressure of Christendom on the People of Israel for 1900 Years* (Boston: The Beacon Press, 1950; republished under the title *Europe and the Jews,* 1960).

(31) Hedenquist, Göte (ed.), *The Church and the Jewish People* (London: Edinburgh House Press, 1954).

(32) Herford, R. Travers, *Christianity in Talmud and Midrash* (London: Williams and Norgate, 1903).

(32a) Heschel, Abraham J., "No Religion is an Island," *Union Theological Quarterly Review* XXI, January, 1966, pp. 117–134.

(33) Isaac, Jules, *Jesus and Israel,* trans. S. Gran (New York: Holt, Rinehart and Winston, 1971).

(34) ———, *The Teaching of Contempt,* trans. H. Weaver (New York: Holt, Rinehart and Winston, 1964).

(35) Katz, Jacob, "Religious Tolerance in the Halakhic and Philosophical System of Rabbi Menahem ha-Me'iri" (Hebrew), *Zion* XVIII (1953), 15–30.

(36) Kaufmann, Yehezkel, *Golah ve-nekhar* (Tel Aviv: Dvir, 1954).

(37) Klausner, Joseph, *From Joseph to Paul,* trans. W. F. Stinespring (Boston: Beacon Press, 1961).

(38) ———, *Jesus of Nazareth: His Life, Times and Teaching,* trans. H. Danby (New York: The Macmillan Company, 1945).

(39) Lapide, Pinchas E., *Three Popes and the Jews* (New York: Hawthorn Books, 1967).

(40) Lauterbach, Jacob Z., "Jesus in the Talmud," in *Rabbinic Essays* (Cincinnati: Hebrew Union College Press, 1951).

(41) Lindeskog, Gösta, *Die Jesusfrage im neuzeitlichen Judenthum* (Uppsala: Almqvist & Wiksells Boktryckeri-a.-b., 1938).

(41a) Loeb, Isidore, "La Controverse religieuse entre les Chrétiens et les Juifs au Moyen Age," *Revue de l'Histoire des Religions* XVII–XVIII (1888), 133–156, 311–337.

(41b) ———, 'Polémistes chrétiens et juifs," *Revue des Études Juives* XVIII (1889), 43–70, 219–42.

(42) Mantel, Hugo, *Studies in the History of the Sanhedrin* (Cambridge, Mass.: Harvard University Press, 1961).

(43) Marquardt, Friedrich-Wilhelm, *Die Entdeckung des Judentums für die christliche Theologie: Israel in Denken Karl Barths* (Munich: Chr. Kaiser Verlag, 1967).

(44) Mayer, Reinhold, *Christentum und Judentum in der Schau Leo Baecks* (Stuttgart: W. Kohlhammer, 1961).

(44a) Merchavia, Ch., *Ha-Talmud bi-re'i ha-natsrut* (Jerusalem: Bialik Institute, 1970).

(45) Moore, George Foot, "Christian Writers on Judaism," *Harvard Theological Review* XIV (1921), 197–254.

(46) ———, *Judaism in the First Centuries of the Christian Era: The Age of the Tannaim* (Cambridge, Mass.: Harvard University Press), Vols. I-II, 1927, Vol. III, 1930.

(47) Neusner, Jacob, Correspondence, *Judaism* XV (1966), 223–226; XVI (1967), 363.

(47a) ———, *Aphrahat and Judaism: The Christian-Jewish Argument in Fourth Century Iran* (Leiden: E. J. Brill, 1967).

(48) Niebuhr, Reinhold, *Pious and Secular America* (New York: Charles Scribner's Sons, 1958); Chapter 7: "Christians and Jews in Western Civilization."

(48a) ———, "The Unsolved Religious Problem in Christian-Jewish Relations," *Christianity and Crisis* XXVI (1966), 279–83.

(49) Olson, Bernhard E., *Faith and Prejudice* (New Haven: Yale University Press, 1963).

(50) Parkes, James, *The Conflict of the Church and the Synagogue*, (Philadelphia: Jewish Publication Society of America, 1961).

(51) ———, *A History of Palestine from 135 A.D. to Modern Times* (London: Oxford University Press, 1949); revised edition: *Whose Land? A History of the People of Palestine* (Baltimore: Penguin, 1970).

(52) ———, "A Reappraisal of the Christian Attitude toward Judaism," *Journal of Bible and Religion* XXIX (1961), 299–307.

(52a) Pfisterer, Rudolf, "Judaism in the Preaching and Teaching of the Church," *Lutheran World* XI (1964), 311–328.

(53) Quervain, Alfred de, *Theologische Existenz Heute: Das Judentum in der Lehre und Verkundigung der Kirche Heute* (Munich: Chr. Kaiser Verlag, 1966).

(54) Rankin, Oliver S., *Jewish Religious Polemics of Earlier and Later Centuries* (Edinburgh: University Press, 1956).

(55) Rosenstock-Huessy, Eugen, *Judaism Despite Christianity* (Alabama: University of Alabama Press, 1969).

(56) Rosenthal, Judah, "The State of Israel and the Christian Church" (Hebrew), in *Mehkarim* (Jerusalem: Rubin Mass, 1966), 578–586.

(57) ———, "The State of Israel in the Light of Christian Theology" (Hebrew), *op. cit.*, 556–577.

(58) Sandmel, Samuel, *We Jews and Jesus* (New York: Oxford University Press, 1965).

(59) Schoeps, Hans Joachim, *The Jewish-Christian Argument: A*

History of Theologies in Conflict, trans. D. S. Green (New York: Holt, Rinehart, and Winston, 1963).

(60) Schürer, Emil, *A History of the Jewish People in the Time of Jesus* (Edinburgh: T. & T. Clark, 1885).

(61) Schwarzschild, Steven S., "Judaism, Scriptures, and Ecumenism," *Judaism* XIII (1964), 259–273.

(62) Simon, Marcel, *Verus Israel* (Paris: E. de Boccard, 1964).

(62a) Siirala, Aarne, "Luther and the Jews," *Lutheran World* XI (1964), 337–347.

(63) Stendahl, Krister, "Judaism and Christianity: Then and Now," in Marty, Martin E., *New Theology No. 2* (New York: The Macmillan Company, 1965, 153–164).

(64) ———, "Judaism and Christianity II: After a Colloquium and a War," *Harvard Divinity Bulletin,* N.S. I (1967), 2–8.

(64a) Tal, Uriel, *Christians and Jews in the "Second Reich" (1870–1914): A Study in the Rise of German Totalitarianism,* in Hebrew (Jerusalem: Magnes Press-Yad Vashem, 1969).

(65) Talmage, Frank, "R. David Kimḥi as Polemicist," *Hebrew Union College Annual* XXXVIII (1967), 213–235.

(66) Tchernowitz, Gershon, *The Relation between Israel and the Gentiles according to Maimonides,* in Hebrew (New York: Bitsaron, 1950).

(67) Trattner, Ernest R., *As a Jew Sees Jesus* (New York: Charles Scribner's Sons, 1931).

(68) Walker, Thomas D., *Jewish Views of Jesus* (London: Allen and Unwin, 1930).

(69) Williams, Arthur Lukyn, *Adversus Judaeos* (Cambridge: Cambridge University Press, 1935).

(70) Winter, Paul, *On the Trial of Jesus* (Berlin: Walter de Gruyter, 1961).

(71) Zeitlin, Solomon, *Who Crucified Jesus?* (New York: Bloch Publishing Company, 1964).

SUPPLEMENTARY BIBLIOGRAPHY

Baron, S. W., "John Calvin and the Jews," in *Harry A. Wolfson Jubilee Volume* (Jerusalem: American Academy for Jewish Research, 1965), English section, 141–163.

———, "Medieval Heritage and Modern Realities in Protestant-Jewish Relations," *Diogenes* XLI (1968), 32–51.

Barth, Markus, *Theologische Existenz Heute: Israel und die Kirche im Briefe des Paulus an die Epheser* (Munich: Chr. Kaiser Verlag, 1952).

Ben-Chorin, Schalom, "Jesus der Jude" in *Das Judentum in Ringen der Gegenwart* (Hamburg: Herbert Reich, 1965).

Fackenheim, Emil, "Samuel Hirsch and Hegel: A Study of Hirsch's *Religionsphilosophie der Juden (1842),"* in A. Altmann (ed.), *Studies in Nineteenth Century Jewish Intellectual History* (Cambridge, Mass.: Harvard University Press, 1964, 171–201).

Fasman, Oscar Z., "An Epistle on Tolerance by a 'Rabbinic Zealot,' " in Jung, Leo (ed.), *Judaism in a Changing World* (New York: Oxford University Press, 1939).

Federici, Tommaso, *Israele vivo* (Turin: Edizioni Missioni Consolata, 1962).

Goldschmidt, Dietrich, *Der ungekündigte Bund* (Stuttgart: Kreuz-Verlag, 1962).

Isaac, Jules, *Génèse de l'antisémitisme* (Paris: Calmann-Lévy, 1956).

———, *Has Anti-Semitism Roots in Christianity?,* trans. D. and J. Parkes (New York: N.C.C.J., 1961).

Israël en de Kerk (The Hague: Lecturbureau der Nederlands Hervormde Kerk, 1959).

Lohse, Eduard, *Israel und die Christenheit* (Göttingen: Vandenhoek & Ruprecht, 1960).

Maritain, Jacques, *Le Mystère d'Israël* (Paris: Desclée, De Brouwer, 1965).

Meisels, Misha, *Mahashava ve-'emet* (Tel Aviv: Mizpeh, 1938–39), Vol. 2.

Oesterreicher, John M. (ed.), *The Bridge: A Yearbook of Judaeo-Christian Studies* (New York: Pantheon Press, 1955, 1956, 1958, 1962).

Rylaarsdam, J. Coert, "Common Ground and Difference," *Journal of Bible and Religion* XLIII (1963), 261–170.

Schultz, Hans Juergen (ed.), *Juden-Christen-Deutschen* (Stuttgart: Kreuz Verlag, 1961).

Synan, Edward A., *The Popes and the Jews in the Middle Ages* (New York: The Macmillan Company, 1965).

Tillich, Paul, *Die Judenfrage: Ein christliches und ein deutsches Problem* (Berlin: Gebrüder Weiss Verlag, 1953).

Weiss-Rosmarin, Trude, *Judaism and Christianity: The Differences* (New York: Jonathan David, 1953).

Wilpert, Paul (ed.), *Judentum im Mittelalter, Beiträge zum Christlich-Jüdischen Gespräch,* Miscellanea Mediaevilia 4, (Berlin: Walter de Gruyter, 1966).

ORIGINAL SOURCES

The following complete texts may be used in conjunction with this volume:

Jewish

Buber, Martin, *Two Types of Faith,* New York: Harper, 1951 (pb).
  Contrasts Jewish faith as trust *in* and Christian faith as belief *that.*

Cohen, Arthur A., *The Myth of the Judeo-Christian Tradition,* New York: Schocken, 1971 (pb).
  A critique of the concept "Judeo-Christian tradition" from a historical and theological point of view.

Kimhi, Joseph, *The Book of the Covenant,* trans. F. Talmage, Toronto: Pontifical Institute of Mediaeval Studies, 1972 (pb).
  A disputation set in twelfth century Provence.

Neubauer, Adolf and Driver, S. R., *The Fifty-third Chapter of Isaiah according to the Jewish Interpreters,* New York: Ktav, 1969, 2 vols.
  A large selection of Jewish commentaries on one of the "suffering servant" passages. Volume one contains the original texts; volume two the English translations.

Rankin, Oliver Shaw, *Jewish Religious Polemic of Earlier and Later Centuries,* New York: Ktav, 1970.
  See Bibliographic Survey.

Troki, Isaac, *Faith Strengthened,* trans. M. Mocatta, New York: Ktav, 1970.
  A disputation set in sixteenth century Lithuania.

Christian

Augustine, St., "Answer to the Jews," in *Treatises on Marriage and*

Other Subjects (Fathers of the Church Series, 27), Washington Catholic University Press, 1955.

Eckardt, A. Roy, *Elder and Younger Brothers,* New York: Schocken, 1973 (pb).
A Protestant call for a revision of the Jewish-Christian relationship on the basis of the view that Christianity does not supersede Judaism.

Justin Martyr, St., "Dialogue with Trypho," in *Complete Writings* (Fathers of the Church Series, 6), Washington: Catholic University Press, 1948.
One of the classic patristic polemical treatises.

Origen, *Contra Celsum,* trans. H. Chadwick, New York: Cambridge University Press, 1965.
A treatise directed against the pagan Celsus but containing a great deal of anti-Jewish material.

Neusner, Jacob, ed., *Aphrahat and Judaism: The Jewish-Christian Argument in Fourth Century Iran,* Leiden: E. J. Brill, 1967.
A translation and study of the Syriac father's "demonstrations" against Judaism.

Ruether, Rosemary R., *Faith and Fratricide,* New York: Seabury, 1974.
A radical reappraisal of Judaism from a Roman Catholic point of view.

Jewish-Christian

Rosenstock-Huessy, E., *Judaism Despite Christianity,* New York: Schocken, 1971 (pb).
The correspondence between Rosenstock and Franz Rosenzweig with valuable introductions.

INDEX TO BIBLICAL AND RABBINIC PASSAGES

HEBREW BIBLE

(Citations follow the numbering in the Masoretic Text. When the Vulgate numbering differs it is given in parentheses.)

NEW TESTAMENT

RABBINIC PASSAGES

GENERAL INDEX

397